PAPERS
OF THE
PEABODY MUSEUM OF ARCHAEOLOGY AND
ETHNOLOGY, HARVARD UNIVERSITY
VOL. 59, NO. 2

THE FREMONT CULTURE

A STUDY IN CULTURE DYNAMICS
ON THE
NORTHERN ANASAZI FRONTIER

Including
THE REPORT OF THE
CLAFLIN-EMERSON EXPEDITION
OF
THE PEABODY MUSEUM

BY

JAMES H. GUNNERSON

WITH APPENDICES BY
WALTON C. GALINAT AND JAMES H. GUNNERSON
AND
MARGARET A. TOWLE

PUBLISHED BY THE PEABODY MUSEUM
CAMBRIDGE, MASSACHUSETTS, U.S.A.
1969

A current list of all publications available
can be obtained by writing to the

Publication Department
Peabody Museum
Harvard University
11 Divinity Avenue
Cambridge, Massachusetts 02138

THE FREMONT CULTURE
A STUDY IN CULTURE DYNAMICS
ON THE
NORTHERN ANASAZI FRONTIER

Including
The Report of
THE CLAFLIN-EMERSON EXPEDITION
OF
THE PEABODY MUSEUM

PAPERS
OF THE
PEABODY MUSEUM OF ARCHAEOLOGY AND
ETHNOLOGY, HARVARD UNIVERSITY
VOL. 59, NO. 2

THE FREMONT CULTURE

A STUDY IN CULTURE DYNAMICS
ON THE
NORTHERN ANASAZI FRONTIER

Including
THE REPORT OF THE
CLAFLIN-EMERSON EXPEDITION
OF
THE PEABODY MUSEUM

BY

JAMES H. GUNNERSON

WITH APPENDICES BY
WALTON C. GALINAT AND JAMES H. GUNNERSON
AND
MARGARET A. TOWLE

PUBLISHED BY THE PEABODY MUSEUM
CAMBRIDGE, MASSACHUSETTS, U.S.A.
1969

PRINTED BY THE CRIMSON PRINTING COMPANY
CAMBRIDGE, MASSACHUSETTS, U.S.A.

TO WILLIAM H. CLAFLIN AND RAYMOND EMERSON

Who early had convictions as to the
archaeological potential
of eastern Utah

PREFACE

THIS monograph is two things. It is a synthesis of results of survey and excavation in the Northern Periphery of the American Southwest in the 1950's by the author, Dr. James H. Gunnerson. It is also a report of the archaeological reconnaissance and test excavations made by the Claflin-Emerson expedition of the Peabody Museum, Harvard University, from 1927 through 1931. The former will speak for itself as it takes its place among the serious considerations of the prehistory of Utah inaugurated by Noel Morss and Julian Steward. The latter, since the field work was done so many years ago, merits further explanation.

The Claflin-Emerson expedition grew out of the devotion of two Boston businessmen, William H. Claflin and Raymond Emerson, to the history of the American Indian. A boyhood fascination with the prehistoric artifacts of New England and of Stallings Island, Georgia, whetted by an interest in the more remote regions of the American West, led Mr. Claflin to transform an intriguing hobby into a scientific enterprise. His friend, Raymond Emerson, shared these interests and in addition was a skilled surveyor. They were abetted and advised by Dr. A. V. Kidder, whose influence lay in the background of so many of the important developments in Southwestern archaeology during the first half of the century. To this combination was added the enthusiasm of Donald Scott, who had returned to the academic halls of Cambridge after a successful career as a publisher in New York.

The bare details of the various expeditions are set down on pages 23–24, below. The plan was to conduct a rapid reconnaissance of eastern Utah from the Arizona line to the border with Wyoming. A gentleman's agreement was entered into with the University of Utah under which the Peabody Museum would be responsible for a survey of the eastern part of the state and the University would take care of the central and western sections. The Museum has a long history of work in Utah going back to 1875–77, when Dr. C. C. Parry excavated on the Santa Clara River in Southwestern Utah and Dr. Edward Palmer at Paragonah in south-central Utah. The shift to eastern Utah was made because of the almost total lack of knowledge of that section.

The surveys of the Claflin-Emerson expedition, although extensive, did not by any means cover the entire eastern part of the state. Concentration was upon the river valleys and, except for Donald Scott's original survey of the Kaiparowits Plateau, little was done on the mesa tops. Surveys in the lower reaches of Ashley Creek, Brush Creek, and the Duchesne River flowing out of the foothills to the south were the only activities in the Uintah Mountain section. A few tributaries where sites are now known to exist were bypassed, including Price River and Thompson Wash, and little was done on the San Rafael River, nor were any surveys made on the eastern edge of the Tavaputs Plateau or in the vicinity of Watson and Dragon. By and large, however, at least a quick look-see was given to most areas. The extreme southeastern part of the state in San Juan County was omitted because the prehistoric inhabitants there were part of the Mesa Verde division of the nuclear Pueblo area. That region was sampled in 1931–33, immediately after the conclusion of the Claflin-Emerson surveys (again at the suggestion of Dr. Kidder) and is described in the report on Alkali Ridge (Brew 1941).

The most important contribution of the Claflin-Emerson expedition was the definition of the Fremont culture based on survey and excavation in the Fremont and Dirty Devil region west of the Colorado River by Noel Morss (Morss 1931). This provided a framework upon which subsequent discoveries could be hung and introduced order where previously there had been only chaos or ignorance. *The Ancient Culture of the Fremont River in Utah* is a fine example of the contribution which can be made by an intelligent scholar even though he is not classified as a "professional." Although Noel Morss studied anthropology in college, he went into the law and belongs to that profession especially peculiar to New England called "trustees." His monograph is one of the more important reports in Southwestern archaeology. Without it, this paper could not have been written with the coherence and effective theoretical value manifest in the following pages.

The remainder of the notes, photographs, and specimens from the Claflin-Emerson surveys have languished ever since in the files and storage of the Museum, awaiting the "right" man to put them to work. This is a fate not unusual to collections of scientific data in archaeology and other professions. The scientific leader of the expedition was Henry B. Roberts, who was in charge in the field during two major seasons of the survey (1929 and 1930) and visited the field party in northeastern Utah in 1931. While working on his report he was afflicted with a serious illness which forced the termination of a most promising archaeological career.

Dr. James H. Gunnerson, the author of this report, was an ideal scholar to pick up the reins. His original training in archaeology was in the Missouri Basin under Professor John L. Champe at the University of Nebraska. After his graduate student residence at Harvard University he spent six years as an archaeologist on the staff of the University of Utah. This report, which includes his Ph.D. thesis, incorporates the Claflin-Emerson data in a useful way that would not have been possible at the time the material was collected. The delay has been unfortunate, as are all circumstances that prevent information in being from reaching the hands of those scholars who might use it, but the material itself has not suffered from it. It is now presented in a theoretical context which gives it the maximum application to the problems of the Northern Periphery of the Southwest.

This monograph, the publication of which has been made possible by generous gifts from Mr. and Mrs. William H. Claflin and Mrs. Donald Scott, relates the prehistory of eastern Utah to the Pueblos which bound it on the south and to the cultures of the Great Basin on the west and north. It is a fitting tribute to the men who forty years ago realized the importance of the remnants of ancient peoples who wrested a meager living from the rugged canyon country of the Green and Colorado Rivers.

J. O. Brew
Cambridge, Massachusetts
September 6, 1968

INTRODUCTION AND ACKNOWLEDGEMENTS

THIS study has four related purposes. It traces the development of theories concerning trans-Colorado Puebloan archaeology. Next it presents for the first time a full description of the Claflin-Emerson expedition of the Peabody Museum which worked in eastern Utah from 1927 through 1931. Then it proceeds to a functional synthesis of the Fremont culture that incorporates these new data. Finally, it discusses the dynamics of the growth and decline of the Fremont culture.

In brief, it suggests that the introduction of a new race of maize into the Southwest caused a population increase that resulted in a movement of people northward from the Virgin Branch of Anasazi into an area in which hybrids of the new maize made possible, for the first time, successful maize horticulture. This northward spread of people is here interpreted as the vigorous frontier movement of a resourceful population that had remained unspecialized through the retention of many old traits, including hunting and gathering techniques, after the adoption of new traits.

The people on the northern frontier of Anasazi developed the distinctive Fremont and Sevier cultures, which dominated the northern three-fourths of Utah from *ca.* A.D. 950 to *ca.* A.D. 1200. Then, apparently as a result of worsening climatic conditions, deculturation took place, changing all the horticulturalists north of the Colorado River into hunters and gatherers, probably the Plateau Shoshoneans of historic times.

This paper, prepared while the author was at Harvard University, was submitted in essentially its present form in partial fulfillment of the requirements for the degree of Doctor of Philosophy in Anthropology at Harvard University. Its preparation was made possible by the assistance of the faculty and staff of the Department of Anthropology and the Peabody Museum. The Director of the Museum, Dr. J. O. Brew, made available the material and information collected by the Claflin-Emerson expedition and provided laboratory and office space for its study. Mr. Donald Scott, Director

Emeritus of Peabody Museum, placed the resources of his personal library and his extensive file on pictographs at the disposal of the author. Previously, under the direction of Mr. Scott, the site plans and profiles that appear in this volume had been drafted, much of the site location data had been placed on base maps, the 1931 field notes had been edited and typed, and work copies of the artifact catalogues had been prepared. All this basic work expedited the preparation of the report of the Claflin-Emerson expedition. The photographs for figures 31*A* and 39–46 were taken by the author. The other photographs were taken by various members of the Claflin-Emerson expedition parties.

During the final year of work on the thesis, the author was awarded a Thaw Fellowship by the Peabody Museum and a research grant by the Department of Anthropology.

Three botanists from the Botanical Museum of Harvard University made substantial contributions to the present work: Drs. Margaret A. Towle and Walton C. Galinat identified plant materials and Dr. Paul C. Mangelsdorf provided valuable advice and encouragement to Dr. Galinat and me in our study of Fremont maize and our re-examination of the entire problem of Southwestern maize.

In describing sites it became necessary to secure additional information on local place names and site locations in Nine Mile and Barrier Canyons. Mr. and Mrs. Howard Price of Nine Mile Canyon, Price, Utah, and Dr. Dean Brimhall of Fruita, Utah, provided this needed information, and Dr. Brimhall further contributed to my knowledge of the Barrier Canyon pictographs by sharing his information and photographs and by personally taking me to view them.

The basic contribution, of course, was that made by Mr. and Mrs. William Claflin and Mr. and Mrs. Raymond Emerson, who in 1927 recognized the need for an extensive archaeological survey of eastern Utah and made funds available for Peabody Museum to carry out such a project. Generous gifts from Mr. and

Mrs. William H. Claflin and Mrs. Donald Scott made possible the publication of the results of the expedition.

This paper has profited from the careful reading and constructive criticism of my thesis committee, which consisted of Dr. J. O. Brew (Chairman), Dr. William R. Bullard, Mr. Watson Smith, and Dr. Evon Z. Vogt. Mrs. Naomi Stratton provided valuable advice on details of manuscript preparation while the paper was being written. My wife, Dolores A. Gunnerson, served as a ready audience and a sage critic upon whom I could try out new interpretations, ideas, and speculations. Mrs. Evelyn Brew painstakingly edited the manuscript for publication and saw it through the printing process. Without her contributions this monograph would not have appeared when it did. Dr. J. O. Brew reread the manuscript while it was being prepared for publication and supplied additional information such as the identification of people in the field photographs.

To all of these people I wish to express my gratitude.

September 20, 1968

JAMES H. GUNNERSON

CONTENTS

PREFACE vii

INTRODUCTION AND ACKNOWLEDGE-
MENTS ix

PART 1. A HISTORY OF TRANS-COLO-
RADO PUEBLOAN ARCHAEOLOGY . . 5
Early work 5
Recent Work in the Virgin Area . . . 7
    A Summary Description of the Virgin
    Branch 9
Recent Work West of the Wasatch . . . 11
    A Summary Description of the Sevier
    Culture 12
Recent Work East of the Wasatch . . . 14
Recent Interpretations 18

PART II. THE CLAFLIN-EMERSON EX-
PEDITION 23
Introduction 23
    Organization of the Project 23
    Geography of the Area Investigated . . 24
    Nature of the Sites Discovered . . . 25
    Contributions of the Project 26
    Presentation of the Data Recovered . . 27
Kaiparowits Plateau 27
    E 11-1 30
    E 11-2 30
    E 11-3 30
    E 11-6 31
    E 11-7 31
    E 12-2 31
    E 12-3 31
    E 12-4 32
    E 12-6 32
    E 12-7 32
Escalante Drainage 33
    E 2-1 33
    E 6-1 33
    E 6-2 33
    E 12-1 33
    H 9-3 34
Glen Canyon 34
    H 6-1 34
    H 6-2 35
    H-6-3 35
    H 7-1 35
    H 7-2 35
    H 7-3 35
Trachite Creek–North Wash 36
    H 3-1 36

H 3-2 36
H 3-3 36
H 3-4 36
H 3-5 37
H 3-6 37
H 3-7 37
H 3-8 37
Ruin Park–Salt Creek–Fort Bottom . . . 38
LS 13-1 39
LS 13-2 41
LS 13-3 41
LS 13-4 41
LS 13-5 43
LS 13-6, 7, 8, 9, 10 43
LS 13-11 43
LS 13-12 43
LS 13-13 43
LS 14-1 44
LS 14-2 44
LS 14-3 44
LS 14-4 44
LS 14-5 44
LS 14-6 44
LS 14-7 44
LS 14-8 44
LS 14-9 45
LS 14-10 45
LS 14-11 45
LS 14-12 46
LS 14-13 46
LS 9-1: Fort Bottom Ruin 46
Dirty Devil River–Waterhole Flat 47
SR 10-1 47
SR 10-3 48
SR 10-4 48
SR 15-1 48
SR 15-2 49
SR 15-3 49
SR 15-4 49
SR 15-5 49
SR 16-1 49
SR 16-2 49
SR 16-3 51
SR 16-4 51
SR 16-5 53
SR 16-6: Cottonwood Cave 53
SR 16-7 58
SR 16-8 58
SR 16-9 59
SR 16-10: Red Snake Cave 59
SR 16-11 61

SR 16-12: Red Point 61
SR 16-13 61
LS 13-14 61
LS 13-15 62
Barrier Canyon 62
SR 8-1 63
SR 8-2 63
SR 8-3 63
SR 8-4 63
SR 8-5 63
SR 8-6 63
SR 8-7 65
SR 12-1 65
SR 12-2 65
SR 12-3 65
SR 12-4: The Great Gallery 65
SR 12-5: Horseshoe Shelter 67
Fremont River Drainage 73
FL 11-1 74
FL 11-2 74
FL 12-1 74
FL 12-2 74
FL 12-3 74
FL 12-4 74
FL 12-5: Deer Bone Cave 75
FL 12-6 76
FL 12-7 76
FL 15-1 76
FL 15-3 76
FL 16-1 76
FL 16-2 77
FL 16-4 77
Muddy River Drainage 78
FL 4-1 78
FL 4-4 79
FL 4-5 79
FL 4-6 79
FL 7-1 80
Desolation Canyon 80
ET 5-1 81
ET 5-2 81
PR 8-1 81
PR 8-2 81
PR 8-3 82
PR 8-4 82
PR 12-21 82
PR 12-22 82
Range Creek Canyon 82
PR 12-1 83
PR 12-2 83
PR 12-3 83
PR 12-4 83
PR 12-5 84
PR 12-6 84
PR 12-7 84
PR 12-8 84
PR 12-9 84
PR 12-10 85

PR 12-11 85
PR 12-12 85
PR 12-13 85
PR 12-14 85
PR 12-15 85
PR 12-16 85
PR 12-17 86
PR 12-18 86
PR 12-19 86
PR 12-20 86
Nine Mile Canyon 87
PR 3-1 87
PR 3-2 87
PR 3-3 87
PR 3-4 88
PR 3-5 88
PR 4-1 88
PR 4-2 88
PR 4-3 88
PR 4-4 88
PR 4-5 89
PR 4-6 89
PR 4-7 89
PR 4-8 90
PR 4-11: Nordell's Fort 90
PR 4-12 90
PR 4-13 90
PR 4-14 90
PR 4-15 90
PR 4-16 91
PR 4-17 91
PR 4-18 91
PR 4-19 91
PR 4-20 91
PR 4-21 92
PR 4-22 92
PR 4-23 92
PR 4-24 92
PR 4-25 92
PR 4-26 94
PR 4-27 94
PR 4-28 95
PR 4-29 95
PR 4-30 95
PR 4-31: Rasmussen Cave 97
    Fremont Component 97
    Basketmaker-like Burial 101
PR 4-32 104
Florence and Chandler Creeks 105
ET 9-4 105
ET 9-5 105
ET 9-6 105
ET 9-7 105
ET 9-8 105
ET 9-9 106
ET 9-10 106
Hill and Willow Creeks 106
ET 6-1 106

ET 6-2 107
ET 6-3 107
ET 6-4: Pinnacle Rock 107
ET 6-7: Long Mesa, Fortification Rock . 107
ET 6-8 111
ET 6-9 111
ET 6-10 111
ET 6-11 111
ET 6-12 111
ET 6-13 112
ET 6-14 112
ET 6-15 112
ET 6-16 112
ET 6-17 112
ET 6-18 112
ET 6-19 113
ET 6-20 113
ET 6-21 113
ET 6-22 113
ET 6-23 113
ET 6-24 113
ET 6-26: Rock House, Eight Mile Ruin . 114
ET 9-1 114
ET 9-2 114
ET 9-3 114
ET 10-1 114
ET 10-3 114
ET 10-4 116
ET 10-5 116
ET 10-6 116
ET 10-7 116
Uinta Mountain Foothills 116
U 16-1 to U 16-7: South Myton Bench . 117
U 11-1 118
A 6-1: Well Cave 118
A 6-2 119
A 6-3 120
A 6-5 120
A 6-6 120
A 6-7 120
A 7-1 120
A 7-2 121
A 9-1 121
A 9-2 122
A 9-3 122
A 12-1 122

PART III. A FUNCTIONAL SYNTHESIS
OF THE FREMONT CULTURE . . . 133
Geography 133
The People 134
Food Quest 135
    Animals Hunted 135
    Plants Gathered 135
    Hunting Implements 136
Horticulture 136
    Plants Cultivated 136

Horticultural Implements 137
    Irrigation 137
Food Storage 138
Food Preparation 139
Drugs and Narcotics 140
Amusement 141
Weaving and Cordage 141
Basketry 141
Leather 143
Ceramics 143
Exploitative Activities 145
Processing of Basic Materials 145
    Bone 145
    Wood 146
    Stone 146
Architecture 146
    Pithouses 147
    Surface Structures 148
    Sheltered Structures 149
    Ceremonial Structures 150
Settlement Pattern 150
Tools 151
    Weapons 151
    Cutting Tools 152
    Perforating Tools 153
    Abrading Tools 153
    Milling Devices 153
    Pounding Tools 153
    Firemaking Equipment 153
Dress and Adornment 154
    Clothing 154
    Adornment 155
Exchange 156
Social Structure 156
Burial Customs 157
Art 158
    Pictographs 158
    Figurines 159
    Pottery 160
Religion 161
Summary 162

PART IV. FREMONT CULTURE DY-
NAMICS 167
Age of the Fremont Culture 167
Origin of the Fremont Culture 170
Fremont Relationships 170
    Routes Connecting the Virgin and Fremont
        Areas 178
    Cause of the Pueblo II Expansion . . . 179
    Predecessors of the Fremont People . . . 180
The Fate of the Fremont Culture . . . 181
The Lexico-Archaeological Matrix of the
    Fremont Culture 193

SUMMARY 195

APPENDIX I. FREMONT MAIZE. by Walton C. Galinat and James H. Gunnerson . . 198

APPENDIX II. USE OF PLANT MATERIALS OTHER THAN MAIZE. by Margaret A. Towle 207

APPENDIX III. THE RASMUSSEN CAVE SKELETON: OBSERVATIONS AND MEASUREMENTS by James H. Gunnerson 209

BIBLIOGRAPHY 211

LIST OF TABLES

1. Distribution of specimens from sites reported in this paper 124
2. Characteristics of all maize ears and cobs from sites investigated by the Claflin-Emerson expedition. 199
3. Characteristics of selected ears of maize. . 202
4. Distribution of specimens of identified plant materials. 207

LIST OF LINE-CUT FIGURES

1. Map of Utah and contiguous areas . . . 4
2. Locations of sites herein reported . . 28, 29
3. Plan of Site LS 13-2 40
4. Plan of Site LS 13-5 42
5. Plan and profile of structure at Site SR 16-3 50
6. Plan of Site SR 16-5 52
7. Plan and profile of Site SR 16-6 . . . 54, 55
8. Plan and profile of structure at Site LS 13-14 60
9. Plan of Site SR 12-1 64
10. Plan of Site SR 12-5 66
11. Plan of Site PR 4-25 93
12. Plan of Site PR 4-31 96
13. Plan of Site ET 6-4 108
14. Plan of Site ET 6-7 110
15. Plan of Site ET 6-26 115
16. Plan of Site A 9-2 123
17. Location of Plateau Shoshonean people ca. A.D. 1700 183
18. Location of Virgin, Sevier, and Fremont cultures ca. A.D. 1050–1150 183
19. Comparison of Shoshonean glottochronology with suggested archaeological reconstruction 184

LIST OF OFFSET HALF-TONE FIGURES

20A. Structure at Site LS 13-2 in Ruin Park
20B. Portion of Structure at Site LS 13-4 in Ruin Park
21A. Structures at Site LS 14-11 in Salt Creek Canyon
21B. Detail of construction at Site LS 13-12 just north of Ruin Park
22A. Two-story storage structure at Site LS 13-11 in a tributary of Salt Creek Canyon
22B. Remains of structures at Site LS 14-10 in Salt Creek Canyon
23A. Distant view of Fort Bottom Ruin (LS 9-1)
23B. Fort Bottom Ruin (LS 9-1)
24A. Structures at Site SR 8-5 on Woodruff Bottoms
24B. Cists 2, 3, 7, and 8 at Cottonwood Cave (SR 16-6)
25A. Pictographs at Site H 3-4 in North Wash
25B. Pictographs at Site FL 4-1
26A. General view of Great Gallery in Barrier Canyon (SR 12-4)
26B. Continuation to right of figure 26A
27A. Details of figures in Great Gallery (SR 12-4)
27B. Details of figures in Great Gallery (SR 12-4)
27C. Details of figures in Great Gallery (SR 12-4)
28A. Details of figures in Great Gallery (SR 12-4)
28B. Details of figures in Great Gallery (SR 12-4)
29A. Details of figures in Great Gallery (SR 12-4)
29B. Details of figures in Great Gallery (SR 12-4)
30A. Details of figures in Great Gallery (SR 12-4)
30B. Details of figures in Great Gallery (SR 12-4)
31A. Small pictograph figures resembling Fremont figurines at unnumbered site in Barrier Canyon
31B. Pictographs at Horseshoe Shelter (SR 12-5)
32A. Excavation in progress at Horseshoe Shelter (SR 12-5)
32B. Ring of basalt boulders outlining a structure prior to its excavation at Site FL 11-2 near Torrey, Utah
33A. Nordell's Fort (PR 4-11), located on end of narrow ridge overlooking Nine Mile Canyon
33B. Storage structure at Site PR 4-13, in Nine Mile Canyon
34A. General view of Rasmussen's Cave (PR 4-31), facing northwest
34B. Burial in situ at Rasmussen's Cave (PR 4-31)

35A. Crude stone walls at Site ET 6-2 in Hill Creek Canyon
35B. Small stone-and-adobe storage structure at Site ET 6-3, near mouth of Horsecorn Canyon
36A. General view of Long Mesa Ruin (ET 6-7)
36B. Details of masonry at Long Mesa Ruin (ET 6-7)
37A. General view of Rock House Ruin (ET 6-26)
37B. Details of masonry at Rock House Ruin (ET 6-26)
38A. Ascent to Pinnacle Rock (ET 6-4)
38B. Excavation at Site A 9-2
39.   Miscellaneous artifacts
40.   Miscellaneous artifacts
41.   Artifacts found with burial at Site PR 4-31
42.   Chipped stone artifacts from Myton Bench sites
43.   Representative chipped stone tools from sites with Fremont culture components
44.   Miscellaneous containers
45A. Eight-rowed cobs from Fremont and Kayenta sites
45B. Dent maize from various prehistoric sites in the Fremont area
45C. A comparison of the most Zapalote Chico–like specimen in the collection studied with a modern ear of Zapalote Chico
46.   Skull from burial at Site PR 4-31
47A. Pack train on top of Water Pocket Fold
47B. Starting down from the top of Water Pocket Fold
47C. Quicksand in Hoxie Creek
47D. Pack train coming out of Hoxie Creek
48A. A current ferry over the Green River
48B. Donald Scott in The Devil's Pocket
49A. William H. Claflin in The Muley Twist
49B. Dave Rust in Water Pocket Fold
50A. A Colorado River trail
50B. Climbing to a cliff ruin
51A. Pack train on a Green River trail
51B. Expedition camp in the Uinta foothills

THE FREMONT CULTURE

A STUDY IN CULTURE DYNAMICS

ON THE

NORTHERN ANASAZI FRONTIER

Including
The Report of
THE CLAFLIN-EMERSON EXPEDITION
OF
THE PEABODY MUSEUM

PART I

TRANS-COLORADO PUEBLOAN ARCHAEOLOGY

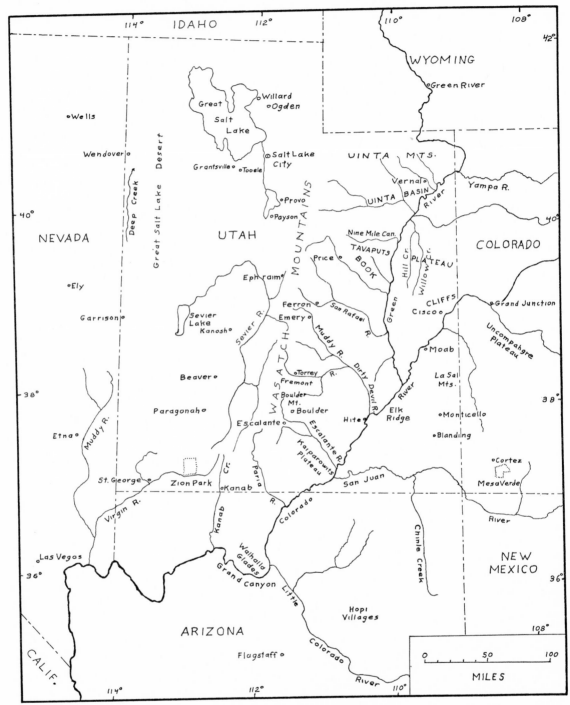

Fig. 1. Map of Utah and contiguous areas.

A HISTORY OF
TRANS-COLORADO PUEBLOAN ARCHAEOLOGY

THE investigation of Puebloan remains north of the Colorado River began nearly a century ago, and most archaeologists who have worked in the area since have speculated on the cultural position of the sites there. Since the ultimate concern of this paper is culture dynamics in the trans-Colorado regions, the history of these speculations, interpretations, and theories is of more importance here than a chronological account of field work as such. To be sure, theory must be based on, and evaluated in terms of, data. But the data are, for the most part, available in detail elsewhere. Moreover, at any given point in the archaeological history of an area the interpretation (and therefore the apparent significance) of the data is likely to be determined largely by the theory most popular at the time.

The treatment of the early history of trans-Colorado archaeology that follows will deal with the region as a whole because the first work was scattered and relatively small in amount. By the early 1930's, however, enough work had been done north of the Colorado so that three major archaeological subareas could be differentiated. Therefore, it seems appropriate not only to begin the discussion of recent history at this date, but to consider the recent history of each subarea separately. Finally, the last section of Part I will relate interpretations based on data from sites and subareas to recent attempts at broad synthesis involving culture dynamics in the trans-Colorado Puebloan area.

EARLY WORK

The first archaeological work reported for the trans-Colorado area was that done in 1872 in conjunction with the U.S. geographical and geological explorations and surveys west of the one hundredth meridian. Severance (1874) briefly reported that "At Provo, Utah, several careful excavations were made in a number of mounds scattered over the plain on which the town stands, and a mass of miscellaneous objects secured" which he proceeds to enumerate. He also noted the site at Paragonah, Utah, with its "four or five hundred mounds" some of which had previously been dug into, and recommended this site for further investigation. At Beaver, Utah, he "probed to a slight degree" into a compact cluster of mounds and concluded that the remains were much like those found at Provo. All these sites are in what is now called the Sevier area.

The first excavations on behalf of a private institution were those of Dr. C. C. Parry, who in 1875 obtained a collection of artifacts from a mound near St. George, Utah, for the Peabody Museum of Harvard University (Put-nam, 1876). At about this same time, under the sponsorship of the Peabody Museum and the U.S. National Museum, Dr. Edward Palmer excavated a mound near St. George and a cave near Kanab, Utah, in what has come to be known as the Virgin area, as well as mounds near Payson and Paragonah, Utah, in the Sevier area. Moreover, he studied the Paiutes of southern Utah (Palmer, 1876, 1878; Putnam, 1880, *passim;* Heizer, 1954). Although his reports are primarily descriptive, Palmer recognized that the pottery from the cave and the mounds was probably related to that found at Pueblo sites elsewhere in the Southwest. On the other hand, he observed that some of the nonceramic artifacts from the cave near Kanab resembled objects then being used by Paiutes and other non-Pueblo Indians.

Holmes (1886), in describing pottery of the Southwest, apparently based his descriptions of pottery from southwestern, central, and northern Utah on the collections made by Palmer. He illustrated a number of specimens and noted the similarity of the pottery from along the Virgin River to that from near Kanab, Utah, and to that from the Four Corners area. He also commented on the differences in the pottery of western Utah from south to north.

The first attempt at a summary of Utah archaeology was apparently that by Henry Montgomery (1894), a professor of natural history at the University of Utah, who had investigated a number of sites in various parts of western Utah, including Beaver, Iron, Juab, Piute, Tooele, Salt Lake, Utah, and Millard counties. His personal observations in eastern Utah were confined to Nine Mile Canyon in Carbon County (at that time part of Emery County), but he also described material collected by others in San Juan County, southeastern Utah. Montgomery commented on the great similarity of all the sites in western Utah and, after describing a few, such as the already much-excavated site at Paragonah, concluded that there was no need to describe others. He attributes the sites in all parts of Utah, along with those in Colorado and Arizona, to the same people. After discussing masonry towers near Nine Mile Canyon, he reflects (Montgomery, 1894, p. 340) that, "Utah, being on the outskirts of the country occupied by a great nation whose headquarters were probably in Mexico, might properly be expected to be provided with a considerable number of military posts or watch stations such as those herein described." This statement may reflect the popular local beliefs of the day that assumed a relationship between the ruins of the Southwest and the Aztecs of Mexico. Such thinking is immortalized in various place names in the Southwest, such as Montezuma Creek in Utah, Montezuma's Castle in Arizona, and the town of Aztec, New Mexico.

A landmark in the history of trans-Colorado archaeology was Nusbaum's report in 1922 of his excavations at Cave du Pont, near Kanab, Utah. This important Basketmaker II site, since dated by dendrochronology at A.D. 217 by Stallings (1941), is still the best source of information on the Basketmaker II phase in the Virgin area.

Another major contribution to archaeology north of the Colorado River was the six years of work by Judd, started in 1916. His survey, with accompanying excavations, took him from the north rim of the Grand Canyon through central Utah to the eastern shore of the Great Salt Lake. Therefore he, too, sampled remains of both the Virgin and the Sevier cultures. During this period a number of preliminary reports appeared (Judd, 1916, 1917, 1918, 1919, 1920) although his final summary was not published until 1926.

About the time that Judd was starting his work in western Utah, Fewkes (1917 b) described ruins (spectacular by local standards) along Hill Creek in northeastern Utah. However, he was far more concerned with the function of these stone structures ("towers") than with their cultural affiliation. He apparently took it for granted that they were remains of a Puebloan occupation.

Meanwhile, even more archaeological work had been done elsewhere in the Southwest and Kidder, by 1924, was able to outline Pueblo culture history with so much precision that his broad formulation has never been significantly altered. In his classic introduction to Southwestern archaeology, Kidder (1924) designated the area north of the Colorado River which contained Pueblo or Pueblo-like sites as the "northern peripheral area of the Southwest" and described its archaeology primarily on the basis of information presented by Judd in his various preliminary reports. Many archaeologists feel that calling this area the "Northern Periphery" obscures its significance, and confusion has arisen because some workers (Steward, for example) later used the term with a meaning different from Kidder's. Nevertheless, the name has never been completely replaced.

During the dozen years that followed Kidder's "Introduction," there was increased archaeological activity in all parts of the "Northern Periphery." In 1926, Judd published a summary of his own work which indicated his belief that the area had been inhabited by ancient Pueblo people and that their culture was "definitely and directly related to those pre-Pueblo and Pueblo cultures represented by the prehistoric ruins in northern Arizona, New Mexico, and Colorado." He noted a gradation from south to north with a "higher degree of culture" in the south. Originally, he thought that this change represented "a gradual culture development from north to south," but he eventually concluded that the evidence could also be interpreted as a "cultural retrogression from south to north" (Judd, 1926, p. 152). As recently as 1940, however, Judd still thought that the prehistoric cultures of western Utah might have originated to the north (Judd, 1940, pp. 428–429).

In southeastern Nevada, archaeological work was conducted in the late 1920's and early 1930's by Harrington (1926 a, 1926 b, 1927, 1928, 1930; for other Harrington publications see Shutler, 1961, p. 78), Hayden (1930), and Schellbach (1927). Harrington, the most active of this group, recognized a culture history starting with a Basketmaker phase that possessed pithouses but lacked pottery, and ending with a phase characterized by large masonry pueblos and a well-developed ceramic complex. Harrington (1930) named two phases, or "stages" as he called them. The earliest Pueblo (post-Basketmaker) phase he called the "Lost City stage" and the final phase, the "Mesa House stage," for the type site.

After Judd, the next archaeologist to make substantial contributions to the data on western Utah was Steward (1931, 1933 a, 1933 b, 1936), who excavated at several sites. By 1933 he had enough information on the entire state to divide it into its major archaeological sub-areas and to pose a number of basic problems with regard to interpretation of the data (Steward, 1933 b). In broad outline, much of Steward's interpretation of trans-Colorado Puebloan archaeology, the first soundly based synthesis, still stands. The development of his thinking is somewhat difficult to follow (possibly because the publication dates of his articles do not reflect the sequence in which they were written). However, when he wrote his 1933 b article he apparently still considered the area drained by the northern tributaries of the Colorado west of the San Juan River (his Area 4) part of the Northern Periphery. But he noted that Area 4 showed more similarities to the Anasazi culture south and east of the Colorado than did any other part of the Northern Periphery, and suggested that it might eventually be desirable to designate it as a "Western Periphery." Steward split the rest of Utah north of his Area 4 by a north–south line along the crest of the Wasatch Mountains. With an east–west line he in turn divided the region west of the Wasatch into two parts of nearly equal size. Most of the southern part of western Utah, Area 3, drains into Sevier Lake, and most of the northern part, Area 2, drains into the Great Salt Lake. Steward designated the region east of the Wasatch Mountains as Areas 1 A (to the north) and 1 B (to the south) with no definite line between them. Except for the fact that he did not show the eastern edge of Area 1 (A plus B) and included part of the Escalante River drainage in it, his Area 1 corresponds to the Fremont area as it was later defined by the author (Gunnerson 1960 a). More recent work in western Utah has tended to minimize the distinction between the areas (2 and 3) set up by Steward there.

Steward's 1933 synthesis represents, to a certain extent, a culmination of early work in trans-Colorado archaeology. Since the present study is concerned with relationships among the three major areas that he delineated, the more recent archaeological work in each area will be considered separately and in some detail in order to provide a basis for later comparisons.

RECENT WORK IN THE VIRGIN AREA

While Steward was finishing his field work in Utah, Gladwin and Gladwin (1934) devised a system for the designation of all cultures in the Southwest in which they suggested two branches of the San Juan (i.e., Anasazi) Stem, the Kayenta and the Nevada. Moreover, they divided the Nevada branch into two phases, the Moapa and the Parawan. Later, Colton (1942) renamed the Nevada Branch the "Virgin Branch" after the Virgin River to give it a name more indicative of its geographical distribution. The Virgin area corresponds closely to Steward's Area 4.

In the meantime, Spencer (1934) had contributed to the information on the central portion of the Virgin area and his report served as a point of departure for Colton's (1952) description of Virgin branch pottery types. In this paper Colton suggested that the Virgin branch be divided into three "foci."

The earliest he called the Muddy River Focus, but for the last two he retained the names Harrington had suggested for his "stages."

At about the time that Spencer was doing his work, a large archaeological program was undertaken in the Zion Park area with funds made available to the National Park Service through the Civil Works Administration. With the exception of two very brief articles (Smith, 1934; Wetherill, 1934), however, the results were not reported until about 20 years later, when Schroeder (1955), salvaging all the information that had survived, provided a major source of data on the eastern half of the Virgin area. Other near-by work consists of a survey of a limited portion of Washington County, Utah, by Rudy and Stirland (1950), the excavation of a rock shelter by Rudy (1954 b), and excavation at two open sites near St. George by Gunnerson (1960 b) and Pendergast (1960).

With the advent of salvage archaeology necessitated by the construction of the Glen Canyon dam, the extreme northeastern edge of the Virgin area was intensively investigated. Surveys in this area have been conducted by Lister (1958 a), Nichols (Suhm, 1959), and Gunnerson (1959 d). Excavations at sites near the Escalante River have been reported by Gunnerson (1959 c), and three seasons' work at the Coombs Site in Boulder, Utah, near the northern edge of the Escalante drainage has been reported by Lister and others (1959 b, 1960, 1961).

Most of the sites investigated by Gunnerson in the Escalante drainage and on the Kaiparowits Plateau, which overlooks it, are Virgin remains of Pueblo II age. Although the differences between these Virgin sites and those in southwestern Utah are difficult to enumerate, the sites in the Escalante area give the general impression of a less solidly developed and slightly simpler manifestation of the Virgin culture. Thus, these Virgin sites appear to have a greater similarity to Fremont sites than do contemporary Virgin remains farther west. Information obtained near Escalante, along with that derived from the literature, led Gunnerson (1960 a) to conclude that the Virgin culture was characterized by the retention of old traits when new traits were adopted.

The easternmost portion of the Virgin area was virtually unknown archaeologically until Steward, in 1932, carried out a survey in the Glen Canyon area and in a strip along the southern edge of Utah between the Colorado River and Kanab. He found the region east of Kanab in southern Utah to be a part "both geographically and culturally, of the Lower Colorado Plateau, that is, the area of southwestern Utah and northwestern Arizona" (Steward, 1941 a, p. 355).

Where the eastern edge of the Virgin area abuts the Kayenta, there appears to be some interfingering and/or blending of these two closely related branches. Colton (1955, 1956) shows that a number of pottery types which center in the Kayenta area extend across the Colorado River into this borderland. It seems likely, however, that the presence of such pottery represents, for the most part, trade or brief occupations by Kayenta people.

Hall (1942) conducted a survey of Walhalla Glades on the north rim at the east end of Grand Canyon and found 273 archaeological sites in a few square miles, a concentration reminiscent of, but even higher than, that found on the Kaiparowits Plateau (Gunnerson, 1959 d). Hall concluded that the area had been occupied from Basketmaker III times into early Pueblo III, with a great population increase in Pueblo II and a gradual shift from exclusively Kayenta to predominantly Virgin affiliations. Since Hall commented on the paucity of information regarding Virgin (Utah) pottery, it is possible that, if he had had data adequate for comparisons, he would have assigned some of the sherds that he classed as Kayenta types to very similar Virgin types such as the Virgin varieties of Tusayan and Moenkopi Corrugated, which appear in Pueblo II times.

Schwartz (1963) has recently reported 48 sites in Nankoweap Canyon, which drains east from the Walhalla Plateau into the Colorado River. All these appear to be of Kayenta affiliation and nearly all are dated between A.D. 1050 and A.D. 1175. Perhaps more enclaves of this sort will be discovered as additional work is done.

A few other sites west and north of the Colorado River have been assigned to the Kayenta branch. The Davis Kiva Site (Gunnerson, 1959 c), located about five miles west of the confluence of the Escalante River and the

Colorado, was probably occupied about A.D. 1150 or a little later. It contained a small, fairly well-built kiva-like structure and a few crudely constructed rooms but relatively little detritus, which suggests a brief slight occupation.

The Coombs Site (Lister, 1959 b; Lister, Ambler and Lister, 1960; Lister and Lister, 1961), located 50 miles northwest of the Davis Kiva Site, is the northwesternmost site to be assigned to the Kayenta branch. Coombs was apparently occupied for no longer than 100 years, beginning about A.D. 1075, but it appears to have been one of the most prosperous communities in the area at the time. It differs from Kayenta sites east of the Colorado River in a number of traits, and many traits that it did share with the San Juan region in general are most characteristic of San Juan Anasazi culture at an earlier date. Moreover, there are many parallels between the Coombs Site and the Virgin branch at about A.D. 1100, including the use of a wide variety of architectural styles and techniques, some of which (for example, jacal above-ground structures) had apparently lost popularity by then in the Kayenta area or at least have not been commonly found at Kayenta sites for which reports are available. Recognizable kivas are absent at the Coombs Site and rare in the Virgin area, but common in the Kayenta heartland. Stone axes and other heavy wood-working tools are scarce at Coombs as at Virgin sites, although stone axes were apparently not common in the Kayenta area either until after 1100. The Coombs axes were not only rare and ineffective in appearance but three of the four found have a notch in or a groove across the poll end (Lister and Lister, 1961, p. 92). This trait puzzled Pendergast (1960, p. 19), who found, at a Virgin site near St. George, a similar specimen that in turn most closely resembled one reported by Schroeder (1955, p. 139) from near Kanab, Utah. Pendergast, following Schroeder, discussed the distribution of axes with notched polls and found them to occur, but only rarely, in southern Nevada, at several places in southwestern Utah, north-central Utah, southwestern Colorado, and eastern Arizona. Woodbury (1954), however, did not include such specimens in his discussion of axes from Kayenta sites in northeastern Arizona. In brief, Virgin influence at the Coombs Site appears to have

been great enough to have introduced most of the traits that differentiate Virgin from Kayenta ca. A.D. 1100. Other traits at the Coombs Site were present in both the Virgin and Kayenta branches at that time.

A major recent contribution to the literature is that of Shutler (1961), who, like Schroeder, salvaged a great deal of old, previously unreported data, which, along with his own field work and a thorough combing of the literature, provided the basis for a summary of the westernmost portion of the Virgin branch. Moreover, his bibliography contains many references to shorter reports by people such as Baldwin, Harrington, and Schroeder who have done work in this far western area during the past thirty years. In setting up a culture sequence, Shutler reverted to "phases," but kept Colton's focus names to designate the latest three. He added a fourth, earlier phase for which he used Gladwin's term "Moapa."

A SUMMARY OF THE VIRGIN BRANCH

The picture of the Virgin branch that emerges from the reports by Shutler, Schroeder, and others is that of a Kayenta-influenced Anasazi culture that developed *in situ* over a long period of time through stages comparable to those established for the other branches of Anasazi: that is, from a prepottery Basketmaker II phase to an early Pueblo III phase. Trade sherds indicate that the Virgin people had relations not only with Kayenta, but also with other areas, especially the lower Colorado River.

The four phases of the Virgin branch in the western part of its area of distribution, with the dates suggested by Shutler (1961, p. 66) and the dates assigned earlier to three of these phases (foci) by Colton (1952, p. 5), are as follows:

Phase	Approximate Dates (A.D.)	
	Shutler	*Colton*
Moapa	? — 500	
Muddy River	500 — 700	600 — 900
Lost City	700 — 1100	900 — 1100
Mesa House	1100 — 1150	1100 — 1150

These phases have been defined specifically on the basis of material from southern Nevada. As yet, no one has determined whether they are applicable to the entire Virgin branch or whether there will be differences elsewhere great enough to warrant establishing other series of phases. The differences that prompted Gunnerson (1960 a, p. 377) to suggest the name "Zion subarea" for the eastern part of the Virgin branch may disappear as additional work is done in all parts of the region. In reporting the material from the Zion Park area, Schroeder (1955) prudently refrained from using the phase names established farther west and discussed his material in terms of Roberts' classification: Basket Maker; Modified Basket Maker; and Early, Middle and Late Developmental Pueblo. These stages can probably be equated with Shutler's phases without too much distortion by letting the Lost City Phase correspond to Early plus Middle Developmental Pueblo.

Although the general development of Virgin culture was very similar throughout the region it occupied, a few features were present in the eastern subarea that appear to have been missing in the western. The two most conspicuous in the archaeological record are black-on-white (slipped) pottery and structures that are almost certainly kivas. Unfortunately, however, the dating of the most kiva-like structure yet found is not too satisfactory. Schroeder (1955), who reported it, was troubled by the fact that on some lines of evidence the site where it occurred appeared to be one of the latest Virgin sites in Zion Park. Yet there were no corrugated or red ware sherds in the part of the artifact collection still extant, and these lacks were also mentioned in the excavation notes. The association of a well-developed and late-appearing architectural style with a stylistically earlier ceramic assemblage is hard to explain unless we assume that the people who occupied this particular site were conservative with regard to ceramics. In any case, this evidence does show that kivas or kiva-like structures were introduced into the Virgin area, probably in Pueblo II times, and that with them appear the first ventilators in pit structures in the Virgin area. Bullard (1962), in a comparative study of pre-A.D. 900 pithouses, could find no mention of ventilators, antechambers, or passage entrances in pit structures in this area. Antechambers and passage entrances have still not been reported for Virgin pithouses of any period.

The information secured from Cave du Pont, with its date of A.D. 217, suggests that the beginning of the development of Anasazi culture may be as early in the Virgin area as elsewhere. Cave du Pont yielded a wide variety of material, including many well-preserved perishable specimens, several ears of corn, slab-lined cists of various sizes, and a number of burials, as well as stone and bone artifacts. Information obtained from Basketmaker cave sites in southern Nevada has been summarized by Shutler (1961).

The open pithouse villages reported by Harrington (1926 a, 1926 b, 1937) were considered Basketmaker II because they lacked both pottery and projectile points of a size suitable for use on arrows. These pithouses have been assigned to the Moapa Phase by Shutler (1961), but cannot be dated more precisely. Thus, the beginning of Basketmaker II in the Virgin area is unknown, but it could predate the time of Christ.

During Basketmaker III times, the Muddy River Phase, dated at A.D. 500–700 on the basis of trade pottery, is characterized by many small pithouse villages, but Basketmaker III material is also found in caves and rock shelters (Shutler, 1961). The pottery made locally during this phase is predominantly plain gray, but some is a black-on-gray that closely resembles Lino Black-on-gray found as trade sherds at Muddy River Phase sites. Small arrow-size projectile points also made their first appearance during this period, replacing dart points. Other forms of artifacts found at Basketmaker II sites continue.

Shutler (1961, p. 68) has suggested that the Lost City Phase (A.D. 700–1100), which accounts for most of the sites that he considered, and appears to represent the period of greatest population density, may eventually be divided into two parts. A number of traits that appear elsewhere in the Anasazi area during Pueblo I times, or *ca.* A.D. 700–900, are missing in contemporary sites of the Lost City Phase. This situation indicates greatly reduced contact between the Virgin branch and the rest of Anasazi during this period or possibly even a complete hiatus in contact. Since much emphasis has been placed on ceramics in the Southwest, this break is made most conspicuous in the Virgin branch by the absence of both neck-banded pottery and pottery painted with designs of Kana-a style. Pueblo II ceramic traits such as corrugation and characteristic painted designs do appear in the later part of the Lost City Phase, showing renewed contact with the east. Fugitive red pigment applied to pottery after firing, a trait most characteristic of Basketmaker III ceramics elsewhere, is found during the Lost City Phase and probably started earlier.

Villages of the Lost City Phase were located for the most part on knolls in the valleys, and, to quote Shutler (1961, p. 68),

"The villages of this phase were combinations of pit and surface houses built with all the varieties of floor and wall construction found in the preceding phase. The rooms were arranged in U-shapes, in straight lines, or in blocks. Bins and storage cists were found within and without the rooms. No room which could definitely be called a kiva has been found in any of these Lost City houses.

"The utility pottery was predominantly plain though corrugated types were introduced late in the phase. The painted types were all black-on-gray and were local imitations of Kayenta types which date from A.D. 700 to 1100.

"The stone artifacts of the Muddy River Phase continued into this phase with new additions. Utah and trough metates were added. Paint grinding stones, stone balls, chipped and ground stone discs, notched stones, a variety of notched and stemmed projectile points, knives and drills, crude choppers, scrapers, and hammerstones were all found.

"Clay and stone pipes, turquoise, shell, stone, and bone beads and pendants, bone awls, spatulae, fleshers and dice were used. The baked clay figurine persisted. Red and yellow ochre and magnesite were used for paint.

"Coiled and twined basketry, matting, cordage, netting and sandals were found; juniper bark, sage brush, yucca, and apocynum were widely used in the manufacture of these things. Cotton was grown and woven into cloth.

"Flexed burials were found in the ash dumps and on and under the floors of abandoned houses. Grave offerings were abundant. Pottery was frequently placed in graves and many of the vessels may have contained food and water. Dog burials were found."

Fewer sites of the final or Mesa House Phase of the Virgin branch are known, although the type site had over 84 rooms dating from this short (50-year) phase. Mesa House was built on a ridge high above the edge of the valley floor, a position with obvious de-fensive possibilities. However, life apparently continued much as before; the people depended upon both corn and squash agriculture and hunting and gathering activities. Architecture remained the same, with both surface and pit structures in use. Corrugated pottery finally increased in popularity at the expense of plain ware. Trade sherds show continued contact with the upper (eastern) Virgin, Kayenta, lower Colorado River, and Patayan areas. The artifact inventory and burial complex remained the same as in the previous phase.

The occurrence of Tusayan Polychrome pottery [dated by Colton (1956) at about A.D. 1150–1300] at a number of sites in Washington County, Utah (Rudy and Stirland, 1950), suggests that the Virgin branch persisted a little later than the A.D. 1150 date suggested by Shutler. Sites yielding Tusayan Polychrome are apparently never large and may represent scattered communities that lingered on after the Virgin branch started to disintegrate. In any case, a terminal date closer to A.D. 1200 may eventually be established for the Virgin branch.

In summary, then, the recognition of the Virgin branch as a distinctive entity has come about very slowly. The earliest investigators tended to lump it with Southwestern remains in general. Kidder considered it peripheral to the Southwest, an opinion that Steward gradually veered away from, but that Wormington still held as late as 1955. The Gladwins designated it as a separate branch in 1934, a classification that Colton obviously agreed with when he changed its name in 1942. Harrington had suggested temporal subdivisions for the western manifestations by 1930 and Schroeder for the eastern part by 1955. And in 1960 Gunnerson recognized that the Virgin branch had acquired its distinctive character because of the additive orientation of the culture, in which a varied repertoire of techniques, artifacts, and practices was built up by the retention of old traits when new traits were added to the complex—a conclusion with which Shutler (1961, p. 9) concurred.

RECENT WORK WEST OF THE WASATCH

Interest in the archaeology of western Utah was stimulated by Steward's interpretations and by his concern with problems that to a large extent had grown out of his widespread excavations in open sites and caves. For a number of years after Steward concluded his field work, however, relatively little archaeology was done in the area, and what was done can be characterized as primarily data gathering. In 1937 Gillin excavated at three open villages near Marysvale, Ephraim, and Tooele in central Utah and the results of this work (Gillin, 1941) constitute the major contribution until after World War II. During the period immediately before the war, limited survey activities were carried out along the middle portion of the Nevada-Utah state line (Malouf, Dibble, and Smith, 1940; Malouf, 1946; Osborne, 1941). Caves continued to attract the attention of archaeologists. Just before and immediately after World War II, excavations were conducted at three caves near the south end of the Great Salt Lake (Smith, 1941, 1952; Enger, 1942).

In 1949 the University of Utah initiated its Statewide Archeological Survey, which had as its first goal a systematic reconnaissance of the entire state. At the time of its inception, the archaeological information regarding Utah was very spotty. Since western Utah was the least well known portion of the state, it was given a high priority and the first thorough reconnaissance of that region was carried out and reported by Rudy (1953). In conjunction with the activities of the Statewide Survey, the University of Utah excavated at one open village site in Nevada just across the state line from the town of Garrison, Utah (Taylor, 1954), and at deeply stratified Danger Cave near Wendover, also on the western edge of Utah, but near the northwest corner of the state (Jennings, 1953, 1957). As adjuncts to Statewide Survey activities, Rudy and Stoddard (1954) described the anomalous archaeological material found on Fremont Island in the Great Salt Lake, and Gunnerson (1956 d) re-examined, in terms of possible Plains relationships, some of the material collected earlier by Steward from caves on Promontory Point at the north end of the Great Salt Lake. Since 1954, the University of California at Los Angeles has conducted excavations for several seasons at the seemingly inexhaustible site near Paragonah in southwestern Utah. A useful report of the first year's work has been published (Meighan et al., 1956). Brigham

Young University has sponsored both survey (Jones, 1961) and excavation (Green, 1961) near Provo, Utah, an area where some of the earliest archaeological work in western Utah was done.

In this area west of the Wasatch Mountains archaeologists have been concerned primarily with two archaeological complexes. The Desert culture, with its simple hunting and gathering economy that completely exploited the environment and never became specialized, had occupied the area during the past 10,000 or more years. The second complex, variously designated as "Puebloid" or "Sevier" or "Sevier-Fremont," contains many Pueblo traits and is the one with which we are most concerned here.

A Summary Description of the Sevier Culture

The general description of the Sevier culture, as presented by Steward (1936), Rudy (1953), and Meighan et al. (1956), has not been significantly altered by subsequent work, but recent views on the cultural position of Sevier vary. Direct dating of Sevier sites is still not possible because wood specimens suitable for dendrochronology have not been recovered. The general consensus of those working in the area during the last twenty to thirty years is that these Puebloan sites were probably all occupied within the period A.D. 500–1270, as suggested by Rudy (1953, pp. 166, 170), for example. The beginning is apparently set at such an early date to allow for the introduction of Basketmaker III-like traits, which were in vogue in the Four Corners area for about two hundred years following A.D. 500. However, since these Basketmaker III traits were never discarded by the people of the Virgin area, with whom the Sevier people had contacts, there is no need to postulate such an early beginning date for the Sevier culture in order to explain them. A date of A.D. 900 is equally plausible.

Steward (1940) suggested that two phases were represented in the Puebloan cultures west of the Wasatch. He thought the simpler cultural remains in the northern part of the area represented the earlier phase and that the presence of later (Pueblo II) traits such as corrugated pottery, which is not common in the northern part, indicated a later phase to the south. Differences in architecture were also interpreted as cultural and temporal variants, with semisubterranean structures thought to be early and surface structures thought to be late. Rudy (1953, p. 166), after his thorough archaeological survey of western Utah and his re-examination of previously published information, conceded that there had been an earlier "Puebloid" occupation to which some later traits had been added in the southern part of the Sevier area, but he could find no evidence for clear-cut temporal distinctions and suggested that the two phases postulated by Steward be dropped until more concrete evidence of such a division was available. Later, Meighan, on the basis of excavations at Paragonah, concluded that at this site and probably at other Sevier sites the adobe surface structures were used for storage while the semisubterranean structures were the dwellings (Meighan et al., 1956, p. 13). Taylor (1957, p. 38) concurs with Meighan, even with regard to the Garrison Site (Taylor, 1954), where he had originally been in doubt about the function of the surface structures. It now seems generally agreed, then, that there was no development from pithouses to adobe houses in the Sevier area; rather, they were used concurrently for different purposes.

Subsistence west of the Wasatch was based on a combination of horticulture and hunting and gathering. The emphasis probably differed somewhat from area to area depending upon local environment. Meighan's conclusion that the surface adobe structures were used for storage requires a moderation of the view expressed by some, Rudy (1953, p. 166) for example, that "only limited horticulture" was practiced by the Sevier people. At sites as widely scattered as those near Paragonah, Willard, and Garrison, Utah, a surplus of something, probably corn, was being amassed that necessitated the building of these multiroomed storage structures.

The most common dwellings in the Sevier area were pithouses and surface jacal structures. When the adobe surface structures were interpreted as dwellings, the pit structures were thought to be kivas, even though there was generally more household detritus in the pit structures than in the surface structures.

Meighan et al. (1956) concluded that there were probably no kivas distinguishable as such in the Sevier area. There may be changes represented in the pithouses, however. The limited sample available shows that ventilators are most common in the southern part of the Sevier area, but the apparently late introduction of ventilators into the Virgin area makes it seem probable that ventilators will not be found in the earliest southern Sevier pit structures.

The pottery of the Sevier culture is in the Anasazi tradition. What Rudy (1953) called "Desert Gray Ware" is found throughout the Sevier area. Within Desert Gray there are a number of types, distinguishable primarily by tempering material and secondarily by surface treatment or decoration. Moreover, these types are geographically limited within the Sevier area. The ware in general is characterized by the predominance of plain gray smooth pottery. Painted designs, when present, are usually on an unslipped surface and hence are called black-on-gray. Decoration, however, is frequently achieved by a variety of approaches to surface manipulation, including incision, punctation, pinching, or the application of pellets or strips of clay. Each of these techniques occurs alone, but often two or more are combined. Such decoration is restricted to the neck or shoulder of the vessel. Surface manipulation on pottery appears to be more common in the northern part of the area than in the south. Corrugation is found in the southern part of the area, but rarely in the north. Where it does occur, it appears to be late. The temporal significance of corrugated pottery has been best demonstrated by Meighan et al. (1956), who showed, primarily by means of stratigraphy, that within the estimated 200-year span represented at the Paragonah site corrugated pottery was absent at first, but gradually increased in popularity, although at most it accounted for only about half the sherds in a few of the lots collected.

Except for ceramics, no Sevier artifacts can be considered truly diagnostic. All the rest are shared with the Virgin and/or Fremont cultures. However, a number of artifacts characteristic of the Sevier culture should be mentioned. Projectile points are generally triangular and are unnotched, side-notched, corner-notched or stemmed. In the southern part of the area, in at least the later part of Sevier, points with very small stems predominate, but in the northern part side-notched points appear to be most numerous. A wide variety of chipped stone blades or knives, both notched and unnotched, were used. Drills, which are not common, usually have simple expanding bases. Ground stone artifacts include a variety of metate types: thin milling slabs, basin metates, trough metates, and the distinctive "Utah" type with a small secondary depression at one end. Manos also show much variety. Stone balls 4 to 6 cm. in diameter are quite common, as are hammerstones. Stone disks and grooved sandstone arrowshaft smoothers are found occasionally. The only stone ornaments are pendants and beads, including some made of turquoise. Bone pendants and beads are found and shells, apparently imported from the Pacific coast, were also used for bead making. Bone awls of several types are common, as are small rectangular bone gaming pieces. Small disks cut from sherds may also have been used as gaming pieces. Perforated sherds, probably used as spindle whorls, and stone "spindle whorls" have been reported but do not occur frequently. Other reworked sherds were apparently scrapers for use in pottery making. Tubular and elbow-shaped pipes were made from both unfired clay and stone. Unfired clay figurines of the same general types found in the Virgin and Fremont areas are often found, although none of the Sevier specimens is as elaborate as the classic Fremont figurines. Very little basketry has been reported from Sevier sites. One specimen from Grantsville (Steward, 1936, p. 55) that may be the only example yet recovered from an open Sevier site is coiled with a single-rod foundation. Pictographs occur throughout the Sevier area, but they are neither as elaborate nor as spectacular as those east of the Wasatch. This may reflect, at least in part, the absence of rock surfaces comparable to those used in the Fremont area.

Over the years, the absence or rarity of a number of Anasazi traits in the Sevier culture has been noted by several archaeologists, who apparently used San Juan Anasazi as a standard for comparison. Gunnerson (1960 a) has already pointed out that differences between Fremont and Anasazi are far less pronounced when Fremont is compared with the Virgin branch, and the same is true of the Sevier culture, whose closest Anasazi neighbor is Virgin. Hence, comparison of the Sevier and Virgin cultures is especially meaningful.

Many artifacts are rare in both Sevier and Virgin. These include polished axes, spindle whorls and neck-banded pottery. Kivas, apparently absent in the Sevier area, are not common in Virgin. Stone masonry is found in the later phases of Virgin culture, but its absence in most parts of the Sevier area can be explained by the absence of suitable stone. The rarity of such Virgin traits as squash and beans and the apparent absence of sandals may reflect the poor preservation of such materials at open sites, although the Sevier people may have worn moccasins as the Fremont people did. The fact that no cotton has been found at Sevier sites could reflect problems of preservation, but it is highly improbable that cotton could have been grown so far north. Environmental factors could also account for lack of evidence of turkeys in the Sevier area. Schroeder (1955, p. 159) concluded that the turkeys possessed by the Virgin people in Zion Park represented imports, since the natural range of these birds did not extend north of the Colorado River.

The human skeletal material collected from the Sevier area is both limited and highly varied. Thus it cannot be used either to support or refute the idea that the Sevier people were of the same physical type as the Anasazi people in general or the Virgin people in particular. However, the cultural trait of occipital and/or lambdoidal flattening of the skull common in the Anasazi area is present in most of the Sevier specimens.

RECENT WORK EAST OF THE WASATCH

In 1928, the region that was later to be called the Fremont area was virtually unknown. Only the two highly interpretive publications by Montgomery and Fewkes were available, and these were more tantalizing than informative.

The Fremont culture was first recognized as a distinctive archaeological complex by Morss (1931), who defined it on the basis of his two seasons' work (done in 1928 and 1929, primarily in the Fremont River drainage) as part of the Claflin-Emerson Peabody Museum expedition. His summary description was as follows:

"This culture was characterized by cave sites with a slab cist architecture similar to that of the Basket-maker and Pueblo I periods; by a distinctive unpainted black or gray pottery; by the exclusive use of a unique type of moccasin; by a cult of unbaked clay figurines obviously related to, but more elaborate than Basket-maker III figurines; by abundant pictographs of distinctive types; and by a number of minor features which tended to identify it as a Southwestern culture on approximately a Basket-maker III level, but which showed consistently a degree of divergence from corresponding features of orthodox cultures. The presence of small amounts of black-on-white and corrugated pottery, with other evidence, showed that this complex was contemporary with Pueblo II in other regions" (Morss, 1931, p. iv).

Morss recognized as Fremont some sites in Nine Mile Canyon, the northernmost part of eastern Utah in which he worked, and suggested that pictographs reported from near Vernal, Utah, were also Fremont. Furthermore, he realized that the Fremont culture was distinct from archaeological manifestations west of the Wasatch Mountains as well as from the full-fledged Anasazi culture in the Four Corners area. Since the material with which Morss worked came predominantly from rock shelters rather than from open sites, he was unaware of many traits that Fremont shared with Anasazi. Therefore, he tended to overemphasize Fremont-Anasazi differences. His observations and conclusions, however, were remarkably astute considering the limited nature of his sample. For example, his surprise at the limited headway made by the Fremont people in ceramics and architecture (Morss, 1931, p. 78) and his statement that "The originality shown in many details of their culture makes it difficult to think of the Fremonters as merely a backward Southwestern tribe" suggest that he felt something lacking in his sample. Certainly, additional work has demonstrated that the Fremont people could and did make pottery and structures that would have been acceptable to their Anasazi contemporaries. This additional work has also corroborated Morss's (1931, p. 77) statement that "So far as they can be evaluated, the influences which moulded the Fremont culture appear to have been Southwestern."

When Steward (1933 b) established his subareas, one of which matches quite closely the area dominated by the Fremont culture, he had available not only the information presented by Morss but also the results of his own excavations in the Uinta Basin (Steward, 1933 a, pp. 32–34). Even so, by accident of sampling, Fremont sites with the strongest increment of Pueblo traits had not yet been excavated. For this reason archaeological manifestations of eastern Utah north of the Colorado River still appeared most to resemble Basketmaker III sites of the Anasazi area with a few Pueblo II traits added.

During the 1930's Albert Reagan, a teacher at the Indian School at Ouray, Utah, took an interest in the archaeology of northeastern Utah and published numerous short articles in many different publications. Most of his work is of questionable value since it is often impossible to distinguish between his observations and his interpretations. A sample of his long list of articles is included in the bibliography of this paper. During the same decade, Leh (1936) conducted and reported a brief reconnaissance in Range Creek Canyon, Beckwith (1931, 1932, 1935) described pictographs from the Uinta Basin and Nine Mile Canyon, and Gaumer (1937, 1939) briefly reported archaeological finds along the Green River.

The next landmark in the history of Fremont archaeology was Gillin's (1938) report of his excavations in Nine Mile Canyon, although Gillin himself did not specifically attribute the material he recovered to the Fremont culture. This work provided a significant amount of new information regarding a variety of open sites in an area intensively occupied by Fremont people and thus began to reveal the basic Pueblo nature of Fremont. In fact, Gillin concluded that there was an ". . . intrusion of Pueblo people responsible for all the structures noted by the 1936 expedition" in Nine Mile Canyon, but he also pointed out that "house types, pottery, and stone work fail to fall into the classical complexes" (Gillin, 1938, pp. 35–36). Gillin's excavations also produced some of the wood samples that, when they were eventually dated by dendrochronology (Schulman, 1948, 1951; Ferguson, 1949), provided some of our best direct dating evidence, placing the age of the Fremont culture at about A.D. 950–1200.

After Gillin's work, the next major contribution to the body of data on Fremont came from a number of sites in Castle Park, a small area along the Yampa River at the extreme northeastern corner of the Fremont area (Baldwin, 1947; Burgh and Scoggin, 1948; Lister, 1951). Since these sites are marginal in nature as well as in location, and since at least two occupations are represented in the caves excavated, the resulting information is difficult to evaluate.

Actually, little more can be said about the cultural affiliations of the sites in Castle Park now than at the time the major reports appeared. One of the occupations was by Fremont people and another was earlier; a third, perhaps early historic, occupation can still not be ruled out. Perhaps the traits from Castle Park that were not specifically associated with preceramic strata, but which have not been reported from Fremont sites elsewhere, will eventually be found at other Fremont sites. Since most of these traits are items of perishable material, their absence elsewhere could be due to the vagaries of preservation. There are other alternatives, however.

Since Castle Park is on the very edge of the area of distribution of the Fremont culture, it is possible that some of the traits not found at Fremont sites elsewhere represent influence from or trade with late survivors of the Uncompahgre complex (the perishable artifacts of which are poorly known) or with some as yet unreported archaeological complex in an adjoining area. It is also possible that these traits, along with some of the Fremont-like traits, represent a later occupation, since a number of them were found in the Great Basin and Plateau areas in early historic times. Some of the material in Mantle's Cave could have accumulated during a transition from Fremont into Plateau Shoshonean, perhaps under some outside influence. Another alternative is that the anomalous items, along with some of the traits that could be Fremont, are earlier than the Fremont culture and were left by a sparse indigenous population that had occupied the area. Such occupations appear to be represented by the Uncompahgre complex (Wormington and Lister, 1956) and by the burial from Site PR 4-31 in Nine Mile Canyon, described later in this report.

The original estimates given by Burgh and Scoggin (1948) and Lister (1951) for the age of the Fremont component, which they considered a laggard Basketmaker culture, now seem too early. Their dates of A.D. 400–800 were based primarily upon two considerations. First, many traits from Castle Park resembled Anasazi traits of A.D. 400–800. Second, this dating was compatible with an estimated cutting date of A.D. 750±50 tentatively given by Schulman (1950) for a beam from a structure in Marigold's Cave assigned to the Fremont culture (Burgh, 1950). This tree-ring date, however, is a tenuous one, and is not supported by dates from other tree-ring specimens. The validity of Basketmaker traits as a basis for an A.D. 400–800 date is negated in Castle Park, as elsewhere in the Fremont area, by the fact that such traits were never discarded. Thus, there is as yet no evidence from Castle Park to support the supposition that Fremont remains there are earlier than those found elsewhere.

The speculations concerning Castle Park sites serve to point up the importance of dendrochronology for the study of Fremont archaeology. Although some of the wood samples had been collected as early as the time of the Claflin-Emerson expedition, the first published tree-ring dates did not appear until 1948, making this year a major landmark in Fremont investigations. From an interpretive point of view, the tree-ring dates from Fremont sites published by Schulman (1948, 1950, 1951), Ferguson (1949), and Smiley (1951) are as important as the archaeological data.

One of the most interesting results of the work in Castle Park was the statement by Anderson (1948) that some ears of corn recovered had their closest parallels in Central Mexico. This comment initiated a period in which various archaeologists sought to find other resemblances between Fremont and the cultures of Mexico, and considered mechanisms and routes by which Mexican traits could have been introduced to the northern part of the Fremont area without leaving traces in the intervening region.

In 1954, Morss published a detailed study of a group of Fremont figurines from Range Creek Canyon, along with a general discussion of figurines in the American Southwest. Morss suggested that Southwestern figurines represent two traditions, a northern and a southern. He felt that Fremont figurines belong to the northern tradition, but that they possibly show some late influence from the southern tradition, which had reached from the Hohokam area to near Flagstaff, Arizona, by about A.D. 1200.

For several years subsequent to the work in Castle Park, Fremont investigations continued to be on the margin of the Fremont area. Hunt (1953) reported Fremont sites from the La Sal Mountain area near Moab, Utah, which is east of the area dominated by the Fremont culture and within a region where Pueblo sites of Mesa Verde affiliation predominated during the time represented by Fremont. Thus, it appears that the La Sals were utilized by both Fremont and Mesa Verde people but that neither group occupied them intensively. Hunt also identified many nonceramic sites as "Fremont?" with the implication that they were possibly ancestral to Fremont, but she has more recently (Hunt and Tanner, 1960, p. 114) acknowledged that the name "Uncompahgre complex" introduced by Wormington and Lister (1956) is more appropriate.

Rudy (1954 a) originally classified some sites in Beef Basin as Fremont, but since these sites were devoid of diagnostic Fremont traits such a classification seems highly unlikely (Gunnerson, 1960 a, p. 376).

The Turner-Look Site on the eastern margin of the Fremont area, excavated over a period of several years and reported by Wormington (1955), has contributed substantially to our knowledge of the Fremont culture. This village had a number of unusual traits, including an exceedingly high percentage (by Fremont standards) of corrugated and Mancos Black-on-white pottery. Evidence of contact with Mesa Verde people at Turner-Look is not too surprising, however, since it is only

about 55 miles from one known Mesa Verde site (LS 9-1 of this report) and may be closer to others as yet undiscovered. The occurrence of non-Fremont traits other than pottery may only reflect the fact that few Fremont villages have been as carefully and thoroughly excavated. Our total sample is not yet large enough to exclude numerous unique traits, and the Fremont culture is, after all, characterized by its great variability.

In 1954, the Utah Statewide Archeological Survey transferred its attention to northeastern Utah. Initially, a thorough reconnaissance was conducted, especially in those areas where the least work had been done previously. After the initial survey, limited excavation was undertaken at several sites that promised to provide the most information about the Fremont culture in the areas where it was apparently best represented. The results of the survey and the early limited excavation were reported by Gunnerson (1957 a).

In conjunction with the Statewide Survey, a University of Utah archaeological field school excavated two Fremont sites near Emery, Utah (Taylor, 1957), where the Fremont culture is especially well developed and clear-cut. Further excavation at Snake Rock, one of the sites tested by the survey in the Emery area (Gunnerson, 1957 c, n.d.), produced a great deal of information which nicely complements that secured by the field school.

Some very unusual material found by a local collector near Ferron, Utah (Gunnerson, 1957 d, 1959 a, 1962 b), may or may not be of Fremont authorship. Included are such items as bone harpoon points, eccentric chipped flint artifacts, and some unusual figurines. Although its relevance, if any, for the Fremont problem is not now obvious, it should be mentioned that the Statewide Survey also provided limited information on what was apparently an early man site near Ferron (Gunnerson, 1956 a).

Not until the extensive survey was completed was it possible to describe any particular Fremont site or subarea as typical or atypical. And the survey revealed that most of the Fremont sites thoroughly investigated previously were either on the margins of the area occupied by the Fremont people or, as in the case of caves and granaries, yielded information on only part of the total Fremont inventory. Therefore, interpretations based on the data had been somewhat misleading.

The first synthesis of Fremont culture based on data from all parts of its area revealed variations and complexities within the culture, but broad intra-areal consistencies were also apparent (Gunnerson, 1956 a). Moreover, the new concept of the Fremont culture that resulted from the Utah Statewide Survey also led to new speculations concerning the relations of Fremont to other parts of the trans-Colorado Puebloan area, and these ideas will be discussed in the brief résumé of hypotheses that follows.

RECENT INTERPRETATIONS

Steward thought that the two cultures here called Fremont and Sevier represented a blending of Basketmaker and Pueblo cultures (e.g., Steward, 1933 b, 1940). In keeping with an idea still commonly held during the period that Steward was writing about Utah archaeology, he apparently considered Basketmaker and Pueblo two entirely separate traditions rather than temporal variations of the same tradition. Accordingly, he reasoned that somewhere Basketmaker and Pueblo sites that had been occupied at the same time would be found near one another. In such an area, the two cultures could have blended, and the culture resulting from the blend could have moved into the Fremont and Sevier areas. Steward once thought that the most likely place for such a fusion was the area north of the Colorado River and east of Kanab, Utah. When he found that the culture history of this area essentially paralleled that in the San Juan area, he concluded that the blending probably took place in northeastern Utah or northwestern Colorado, the only archaeologically unknown areas left outside his Northern Periphery.

About ten years ago, after systematic investigations of all Utah by the Statewide Archeological Survey had begun, the history of the Puebloan cultures of the northern three-fourths of the state again received concentrated attention. Rudy (1953) pointed out two alternatives: either the Pueblo traits had been introduced into this area by migration of Pueblo people who brought the traits with them, or the traits moved in through diffusion and were accepted by hunting and gathering people who had already lived there for a long time. Rudy favored the second interpretation —that his Puebloid people were indigenous hunters and gatherers who had acquired Pueblo traits. This view, which represented a swing of the pendulum away from the interpretations advanced by Steward, gained its widest recognition through the stimulating and much-cited paper by Jennings and Norbeck (1955). This article made a number of very important points with regard to Great Basin prehistory. It pointed out that the way of life in much of the Great Basin had changed very little during the more than 10,000 years of human occupation. The paucity of plant and animal foods in this inhospitable region necessitated the complete exploitation of environment which characterizes the Desert culture as defined by Jennings and Norbeck. Only in the southeastern part of the Great Basin was horticulture possible even during favorable periods. The point is also well made that it was from the Desert culture, using the term broadly, that the horticultural way of life gradually developed over the entire Southwest, and that therefore it completely distorts the picture to imply, through use of the term "Northern Periphery," that the ancient Desert culture of the Great Basin was culturally peripheral to the Southwest. This objection, voiced previously by Rudy (1953), to naming a large archaeological area with great time depth on the basis of a relatively brief cultural development in only a part of it, is acceptable.

The Jennings-Norbeck suggestion of continuity from a Desert culture into the specialized horticultural Southwestern pattern as such is reasonable, and the continuity of a Desert culture for thousands of years without significant change throughout most of the Great Basin is demonstrable. These authors are on less firm ground, however, when they favor a similar continuity of people in the intervening Fremont and Sevier areas and interpret the Anasazi traits found there as having arrived by diffusion. And indeed even they, acknowledging Rudy's alternative suggestion, state that "there might have been an actual influx of Anasazi people into the area" (Jennings and Norbeck, 1955, p. 6).

But archaeology needed a new interpretation of these Puebloan cultures because those suggested by Steward had proved unfruitful. And the attractiveness of the Rudy-Jennings-Norbeck interpretation is reflected in subsequent publications by most of the people who have dealt with the Fremont and/or Sevier cultures. For example, Wormington (1955, p. 180) may be thinking along the same lines when she says, "Comparative data would suggest that the Puebloid (Sevier) and Fremont Cultures sprang from the same variant of the generalized Basin Culture and that both acquired certain Anasazi traits, but that, due to different environmental conditions, separation by physiographic barriers which favored independent development, and exposure to different influences, they did not develop in entirely the same way." She also sees in the Fremont culture influence from both Mexico and the Northern Plains. Although she apparently favors diffusion as the most probable means by which traits entered the Fremont area, she does not rule out the possibility of migrations and essentially leaves the mechanism an open question.

The influence of the Jennings and Norbeck article is also evident in the paper (Jennings, ed., 1956) that resulted from the Southwestern section of the *Seminars in Archaeology: 1955*. To avoid the implications of the term "Puebloid" for the western Puebloan remains and to reflect the close similarities between them and the Fremont culture, the name "Sevier-Fremont" was substituted. The seminar interpreted both Fremont and Sevier-Fremont as having developed during hundreds of years from a Desert culture base with the addition of various Anasazi traits. This thinking is also reflected by Taylor (1957), who served as recorder for the seminar, and again by Jennings (1960) in a semi-popular article.

However, Meighan, another member of the 1955 Southwestern Seminar, presented a radically opposing view in a volume published the following year (Meighan *et al.*, 1956, p. 21) where he suggested that the people who settled the Paragonah Site, which the Seminar had specifically included in Sevier-Fremont,

were Arizona colonists from south of the Colorado River.

More recently Gunnerson (1960 a), after several years' work in the Fremont and Virgin areas, suggested that the Fremont culture (and probably the Sevier) represents a Pueblo II expansion from the Virgin area, where many earlier (Basketmaker) traits had been retained after new (Pueblo) traits were added to the cultural assemblage. This interpretation will be examined later in more detail.

Opinions on the fate of the Fremont and Sevier people have differed as much as those concerning their origin. Probably every anthropologist who has worked in the region they inhabited has considered the possibility that these prehistoric farmers gave up their settled way of life to become the Plateau Shoshoneans found in the area by the first white explorers. Steward (e.g., 1940), however, favored an exodus of horticultural people and their replacement by speakers of Plateau Shoshonean. As recently as 1955 he ruled out the possibility that the Shoshoneans represent deculturated Puebloan people. Wormington (1955) postulated that the Fremont people moved south and joined the Hopi. Schroeder (1961) and Shutler (1961) both felt that the Southern Paiute, bringing their distinctive pottery, moved into the Virgin area prior to its abandonment by the Virgin people, who, they thought, may also have joined the Hopi.

Apparently Shimkin (1940) was the first anthropologist to support strongly the idea that the Plateau Shoshoneans are deculturated Puebloan people. This theory has been endorsed more recently by Rudy (1953), Jennings and Norbeck (1955), Taylor (1957), and Jennings (1960), perhaps because it emphasizes the overriding influence of the Basin environment and has the Sevier-Fremont people concluding their history much as these archaeologists suggest they began it—as hunters and gatherers. Gunnerson, after considering linguistic data presented by Romney (1957), Hale (1958), and Lamb (1958) in the light of what is known of trans-Colorado archaeology, has tentatively suggested:

"(1) that the Virgin-Branch Anasazi people were proto Plateau Shoshoneans; and (2) that the Fremont and Sevier people . . . are represented historically by the Ute-Southern Paiute and Shoshone-Comanche respectively, while the Virgin-Branch people themselves are represented by the Northern Paiute" (Gunnerson, 1962a).

Since 1931, that is, during the period that theories concerning trans-Colorado Puebloan archaeology have been developing and changing, one large body of relevant material from the Fremont area has remained unexploited—the artifacts and information (except that reported by Morss) obtained between 1928 and 1931 under the auspices of the Claflin-Emerson Peabody Museum expedition. Since the majority of sites represented by this collection were never resampled by other workers, it has seemed certain that study of the material would lead to new conclusions and/or serve to corroborate previous ones. Thus, at an important point in the development of theory on trans-Colorado archaeology, there has been readily available in the Claflin-Emerson material the results of four seasons' field work against which to test hypotheses.[1]

[1] Since early 1963 when the manuscript for this paper was completed, additional archaeological work has been done in the area considered. However, this manuscript has not been revised to include references to work published while it was in various stages of preparation for publication, in part because I do not feel that the results of subsequent work warrant any significant changes in the interpretations presented here. Judging from the wide range of interpretations and the general disagreement among the participants at the session on Uto-Aztecan prehistory at the 1966 Annual Meeting of the Society for American Archaeology, some of the interpretations included in this paper will not be universally accepted. On the other hand, none of the alternative suggestions has been generally accepted, and this work, which takes into account the wide variety of information from archaeology, ethnology, linguistics, ecology, botany, and history, remains the most comprehensive, internally consistent, interpretation of the evidence relevant to the Fremont Culture. Since any broad interpretation is in reality a greatly simplified model, there are certain to be weak spots and strains, but the goal here has been to utilize as much information as possible and at the same time to do as little violence as possible to the body of data as a whole. Recent controversies have served principally to emphasize the importance of Fremont in the reconstruction of Inter-Mountain prehistory and it is to be hoped that someone will soon reexamine the Fremont problem in its entirety, taking into consideration all of the evidence, old and new, and evaluating all the interpretations.

PART II

THE CLAFLIN-EMERSON EXPEDITION

THE CLAFLIN-EMERSON EXPEDITION

INTRODUCTION

IN 1927, at the suggestion of A. V. Kidder, William H. Claflin, Jr., and Raymond Emerson took a pack trip through portions of southeastern Utah west of the Colorado River, an area then virtually unknown to archaeologists. During their brief explorations they visited several archaeological sites, including the now well-known one at Boulder, Utah, and heard of additional sites on the Kaiparowits Plateau and in the Fremont River drainage (Claflin, n.d.). Their recognition of the archaeological importance of the area between the Colorado River and the Wasatch Plateau prompted them and their wives to sponsor an extended reconnaissance program to be carried out by the Peabody Museum of Harvard University, where Claflin was Curator of Southeastern Archaeology.

ORGANIZATION OF THE PROJECT

The general plan of the Claflin-Emerson expedition was to survey the western drainage of the Colorado River, as well as a narrow strip on the east side of the Colorado River from the Kaiparowits Plateau nearly to Moab, Utah, and the drainage of the Green River as far north as the Uinta Mountains. Limited excavation was also to be carried out at selected sites. Since automobile roads were (as they still are) few and far apart, horses and pack animals had to be used for transportation. Three towns, Escalante, Moab, and Green River, Utah, were chosen as points of departure for the pack trains. However, much of the region surveyed, especially in the southern half, is so rough as to be inaccessible even by horseback, or so barren that camp had to be moved frequently in order to ensure a supply of feed and water. Not until the northern part of the Uinta Basin was reached was it feasible to use automobiles.

Thus, many parts of the area visited by the Claflin-Emerson expedition have been inaccessible to more recent archaeological parties dependent on trucks or jeeps for transport and have therefore never been resampled. Only the necessity of conducting salvage archaeology has led to the re-examination of other formidable sections of the region.

Donald Scott, then Assistant Director of the Peabody Museum, initiated field work under the Claflin-Emerson program during the spring of 1928 with a reconnaissance of the Kaiparowits Plateau and the drainages of the western tributaries of the Colorado River between and including the Escalante River and the Fremont River. During the summers of 1928 and 1929, Noel Morss, following some of the leads provided by Scott, carried out more intensive work along the Fremont River that included excavation as well as survey. He also did limited work in Nine Mile Canyon, in Thompson Wash near Thompson, Utah, and at Boulder, Utah. The work done by Morss was promptly reported (Morss, 1931), and defined the Fremont culture as described above.

Also during the summer of 1929, concurrently with the work being done by Morss, a second party under the direction of the late Henry Roberts conducted survey activities with limited excavation in the drainages of the Muddy River, the Dirty Devil River, North Wash, Barrier Canyon, and smaller tributaries of the Colorado River between these last two.

In the summer of 1930 the only Claflin-Emerson party in the field, again under Roberts, concentrated its survey and excavation activities in an area lying on both sides of the Colorado and Green rivers from the mouth of the Dirty Devil River north to the mouth of Barrier Canyon. On the west side of the rivers, the areas most intensively investigated were Waterhole Flat, which lies north of the Dirty Devil and west of the Colorado River, and Barrier Canyon. On the east side of the rivers, activities centered in Ruin Park, directly across the Colorado River from Waterhole Flat, and along Indian Creek just to the north. Originally, Roberts was to have been in charge of all remaining phases of the Claflin-Emerson project, but commitments to the Carnegie Institution of Washington compelled him to withdraw from field work at the end of the summer of 1930. An arrangement was made between the Museum and the Carnegie Institution which would have permitted Roberts to devote half time to the completion of the report during 1932 and 1933 but this plan had to be abandoned because of illness.

In 1931, during the fourth and final summer of the Claflin-Emerson expedition, Donald Scott was the leader of the expedition, with J. O. Brew serving as his technical assistant. This season, the reconnaissance covered the Green River and its tributaries from Green River, Utah, north to the Uinta Mountains. As in previous years, field activities included excavation at selected sites.

In addition to the supervisory personnel already mentioned, several others participated in the field activities for one or more seasons and information is recorded in the notebooks of many of these men as well as in those of the supervisors. Thus, other important contributors to the success of the project include Robert Sanderson, Lyon Boston, Alfred Kidder II, Donald Scott, Jr., William Bowers, Waldo Forbes, and James Dennison. David Rust of Provo, Utah, who had guided Mr. Claflin and Mr. Emerson on their 1927 trip, served as guide for the expedition in each of the four years.

Geography of the Area Investigated

The region investigated by the Claflin-Emerson expedition comprises about three-fourths of the part of Utah east of a north–south line drawn through the middle of the state. The one-fourth not investigated is a triangle in southeastern Utah bounded by the Colorado and Arizona state lines on two sides and by the Colorado River on most of the third side. A little work was done just east of the Colorado River. All of the area explored, some 30,000 square miles, is drained by the Colorado River and is part of the Colorado Plateau. Elevations vary from less than 4000 feet in Glen Canyon, where the Colorado River leaves Utah, to over 13,000 feet in the

highest parts of the Uinta Mountains on the northern edge of the area investigated. Most of the area has an elevation between 5000 and 7000 feet. Exceptions are the deep canyons, the east–west Tavaputs Plateau, and the mountains that rim the area on the west and north.

The largest river in eastern Utah is the Colorado, which heads in the Rocky Mountains in Colorado. Its major tributary, the Green, is nearly as large. These rivers, which for the most part flow through deep canyons in Utah, carry a great deal of water in the spring and early summer. By early fall, however, their flow is greatly reduced. In few places could they have been diverted for irrigation by the aboriginal population. When they are full, they are raging torrents and, when they are low, their level is much below possible farm land. Perhaps in a few places these rivers might provide subirrigation for the sandy terraces occasionally found along them, but such terraces do not seem to have been extensively utilized.

Many tributaries of the Colorado once contained alluvial fill on top of which streams meandered. Most of these have been scoured out within the past eighty years, a process that is still going on; apparently, however, such fill was present in most of the tributary canyons during the A.D. 900–1200 period of maximum population.

The extensive portion of the region that is between 5000 and 7000 feet in elevation is for the most part sandy and rocky, with sparse vegetation. This is not surprising, since the average annual precipitation is only six to ten inches and only about half of that amount falls in warm weather. Since there is higher precipitation in the mountains, much of it in the form of snow, one finds a series of oasis-like spots where small streams carrying melt water emerge from the mountains. The average growing season varies from about 80 days along the foot of the mountains to about 170 days along the Colorado River. In the areas where rainfall is highest, which are also the areas that benefit from melting mountain snow, the growing season is only about 80 to 120 days (Alter, 1941).

Over most of eastern Utah, at elevations of about 7000 feet, moderately heavy stands of pinyon pine and juniper are encountered. Above these conifers, quaking aspen and ponderosa pine occur.

Nature of the Sites Discovered

Most of the archaeological sites located by the Claflin-Emerson expedition are in what has come to be known as the Fremont area, here defined as that portion of eastern Utah and northwestern Colorado in which the preponderance of the archaeological sites are assignable to the Fremont culture. For the most part, this area is bounded by natural features which would have constituted partial barriers to the free movement of people to and from adjacent areas. To the west and north are the Wasatch and Uinta mountains, respectively. On the south is the rough terrain at the southern edge of the Fremont River drainage. The southern part of the eastern boundary is approximated by the deep canyon of the Colorado River, and the northern part, which is poorly defined, apparently lies just to the east of the Colorado–Utah state line in the rough country between the Colorado and Yampa rivers. The Claflin-Emerson expedition visited none of the few Fremont sites east of the Colorado River (e.g., in the La Sal Mountains) in the area containing predominantly Mesa Verde sites. It did, however, record a number of small Fremont sites in the Waterhole Flat–lower Dirty Devil River area where the sites are about equally divided between the Fremont and the Mesa Verde cultures.

Within the Fremont area as here defined there are a few non-Fremont sites. In Barrier Canyon, which is just north of the Waterhole Flat area and just across the Colorado River from the northwesternmost corner of the Mesa Verde area, there is evidence of Mesa Verde occupation at two sites, and it is not possible to tell on the basis of information collected whether the sites at and just below the mouth of Barrier Canyon were Fremont or Mesa Verde. At Horseshoe Shelter (SR 12-5) in Barrier Canyon there was either a mixed Fremont–Mesa Verde occupation, or separate occupations, by these two groups, and probably an earlier Basketmaker occupation as well. Unfortunately it is not possible to reconstruct the history of this site or even to distinguish between the various artifact complexes except on typological grounds. In any case, it is only in the southeastern corner of the Fremont area that there is significant overlapping with sites of other contemporaneous cultural traditions.

Elsewhere in the Fremont area, the only sites yielding material that can be assigned definitely to non-Fremont occupations are Rasmussen Cave (PR 4-31), which contained a Basketmaker II–like burial below evidence of a Fremont occupation; and several poorly delimited sites near Myton, Utah (U 16-1 through U 16-7), that yielded a crude percussion-flaked stone complex.

The rest of the sites in the Fremont area are assigned to the Fremont culture with varying degrees of certainty. Sites yielding a predominance of sherds assignable to either variety of Turner Gray (Emery or Uinta) are considered unquestionably Fremont. Nonceramic sites at which evidence of horticulture and/or architecture has been found are considered probably Fremont, as are pictograph sites characterized by the distinctive anthropomorphic styles thought to be of Fremont origin. The few other sites in the Fremont area are considered possibly Fremont, although the amount of information contributed by these is so small that their assignment is not crucial.

The Claflin-Emerson expedition also covered a considerable region to the south of the Fremont area. To the southeast, the Ruin Park–Salt Creek Canyon area contains evidence of a heavy late (Pueblo II–III) Mesa Verde occupation. The Kaiparowits Plateau appears to have been occupied almost exclusively by Virgin branch people. Elsewhere in this southern section, however, the archaeology is much more complex in spite of its meagerness, and even now, after a great deal of additional work, the picture is far from clear. Immediately to the northeast of the Kaiparowits is the drainage of the Escalante River in which most of the sites appear to belong to the Virgin branch, but which also contains a few Kayenta sites and some sites that are either Fremont or Virgin with strong similarities to Fremont. In the Glen Canyon of the Colorado River and in the lower reaches of its tributaries above the Escalante River as far north as Barrier Canyon, the situation becomes more complicated. Sites in Glen Canyon are for the most part Mesa Verde to the north and Kayenta to the south, with the dividing line apparently moving south during the course of time (that is, with Mesa Verde gaining ground at the expense of Kayenta), but neither the boundary nor the typological distinctions between the two cultures are sharp here. Fremont and Virgin influence in Glen Canyon proper was apparently slight. In the area drained by the lower reaches of the Dirty Devil River, where both Fremont and Mesa Verde cultures are represented, little Virgin and Kayenta influence was found.

CONTRIBUTIONS OF THE PROJECT

The contributions made by the Claflin–Emerson expedition are several. It substantially augmented the data on Fremont artifacts by adding some entirely new traits to the inventory, disclosing new variations on architecture and basketry, and providing new information on the distribution of traits already known. Moreover, the expedition has made available a collection of maize specimens that has stimulated new ideas on the development and spread of maize in North America, and has, as a result, provided a plausible explanation for the existence of both the Fremont and Sevier cultures. The project also provided information on some of the northwesternmost Mesa Verde sites, and the study of pottery from these sites has suggested the possibility of the diffusion of some Mesa Verde traits to Fremont. Since some Kayenta and Virgin sites occurred in the area surveyed, the expedition has contributed a limited amount of information on these complexes. In addition, it has extended our knowledge of the geographical boundaries of the cultures enumerated above, and has made it possible to describe the nature of the borderland between Fremont and Mesa Verde.

A few sites investigated by the Claflin-Emerson expedition revealed the presence of a Basketmaker-like culture. Some specimens from this complex serve to link it with similar manifestations in other areas, and stratigraphy shows that it preceded Fremont. One interesting burial revealed that tailored skin clothing was worn by these Basketmaker people. An even earlier complex may be represented at small sites on the Myton Bench, in the Uinta Basin, where crude percussion-flaked blades or choppers were found on the surface. Since this material was mixed in some places with small amounts of Fremont pottery and even later material, it may not be as old as it appears on the basis of typology.

If the final report had been written soon after the field work was completed, much could have been said regarding each of these problems and the publication would have been a welcome contribution. But writing the report at that time would have been a baffling experience, because much of the information was from areas where as many as four different archaeological complexes were represented. Adequate interpretation of the mixtures of rather similar material related to distinct but poorly known cultural developments whose most outstanding manifestations lay elsewhere would have been frustrating to say the least. Furthermore, by pure chance, some of the areas most intensively occupied by the Fremont people had not been sampled.

Meanwhile, in the decades that have elapsed between the termination of the field work and the beginning of this, the final report of the Claflin-Emerson expedition, additional work has been done both in northeastern Utah and in the surrounding areas. And, with the insight gained from a greater knowledge of the various culture complexes involved, it is now possible to interpret the important data gathered between 1928 and 1931 more meaningfully than it could have been interpreted then. Thus, while delay in reporting field work is not usually advantageous, there have been some fortuitous compensations in this case.

All the work carried out under the Claflin-Emerson project except that done by Morss is reported here. Descriptions of sites are based primarily on the field notes, maps, plans, photographs, sketches, and unpublished preliminary reports made by the original investigators. In a few cases these data have been supplemented by the author's personal knowledge of a site. The specimens described were all collected by the Claflin-Emerson parties. As could be expected, some difficulties have arisen in the reporting of work done so long ago and by someone else, especially since the original field man expected to utilize his notes personally. In some instances, data of one sort do not check with data of another. Some sites have had temporary field designations as well as permanent site numbers and it is not always possible to equate the two with certainty when some of the data carry one designation and some another. In a few cases it has been possible to detect and correct errors introduced in changing from field to permanent site designations. Where the association of a collection of specimens with a site is uncertain the site description indicates the fact. Also, there is reason to believe that some field notes were never deposited in the files and have since become lost. In such cases, it has been necessary to place more reliance on map, photographic, and specimen data that could not be checked against the notes. Many brief or cryptic notes that would have had significance for the person who made them were meaningful to the author only because he had spent much of six years doing field work in the same general areas.

In spite of the various problems encountered, virtually no data were found to be unusable. In a few instances, sites for which there are no other data were assigned numbers and located on maps. Such sites were probably recorded by the archaeologists on the basis of information from local persons, but not visited; they have been omitted from this report.

PRESENTATION OF THE DATA RECOVERED

In the following section the sites investigated by the Claflin-Emerson parties will be grouped for the most part according to river drainages, and the descriptions will, in general, proceed from south to north. Figure 2 shows the locations of sites and Table 1, which follows the site descriptions, is an index to the distribution of specimens by sites.

The site designation system is based on longitude and latitude: each one-minute quadrangle is represented by a one- or two-letter symbol derived from the name of the corresponding U.S. Geological Survey topographic maps as follows.

Symbol	Quadrangle Name	Longitude South Side	Latitude East Side
A	Ashley	40	109
E	Escalante	37	111
ET	East Tavaputs	39	109
FL	Fish Lake	38	111
H	Henry Mountains	37	110
LS	La Sal	38	109
PR	Price River	39	110
SR	San Rafael	38	110
U	Uinta	40	110

Each one-minute quadrangle, in turn, was divided into sixteen smaller quadrangles, fifteen seconds to a side, numbered consecutively in rows from left to right and from top to bottom. Within each of these smaller quadrangles sites were numbered consecutively, usually in the order in which they were found. Since the best maps available at the time of the Claflin-Emerson expedition were only reconnaissance maps and quite inaccurate, a number of sites for which the location was determined with reference to streams shown on the maps were given numbers assigning them to the wrong quadrangle. When such errors were found, the original erroneous site numbers were usually preserved and the description calls attention to the error. Considering the roughness of some of the terrain and the difficulty of travel, it is surprising that these maps, made long before aerial photography was used, are as good as they are, and that the archaeological parties were able to provide such good information as they did.

KAIPAROWITS PLATEAU

The Kaiparowits Plateau extends from the Colorado River opposite the mouth of the San Juan northwest to join the Escalante Mountains, a southern extension of the Wasatch Plateau. The nearly level top of the Kaiparowits has a maximum width of about 5 miles, and for most of its 50-mile length it is much narrower. The northeast edge of the plateau, which is a straight line and is therefore called the Straight Cliffs, drops nearly vertically for 2000 feet to a strip of near-desert about 10 miles wide that separates it from the Escalante River. Virtually all the drainage from the top of the plateau is to the south, so that the southwest edge is very rough and ragged as compared to the straight northeast edge. The top

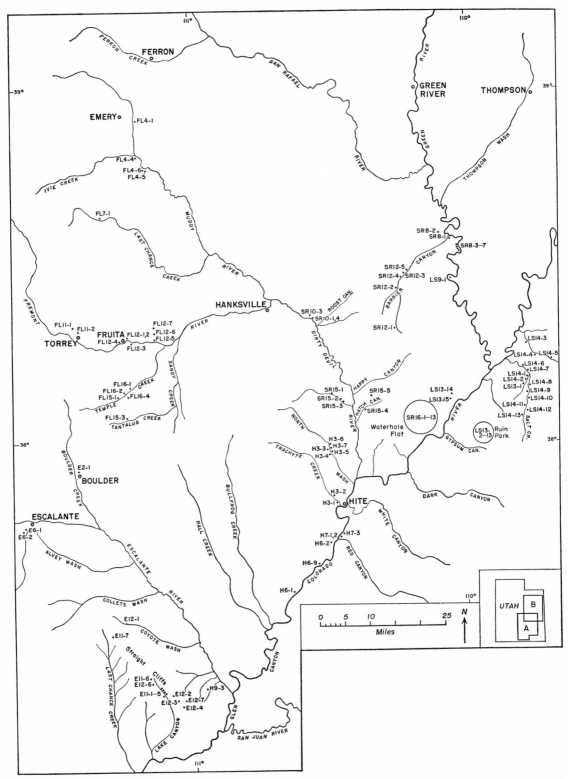

FIG. 2A. Locations of sites herein reported.

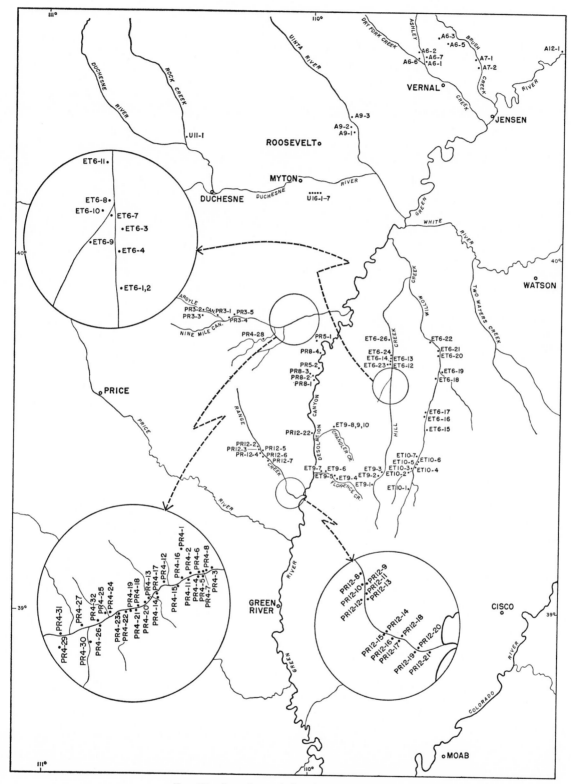

Fig. 2B. Locations of sites herein reported.

of the plateau is characterized by low ridges or knolls, topped with pinyon and juniper, and separated by sandy, sage-covered flats. Near the heads of the canyons that cross the plateau and just under the northeast rim are several good springs.

A recent archaeological survey of the Kaiparowits Plateau (Gunnerson, 1958, 1959 d) revealed numerous sites, primarily of two types. Open sites consisting of one or a few rooms are situated on most of the ridges on top of the plateau; and smaller masonry structures, most of which probably served for storage, are just under the rim, especially along the irregular southwest side. The Gunnerson survey, by no means exhaustive, covered approximately 10 square miles and recorded 250 sites, nearly all of which were small and lacked evidence of long occupation. These sites have been assigned to the Virgin branch Anasazi of Pueblo II–early Pueblo III times, but they show definite simplifications suggesting that they are culturally as well as geographically intermediate between Virgin and Fremont. The relatively few sites found in the brief time devoted to the Kaiparowits by the Claflin-Emerson expedition are representative of the larger sample recorded later and do not change the archaeological picture.

E 11-1

Within a distance of about 4 miles along Lake Canyon, starting from a point about 2 miles above its mouth, five rock shelters containing structures were found. Four of these are on the north side of the canyon, the fifth on the south side. These five sites were assigned numbers E 11-1 through E 11-5, although more recent maps suggest that they should carry E-12 numbers. Only three of the sites (E 11-1, 2, 3) were entered and described.

In the first site, the remains of three semicircular structures, all built against the back wall of the shelter, were observed. One of these is 2.3 m. wide along the cliff face and extends out 1.7 m. from it. The wall, 1.2 m. high, is constructed of stone slabs of varying sizes chinked with adobe. A doorway 35 cm. wide and 55 cm. high has a stone-slab sill and a stone-slab lintel under which there are three poles to provide additional support. The sides

of the doorway are of smooth adobe. Poles and stone slabs, probably from the roof, were found inside the structure. The second room was of similar construction except that the wall was built all the way to the ceiling of the shelter. This wall, 1.2 to 1.5 m. high, was plastered with adobe on the inside. A doorway, again 35 cm. wide and 55 cm. high, has a lintel composed of four sticks and a sill consisting of a stone slab. Along the middle of the sill is a ridge of adobe which, together with a vertical pole at either side of the doorway, had apparently served as a door jamb.

The third room was like the first two, except that a portion of the wall, where it extended over the edge of the shelter floor, was partially supported by a pole in its base. The pole roof is still in place.

E 11-2

This site, a rock shelter about 10 m. long but only about 1 m. high, contains two semicircular structures built against its back wall. The larger and first-built room extends 3.4 m. along the cliff and is 1.8 m. wide. The wall, still standing about 60 cm. high, is constructed of large blocks of stone, and adobe. The portion containing the doorway is partially demolished. The second room, built in part against the first, is about 1.8 m. long and 1.2 m. wide. The doorway is 35 cm. wide and 44 cm. high, and both its sill and lintel are single stone slabs. A vertical stick at one side of the doorway helped support the lintel.

E 11-3

The four structures at this site are all semicircular and built against the back wall of the shelter. The largest, about 1.8 by 2.4 m., was constructed of alternate courses of medium-sized stone slabs and adobe mortar. Its doorway, 42 cm. wide and 56 cm. high, has a lintel of three sticks and a flat stone sill. The second room, 1.8 by 1.5 m., was constructed of smaller stone slabs and was almost completely plastered both inside and outside. The doorway, partially broken out, had been about 50 cm. square with a stick lintel and a stone sill. The third room, about 1.2 m. in width, depth and height, was also built of small stones and adobe in courses with adobe plaster. On a projection somewhat above the floor of the shelter, between these last two structures and built against the walls of both, is a small bin about 30 cm. across.

SPECIMENS (from E 11-1, 2, 3)

Pottery sherds	
North Creek Corrugated	5

E 11-6

At an open site about 1 mile northwest of the lake on the Kaiparowits Plateau were found the remains of one structure, about 2.5 m. square, still standing about 1 m. high. Construction is of rock slabs of moderate size and no evidence of adobe mortar could be found. Near by are scattered rocks, suggesting that there had formerly been four or five other rooms.

SPECIMENS

Pottery sherds	
Moenkopi Corrugated	6
Washington Corrugated	4
North Creek Corrugated	1
Escalante Gray	6
Emery Gray	1
North Creek Black-on-gray	2
North Creek Gray	5

E 11-7

Along the Thirty-five Mile Trail (Upper Trail) to the Kaiparowits Plateau, which starts up the Straight Cliffs near the head of Coyote Wash, is a pictograph panel, not far from which there is a small stone-slab structure in a rock shelter. The pictographs, about 60 m. below the top of the Plateau, consist of ten figures painted in red. One, anthropomorphic, has a square head on a triangular body from each corner of which two parallel lines slope outward. The structure, about 30 m. below the top of the Plateau, is about 2 m. square with nicely squared corners. It still stands about 75 cm. high and was not entered. This may be site 42Ka770 described by Gunnerson (1959 d, p. 403).

E 12-2

About 2 miles southeast of the lake is another open site with a structure, about 5 by 6 m., which has a partition dividing it into two rooms, each about 3 m. wide. The walls, constructed of moderately large stone slabs,

stand from 15 to 60 cm. high. There is some evidence to suggest that each of the two rooms might once have been divided into two roughly square rooms.

E 12-3

A rock shelter just under the rim of the Straight Cliffs about 1.5 miles northwest of the head of Fifty Mile Trail contains the ruins of several structures. Access to the shelter can apparently be gained only by following first along the top of a steep slope and then along a narrow ledge for a distance of about 0.2 mile. The shelter is about 50 m. long and 3 to 4 m. deep. At the south end of the shelter is a semicircular room for which a 4-m. section of cliff forms the straight back wall. The wall, constructed of stone slabs of varying sizes laid in adobe mortar, extends out 2.5 m. from the back of the shelter and stands to a maximum height of 3 m. The sloping ceiling of the shelter forms the back part of the roof of the room and parallel poles covered with adobe form the front part. In the center of the wall is a doorway 30 cm. wide and 45 cm. high with a stone slab for a sill and three split cedar poles for a lintel. Abutting the wall of this structure is a short section of wall about 1.3 m. long and 1 m. high, apparently part of a second structure.

About 2 m. from these first two structures and near the front of the shelter is a U-shaped room about 3 m. long, 1.5 m. wide (at the straight end), and 1.1 m. high. The floor of this room was excavated into the sloping floor of the shelter so that the roof at the rear is only slightly above the floor level of the shelter and the front edge of the room floor was not excavated at all. Wall construction was of stone slabs laid in adobe mortar. The portion of the roof that remains shows that it was constructed of cedar poles about 6 cm. in diameter resting on top of the walls and spanning the short dimension of the room. On top of these poles were willow poles 1 to 2 cm. in diameter, on which was a layer of adobe turtlebacks.

Another semicircular room built against the back wall of the shelter near the middle extends about 2 m. along the cliff, is 1 m. wide, and still stands 1.2 m. high. At the north end of the shelter are the remains of probably two more similar structures, one of which was about 2 m. long where it joined the cliff.

SPECIMENS

Pottery sherds
Moenkopi Corrugated	10
Moenkopi Corrugated, Coombs variety	5

Probably four vessels are represented, one of which is of the Coombs variety.

E 12-4

About 300 m. southeast of Moki Seep (an excellent spring just under the rim of the Straight Cliffs about 1.5 miles southeast of the top of Fifty Mile Trail) is a rock shelter under the cliff rim. Against the back of this shelter, which is about 15 m. long and 2.5 m. deep, is a semicircular room 4 m. long and extending out 1.2 m. from the wall of the shelter. The wall, very roughly and irregularly constructed of pieces of stone and much adobe, stands about 1.2 m. high—to within about 45 cm. of the ceiling of the shelter. At floor level in the middle of the wall is a doorway 40 cm. wide and 60 cm. high, with single stone slabs forming both the sill and the lintel. The remains of two smaller semicircular rooms flank the room just described. One end of the wall forming each of the small rooms had abutted the wall of the central room and the other end joined the cliff wall.

A well-made corrugated pot, found but not collected, was 30 cm. high, had a maximum diameter of 30 cm. and a neck diameter of 20 cm. Corrugation was varied to provide a decorative band around the neck.

The following specimens were found scattered on the plateau above Moki Seep over an area about 0.2 mile in radius.

SPECIMENS

Pottery sherds
Virgin Black-on-white	1
North Creek Gray	1
Jeddito (?) Black-on-yellow	1

Chipped Stone
Point or blade fragments	3

E 12-6

In the flat lands to the west of the lake at the head of Lake Canyon are several elevations about 15 m. high and averaging 120 to 150 m. by 60 m. in area. On these, building stones were scattered over areas of perhaps 12 by 30 m. Often individual rooms were outlined by single courses of rocks, and some wall remnants stood as high as 1 m. Pottery is relatively abundant at these sites.

SPECIMENS

Pottery sherds
Middleton Black-on-red	2
Middleton Red	2
Virgin Black-on-white	9
Tusayan White ware	1
North Creek Gray	1
Moenkopi Corrugated	3
Washington Corrugated	9
Emery Gray	2

Chipped stone
Projectile point	1

Some of the Washington Corrugated sherds appear to be tempered with crushed sandstone or with sand from recently disintegrated sandstone, since much cementing material still adheres to many of the sand particles. Both Sosi and Dogoszhi styles of decoration are found among the Virgin Black-on-white sherds.

The projectile point, crudely made of red jasper, is side-notched. The tip and perhaps the end of the base are missing. It appears to have been about 2.4 by 1.0 cm. originally.

E 12-7

About halfway up the Straight Cliffs along the lower (Fifty Mile) trail, a small rock shelter was entered by means of ropes and was found to contain remnants of a structure and some detritus. A retaining wall had been constructed of poles and the space behind filled with stone and adobe to provide a level floor. Other similar shelters were seen near by, but they were not entered.

SPECIMENS

Pottery sherd
North Creek Gray	1
Mat fragment	1

The mat fragment is woven from flat yucca stalks each about 8 mm. wide, in a simple over-two, under-two twill pattern. The fragment, which is 8 by 17 cm., shows none of the original edges of the mat.

ESCALANTE DRAINAGE

The Escalante drainage shows many contrasts. The lower half of the Escalante River flows through a deep, narrow, steep-sided canyon that can be entered in few places. Numerous short tributaries join it from the exceedingly rough and barren area to the north, and fewer, but for the most part larger, tributaries come in from the south from the foot of the Straight Cliffs, the northern edge of the Kaiparowits Plateau. Only one of these southern tributaries, Collet's Wash, actually heads on the Kaiparowits. The upper, larger tributaries of the Escalante River head in the Escalante Mountains and on the south side of the Aquarius Plateau, also known as Boulder Mountain. Where the Escalante River emerges from the mountains, its valley is broad and level, with enough alluvial fill to permit modern farming with the aid of irrigation water taken from the stream. The two present-day settlements in the Escalante drainage are Escalante, at an elevation of 5800 feet, and Boulder, about 1000 feet higher. Escalante has an average growing season of 134 days and an average annual precipitation of just under 12 inches (Alter, 1941, p. 1148). Near these two favorably situated communities is evidence of the heaviest aboriginal population. In the lower part of the drainage, archaeological sites are to be found primarily where there is alluvial fill that could be farmed.

The cultural affiliation of sites in the Escalante drainage, like that of sites on the Kaiparowits, is predominantly with Virgin Anasazi. A few sites may be Fremont. Other sites, such as H 9-3, are probably Kayenta outliers. The most anomalous site in the Escalante drainage is the large Coombs Site (E 2-1) located in the town of Boulder. Lister (Lister *et al.*, various), who supervised the excavation of this site, considers it primarily Kayenta with numerous variations from the customary Kayenta complex. To a large extent, however, these variations are the differences that distinguish Virgin branch sites from Kayenta sites.

A few sites in the Escalante drainage show evidence of occupation prior to the Pueblo II-III period represented by the majority. Of these, some are assignable to the Virgin branch

at an early ceramic level, while still others are unquestionably preceramic (Gunnerson, 1959 c).

E 2-1

This site, a large village located on the north edge of the town of Boulder, was visited a number of times by Peabody Museum parties. The limited work done there was reported by Morss (1931, pp. 2-3). The excellent reports by Lister and various coauthors (1959, 1960, 1961) on recent excavations at this site (the Coombs Site) make additional description superfluous.

E 6-1

South of Escalante, on the left side of, and about 60 m. above Alvey Wash are the remains of three small structures on ledges under protective overhangs. The best-made utilizes bedrock for its ceiling, back wall, and most of its floor. The other three walls are carefully constructed of layers of rock about 1.5 cm. thick alternating with layers of adobe about 10 cm. thick. The front wall, slightly curved, is about 1.5 m. long and 1.4 m. high; the side walls are 0.8 m. long, and all walls are smooth on the inside. A doorway through the west wall is 30 cm. wide and 45 cm. high and has a stick lintel and a stone-slab sill. The sides of the doorway are of smoothed adobe. At one corner, the wall is supported by two poles, each 8 cm. in diameter, which extend under sections of the walls resting on bedrock. A section of adobe floor is also supported by these poles. The other two structures, one of them almost completely demolished, were of similar construction but more crudely made.

E 6-2

About 0.5 mile up Alvey wash from E 6-1 and on the same side are a few pictographs of men about 20 cm. tall painted in red. One of the men is on horseback.

E 12-1

This site is about 200 m. west of Coyote Holes, a source of poor water along Coyote Creek, a western tributary of the Escalante River. Here, pecked into a large rock slab in a small rock shelter, are outlines of feet about 25 cm. long—two in one place and one in another. About a dozen narrow sharpening (?) grooves have been ground into the same rock.

H 9-3

This site is a large rock shelter on the west side of Davis Gulch, a western tributary entering the Escalante River near its mouth. The most notable structure, probably a kiva, was built at the outer edge of the floor of the shelter so that there is here a free-standing wall, although at the rear the roof of the room is at the level of the shelter floor. The room is circular, 2.6 m. in diameter and 2.1 m. deep, with a niche in one wall and a pole-and-adobe roof. Four or five crudely built rooms are located against the cliff face. The excavation of this site has been subsequently reported by Gunnerson (1959, pp. 117–147).

SPECIMENS

Pottery sherds
Flagstaff (?) Black-on-white	2
Moenkopi Corrugated	3
North Creek Gray	3
Cucurbita fragments	2

GLEN CANYON

The Claflin-Emerson expedition did little more than touch the Glen Canyon of the Colorado River. The data obtained from this limited reconnaissance, however, reflect at least partially the complex archaeological picture revealed by the recent extensive salvage archaeology in and surrounding the area to be flooded behind the Glen Canyon dam. These earlier discoveries are described here in order to put them on record.

Work in Glen Canyon prior to 1959 has been reviewed by Adams (1960) and subsequent to 1959 there have appeared several reports relevant to that portion north of the mouth of the Escalante River with which the Claflin-Emerson expedition was concerned (Lipe, 1960; Lipe et al., 1960; and Sharrock et al., 1961). Ecological studies and a survey of vegetation have been made in Glen Canyon, in part to assist with archaeological interpretations, by Woodbury and others (1959 a, 1959 b).

Much of Glen Canyon is 1000 feet deep and along most of its length the walls consist of a series of nearly vertical cliffs. In some places there are alluvial bars along the Colorado River or low benches at the bases of the canyon walls that are accessible from the river. Often, however, the river flows at the foot of a cliff, preventing travel by land along the river. Furthermore, there are not very many places where it is possible to get horses down to the bottom of Glen Canyon and even fewer where they could be taken across the river and up the other side. Thus Glen Canyon would serve as an impediment even to foot travel and it probably was never more than sparsely occupied. Glen Canyon was apparently either a border area between cultures or a cultural no-man's land. In early historic times, it was utilized to some extent by Hopis, Paiutes, and Navajos. In prehistoric times peoples of Mesa Verde, Kayenta, Virgin, and Fremont affiliation came in contact with one another there. Perhaps the nature of interaction among these peoples will eventually be better understood. The recently collected data cited above strongly suggest that during Pueblo III times more and more of the Glen Canyon area was being dominated by the Mesa Verde people at the expense of the Kayenta people especially.

H 6-1

The remains of several structures were found in the open on a ledge on the north side of Smith Fork Canyon where it enters the canyon of the Colorado River. In front of the ledge, which is about 37 by 14 m., is a steep slope about 7 m. high and behind it rises a vertical cliff. For 12 m. along the edge of the central portion of the ledge is a wall about 30 cm. high composed of one course of rounded rocks. At either end is a crescent-shaped wall three courses high and about 1.5 m. long. In the middle of the ledge a structure 1.8 m. square still stands 1.2 m. high. Construction is of stone slabs laid in uneven courses, with no evidence that smaller stones or adobe had been used as chinking. Care had been taken, however, to keep the insides of the walls even, and the interior corners of the room are rounded. Other lines of rocks, now only one course high, probably represent still other structures. No artifacts could be found at the site.

H 6-2

At the mouth of Ticaboo Creek near Cass Hite's old ranch is a large boulder about 3 m. high, one face of which is covered with petrographs. The most interesting are two humpbacked flute players standing with their knees bent; but their legs are not crossed and they are not phallic. Other elements are zigzag lines, sinuous lines, circles, spirals, animals, and anthropomorphic figures, including a man shooting a bow and arrow.

H 6-3

On a promontory which overlooks the Good Hope Bar and which has an excellent view of the Colorado River, a few sherds were found at the base of a boulder. No other evidence of occupation could be found.

SPECIMENS

Pottery sherds
Mancos (?) Black-on-white with outside corrugated	1
Mancos Corrugated	3
Tusayan (?) Corrugated	10
North Creek Gray	1
Jeddito Black-on-yellow	1

The Tusayan (?) Corrugated sherds appear to be tempered with crushed sandstone.

H 7-1

This site is located on the east side of the Colorado River about 0.3 mile above the mouth of Red Canyon. It is situated on the first bench back from the river and consists of an L-shaped ruin 18 by 13 m., probably containing six to eight contiguous rooms and enclosing a depression 5.5 m. in diameter. The walls, of rather crude masonry, still stand as high as 1.2 m. The outside corners are square, but the inside corners are somewhat rounded. This site, together with H 7-2, has since been excavated by Lipe (1960, pp. 114–138), who treated them as a single site, the Loper Ruin or 42 Sa364.

SPECIMENS

Pottery sherds
Mesa Verde White ware	5

H 7-2

The edge of the bench upon which H 7-1 is situated is somewhat undercut in places and several rooms had been built against its face in order to take advantage of the protection afforded by the overhang. One section of wall, perpendicular to the cliff and still standing 3 m. high, has the ends of three cedar poles, each about 8 cm. in diameter and spaced about 8 cm. apart, projecting from it about 1.5 m. above the bottom. These had apparently formed part of the floor of a second story. The walls had been built of stone slabs and blocks laid in adobe mortar. Only the portion of the walls (about 1 m. long) protected by the overhang still stands.

SPECIMENS

Pottery sherds
Mesa Verde White ware	6
Mancos (?) Black-on-white, corrugated exterior	1
Mancos Corrugated	6
Moenkopi Corrugated	2
Corncob	1

There is some question as to whether the Moenkopi Corrugated sherds might be sand-tempered Mancos Corrugated and whether the sherd that is both painted and corrugated could not better be classified as a corrugated McElmo sherd.

H 7-3

About 0.2 mile north of H 7-2, and situated in a 10-m.-wide rock-shelter in the face of the same bench, is a ruin composed of nine contiguous rooms. The rooms had been irregular in shape and ranged from 0.6 to 2.4 m. across. The walls, now standing to a maximum height of 60 cm., were roughly laid up of irregular stones about 25 cm. in diameter. Although the shelter has been used by cattlemen for the storage of feed, many of the floors seem to be undisturbed.

SPECIMENS

Pottery sherd
Mesa Verde (?) White ware	1

TRACHITE CREEK–NORTH WASH

Both Trachite Creek and North Wash (Crescent Creek) head on the Henry Mountains and flow southeast to join the Colorado River about 7 and 2 miles, respectively, below the mouth of the Dirty Devil River. Hite, Utah, is situated at the mouth of Trachite Creek and the road from Hite to Hanksville goes up North Wash, crossing its bed many times. The variety exhibited by the little material collected in North Wash suggests that in prehistoric times, also, it served as a means of access to the Colorado from the west. White Canyon, which joins the Colorado opposite the mouth of Trachite Creek, provides an equally easy access to the Colorado from the east.

The limited amount of material collected in these two canyons does not show that they were strongly dominated by any particular group or that they ever had a significant population. Considering the paucity of land suitable for horticulture, the latter is not surprising.

H 3-1

On the left side of Trachite Creek, about 2 miles above its confluence with the Colorado River, is a large boulder with a flat surface upon which several pictographs could be discerned, apparently under the weathering on the surface. Several square-shouldered triangular-bodied anthropomorphic figures, some partially superimposed upon others, had apparently been painted in white. The two best-preserved figures are 0.82 and 1.04 m. tall and 47 and 55 cm. wide, respectively. The larger of the two had some sort of headdress represented by 24 short vertical lines.

H 3-2

On the right bank of Trachite Creek, about 2.5 miles above its mouth, is a large boulder on three sides of which are numerous pictographs, all pecked. Included among the figures is a snake 1.1 m. long; several anthropomorphic figures, about 30 cm. tall, with triangular, trapezoidal, square, rounded, and "stick" bodies; sheep or goats; a pair of six-toed footprints; and various geometric designs.

H 3-3

About 200 m. above Hogg Spring, which is about 10 miles up North Wash (Crescent Creek) from its mouth, are two pictographs. One is a snake 3.1 m. long, the front part of which is painted while the tail portion is pecked. The other is a plain trapezoidal-bodied, square-shouldered anthropomorphic figure about 1.5 m. tall.

H 3-4

This site, a large rock shelter about 200 m. high, with a floor about 120 m. long and 2 to 7 m. wide, is located about 0.25 mile south of Hogg Spring. Near the south end of the shelter and about 3 m. above its present floor is a very impressive anthropomorphic figure (fig. 25A) painted in a mahogany red. It has a trapezoidal body with rounded shoulders and a nearly circular head. Decoration, painted in white, consists of a diadem of nine dots, two parallel rows of thirteen dots across the forehead, a double row of smaller dots down either side of the face, and two parallel rows of 19 and 21 dots across the upper part of the chest, below which are ten vertical lines extending about halfway down the body. Beside this figure is an elliptical-bodied quadruped painted the same color and about one-third as high. The animal appears to have had appendages crudely added in a lighter paint at a later date to make it more closely resemble a mountain sheep. Near the middle of the shelter are pecked two figures of sheep, one with an oval body, the other with a trapezoidal body, 24 and 27 cm. long, respectively. The hoofs of both are clearly shown cloven.

Several crude walls are present in the shelter, all of irregular stones laid without spalls or adobe and none more than 60 cm. high. One or two are roughly circular, 1.2 to 1.8 m. in diameter; three or four are more or less incomplete squares, 1.5 to 2.1 m. on a side; and others are simply straight walls between large fallen rocks and the back wall of the shelter. A test pit revealed a layer of adobe 8 cm. thick about 45 cm. below the surface, under which was a layer of clean white grass.

This site was investigated by a second Peabody Museum party which excavated two of the structures. Both were built of loosely piled sandstone blocks, some of which had apparently fallen from the roof of the shelter. No mortar had been used. One of the rooms, semicircular, with the back wall of the shelter serving as its rear wall, is 4.9 m. long along the cliff and has a maximum width of about 2.3 m. A fireplace containing two stone slabs was found in the approximate center. Near one end of the back wall was found a storage bin about 60 by 90 cm., constructed of four stone slabs. A moccasin was found in one of the rooms.

SPECIMENS

Moccasin fragment	1

This fragment, which is mostly sole, shows evidence of a great deal of repairing. In one place near what was probably the heel, there appear to be eight layers of hide. Between two of them there is a thin layer of juniper bark fiber. Not too much can be determined about the construction of the moccasin. It appears to have been made from two layers of deer or antelope hide. The sole was brought up and puckered over the toes (and presumably along the side of the foot). The inner layer of hide had the hair side inside and at least part of the hair had been left on. The original sewing, along the pucker at least, was with sinew, but most if not all of the repair work had been done with plant fiber cord, probably yucca. In any case, the moccasin was not of Fremont style, but resembles the Basketmaker II type described by Guernsey (1931, pp. 66–8).

H 3-5

On the east side of Crescent Creek and about 400 m. above Hogg Spring is another large rock shelter at the top of a very steep slope. On the back wall of the shelter are two anthropomorphic figures with trapezoidal bodies and square heads, painted in red. One is 27 by 46 cm., the other 23 by 56 cm. From the top of the head of one, three straight lines extend 8 cm. to the left. Legs and arms are depicted by narrow, nearly straight lines.

H 3-6

About 0.5 mile above H 3-7 is another rock shelter about 30 ft. across that showed meager evidence of occupation.

SPECIMENS

Pottery sherd	
Tusayan Corrugated	1
Stone flake	1

H 3-7

Two smaller rock shelters adjacent to one another are just a little way up the canyon from H 3-5. Very little evidence of occupation could be found.

SPECIMENS

Pottery sherds	
Mancos Corrugated	2

H 3-8

Another site in Crescent Canyon, not far from H 3-4, yielded an unusually wide variety of pottery for the area. The exact location of this site, a rock shelter, is not known so it could conceivably be one of the other sites already described from Crescent Canyon.

SPECIMENS

Pottery sherds	
Flagstaff Black-on-white	2
Tusayan Black-on-red	2
Tsegi Orange ware	1
Moenkopi Corrugated	8
Mesa Verde (?) Corrugated	3
Emery Gray	6
Chipped Stone	
Blades	3
Drill	1
Blade or point fragments	2
Bone	
Awl	1
Splinter	1

The Flagstaff Black-on-white sherds are from two different vessels. One had been quite large and had had a strap handle, apparently horizontal. The other sherd shows evidence of grinding on one edge as if it had been re-used as some form of tool. The sherd identified as Tsegi Orange ware has traces of a red slip, but no black paint is present. The two black-on-red sherds are from different vessels, one a bowl, the other a jar. All the Emery Gray sherds are from jars, of which at least three appear to be represented. On one is a portion of a handle that had been attached by a riveting technique in which the end of the handle had been inserted through a hole in the vessel wall.

Two of the blades are nearly identical in shape and size (4.1 by 1.6 by 0.4 cm.). Their outline is that of a scalene triangle with slightly convex sides and a straight base. The base lacks about 10° of being perpendicular to the long axis of the blade. One blade is of opaque white flint, the other of translucent gray-tan chalcedony. The third blade, beautifully chipped from gray-to-tan translucent chalcedony, is complete and measures 10.5 by 2.9 by 0.6 cm. One end comes to a very sharp point, the other to a rounded point. The broadest part of the blade is slightly closer to the sharp point than to the rounded point. The other chipped stone artifacts are of similar material. The drill, which is triangular with concave sides and a straight base, is 3.2 by 1.6 by 0.6 cm. One fragment may be from a blade similar in shape to the two complete ones, but somewhat larger. The other fragment is the tip of a slim, delicately chipped, serrated point.

The bone awl, made from a splinter of long bone by simply sharpening one end and leaving the other end rough, measures 9.1 by 0.6 cm. It shows much polish, apparently from use. The other bone splinter appears to have been the butt of a similar awl.

RUIN PARK–SALT CREEK–FORT BOTTOM

The only area investigated by the Claflin-Emerson expedition in which there had been a substantial occupation by people with Mesa Verde culture is a narrow strip on the east side of the Green and Colorado rivers from about the mouth of Gypsum Canyon (38° north latitude) north to about the San Juan–Grand County line (38°30′ north latitude). This lies at the northwestern edge of the area solidly occupied by Mesa Verde people. The Mesa Verde occupation of the strip in question does not, however, appear to have antedated Pueblo II times. Farther to the west, across the Colorado and Green rivers, the few sites showing a very light use by Mesa Verde people were probably temporary.

The Ruin Park–Salt Creek area lies on the northwest side of Elk Ridge—between it and the Colorado River. Elk Ridge, located 30 miles west of Monticello, Utah, is nearly 9000 feet high and on it head many streams that flow into the San Juan River to the south and the Colorado River to the west. On the northwest side of Elk Ridge are a number of nearly level open parks such as Beef Basin and Ruin Park at elevations between 6000 and 7000 feet. These parks are drained by steep, rough canyons which, in some cases, descend to the 4000-foot elevation of the Colorado River in less than ten miles.

In Ruin Park, the main vegetation is sagebrush, which attests to the relative richness of the soil. On the ridges that break up this park land there is a good stand of pinyon and juniper with scatterings of pine and mountain mahogany. At higher elevations on Elk Ridge the trees get thicker and afford a habitat which supports many deer and elk, hence the name. Precipitation information is not available for the immediate area, but Blanding and Monticello slightly to the east (at about the same elevations) average about 15 inches and 17 inches per year, respectively. June, May, and April are, in that order, the driest months (Alter, 1941). By also projecting the average growing seasons of 147 and 136 days for Blanding and Monticello to Ruin Park, one sees the possibility for maize agriculture there.

These parks, and to a lesser extent the area on the south and east sides of Elk Ridge, are rich in archaeological sites which have received relatively little scientific attention. The most extensive work has been reported by Rudy (1955). Other work, almost exclusively survey, has been reported by Baldwin (1949), Cummings (1910), Steen (1937), Gunnerson (1956 a, 1956 b, 1960 a), and Sharrock and Keane (1962).

In the canyons to the north of Ruin Park are archaeological sites which have received even less attention. One of the earliest published reports of archaeological sites in Utah describes and illustrates ruins in what was called "Labyrinth" Canyon, and which must be Indian Creek to judge by the map (Newberry, 1876, p. 95). Except for a brief summary by Pierson (1962) and two articles by Henderson (1946 a, 1946 b), there are apparently no other published references to the archaeology of either Salt Canyon or Indian Creek Canyon.

All the sites in the Ruin Park–Salt Creek area seem to date from late Pueblo II–early

Pueblo III times, perhaps from between A.D. 1150 and A.D. 1250. The dating, based primarily on ceramic evidence, is somewhat tenuous since the black-on-white sherds do not match the published type descriptions closely. Rudy (1955) was plagued by the fact that, with regard to pigment and design elements, pottery from the contiguous Beef Basin failed to match the published descriptions of Mancos Black-on-white, Mesa Verde Black-on-white, or McElmo Black-on-white, types to which it was most closely related. In the present study, an attempt to follow the descriptions provided by Abel (1955) would have resulted in lumping all the Mesa Verde White ware sherds as McElmo Black-on-white. Many of these sherds could better have been called Mesa Verde Black-on-white, except that they all have a thin slip instead of the thick slip attributed to Mesa Verde Black-on-white. Because it would probably distort the picture to classify all of the Mesa Verde White ware sherds as McElmo Black-on-white and since the present collection is too small to justify the establishment of new types or varieties, it seems best for now to leave the identifications at the ware level. It is likely that, once the current intensive studies of ceramics from near the heart of the Mesa Verde area have been completed, these ceramics from the western edge of the Mesa Verde area can be re-examined and classified more meaningfully.

Other problems are also encountered in classifying the pottery from this western Mesa Verde periphery. Nearly all the painted ware contains significant amounts of sand, crushed sand, or crushed rock. One problem created by the occurrence of crushed rock in black-on-white pottery, especially here on the boundary between Mesa Verde and Fremont, is the possibility of mistaking small sherds of Emery Black-on-white for Mancos Black-on-white or Mesa Verde White ware and vice versa, since the use of crushed rock for tempering is one of the diagnostic traits of Fremont pottery.

Moreover, much of the corrugated ware from these Mesa Verde sites is tempered with sand rather than with the traditional crushed rock. Since sand as opposed to crushed rock is the most distinctive difference between Mesa Verde and Kayenta corrugated pottery, this variation leads to classification problems. Where a ceramic sample is small, it could be difficult to decide to which of these two branches a site should be assigned. Furthermore, the possibility arises that some corrugated trade sherds found at Fremont sites may have been classified as Tusayan Corrugated when in reality they had a Mesa Verde origin. The most probable explanation of sand tempering in Mancos Corrugated sherds is diffusion of this trait from Kayenta, since the Mesa Verde–Kayenta boundary is not at all sharp along the Colorado River.

The variation in architecture is also difficult to explain. Whereas some of the masonry in Ruin Park is of high quality, although not as uniform as the best Anasazi architecture, the structures at some of the sites in Salt Canyon, presumably occupied about the same time, are exceedingly crude. It is fruitless to speculate as to whether the crude dwellings were built by marginal citizens or whether they represent temporary habitations, quickly built to take advantage of the protection provided by rock shelters while more substantial buildings were being constructed at open sites. Beyond Ruin Park to the north and west few pretentious structures are found, although there is one moderately well built Mesa Verde structure (LS 9-1) at Fort Bottom, about 30 miles farther north.

Sites LS 14-6 through LS 14-13, located along Salt Creek, should in reality have been given LS 13- numbers and some of the Ruin Park sites with LS 13- numbers should probably have been given AB 1- (for Abajo) numbers. These errors came about because of inaccuracies on the best maps available at the time of the survey (1929).

LS 13-1

In Lost Canyon near Cave Spring there are several rock shelters containing small structures. At this particular site there are the remains of four curved structures built of medium-sized stone slabs laid in heavy mortar. One is circular, free standing, and 1.4 m. in diameter. A second, also circular, but built against one wall of the shelter, is 1 m. in diameter. A third, semicircular and utilizing the wall of the shelter as one of its walls, is 1.3 by 1.1 m. The fourth structure is built on

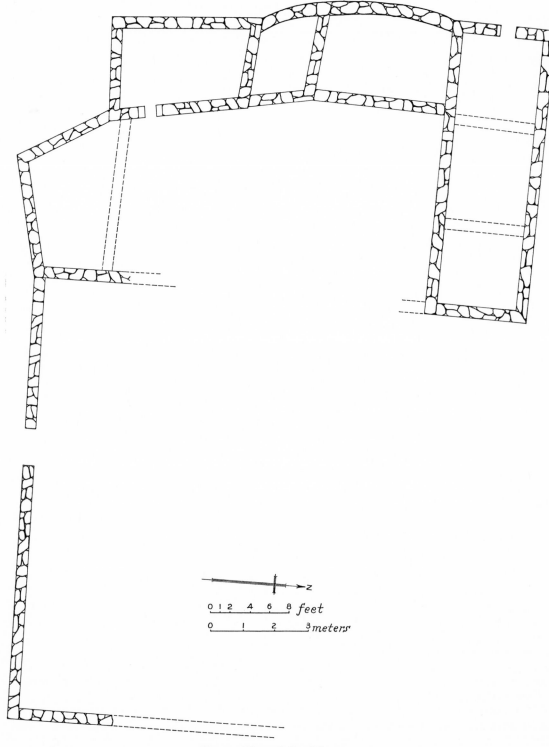

Fɪɢ. 3. Plan of Site LS 13-2.

a narrow ledge about 14 m. from the main part of the shelter and utilizes the cliff face as part of its back wall. Its long axis is 1.8 m. and parallels the cliff, the short axis is 1.5 m. long, and the wall averages about 33 cm. in thickness. There is a doorway about 45 cm. wide part way up one of the end walls.

SPECIMENS

Pottery sherds	
Mesa Verde White ware	4
Mancos Corrugated	6
Mesa Verde Corrugated	1
Tusayan Corrugated	2
Anvil for fire drill	1
Horn sickle (?)	1
Juniper bark ring	1

The Tusayan Corrugated sherds are so identified primarily because of their sand temper. Perhaps they should be considered a sand-tempered variety of Mancos Corrugated.

The fire-drill hearth is a piece of stick 2 cm. in diameter. A hole 7 mm. in diameter has been burned into the stick with a fire drill. A narrow slot has been cut into the hole to hold the tinder.

A piece of mountain sheep horn had been cut down at its base to form a handle and the mid-portion ground down on one side to provide a sharp edge, presumably to serve as a sickle. The sharp edge does not show a great deal of polish, however. The specimen, badly eaten by insects, has perhaps 10 cm. of the tip missing.

The coil of juniper bark is about 15 cm. in diameter and could have served as a pot rest.

LS 13-2

Many ruins were seen in the Beef Basin–Ruin Park area, but specimens were collected and data recorded at only a few selected sites in Ruin Park. Subsequent excavation in Beef Basin carried out and reported by Rudy (1955) has provided more detailed information on the area.

Site LS 13-2 (figs. 3, 20A), the largest site in Ruin Park, is on the north side at the west end. This structure is built of large unworked, but frequently square-cornered, sandstone blocks. Scant use was made of mortar, but many small pieces of stone were used as chinking. The north wing still stands one and one-half stories high and may have been as much as three stories high. One T-shaped doorway is preserved. The rest of the structure was probably only one story high. The entire building is U-shaped with the opening to the east, and measures about 15 by 11 m. There is no evidence of a kiva near it. However, about 25 m. to the east is a round tower, apparently with a double wall, about 2.5 m. in diameter and still standing 1 m. high.

SPECIMENS

Pottery sherds	
Mesa Verde White ware	47
Mancos Corrugated	13
Mancos (?) Corrugated	
(sand-tempered)	14
Mesa Verde White ware or Mancos	
Black-on-white (no paint)	17

LS 13-3

At the south edge of Ruin Park, on a bench overlooking it, is a ruin with a U-shaped house block opening to the north and a single kiva to the northwest of it. In size and quality of masonry this house block is similar to that at LS 13-2. One of the earlier rooms, at the southwest corner, is essentially square with rounded corners and had been two stories high. The other living rooms have square corners, and doors, where present, are square or rectangular. Someone had dug into the kiva previously, revealing six pilasters, and a ventilator on the southeast side.

SPECIMENS

Pottery sherds	
Mesa Verde White ware	47
Mancos Black-on-white	9
Mancos Corrugated	12
Mancos (?) Corrugated	
(sand-tempered)	13
Gallup Black-on-white	1
Mesa Verde White ware or Mancos	
Black-on-white (no paint)	7

LS 13-4

This site, located about 0.25 mile east of LS 13-3, also has masonry (fig. 20B) similar to that at LS 13-2. There is no kiva in evidence, but a round tower is incorporated in the main house block. The other seven to nine rooms in the block tend to be rectangular, although three are off-square because of their joining the round tower. A second unit consisting of two rooms, one with a rounded wall,

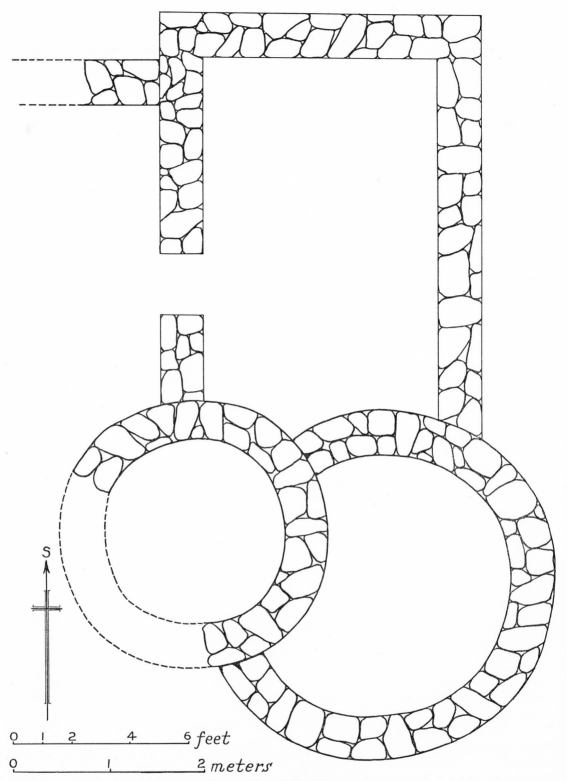

S

0 1 2   4   6 *feet*

0   1   2 *meters*

Fig. 4. Plan of Site LS 13-5.

is close by, but apparently was never attached to the larger block. There is a small accumulation of refuse to the east of the houses.

SPECIMENS

Pottery sherds

Mesa Verde White ware	30
Mancos Black-on-white	13
Mancos Corrugated	5
Mancos (?) Corrugated (sand-tempered)	4
Mancos Black-on-white, corrugated exterior	1
Mesa Verde White ware or Mancos Black-on-white (no paint)	7

LS 13-5

This site, near the middle of Ruin Park, consists of a three-room structure (fig. 4) made of unworked stone blocks that have, however, been selected with unusual care. The first room built is round, about 2 m. in diameter. Against this was constructed a second circular room about 2.5 m. in diameter and, finally, a square tower, still standing two and one-quarter stories high, was built abutting the two circular rooms. The tower, 2.4 by 3.2 m., has walls that are very smooth on the outside and very rough on the inside. A section of wall suggests that another room had been built against one side of the square tower. A section of cedar beam had apparently been collected from this ruin at some time in the past.

SPECIMENS

Pottery sherds

Mesa Verde White ware	35
Mancos Black-on-white	11
Mancos Corrugated	3
Mancos (?) Corrugated (sand-tempered)	23
Sosi Black-on-white	4
Mesa Verde White ware or Mancos Black-on-white (no paint)	4

LS 13-6, 7, 8, 9, 10

At the highest point on the south side of Ruin Park are the ruins of a tower or a rectangular room about 4 by 2 m. On a shelf just under the east side of this knoll is a round structure, perhaps a tower or kiva, and near by are other ruins with one to several rooms.

SPECIMENS

	LS 13-6	LS 13-7	LS 13-8
Pottery sherds			
Mesa Verde White ware	17	32	6
Mancos Black-on-white	4	13	–
Mancos Corrugated	–	2	7
Mancos (?) Corrugated (sand-tempered)	–	6	1
Tsegi Orange ware	–	3	–
Mesa Verde White ware or Mancos Black-on-white (no paint)	–	–	8

LS 13-11

North of Ruin Park in the wall of Spring Canyon, a tributary of Salt Creek, is a well-preserved, two-story storage structure (fig. 22A), built from floor to ceiling in a shallow rock shelter. The structure utilizes the back wall of the shelter as one wall; the other three walls are constructed of rocks laid in an abundance of adobe mortar. The entrances to both stories are in one end, one directly above the other. The lower doorway has large stone slabs for both sill and lintel and has an adobe jamb on both sides and across the top. The upper doorway extends to the roof of the shelter. The lower room is about 1 m. wide and 2 m. long and the upper room, formed by a continuation of one end wall and part of the side wall, is about half as long.

LS 13-12

At an open site just to the north of Ruin Park in Bobby's Hole there is a small ruin (fig. 21B), interesting in that the walls are a combination of irregular stones laid up very crudely and four larger stones, each about 0.3 by 0.4 by 1.1 m., set on end at intervals around the wall. The room enclosed is about 4 m. in diameter.

SPECIMENS

Pottery sherds

Mesa Verde White ware	8

LS 13-13

In Pap's Pasture, just north of Ruin Park, is a small cliff ruin rather carefully constructed of moderately large to large slabs, carefully chinked with small pieces of rock and perhaps a little adobe. In general, the slabs, which decrease in size from the bottom of the wall up, have been carefully selected but not dressed. The doorway, in the center of one wall, has a stone sill a little above floor level, and a stone lintel. The roof is now mostly gone; it consisted of a few large rafters which supported closely spaced smaller poles that had probably been covered with adobe.

SPECIMENS

Pottery sherds
Mesa Verde White ware	11
Mancos Corrugated	5
Mesa Verde White ware or Mancos Black-on-white (no paint)	3

LS 14-1

This site, Cave Spring, is located in Salt Creek Canyon at the mouth of Lost Canyon. Pictographs at the site include three figures painted in red; they are probably anthropomorphic, but very poorly executed.

SPECIMENS

Pottery sherds
Mancos Black-on-white	3
Mesa Verde White ware	3
Unidentified	4
Chipped Stone blade	1

The unidentified sherds are probably undecorated sherds from vessels of one of the other two types.

The blade, 8.8 by 5.7 by 1.2 cm., is triangular (scalene) with convex sides. It is of dark brown quartzite and was chipped primarily by the removal of large flakes.

LS 14-2

A moderately well-built structure was found under a protective overhang in the wall of Lost Canyon. A wall forming about two-thirds of a circle abuts the rear wall of the shelter at either end, enclosing an area about 1.5 m. in diameter. The wall, consisting of stone slabs laid in adobe mortar, is well constructed and still stands about 1 m. high. The doorway, in one side, has a stone slab sill about halfway up the wall and apparently once extended to the roof, which is now missing.

LS 14-3

This pictograph site, located along Indian Creek, contains several featureless, undecorated anthropomorphic figures with square heads and some small-headed sheep with rounded bodies. A few more or less geometric designs were also present.

LS 14-4

This site, located near LS 14-3 on Indian Creek, consists of a platform constructed by laying poles across two narrow ledges on either side of a wide place in a triangular crevice. The platform, about 2 by 2 m., was undoubtedly built for storage purposes.

LS 14-5

This site, located in the canyon wall of Indian Creek, consists of the remains of a structure situated in a small niche which it had nearly filled. The room, now very poorly preserved, had walls constructed of irregular stone slabs roughly laid, apparently without the use of mortar, but chinked on the inside with adobe. The roof had been supported on poles that rested on the walls.

LS 14-6

In Salt Creek Canyon, about 0.25 mile below Peek-a-boo (a natural arch), there are pictographs of many hands painted in red, white, yellow, and black.

LS 14-7

At Peek-a-boo, in Salt Creek Canyon, there is a row of at least 60 white dots directly above two circular figures, probably anthropomorphic. At the top of one of these is a round head on a thin neck, and projecting from the bottom are two straight lines, probably legs. The circular body is almost entirely covered with small squares. The other figure has a larger nearly square head but no legs, and is decorated with vertical lines alternating with rows of dots. The white figures had been painted over red figures, now very faint.

LS 14-8

This site, Cedar House, is located about 5 miles above Peek-a-boo, in Salt Creek Canyon, and gets its name from a structure about 3 by 2.5 m. and 1.2 m. high that was constructed of cedar poles, essentially by cribbing them. The sides were then covered with adobe, and flat stone slabs were set on edge at the base of the walls. The structure was roofed with long cedar poles covered with adobe and stone spalls.

SPECIMENS

Pottery sherds	
Mesa Verde White ware	7
Mancos Corrugated	2
Metate	1
Plaited mat fragment	1

The fragment of mat is plaited in an over-two, under-two twill pattern. The elements, stems of phragmites, are about 1 cm. wide.

The metate, observed but not collected, is thick and rectangular and has a deep trough.

LS 14-9

About 2 miles farther up Salt Creek Canyon from LS 14-8, and just to the west of a spring that bubbles up in the creek bed, is a pictograph panel containing a series of angular snakes painted in white.

LS 14-10

Several small structures (fig. 22B) are located under an overhang in Salt Creek Canyon about 8 miles above Peek-a-boo. Two of these structures, built against the cliff face, were constructed of irregular stone slabs, apparently without the use of adobe mortar. At least one of the rooms had been chinked with adobe and still has a roof consisting of parallel cedar poles resting on top of the wall and covered with a layer of grass and a layer of adobe. This structure, essentially circular, is about 75 cm. in diameter, and has a nearly square doorway with a single-stick lintel. A second room consists of two parallel walls about 2.2 m. apart, extending from the cliff face to two large boulders about 3 m. away. The roof is missing, but a doorway 0.5 m. wide and 1.4 m. high, with a lintel composed of three cedar poles, is preserved. A third structure, 2.5 m. in diameter, and a small cist in the floor of the shelter, partially covered with a pole-and-adobe roof with a square opening, are also present.

LS 14-11

This site (fig. 21A), containing ten habitation rooms or houses plus a number of smaller storage rooms, occupies an overhang about 40 m. long, situated on the west side of and about 30 m. above Salt Canyon, about 2 miles below its fork. The floor of the shelter was very irregular and had been leveled in places with poles and rocks. The houses tend to be square or square with rounded corners and were constructed of rough, unshaped stone slabs laid in heavy mortar. At floor level in the front wall of each house is a small ventilator, directly in front of which is the fireplace. The roofs were apparently constructed of cedar poles, rushes, and adobe, and in some instances rather large stones were also incorporated. The houses, some of which were set into the fill of the shelter, range in size up to about 3.7 m. square. Most of the storage rooms are semicircular, utilizing the cliff wall for their straight side, and are constructed of rough stone slabs laid in much mortar. A few, however, are square.

On the back wall of the shelter are some pictographs. Among them are trapezoidal-bodied anthropomorphs with decorations suggestive of necklaces and sashes, sheep, geometric designs resembling pottery decoration, and negative-painted hands.

SPECIMENS

Pottery sherds	
Mesa Verde White ware	30
Mancos Black-on-white	6
Mancos Corrugated	10
Mancos (?) Corrugated (sand-tempered)	4
Unpainted portions of black-on-white vessels	14
Perforated pottery disk	1
Sandal	1
Ring pot rest	1
Reed mat fragment	1
Cord fragments	9
Yucca chain	1
Cucurbita fragment	1
Corn stems	4

A disk has been roughly shaped from what is probably an unpainted portion of a painted vessel. Since there are several spalled areas on the surfaces, it seems likely that the piece was not considered worth finishing. A biconical hole through the middle suggests that in making disks from pottery sherds, the hole was drilled before even the rough shaping was started. The specimen is about 4 cm. in diameter.

A square rim sherd (7.4 by 7.4 cm.) from a black-on-white bowl has on it a large spot of black paint suggesting that it was used as a paint dish.

The sandal (fig. 40, *f*) is very similar to Kidder and Guernsey (1919, p. 101) type I, a, 1, except that it is plaited with a plain weave instead of a twill weave. It had apparently been attached to the foot by means of edge loops as described by the same authors (1919, p. 107). The sandal is 27 by 10 cm., has a straight but slightly angled toe and a somewhat rounded, narrow heel. It is made of strips of yucca leaves which average about 1.5 cm. in width.

The pot rest is a ring, 20 cm. in diameter on the outside, 10 cm. in diameter on the inside, and 3 cm. thick, made by bending a long bundle of yucca leaves into a circle and wrapping the bundle with additional yucca leaves.

A fragment of the selvage edge of a twined rush mat was recovered. The rushes (*scirpus*) have a flattened width of about 1 cm. and are held together by a single-ply, Z-spun cord, probably made of *scirpus* fiber. At the edge of the mat, each rush was bent over, passed under the bent-over end of the adjacent rush, and caught under the weft cord as it passed around the rush once removed. Since only one weft cord remains, it is not possible to tell how widely spaced the weft was.

All the samples of cord were two-ply, Z-twist. They varied from 2 to 4 mm. in diameter. Nine of the specimens were made of yucca fiber, the other was probably juniper.

The chain of yucca leaves appears to be the result of children's play. A few yucca leaves were tied end to end with square knots. The long strip was then doubled and tied together with a very loose overhand knot, leaving a loop about 3 cm. in diameter; this procedure was repeated until the long strip was used up and a chain-like specimen, of which about 30 cm. remains, resulted. If any two of the overhand knots were to be pulled tightly together, a granny knot would result.

Four stems from corncobs were found strung on a piece of yucca leaf which in turn had been tied with a square knot. Perhaps several ears of corn had been attached to one another in this manner for storage or transporting.

LS 14-12

This site, another cliff dwelling similar to LS 14-11, is located about 0.5 mile farther up Salt Canyon from it. There are three or four single houses and about fifteen smaller storage rooms at the site. On the back wall of the shelter are pictographs including several negative-painted hands and what is probably part of a curvilinear anthropomorphic figure.

LS 14-13

This site, another cliff dwelling similar to LS 14-12, is on the north side of Salt Canyon where the West Fork enters it.

LS 9-1: Fort Bottom Ruin

The ruin at Fort Bottom (fig. 23 *A,B*), which takes its name from an imposing structure, is the northernmost ruin of Mesa Verde affiliation. The site is on a small 120-m.-high butte in a hairpin bend of the Colorado River and is connected with the east wall of the canyon by a very narrow knife-edge ridge about 60 m. high and perhaps 300 m. long. There are two rooms in the 3.4-m.-high main structure or "fort." The first room built is about 2.5 m. in diameter and 2 m. high. A second room of about the same size was later built against the first. A ground-level doorway about 75 cm. high and 45 cm. wide, with a stick lintel, connects the two rooms. On top of the second room had been added a second story that had a doorway (later walled up) leading to the roof of the first room. The walls are of dry-laid, unshaped sandstone-slab masonry and had been plastered on the inside. Some of the plaster remaining in place is slightly reddened, probably from burning. Surrounding the main structure are the ruins of two or possibly three smaller structures, possibly storage rooms. This site has also been visited and reported by Gunnerson (1959 b, pp. 5–6).

SPECIMENS

Pottery sherds
Mesa Verde White ware	4
Mancos Black-on-white	3
Mancos Corrugated	11
Emery Gray	6

Unidentified gray   8
Chipped Stone
    Blade fragment   1
    Point   1

The painted pottery shows varying amounts of crushed rock and sand. The plain gray unidentified sherds are difficult to classify in that they do not match established types exactly. Three of them are nearly black (surface and paste), partially polished, and tempered with moderate amounts of black, slightly vesicular sand. Five gray-to-tan sherds are moderately smooth, unpolished, and tempered with a mixture of sand, crushed rock, and crushed sherds.

The point, which is incomplete, is of pink chalcedony, triangular with a concave base, and has two side notches and a basal notch. It had been about 2.3 by 1.5 mm. The blade fragment is of brown jasper.

DIRTY DEVIL RIVER–WATERHOLE FLAT

Near the town of Hanksville, Utah, the Muddy River and the Fremont River join to form the Dirty Devil River, which flows southeast to enter the Green River about 6 miles north of Hite, Utah. For its first few miles the Dirty Devil flows across relatively level but barren land with an elevation of about 4400 feet. But the river soon entrenches itself in a canyon about 1000 feet deep for much of its length. Tributary canyons entering the mid-portion of the Dirty Devil are almost all from the very rough and rugged area to the east and have their headwaters on the flat barren country that forms the divide between the Dirty Devil and Barrier Canyon. The eastern tributaries of the lower Dirty Devil drain part of the rugged, almost waterless Waterhole Flat, much of which, however, is drained by a number of short canyons that flow directly into the Colorado River. The largest southern tributary of the Dirty Devil, Poison Spring Wash, rises very near the headwaters of Crescent Creek (North Wash) on the eastern slope of Mt. Ellen of the Henry Mountains and enters the Dirty Devil about 15 miles above its mouth.

The general rugged barrenness and low precipitation (about 6 inches annually), which would preclude horticulture without irrigation in the Dirty Devil–Waterhole Flat area, are reflected in the archaeological record. Large or intensively occupied sites could not be found and very few sites showed evidence of structures that could be considered dwellings. More recent work along the lower part of the Dirty Devil revealed only a single, insignificant archaeological site (Lister, 1959 a, pp. 60–61). And the reconnaissance by Gunnerson (1957 a, pp. 77–80) of the Robbers' Roost area to the north located only small sites, most of them probably camp sites.

Archaeological data from the Dirty Devil–Waterhole Flat area show a varied if sparse occupation. The most rewarding site (SR 16-6) was occupied almost exclusively by a Basketmaker II people. Later sites show affiliation with Fremont, Mesa Verde, Virgin, and Kayenta. The data are too few to indicate clearly the relationships among these four cultures in this area. The most plausible explanation is that small groups from each ventured into or across it in the course of trading, hunting, or exploring. The lack of sites yielding evidence of even moderately long occupation seems to rule out a situation in which there was a blending of cultures.

SR 10-1

This site, near the confluence of Buck Canyon and the Dirty Devil, is a rock shelter containing a dripping spring. A little detritus, especially bones, was found but there was no evidence of structures.

The following specimens are probably from this site.

SPECIMENS
    Pottery sherd
        Emery Gray   1
    Quartz pebble, partially perforated   1
    Modified bone   1
    Unmodified bone   4
    Snail shell   1
    Rush matting fragments   3
    Animal and bird remains   3

The sherd appears to be from a bottle or pitcher with a slightly flattened spherical body about 12 cm. in diameter. The only piece of worked stone collected was a light pink, almost round, quartz pebble about 3.2 cm. in diameter and 1.7 cm. thick. It appears to have been at least partially shaped by pecking and grinding, and a conical depression 0.6 cm. deep in the middle of one face is almost certainly artificial.

Five deer metatarsals were collected. Four are not modified, but the fifth has had both ends ground or cut squarely off and the outside ground and polished to form what is essentially a truncated cone 3.5 cm. long with maximum and minimum diameters of 1.6 and 1.0 cm. A round hole 0.3 cm. in diameter passes through the middle of the smaller end, but the larger end is solid except for a portion that appears to have been broken out accidentally. The foot and lower leg of a deer with skin and tendons preserved by desiccation, part of a fledgling eagle, similarly preserved, and a rodent skull were also recovered.

Portions of two or possibly three twined rush mats were collected. Construction techniques are the same in all specimens. Individual rushes (*scirpus*) are held together with Z-twist cords made of *scirpus* fiber. The cords, which are twisted only once between rushes, are 5 cm. apart in two samples and 7 cm. apart in the other. In the most complete specimen, the ends of the rushes are bent back about 3 cm. and tucked into the loop of the weft cord that surrounds the adjacent rush. The weft element is continuous in that it is not tied off and cut at the end of each line but goes back and forth across the mat. At the edge parallel to the rushes, the weft cords are knotted with an overhand knot, twisted loosely together for 5 cm. where they follow the edge of the mat, are knotted again, and start back across the mat in the opposite direction.

SR 10-3

On the north side of the Dirty Devil River just above the mouth of Buck Canyon is a pictograph panel depicting two men, apparently fighting. Each is holding a circular shield in front of himself and has a club (?) raised behind his head. One shield has three short lines extending up from it. Each man also has something, perhaps a horn or a feather, projecting up from the back of his head. The figures are only 16.5 and 19 cm. tall. Also

shown is a man with a bow and arrow shooting at an animal, apparently a buffalo.

SR 10-4

Near the confluence of Buck Canyon and the Dirty Devil is an open site on a ledge that contains the remains of house structures. Construction was apparently of dry-laid sandstone blocks. Although the site is badly eroded, there appears to be about 60 cm. of fill.

Just east of the ledge upon which the structures were built are several red painted anthropomorphic figures 1.0 to 1.2 m. tall. They have squarish bodies and some have what appear to be horns projecting from their heads. Just to the east of these are a number of pecked figures, including mountain sheep.

The following artifacts are probably from this site.

Specimens

Pottery sherds	
Emery Gray	12
Snake Valley (?) Black-on-gray	1
Chipped point	1
Worked bone	2

The point, made of gray flint, is triangular with deep corner notches (fig. 43, *g*). It is 2.8 cm. wide and appears to have been about 5 cm. long (the tip is missing). One of the bone artifacts is a portion of an awl made from an 8-mm.-wide splinter of a mammal long bone. The other is a section of a rib 1.0 cm. wide and 10.5 cm. long. Both ends have been cut off and a notch cut into one side near one end. Its function is not obvious.

SR 15-1

About 5 miles up Poison Spring Wash from its confluence with the Dirty Devil is a small but interesting pictograph panel consisting of pecked figures. In it is a man with a bow as large as he is, shooting close range at an animal, probably a buffalo, which faces him. Behind the animal is a rectangle below which are two concentric circles. Below the man is a spiral with four convolutions terminating on the outer end with a meandering line. There are also two men fighting, very similar to the pair described at site SR 10-3.

SR 15-2

A small rock shelter in Poison Spring Canyon 3 miles from its mouth yielded some evidence of occupation. The remains of a poorly preserved structure were observed and a few artifacts collected.

SPECIMENS

Pottery sherds	
Sevier Gray	4
Emery Gray	1
North Creek (?) Gray	2
Quids	10
Antler tine	1

The quids are of masticated yucca leaves. The antler tine tip, possibly elk to judge by its size, is burned and shows no evidence of having been worked.

SR 15-3

In this small rock shelter, located in Poison Spring Wash about 2 miles above its mouth, nothing was found but a small firepit and a pile of cedar bark and grass. A little way below it were a few pictographs, including a humpbacked flute player.

SR 15-4

This site, a rock shelter, is located in Hatch Canyon about 4 miles above its confluence with the Dirty Devil. In the shelter are the remains of two semicircular cists, each about 1 m. in diameter, which had utilized the back wall of the shelter as one wall. All that remains of the constructed walls are thin stone slabs, many of them still standing on edge.

SR 15-5

This site, a rock shelter containing two cists, is located on the north side of the north branch of Hatch Canyon, between it and Happy Canyon. It is situated in the side of a bald-face hill on top of a mesa. The cists are pits in the shelter fill that had been partially lined with vertical stone slabs. There apparently never had been slabs on the east side of either. One cist, about 1.2 by 0.9 m., had incorporated three slabs; the other, about 1.2 by 1.5 m., had incorporated five slabs. The specimens are all from the former; the latter, however, was lined with cedar bark.

SPECIMENS

Animal fur	1
Tanned hide strip	2
Hide cord	1

The piece of hide, tanned with the fur left on, is 25 by 8 cm. and shows no evidence of use. The two strips of tanned hide, which are about 25 and 30 cm. long and vary from 0.5 to 1.0 cm. wide, had been tied together with a granny knot. They were tanned with the hair removed and are still soft. The fur cord is about 40 cm. long and 0.7 cm. in diameter. It was made by twisting together three narrow strips of rabbit (?) hide (with the fur left on) in a Z-twist.

SR 16-1

The remains of two small structures were found in a 4.5 by 6 m. rock shelter at the head of the first canyon east of the main canyon in Waterhole Flat. These structures are about 1 m. in diameter and about 0.6 m. high. The lower portions of the walls are made in part of stone slabs set vertically and the spaces between are filled with smaller slabs laid horizontally, which continue up to form one course on top of the vertical slabs. The roof is constructed of split cedar poles and sandstone slabs covered with a heavy layer of adobe.

The following specimens are probably from this site.

SPECIMENS

Pottery sherds	
Mesa Verde (?) White ware	2
Mancos Corrugated	6
Emery (?) Gray	3
Chipped blade	1
Chipped point fragment	1

The blade, which is complete, is made of a fine-grain gray quartzite and is 9.0 by 3.3 cm. It is essentially a triangle except that the sides flare slightly at the base. Perhaps the flaring is the result of resharpening the blade while it was still hafted. The point fragment appears to be from a triangular, corner-notched point with serrated sides. It was made from reddish chalcedony and had been about 2.0 by 4.5 cm.

SR 16-2

On a ledge just above the main shelter (SR

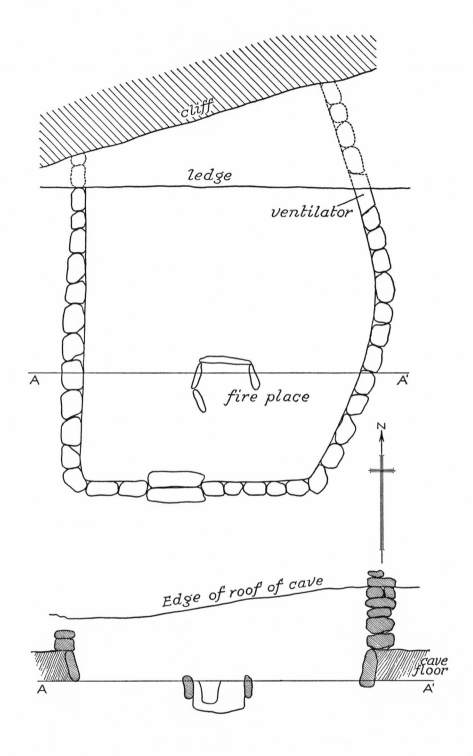

cliff

ledge

ventilator

A   A'

fire place

N

Edge of roof of cave

cave floor

A   A'

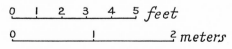

0 1 2 3 4 5 *feet*

0   1   2 *meters*

FIG. 5. Plan and profile of structure at Site SR 16-3.

16-1) are two small, well-made semicircular storage rooms constructed of stone slabs set in an abundance of adobe mortar. Each door frame consists of three cedar poles, two vertical and one horizontal across their tops, tied together with withes where they cross. Both structures are built against the cliff, utilizing it as one wall. The one built first is 2.1 m. long and 1.2 m. wide. The second, built in part against the first, is 1.3 by 1.0 m.

SR 16-3

The best-constructed dwelling found in the Waterhole Flat area is in a rock shelter about 6 by 15 m. This room (fig. 5), about 4.7 by 3.5 m., utilized the back wall of the shelter as one of its walls. A shallow pit had been excavated into the floor of the shelter and lined with vertical stone slabs. Resting on top of these slabs and on the floor of the shelter outside the pit are walls of horizontal slab masonry. The insides of the walls had been chinked with adobe, but no evidence of adobe was found on the outsides. The floor of the room was carefully prepared of puddled adobe. A fireplace, about 65 cm. in diameter and partially surrounded with stone slabs, is situated near the front of the room. It still contained much ash. The doorway through the front wall has a doorstep 70 cm. long, 15 cm. thick, and 15 cm. high, topped with a two-piece stone sill held in place by two cedar poles. Near the rear of one wall is a ventilator. The roof of the shelter, which forms the roof of the room, is about 2 m. high near the front of the structure, but at the rear a ledge projects down to within 30 to 45 cm. of the floor.

The following specimens are probably from this site.

SPECIMENS

Pottery sherds	
Mesa Verde White ware	46
Garfield Black-on-white	1
Mesa Verde Corrugated	1
Mancos Corrugated	3
Tusayan Corrugated	2
Moenkopi Corrugated	2
North Creek Gray	9
Emery Black-on-white	1
Emery Black-on-gray	1
Emery Tooled	1
Emery Gray	8
Worked sherds	2
Stone flake	1

Many of the Mesa Verde sherds contain moderate amounts of crushed rock and sand, often fractured. The sherds identified as Tusayan and Moenkopi Corrugated may actually be sand-tempered Mancos Corrugated. The worked sherds, both Mesa Verde White ware, are probably parts of pottery scrapers.

SR 16-4

A rock shelter at Point of Rocks southeast of Sunset Pass shows evidence of occupation, but no indication of structures. The shelter, which faces west, is about 6 m. long, 4 m. deep, and 3 m. high. It has about 60 cm. of sandy fill composed of two layers containing charcoal and detritus, separated by and covered with layers of clean sand. About 5 m. in front of the shelter is a stone-slab-lined fire box about 1.2 m. in diameter and 1 m. deep, partially filled with ash.

In addition to the specimens listed below, which probably came from this site, seven manos and one metate were observed. The manos were crude and shaped on one side only, but three were provided with finger grips. The metate consists of a flat stone slab, roughly shaped and slightly pecked on the grinding surface.

SPECIMENS

Pottery sherds	
Emery Black-on-white	2
Emery Black-on-gray	6
Emery Gray	8
Tusayan White ware	2
Pottery disk	1
Chipped stone blade fragment	1
Bone fragments	9
Bone flaker (?)	1

The black-on-gray sherds (all from one bowl) and the black-on-white sherds (from two bowls) are decorated with parallel encircling lines. One of the black-on-white sherds had been ground to form a disk 3.4 cm. in diameter. The chipped stone fragment is the square base of a gray chalcedony blade 3.1 cm. wide. Some of the bone fragments had been worked and appear to be from awls. The flaker (?), 10.5 cm. long and poorly preserved, comes to a blunt point at each end.

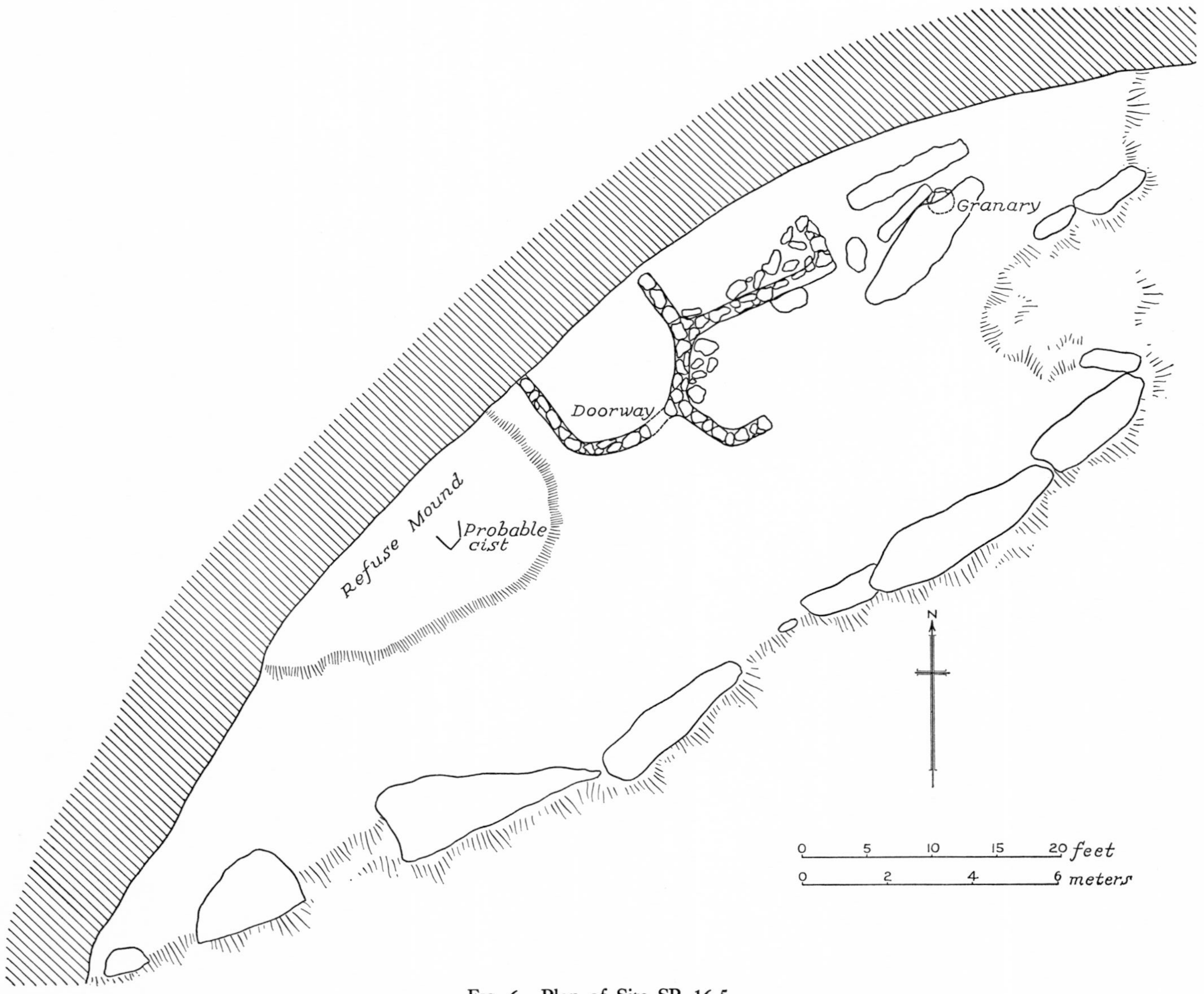

Granary

Doorway

Probable cist

Refuse Mound

N

0   5   10   15   20 feet

0   2   4   6 meters

Fig. 6. Plan of Site SR 16-5.

SR 16-5

This site, located on the east side of Willow Tank Canyon near Willow Tank, is a rock shelter containing a four-room structure (fig. 6) and a smaller storage bin. The structure was built of irregular, unshaped stones of varying sizes that had been loosely laid. The most complete room, and probably the earliest, is semicircular, about 2.6 by 3 m., and utilizes the back of the shelter as one wall. Sections of the walls of at least two other rooms adjoin this structure. In one room, a possible bed, covering an area about 1 by 1.1 m., consisted of a layer of cedar bark on top of a layer of Brigham's tea stems which, in turn, was on a layer of twigs. Directly west of the structure was a refuse dump 1 to 1.2 m. deep that contained charcoal, ash, and flint chips, but no sherds. The pottery was all found on the surface of the site. The storage bin, built between two large boulders, is 46 cm. in diameter at the top and 62 cm. in diameter at the bottom, and is now standing 60 cm. high. Part of a cist 66 cm. in diameter was found in the refuse deposit, about 1 m. below the surface.

The large amount of nonceramic refuse and the cist suggest a rather long or heavy early occupation followed by a less intensive occupation which left the masonry structures and the sherds.

SPECIMENS

Pottery sherds
Emery Gray	76
Emery Tooled	2
Emery (?) Black-on-white	1
Emery (?) Corrugated	1
Unidentified gray	2

Chipped stone
Point and blade fragments	5
Scraper	1

The one painted sherd has a very thin slip and is decorated with broad parallel lines; the tooled sherds are decorated with fine scoring. The unidentified sherds are from the concave bottom of a vessel, are tan to gray, and are sherd-tempered.

Two of the blade fragments are from unnotched, triangular (slightly scalene) blades with straight to slightly convex sides. One, of red jasper, is 3.3 cm. wide and had been about 6 cm. long. The other, of gray chalcedony, is 2.1 cm. wide and had been about 4.5 cm. long Another fragment (fig. 43, h), from a triangular blade with side notches, a concave base, and rounded basal corners, is 2 cm. wide and had originally been about 5.3 cm. long. A smaller base was from a point with concave sides and a constricted, rounded stem. The point (fig. 43, n) is 1.7 cm. wide and had originally been about 3.3 cm. long. Its stem is 0.9 cm. wide at the end and constricts to 0.8 cm. in width. An even smaller triangular red jasper point apparently had never been finished because of asymmetry or damage during manufacture. It has one corner notch (the other basal corner is a right angle) and had been about 1.3 by 2.1 cm. An artifact of gray and white chalcedony has one carefully chipped scraper edge and, in general, resembles a snub-nosed scraper.

SR 16-6: Cottonwood Cave

This site, of Basketmaker affiliation, is a long curved rock shelter, about 6 m. deep at its deepest, located about 2.5 miles southeast of SR 16-5. In front of the nearly level floor of the shelter is a talus cone about 3 m. high. In the sandy floor of the shelter are the remains of at least nine cists (figs. 7A,B, 24 B). All but one of these cists are of the usual type in which a pit has been lined with nearly vertical stone slabs. The measurements of the most complete cists are as follows:

Cist No.	Diameters (cm.) North–South	East–West	Depth (cm.)	Number of Slabs used
1	61	74	49	6
2	70	67	91	7
3	62	70	81	4
4	118	84	61	8
5	84	76	70	8
6	107	79	91	5

The one unusual cist (no. 3) is square, with one vertical slab on each side forming the lower part of the pit lining. Above the slabs two courses of horizontal rocks had been laid and the whole cist roofed over with cedar poles, adobe, and stones, except for a rectangular opening 40 by 46 cm., which was fitted with a stone slab cover. This cist had been sealed with a mixture of adobe and cedar bark. In the cist were found a miniature vessel, a scrap of feather cloth, and some cedar bark.

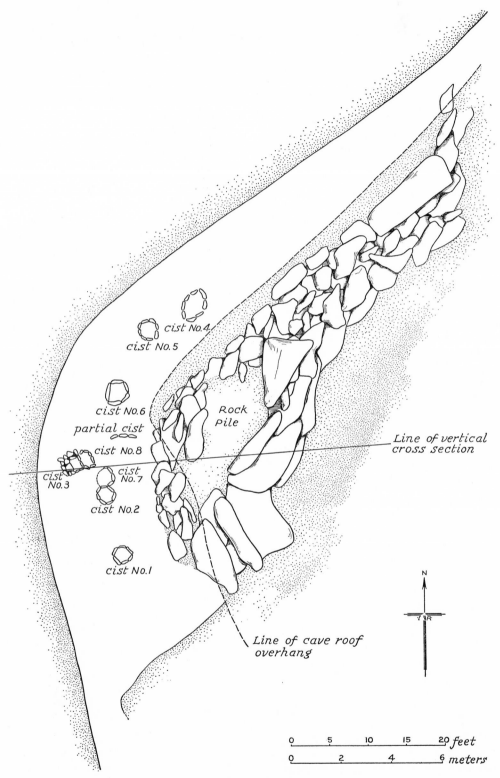

cist No.4

cist No.5

cist No.6

partial cist

cist No.8

cist No.3

cist No.7

cist No.2

cist No.1

Rock Pile

Line of vertical cross section

Line of cave roof overhang

N

| 0 | 5 | 10 | 15 | 20 feet |

| 0 | 2 | 4 | 6 meters |

FIG. 7*A*. Plan of Site SR 16-6.

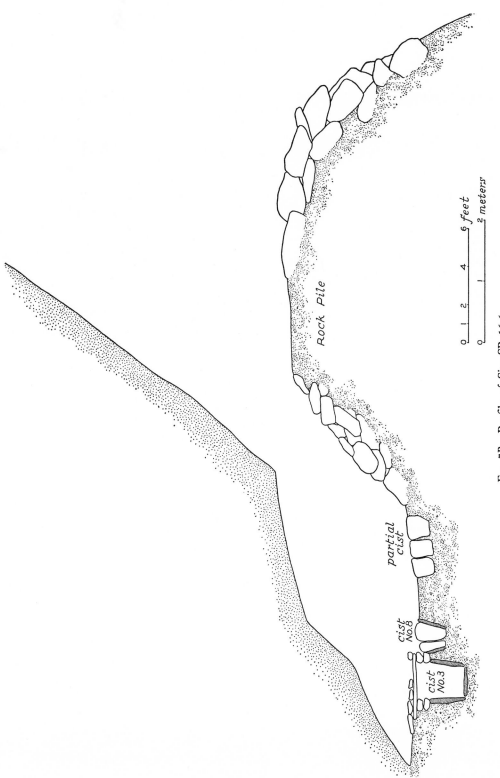

Fig. 7B. Profile of Site SR 16-6.

Very little was found in the fill of the other cists. A 30-cm.-thick layer of cedar bark was found in the bottom of Cist 1, and cedar bark chinking was found between the stones in Cist 4. The rest of the specimens came from the fill of the shelter in the area containing the cists.

At the north end of the shelter, about 4 m. above the present floor, are a number of figures painted in red and decorated with white. Preservation is poor since the rock face upon which they were painted has scaled quite badly. The largest figure, 1.2 m. tall, has a rectangular body and a nearly square head. Arms had not been represented, but there is evidence of legs. The eyes are shown, and pendant from the area of the nose are slightly sinuous lines about 50 cm. long. Across the top of the head and extending a short way down either side is a double row of small dots. On the left half of the chest is an area covered with about seven rows of somewhat larger dots, and along the left side is a curved row of large dots extending from the shoulder to the midpoint of the body, below which is a double row. A second figure is about 1 m. tall, has an oval body, a semicircular head, and short legs. Facial features are lacking, but dots across the top of the head and down the sides to the chest suggest long hair. A third figure, mostly obliterated, is apparently a portion of an anthropomorph of about the same size.

SPECIMENS

Pottery sherds	
Unidentified gray	7
Miniature pottery vessel	1
Chipped stone	
Blades	2
Scrapers	2
Used flake	1
Blank (?)	1
Red paint	1
Worked bone	2
Wooden sickle (?)	1
Twig animal figure	1
Basketry	3
Twined bag	1
Buckskin pad	1
Sandal	1
Sandal innersole	1
Feathercloth fragment	1
String	X
Braided yucca leaves	X
Pine gum	X
Deer skin	X
Yucca spines	X
Twigs	X
Corn ears in bark bundle	5

The unidentified pottery sherds were found on the surface at the back of the shelter. All appear to be from one jar about 15 to 20 cm. in diameter with a neck perhaps half that diameter. A handle had extended from the junction between the neck and body probably to the lip. The sherds are about 3 mm. thick except where unobliterated coils under the shoulder increased the thickness. The surface is brown to black and quite well polished. The core is very light gray and the tempering consists of subangular fragments of light and dark igneous rock and very fine sand. It is probably assignable to Tusayan Gray Ware, and possibly to Escalante Gray. In any case, there is little question but that these sherds are intrusive.

The miniature vessel, a hemispherical bowl, was found in the bottom of Cist 3. It is 5.4 cm. in diameter and 2.5 cm. deep, and the walls are about 0.4 cm. thick. It appears to have been lump modeled, is unsmoothed and poorly fired. The outside, in fact, cracked or crazed very deeply as it dried. The color is dark gray to buff and the paste contains a little sand, perhaps accidentally included. This piece is the only pottery that appears indigenous to the site.

The two points or blades are of the same general outline—triangular with slightly convex sides and a rounded stem. The larger, of gray, fine-grain quartzite, is 8.4 by 2.4 cm. and the smaller, of gray chalcedony, 4.1 by 2.0 cm. The stems are 8 and 9 mm. long, respectively. On the bases of both are traces of pitch or gum with which they had probably been hafted.

Two large flakes show unifacial chipping along one side and one end to provide a scraping edge. On neither specimen is the chipping steep. Another large flake shows use-retouch along one edge, and still another thicker piece of chipped stone may have been intended for a blank that proved to be unworkable.

Two metates were observed at the site but

not collected. These consisted of flat stone slabs that had not been modified except for pecking on the grinding surfaces.

The red paint (fig. 39, *f*) appears to be pigment that had been molded into a cylinder 11.5 by 3.8 cm. Encircling it are two sinuous, double rows of very small punctations. There is no evidence of wear or grinding to suggest how the cylinder was used, although the end could have been rubbed over a surface such as moist skin without any evidence being left. It seems more likely that the form simply represents a convenient way of storing pigment.

One bone artifact, probably a flaking tool, was made from the proximal end of a deer or antelope ulna that has been slightly modified to form a handle and very carefully ground and smoothed to form the blunt point. This specimen is 11.5 cm. long. The other bone artifact is fragmentary, but shows a great deal of work. It consists of a thin (5 mm.) but relatively wide (4.7 cm.) flat section cut possibly from a deer tibia, parallel to the long axis. It has been ground so much in order to flatten it that the cancellous portion of the bone shows on both surfaces. The edges show a great deal of polish. This specimen could have been the butt of a very nicely finished awl, but with the point missing, the original form is not determinable.

The wooden sickle (?) (fig. 40, *b*) is 40 cm. long and 4 cm. wide. About 22 cm. from the end that had served as a handle the specimen constricts to 1.6 cm. in width, and, extending for 6 cm., there is a series of 6 notches, each about 5 mm. wide and 5 mm. deep. The sickle is nearly flat but slightly bowed so that the notches are on the right side when held with the bow down. The edge opposite the notched edge also shows a great deal of polish and may once have had notches that were worn completely off. The 11 cm. beyond the notches shows some polish, especially on the convex side, but less than the notched, constricted portion.

The twig animal figure (fig. 39, *g*) is very much like a type that has been reported several times, especially from the Grand Canyon area (Wheeler, 1939, 1942, 1949; Farmer and de Saussure, 1955; Gunnerson, 1955; Schwartz *et al.*, 1958). It differs, however, in that the

unsplit end of the willow twig from which the animal is made projects 7 cm. down through the abdomen, perhaps to form a handle or support. Within the body of the animal, the twig is split. One half was bent forward about 1 cm., then down for about 3.5 cm. to form the front leg, was doubled back on itself, and continued up for another 3.5 cm. to form the neck, and then doubled back on itself again. The other half of the twig was bent back for 1.5 cm., then bent down for 3.5 cm. to form the rear leg, then doubled back on itself. The first half of the twig, after it was doubled back along the neck, was coiled horizontally around the legs to form the body. The second half was then coiled vertically around the body, then horizontally around the neck, and finally it was fashioned into a head, most of which is now missing. The body is 5 cm. long and 3 cm. high. The animal stands 8 cm. high, exclusive of the handle or support.

Portions of probably four baskets were recovered from this cave. Three of these were coiled with a half-rod, probably willow, and a yucca bundle foundation. The sewing was done with bark, probably willow, and stitches are not interlocked and are not usually split. There are about 3 stitches per cm. and 1.5 to 2.5 coils per cm. Several sections of what was probably one basket suggest that it was a shallow bowl and somewhere around 40 cm. in diameter. The middle of a basket from Cist 8 has in it a thick layer of what looks like burned mush.

Two fragments from Cist 4, probably from a single basket, were made by the technique that Mason (1904, pp. 257-8) calls "Fuegian coiled basketry." The binding material makes a full turn around itself at each stitch (the stitches are about 1 cm. apart), causing the warp elements to be about 3 mm. apart. The result is a very open weave such as that found in "sifter" baskets.

The fragmentary "twined" bag is so crudely constructed and made of such rough material (yucca leaves) that it is difficult to tell exactly what technique was used. In fact, construction appears almost haphazard. In one portion it somewhat resembles Mason's (1902, pp. 230–1) wrapped work, except that where the warp and weft elements cross each other, one is knotted with an overhand knot around the other. This could be considered some sort of variation on openwork coiling. No fragments can be certainly identified as having come from either the middle of the bottom or the edge of the bag. The general size of the pieces, however, suggests that the bag had been 25 cm. in diameter.

The sandal (fig. 40, *h*) found in this cave looks almost like an attempt to make a moccasin entirely from plant material, since the foot would be entirely covered by it. The foundation consists of an oval hoop made from a twig about 5 mm. in diameter. Tied to this and crisscrossing it in a more or less haphazard manner are yucca leaves. In various places where these cross one another, they are tied or wrapped together. Other strips of the same material form a few loops along either side of the foot and these in turn are laced together by a strip of the same material that crosses the top of the foot in a zigzag manner four times and then attaches to the heel of the sandal. Some of the fibrous strips appear to pass through the layer of soft grass about 1 cm. thick that entirely lines the sandal and apparently was not removable. The outside dimensions are 24 by 14 cm.

A pad of grass like that which lines the sandal appears to be a removable innersole, since there is smoothly caked dirt where the heel and the ball of the foot would have been. Another wad of the same material, about the same size but showing no evidence of use, was also recovered.

The buckskin pad (fig. 40, *e*), possibly an umbilical pad, is a rectangular pillow 13 by 7 by 4 cm., stuffed with a soft grass and sewed neatly along the edges with two-ply, Z-twist cord of plant fiber. Near one end are two loops 2.5 cm. long made by passing narrow strips of buckskin through holes and knotting the ends. On the same side of the pad as the loops are three somewhat worn depressions across the pad perpendicular to the long axis, as though the pad had been held in place by three straps or bands. One of these depressions passes under the loops. The buckskin is still soft.

Three pieces of cord from a feather robe were recovered. The core of the cord was a two-ply, Z-twist cord of yucca fiber. Around this was wound a layer of split feathers. Each feather section was held in place by having one end tucked into the adjacent wound feather and the other end held under itself. There is no evidence of an additional wrapping of cord over the feathers.

Several pieces of cord made from plant fibers were recovered. These were all Z-twist and ranged in diameter from 2 to 12 mm. Two of the 2-mm. cords were twisted to a long tapering point. Some of the smaller cords are of yucca or Indian hemp but most of the cords are of juniper bark.

Raw materials found in the cave included deer hide (mostly from the legs), a bundle of yucca spines, two lumps of pine pitch, a lump of a black brittle pitch on a stick, a lump of clay, a scrap of buckskin, a few split twigs or withes, and a small bunch of Indian hemp fiber.

SR 16-7

This site, located in a small canyon on the east side of Waterhole Canyon, showed evidence of occupation. The following specimens were collected.

SPECIMENS

Pottery sherds	
Emery Gray	9
North Creek Gray	3
Tusayan Corrugated	14

SR 16-8

About two miles southeast of SR 16-10 in the side of Cottonwood Canyon a rock shelter showing evidence of occupation was found. The following specimens are probably from this site.

SPECIMENS

Pottery sherds	
Emery Gray	10
Emery Tooled	1
Mancos (?) Black-on-white	3
Chipped stone	
Blade and point fragments	6
Modified flakes	4

The Emery tooled sherd has on it a row of slightly overlapping clay pellets applied at the junction of the body and a straight vertical rim. Each pellet is about 0.7 by 1.2 cm., and has a round punctation near one end.

Included in the Emery Gray sherds are two handles, one apparently a horizontal strap handle from a jar, and the other (oval in cross section, 1.4 by 1.7 cm. and nearly straight) from either a pitcher or a ladle. The possible Mancos sherds are probably from two jars and one bowl.

The blade and point fragments are all either tips or midsections and not diagnostic. Two midsections about 2.1 cm. wide were probably from very simple blades about 5 cm. long.

SR 16-9

A site near Chaffin's Pond in the central part of Waterhole Flat yielded a little evidence of occupation.

SPECIMENS

Pottery sherds
Mesa Verde White ware	1
Mancos Corrugated	4
Chipped stone	
Blade	1

The Mesa Verde sherd is a portion of a large water or storage jar that had been decorated on the upper half of the body. The vessel is not well finished and the design, although rather intricate, was not well executed. The corrugated sherds are of an even poorer quality.

The blade, of red jasper, is 7.3 by 4.6 by 1.0 cm. and is more or less almond-shaped.

SR 16-10: Red Snake Cave

This rock shelter, located on the west side of Willow Tank Canyon, is situated in a white ledge about 13 m. above a side canyon entering from the northwest. The back of the shelter is walled off with a loosely laid wall of irregular stones reinforced in a haphazard manner with cedar logs. Behind the wall, the floor of the shelter had been leveled off and covered with grass and adobe. Debris was quite shallow in the shelter and no refuse deposit remained in front of it. The following specimens are probably from this site.

SPECIMENS

Pottery sherds
Tusayan Corrugated	64
Emery Gray	7
Soft red unidentified	39
Clay animal head	1
Chipped stone points	2
Chipped stone scraper	1
Atlatl weight (?)	1
Hammerstones	3
Worked sticks	21
Cord	3
Perforated shell	1
Cucurbita fragment	1
Pine gum	X
Quids, chewed yucca	3
Fiber	X

There is nothing particularly noteworthy about either the Tusayan Corrugated or the Emery Gray. The soft red sherds, probably all from one vessel, had been only slightly fired if at all. This ware varies in thickness from 0.7 to 1.4 cm., was made of untempered clay by coiling, was moderately well smoothed on the outside, and had had a handle. The outer surface is reddish gray, apparently darkened by soot.

The animal head (fig. 39, e), modeled from red clay and unfired, could be an attempt to represent a dog, but it looks more like a herbivore with a pointed nose. Eyes are represented by slightly raised bumps with a small punctation in each. Nostrils are also represented by punctations and the ears, erect and pointed, are modeled. Small rough areas behind the ears may be where antlers had been attached. The head is 3.8 cm. long and 1.9 cm. thick just behind the eyes. A section of neck, 1.2 cm. long, terminates in a roughly broken end.

Two red jasper points were recovered, both nearly complete. One, triangular with a concave base and serrated sides, had been 3.7 by about 1.5 cm. The other has deep corner notches and had been about 2.7 by 1.9 cm. What appears to be the scraping edge of a white chalcedony snub-nosed scraper was also found.

The possible atlatl weight is essentially cylindrical, except that it tapers slightly toward both ends, which are rounded, and it has one flat side. The piece is carefully shaped and, where the nonhomogeneous rock permits, it is well smoothed. It is 5.6 cm. long and has a maximum diameter of 2.0 cm.

Most of the pieces of worked sticks, which range from 3 to 9 mm. in diameter, appear to be scraps that have been cut off. In some

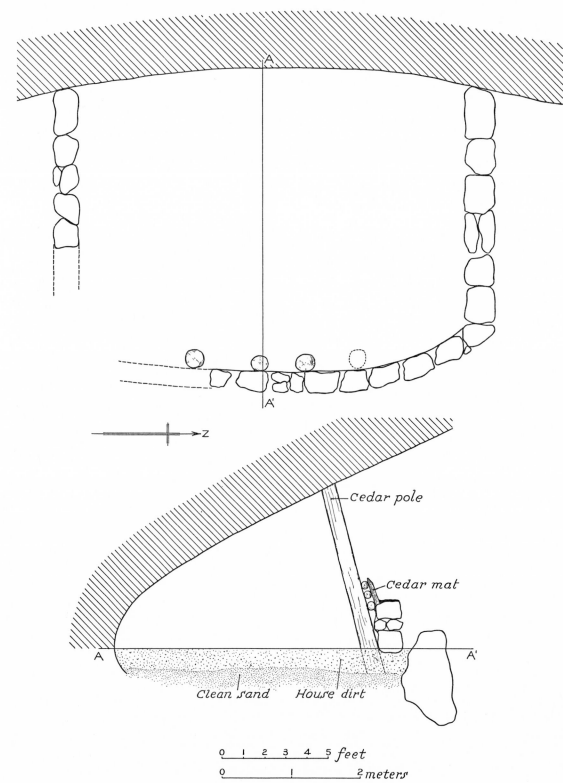

FIG. 8. Plan and profile of structure at Site LS 13-14.

cases the end opposite the cut is well smoothed and rounded, in others it is rough. One piece has a cleft 1 cm. deep and 0.2 cm. wide, as if it had been the end of an arrow and had had a point hafted in it. One piece 23 cm. long was tapered gradually at both ends. Three 3-mm. sticks from 9 to 15 cm. long were carefully tapered at one end, and one was battered at the other. Another stick had four turns of sinew around it. Three short sections of cut reed (*phragmites*) were also found. Three larger sticks, apparently pokers, were charred on one end.

The three pieces of cord are all two-ply, Z-twist. Two are made of yucca fiber and one of Indian hemp fiber.

The shell, which had apparently been perforated so that it could be used as a bead, is 1.4 by 1.1 cm. and has a hole 4 mm. in diameter through it.

SR 16-11

Just north of site SR 16–3 is a rock shelter with a niche in the back wall which had been walled up to form a small storage room about 2 m. deep, 1.2 m. wide, and 1 m. high. The well-built masonry wall has a 40 by 50 cm. doorway approximately in the middle. A jamb to accommodate a stone-slab door reduces the opening to about 25 by 32 cm. Two poles 8 cm. in diameter form the lintel.

SR 16-12: Red Point

A rock shelter located near Red Point at the southwest side of Waterhole Flat in the vicinity of a spring looked promising, but several hours of excavating failed to produce much cultural detritus.

Specimens

Fur cloth fragment	1
Worked bone	1

The fur cloth fragment, 30 by 30 cm., has two-ply, Z-twist warp made by twisting together narrow strips of rabbit skin with the fur left on. The weft of this twined fabric is also two-ply, Z-twist, but is of juniper fiber. The selvage consists of a cord about 2.5 cm. in diameter made by winding a strip of rabbit skin around a yucca-fiber cord. The warp,

which had probably been continuous, was attached to the selvage cord by a yucca-fiber cord that was wound around the selvage and on each turn caught a bight of the warp.

The worked bone is a section of the nasal bones of a large mammal (fig. 39, *h*), 18 by 7.6 cm. Shallow notches about 3 mm. apart were cut all along both sides and two holes were drilled through the specimen along the mid-line, 0.8 cm. from one end and 4.3 cm. from the other. Much of the rough inner side has been carefully cut or ground down. The specimen comes to a blunt point at one end; the other end appears to be broken off. Nothing about the specimen suggests any obvious use.

SR 16-13

In a rock shelter on the east side of Red Point are three log structures, one well preserved, that could be aboriginal; however, they may be recent. The structures, each about 1.6 by 1.6 m., had been made by cribbing cedar logs and covering the top with split cedar poles. The walls had been chinked with cedar bark, stones, and adobe. No ax marks could be found on the logs; all had apparently been felled by burning.

Potsherds, including black-on-whites, worked flint, and a mano were found at the site, but these artifacts were not necessarily contemporaneous with the structures.

LS 13-14

Just to the east of Waterhole Flat is Big Flat, in a very rough area known as Erney Country. In a rock shelter at the north end of Big Flat are the remains of an unusual room (fig. 8), 3.8 m. wide, that utilized a 5.5 m. length of the back wall of the shelter as one wall. The lower part of the front wall had been constructed of sandstone blocks crudely laid without use of adobe. Several poles wedged between the floor and the 2-m.-high ceiling of the shelter on the inside of the stone wall had supported the upper part of the wall, which had apparently consisted of a coarse cedar-bark mat. There is a small refuse dump in front of the shelter.

The following specimens are probably from this site.

SPECIMENS

Pottery sherds	
Mancos Black-on-white	1
Mesa Verde White ware	8
Mesa Verde Corrugated	6
Mancos Corrugated	2
Lino (?) Gray	1
Emery Gray	3
Chipped points or blades	7
Flake	1

The points or blades represent a wide variety of colors of flint, chalcedony and jasper. Five of them (some incomplete) are triangular with straight to slightly convex sides and bases, and side notches. They range in size from 1.9 by 1.7 cm. to 2.5 by about 4.8 cm. The other two, both about 3.3 by 1.9 cm., are almond-shaped.

LS 13-15

In a small high rock shelter in Erney Country, a lone complete pottery water jar was found with no other evidence of occupation present.

SPECIMENS

Pottery Jar, Mesa Verde White ware	1

This complete water or storage jar is 30 cm. high and has a maximum diameter of 29 cm. Decoration is restricted to the upper half of the body; the neck, 7 cm. high and 11 cm. in diameter, is undecorated. The painted design consists of three equally spaced circular areas, each about 14 cm. in diameter. The designs within the circles all follow the same general layout—a heavy cross and four wedges. Each of the twelve wedges is filled with two opposed stepped elements. One cross is filled with a checkerboard design, one with opposed barbed lines separated by a wide zigzag line, and the third with a combination of these motifs. The areas between the circles are filled with diagonal parallel lines, some of which are joined by short cross lines to produce a stepped motif. Line widths average about 4 mm. The painted area is framed by a single continuous line at the junction of the neck and body and by two parallel lines just below the line of greatest girth. These two lines are interrupted by two undecorated horizontal strap handles. Painting was only moderately well executed on a very thin slightly crazed slip. The vessel itself is well made and symmetrical.

BARRIER CANYON

Barrier Canyon, also known as Horseshoe Canyon, is surrounded by relatively level but nearly barren, sand-dune-spotted range land with an elevation of about 6000 feet. The main part of the canyon is steep-sided and, in its 15-mile length, the canyon floor drops from 5000 to 4000 feet, where it joins the Green River 30 miles south of Green River, Utah. Barrier Canyon, which is for the most part dry, drains to the northeast and is the only significant western tributary of the Green River between the San Rafael River and the Dirty Devil River. The few springs in Barrier Canyon are small; the scanty alluvial fill is very sandy and not especially rich. Average annual precipitation at Hanksville, 30 miles to the west, is 5.34 inches and at Green River, about the same distance north, it is 6.13 inches (Alter, 1941, pp. 1147, 1150). Since the terrain around Barrier Canyon is very similar to that around these two towns, one can expect the precipitation to be comparable. Thus,

neither the canyon nor the surrounding area is well suited for farming. Some of the bottom land along the Green River at and below the mouth of Barrier Canyon could, however, be used for horticulture by means of either artificial irrigation or natural subirrigation from the river. The area at the mouth of Barrier Canyon, as well as Woodruff Bottoms about 6 miles to the south, was included in the reconnaissance.

The archaeological remains in Barrier Canyon and near-by areas are interesting but somewhat baffling. In the canyon itself, there is a large spectacular pictograph panel with many life-size anthropomorphic figures plus a number of smaller panels only some of which are here reported. In an attempt to learn more about the probable artists, a search was made for occupation sites in the canyon, but only one (SR 12-5) was found. This site, when excavated, was not as informative as had been hoped because it had apparently been occupied briefly three times, once by preceramic Basketmakers, once by Fremont people, and once by Mesa Verde people. The material from the last two groups may represent a mixed occupation.

A site at the head of Barrier Canyon and a few at its mouth and on Woodruff Bottoms contained habitation and storage structures, but the small amount of detritus that they yielded suggests only limited occupation. Archaeological survey in the surrounding Robbers' Roost area (Gunnerson, 1957 a, pp. 77–80) revealed a number of small, lightly occupied sites, mostly near the few springs in the area. These sites were probably temporary camps, possibly used for hunting antelope, which at one time were very numerous in the area, or for collecting jasper, which is also abundant. With the lack of evidence of significant habitation sites, one can only conclude that Barrier Canyon with its magnificent pictographs was some sort of remote ceremonial center or retreat.

SR 8-1

At the mouth of Barrier Canyon four structures and some pictographs were found. Three of the structures consist of horizontal stone slabs laid in abundant adobe mortar and were roughly plastered with adobe. They average about 1 m. square and are from 0.6 to 1.2 m. high. One is on a ledge that can be reached only by means of a rope from above. Another has a pole-and-adobe roof. At the point of the confluence of the two canyons is a larger rectangular room, probably a house, 2.4 by 1.5 m., with walls still standing about 0.9 m. high.

Directly above this house are a number of rather amorphous figures painted in red and white. The panel is dominated by a central arc, opening down, consisting of two lines, one solid and the other partly solid and partly a row of dots. Some of the other figures are probably anthropomorphic and animal forms. Just to the south of this panel are a number of very faint sheep and deer pecked into the face of a rock.

SR 8-2

About 5 miles west of the mouth of Barrier Canyon and about 1.5 miles north of the canyon is Keg Knoll. A rock shelter in the side of the knoll shows a little evidence of having been occupied.

SR 8-3

Woodruff Bottoms, located on the west side of the Green River about 6 miles below the mouth of Barrier Canyon, is a broad, low, sandy flat that slopes gently from the river to the base of the canyon walls. A number of large boulders strewn over the bottom have had structures built on them. Site SR 8-3, situated on a boulder about 3 m. high, apparently consisted of only one room. Construction is of moderately large irregular slabs and chunks of stone chinked with smaller stones. Originally, the walls had probably also contained some adobe.

SR 8-4

Also at Woodruff Bottoms several smaller structures, probably used for storage, had been built under slight overhangs and in niches under sloping rocks. This site, an example of such a structure, consists of a curved wall enclosing a space about 1.5 m. across. The wall is constructed of moderately large irregular stone blocks and chinked with smaller stones and adobe. It is now standing about 0.8 m. high.

SR 8-5

The largest site (fig. 24A) found at Woodruff Bottoms is similar to SR 8-3 and consists of at least four and possibly six rooms which nearly cover the top of a boulder about 6 by 9 m. and 5.5 m. high. Construction is of rough sandstone blocks chinked with small stones and adobe. The maximum height of the remaining walls is about 1 m.

SR 8-6

On one nearly vertical rock face at Woodruff Bottoms are two petrographs, apparently aboriginal, that had been produced by rubbing. A small area in the center of each was pecked. One figure is a circle divided into four equal segments by a horizontal and a vertical line. Two opposite quadrants have been filled in by rubbing and the other two left plain. The other figure, now partly scaled off, consists of a broad line forming about half a circle

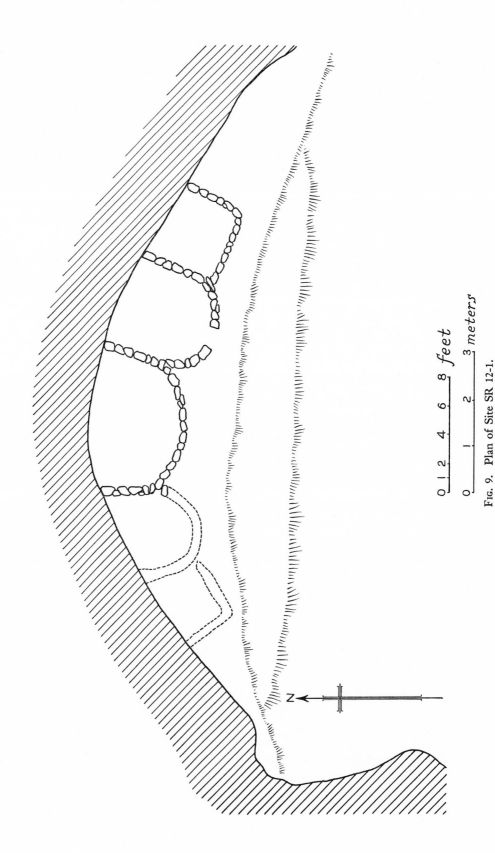

0 1 2 4 6 8 *feet*

0 1 2 3 *meters*

Fig. 9. Plan of Site SR 12-1.

with rays or spokes toward the center where there is another arc or part of a solid circle.

SR 8-7

The pictographs observed and photographed at this site are long-horned mountain sheep, the most common type found at Woodruff Bottoms.

SR 12-1

The remains of five contiguous rooms (fig. 9) were found on a ledge protected by a large, hemispherical, south-facing rock shelter situated just under the rim in the ridge which forms the divide between the heads of Barrier Canyon and Spur Fork Canyon. Each room is built against the back wall of the shelter and has a curved front wall. Construction is of sandstone blocks loosely piled without the use of mortar. The walls are crudely made and none is over 1.2 m. high. No evidence of a roof is preserved. A spring and a little flat land suitable for farming are near by.

SPECIMENS

Pottery sherds	
Mesa Verde White ware	11
Mancos Corrugated	6
Emery Gray	2
North Creek (?) Gray	1
Unidentified	2
Points	3
Drill	1
Blade Fragments	2
Perforated shell	1

The Mesa Verde sherds contain an unusually large amount of crushed rock and sand, some of it fractured. The unidentified sherds, which have a white outside slip but are not painted, may also have been Mesa Verde White ware.

Two chipped stone points are essentially triangular with side notches. A complete one of gray chalcedony is 3.0 by 2.5 cm. and comes abruptly to a point. Another, of red jasper, has a slightly convex base, is 1.9 cm. wide, and appears to have been about 4 cm. long. One small, nearly complete gray chalcedony point was triangular with a concave base, 1.1 by about 2.9 cm. The drill fragment consists of just the point, 2.5 cm. long and 0.7 cm. in greatest diameter.

The shell, 1.7 by 1.4 cm., appears to have been ground and polished on all edges and to have had a hole 4 by 5 mm. ground through it near the center. It was probably a bead.

SR 12-2

About 15 miles above the mouth of Barrier Canyon, nearly halfway up its north wall and opposite the mouth of Spur Fork Canyon, is a small rock shelter in the rear of a larger rock shelter at the top of a steep talus slope. Limited testing in the shelter revealed only sparse evidence of occupation.

SR 12-3

About 1.25 miles up Barrier Canyon from where the Jeep road crosses it is a large, deep rock shelter about 125 m. across the front with a floor only about 3 m. above the stream bed. On the back wall are some very crude pictographs, mostly anthropomorphic, which appear to have been painted with red mud rather than with the better paint used for most of the panels. Many of the figures have a trapezoidal to triangular body with a projection at the top to represent a head. A few of the better-executed and larger figures (up to about 60 cm. tall) have headdresses depicted, and their bodies are covered with vertical lines rather than filled in solid.

SR 12-4: The Great Gallery

This site, the Great Gallery of Barrier Canyon, is probably the most spectacular pictograph site in Utah if not in the entire United States. Perhaps the most surprising thing about this site is that none of the figures have been significantly damaged by vandals as have so many other pictographs. This panel is located on the back wall of a shallow but high rock shelter on the north side of Barrier Canyon, about 4 miles above the Jeep road that crosses it. The floor of the shelter, which is easy to climb to at one point, is a ledge about 8 m. above the floor of the canyon. The bottoms of the painted figures are 3 to 5 m. above the floor of the shelter. For a distance of about 30 m. along the vertical back wall of the shelter is an almost continuous row of red anthropomorphic figures, many of them about life-size and some elaborately decorated. In addition to the colossal figures that dominate

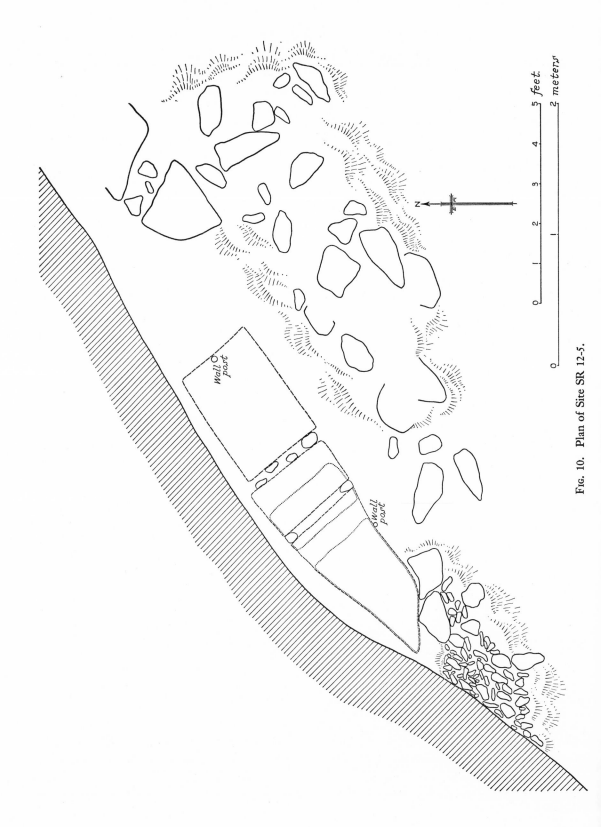

Wall post

Wall post

N

0   1   2   meters

0   1   2   3   4   5   feet.

FIG. 10. Plan of Site SR 12-5.

the panel, there are also smaller anthropomorphic and animal figures.

The details of the figures can be understood best by referring to the photographs (figs. 26A–30B), but a few general comments are in order. Many of the figures were painted over areas that had been carefully smoothed, apparently by rubbing with a straight piece of stone such as was found at the site excavated near by (SR 12-5). In at least one instance this smoothing had apparently partially obliterated some small pecked figures of sheep or goats, and paint from the subsequent anthropomorphic figure extends into some of the pecking.

As can be seen in the photographs, the panel is dominated by large anthropomorphic figures of two general styles: solid red figures with narrow rounded shoulders, and broad, square-shouldered figures with very elaborate and detailed decoration in red, white, and green, probably representing either ornamented clothing or body painting. Facial features, when present, consist only of large round eyes usually left unpainted in a red face, but sometimes the eyes are painted red when the face is white. In some figures the eyes were pecked into the rock prior to painting. In none of the large figures are arms or legs shown.

The smaller anthropomorphic figures, ranging from 15 cm. to 1 m. tall, show far more variety than do the large figures. Both of the styles described above occur, but the decoration is not as elaborate as on the large broad-shouldered figures. There is one solid red non-phallic humpbacked flute player about 0.6 m. high. Two figures about 26 cm. tall, one with a long staff, are facing each other, and to judge by the well-depicted movement, they appear to be fighting. About 30 cm. from these two men and drawn to about the same scale is a circle of ten animals, possibly antelope, which have been painted very carefully and show a great deal of very graceful motion in various directions. Just below them and possibly part of the same scene is another animal that could be a dog. The movement of these exquisite little animals and of the men contrasts markedly with the stiff, awesome, grandiose massiveness of the large anthropomorphs that dominate the panel.

This pictograph panel was carefully copied by the Utah Art Project of the WPA and a full-size reproduction was shown soon afterwards at the Museum of Modern Art in New York City in an exhibition prepared by the Indian Arts and Crafts Board of the United States Department of the Interior. A publication that grew out of this exhibition includes one photograph of the panel (Douglas and D'Harnoncourt, 1941, 24). The reproduction is now at the Denver Museum of Natural History. A smaller copy of the entire panel and of many of the individual figures or groups of figures was made by the same project and is in the Museum of Anthropology at the University of Utah. Photographs of small parts of this panel were also published by Steward (1937 a, pl. 4b) and Henderson (1957, p. 9) and figures from it served as cover designs for five numbers of *Utah Archeology* (vol. 4, no. 2; vol. 5, nos. 1–4).

SR 12-5: Horseshoe Shelter

This site, a rock shelter opening to the southeast, is located on the left-hand side of Barrier (Horseshoe) Canyon about 11 miles above its mouth. Whereas pictographs are numerous in this part of the canyon, this is the only site that shows much evidence of occupation. It was excavated in the hope of providing more evidence as to the cultural affiliation of the artists who produced the pictographs, some of which (fig. 31B) are near the area occupied. The nature of the few available notes concerning work at this site makes reconstruction of the excavation procedure as well as of the aboriginal occupation somewhat speculative. The following description represents what seems to be the most plausible interpretation of the information available.

The site (figs. 10, 32A), which is easily accessible from the canyon floor, was first occupied by people who built three rooms (A, B, C) against the back wall of the shelter. The easternmost room (A) was about 3 by 5 m. and was built almost contiguous to the middle room (B) which was about 3 by 3 m. The west room (C), behind some large fallen rock, was more or less triangular and about 3 by 5 m. A gap of perhaps 1.5 m. separated rooms B and C. There is much uncertainty as to whether all three of these structures were actually rooms. The one most certainly a room, and the one from which the most construction data was secured, is Room A. Except for the butts of two posts, one in the middle of the east wall of the east room (A) and one at the southeast corner of room C, there was no other evidence that could be interpreted as walls or support for the roof. The roof had apparently been constructed of parallel poles extending perpendicular to the cliff wall and covered with a layer of cottonwood bark over which was a layer of cedar bark. Rocks, presumably added to hold this material in place, were found on top of the roof material. The floors had been excavated 8 to 25 cm. into the floor of the shelter, but they had not been specially prepared. No definite hearths were found. A rock-lined cist, however, was found near the back wall of the shelter in the middle of room B. It was about 0.8 by 1.1 m. by 0.5 m. deep and was filled with rubbish, including "many arrow points, (and) two parts of good figurines." (Bower's notes).

The site was then abandoned and, after about 8 cm. of sand had drifted in on the floors, the structures burned.

At a subsequent time, but probably not long after, the site was reoccupied, floors of earth and/or adobe were placed over the refuse in at least some of the three early rooms, and three new rooms (D, E, F) were constructed. Room D, about 3 by 5 m., conformed to the outline of Room A and was directly over it. A gap of perhaps 1.5 m. separated Room D from Room E, which was about 3 by 3 m. and overlapped Room B in part. A similar gap separated Room D from Room F, which was over the west 3 m. of Room C.

It was Roberts' impression that the artifact assemblages apparently associated with these two occupations were essentially the same. A tabulation of the artifacts, however, shows some very striking differences. Except for the ten unidentified sherds from a very crude unfired miniature bowl, not uncommon in Basketmaker II sites, there are only five sherds, and these disproportionately high in painted wares, from Rooms A, B, and C. These five sherds could easily have worked down from upper levels (which yielded 260 sherds) in the very sandy fill which, according to Bower's notes, contained many rat holes. The figurine fragments and other fragments of molded clay, on the other hand, all came from Rooms A, B, and C. The apparently greater abundance of chipped stone artifacts in these lower rooms is less significant, since those in the "site general" category could have been predominantly from the upper level.

In short, the evidence at hand suggests that there may have been a nonceramic occupation of the site prior to its occupation by Fremont and/or Mesa Verde Pueblo II-III peoples. On the other hand, there may have been only two occupations, Fremont and Mesa Verde, or even a single mixed occupation. The cultural affiliation of the Barrier Canyon artists was, unfortunately, not clarified by this excavation.

In addition to the structures, there were also both broad and narrow grooves worn in sandstone, apparently from either manufacturing or sharpening artifacts, and red painted pictographs. The figures were, for the most part, triangular-bodied anthropomorphs about 20 to 30 cm. tall. Heads, some with horns or headdresses, are relatively small and a few figures have arms. Some of the bodies are decorated with either vertical or horizontal lines or dots. The figures at best are only moderately well executed and one group of two deer with large horns, a buffalo with a very small head, and a hunter with a bow and arrow are very crudely painted.

| | Rooms | | | | | | | | Site | |
	A	B	C	ABC	D	E	F	DEF	Gen	Total
SPECIMENS										
Pottery sherds										
Mancos Black-on-white	2	–	–	–	–	–	–	13	–	15
North Creek Black-on-gray (?)	–	–	–	–	–	–	–	2	–	2
Emery Black-on-gray	1	–	–	–	–	–	–	1	–	2
Tsegi Red-on-orange	–	–	–	–	–	–	–	1	–	1
Mancos Corrugated	–	–	–	–	–	–	–	61	–	61

Specimens	Rooms							DEF	Site Gen	Total
	A	B	C	ABC	D	E	F			
Pottery Sherds										
Sand-tempered	–	–	–	–	–	–	–	39	–	39
Sandstone-tempered										
Corrugated	–	–	–	–	–	–	–	1	–	1
Emery Corrugated	1?	–	–	–	–	–	–	6	–	7
Emery Tooled	1	–	–	–	–	–	–	1	–	2
Mancos Black-on-white (?) (no paint)	–	–	–	–	–	–	–	7	–	7
Emery Gray	–	–	–	–	–	–	–	116	–	116
Escalante Gray (?)	1	–	–	–	–	–	–	3	–	4
North Creek Gray (?)	–	–	–	–	–	–	–	7	–	7
"Shoshoni" ware (?)	–	–	–	–	–	–	–	1	–	1
Unidentified, unfired	10	–	–	–	–	–	–	–	–	10
Reworked sherds	1	–	–	–	–	–	–	1	–	2
Figurine fragments	2	2	1	–	–	–	–	–	–	5
Fragments of modeled clay	2	2	–	16	–	–	–	–	–	20
Stone										
Points and small blades										
Triangular, notched	–	–	1	–	–	–	–	–	2	
Triangular, concave base	2	–	1	2	–	1	–	–	2	
Triangular, straight base	–	–	2	10	–	–	–	–	16	
Lanceolate, straight base	–	–	–	4	–	–	1	–	15	
Lanceolate, concave base	1	–	–	–	–	–	–	–	1	
Tips and midsections	–	–	–	27	–	–	–	–	40	
Flake blades	2	–	1	–	–	–	–	–	–	
Large blades	1	1	–	–	–	–	–	–	3	
Small choppers	8	–	1	–	2	1	–	–	17	
Large choppers	–	–	–	–	4	–	–	–	1	
Graver	–	–	1	–	–	–	–	–	–	
Scraper	–	–	–	–	1	–	–	–	–	
Hammerstones	1	–	–	–	4	2	3	–	–	
Abrading stones	–	–	–	–	2	–	–	–	–	
Sharpening stone	–	–	–	–	–	1	–	–	–	
Painted stones	1	–	–	–	1	1	–	–	–	
Pigment (red)	1	–	–	–	–	–	–	–	–	
Bone, Horn, Hide										
Awls	–	1	–	–	5	1	1	–	–	
Flaker	–	–	–	–	–	1	–	–	–	
Beads	–	–	–	–	2	–	–	–	–	
Pendants	–	1	–	–	–	1	–	–	–	
Gaming pieces	–	–	1	–	–	1	–	–	–	
Sickle	–	–	–	–	1	–	–	–	–	
Misc. worked bone	–	–	–	–	1	1	–	–	–	
Skin, hide	–	–	–	–	2	1	–	–	–	
Unworked bone, horn	–	–	–	–	X	X	X	–	X	
Wood, Reed, Fiber										
Sandal	–	–	–	–	–	–	1	–	–	
Basketry	1	–	–	–	–	–	–	–	–	
Matting	–	–	–	–	1	–	–	–	–	
Innersole	–	–	–	–	–	1	–	–	–	
Shredded bark ring	–	–	–	–	1	–	–	–	–	
Arrow fragment	–	–	–	–	–	–	1	–	–	
Arrow foreshaft	–	–	–	–	–	–	1	–	–	
Cord	–	–	–	–	4	–	–	–	–	
Feather cloth, fragment	–	–	–	–	1	–	–	–	–	

| | | | Rooms | | | | | | Site | |
SPECIMENS	A	B	C	ABC	D	E	F	DEF	Gen	Total
Wood, Reed, Fiber										
Tube or bead	–	–	–	–	–	1	–	–		–
Fire-drill hearth	–	–	–	–	1	2	–	–		–
Misc. worked wood	–	–	–	–	2	–	–	16		–
Knotted sticks and fiber	–	–	–	–	X	X	X	–		–
Gourd container	–	1?	–	–	–	–	–	–		–
Toy bow (?)	–	–	–	–	1	–	–	–		–
Crook stick	–	–	–	–	1	–	–	–		–

The Mancos and affiliated pottery from this site is for the most part rather strange. The workmanship on the Mancos Corrugated ware is generally sloppy with very irregular coils. The sand-tempered corrugated sherds, although fewer in number, show greater variation. Some of these sherds have narrow neat bands while others are quite irregularly coiled and indented. On a few sherds the coils have been mostly obliterated through smoothing. At least eight Mancos Black-on-white vessels of greatly varying quality are represented. Included is one rather crude miniature vessel.

The Emery Gray sherds appear to be of about average quality for Fremont sites in the general area. The paucity of Emery tooled and Emery painted sherds and a complete absence of handles are rather surprising.

The identification of the minority types is not very certain. The sherds come close to fitting the descriptions for these types, but any cultural implications are questionable. The unidentified, unfired sherds are all from a single miniature vessel which appears to be the result of a child's play.

Only two sherds had been reworked: a pottery scraper made from a Mancos Black-on-white sherd, and a perforated disk 5.8 cm. in diameter made from an Emery Tooled sherd.

Three of the clay figurine fragments (fig. 39, a–d) fall into the general Fremont type. Two of these (from rooms A and B) are the lower or skirt portions of flat figurines on which the skirt is represented by narrow vertical appliquéd strips of clay. The one from Room A is 4.4 cm. wide near the bottom and constricts to 2.5 cm. where it is broken off at the waist. There appears to have been a belt of very small appliquéd pellets, each with a tiny punctation through it, around the waist.

The other figurine skirt is 3.2 cm. wide near the bottom and constricts to 2.6 cm. where it is broken off, apparently just below the waist. At the top of the skirt is a single narrow horizontal strip of clay forming a sort of waistband. A head of another flat figurine from Room A has a median ridge pinched up to represent the nose, below which are molded two laterally placed nodes to represent breasts. The specimen is broken off just below the breasts where it apparently had constricted. The maximum width of 3.5 cm. occurs just below the nose (just above the breasts). The maximum thickness (at the breasts) is 1.8 cm. and the minimum (between them) is 1.4 cm. The length of the remaining portion is 4.5 cm. There is no evidence of its ever having had additional facial features or head and shoulder ornaments.

Two other figurines, which apparently were originally much alike, were recovered from Rooms C and A. The one from C, the more complete (fig. 39, b), resembles one from the Fremont drainage illustrated by Morss (1954, fig. 21f) in that it is modeled in the round and has stump legs and arms. The heads, unfortunately, are missing from both of the Barrier Canyon specimens. The more complete of these two is 5.1 cm. long and had probably been at least 6 cm. long originally. Some of the other pieces of modeled clay are probably from figurines, but they are too fragmentary or amorphous to be definitely identified.

The chipped stone artifacts from this site are most noteworthy for the large number of projectile points and/or small blades (mostly broken) and for their lack of variety in form (fig. 43, o–w). The two most common types (triangular with straight base and lanceolate with straight base) grade into one another and differ from each other primarily by having their greatest width at the base (triangular) or ahead of the base (lanceolate). If a specimen has essentially parallel sides at the base, it is included in the latter type. Bases that are slightly convex or slightly concave are considered straight. Points or blades of these two types appear to have ranged from about 2.5 to 5 cm. in length and 1.4 to 2.3 cm. in maximum width. All are relatively thin, well chipped on both faces, and of either chalcedony or jasper.

The lanceolate, convex-based blades differ from the types just described in that they have pronouncedly convex bases. The triangular points with concave bases fall within the size range (at the small end) of the triangular points.

The notched point from Room C (fig. 43, *o*) is very delicately chipped, is 2.1 by 1.3 by 0.2 cm., and seems out of place in the assemblage. The other notched points (both broken) are about 3.2 by 2.7 by 0.5 and 2.3 by 1.5 by 0.3 cm. All have straight bases and side notches. The other points from Room C are also small, thin, and delicately chipped. One has a wide trapezoidal basal notch.

Nicely chipped large blades are not common at this site. Bases of two thin blades, one square and 4.5 cm. wide, the other rounded and 3.4 cm. wide, are of uncertain provenience. Two somewhat cruder blades, one 11.5 by 2.9 by 1.0 cm., the other 6.0 by 3.0 by 0.8 cm., from Rooms B and A, respectively, still have on their rounded bases pitch or gum with which they had been held in their handles.

On one flake is a graver point 1.3 cm. long which had been carefully chipped from just one face. The scraper found had scraping edges chipped unifacially along one side and one end of a flake 6.6 by 3.3 by 1.8 cm.

The "abrading stones" from Room D (one of sandstone, the other of chert) appear to have been used to flatten some surface. Perhaps the smoothed areas on which some of the near-by pictographs were painted were prepared with tools of this sort. The sharpening stone from Room F has a round-bottomed groove 1.2 cm. wide and 0.8 cm. deep that appears to have been used to grind some material such as bone.

The small almond-shaped choppers (fig.

43, *y*) are for the most part bifacially percussion-chipped artifacts that show little if any retouching and seldom much evidence of use. They are about 4 to 6 cm. long, are about half as wide as long, and on the average are about half as thick as wide. One end is usually more pointed than the other. They are usually made from thick flakes on which the bulb of percussion is often still visible. Jasper is by far the predominant material.

The large choppers (fig. 43, *x*, *z*) are much like the small ones in shape, proportions, material, and workmanship, but are much larger (9 to 14 cm. long) and show evidence of use or battering along the cutting or chopping edges. The longest specimen in this category is somewhat better made, is slimmer than usual, and could be considered a crude knife.

The piece of painted sandstone from Room A is nearly rectangular, 8.0 by 3.3 by 1.0 cm., and has seven nearly straight parallel lines drawn across it with what appears to be charcoal. The other two painted pieces have red paint on them and appear to be fragments of pictographs that have scaled off.

The bone awls from this site (all broken, many burned) include three types. Most common are splinters of mammal long bones that have been partially smoothed and pointed. Two awls, also made from mammal long bones, had the articulation of the bone left on to provide a handle. A single awl appears to have been made from a section of a rib. The flaker resembles a large splinter awl except that its point is blunt.

One bead, cut from a mammal long bone, is 1.4 cm. long and 1.1 cm. in diameter. Its ends are partially smoothed. The other bead was to have been about the same size, but the ends are still rough. The articular end of a cut bone seems to be a scrap left from the manufacture of such beads. A groove had been cut around the bone until it was thin enough to break.

The gaming pieces, apparently made from sections of mammal long bones, are rectangular with rounded ends and each has one flat and one convex face. The specimen from Room E is 4.5 by 1.2 by 0.3 cm. and was very carefully made and polished. The convex side has three shallow holes, each about 2 mm. in diameter, drilled into it. Circular grooves, apparently ground with the end of a tube 5 mm. in diameter, had been cut concentrically around the two holes nearest the ends of the specimen. The third hole (in the middle) was not so embellished. The other gaming piece, 3.7 by 1.0 by 0.5 cm., has no distinctive markings.

The bone pendants, apparently also cut from sections of mammal long bones, are nicely made and polished, trapezoidal in outline and perforated near the narrow end. The one from Room E is 5.3 cm. long and 0.2 cm. thick. It varies in width from 1.3 cm. to 1.5 cm. It is decorated with 15 shallow holes drilled into one surface. A row of six very small holes crosses it near the perforation and a row of three 1-mm. holes crosses it 1.5 cm. from the other end. Along the center line of the specimen between these two rows is a row of six holes decreasing in size. The other pendant, 4.2 cm. long, 0.2 cm. thick, and varying in width from 0.9 cm. to 1.4 cm., is undecorated.

The sickle (fig. 40, *c*) is made from a nearly flat section of mountain sheep horn. The small end of the horn served as the handle and irregularly spaced shallow notches had been cut on the inside curved edge at the large end. The area around the notches is polished from use. The sickle, designed to be held in the right hand with the convex (outside) surface down, had a chord length of 27 cm.

The sandal (fig. 40, *g*), of which only the mid-section is preserved, is very similar to Kidder and Guernsey (1919, pp. 101–2) type I, a, 2. It is finely woven of strips of yucca leaves 4 mm. wide in a twill (over-two, under-two) pattern. The ends of the strips were trimmed about 1 cm. long on the under side and had become frayed from wear. In addition, several separate loops of the same material were passed through the sandal and left projections on the under side to fray and produce more padding under the arch of the foot and under the toes. Since both ends of the specimen are missing, it is not possible to tell how the heel and toe were finished.

The innersole is a mixture of grass and shredded juniper bark.

The rush matting, of which a selvage section was preserved, is twined and has double warp elements of flattened rushes (*scirpus*).

The weft strands, of single-ply, Z-spun juniper cord, are spaced about 3.4 cm. apart. The ends of the rushes are bent over at an angle, pass through the loop of weft going around the third warp element away and terminate between the two layers of rushes. Thus no ends are exposed and the mat is four layers thick near the edge.

The basketry is coiled, with a half-rod-and-bundle foundation. The stitches, about 5 per cm., are not interlocking, but are occasionally split, probably accidentally. Only a fragment, and that partially burned, remains. The welt is yucca, but the rod and stitching could not be identified.

The cedar-bark ring, probably a pot rest, is about 11 cm. in diameter on the outside and 4 cm. on the inside. A bundle of cedar bark had been bent, so that its ends overlap, into a circle, and this in turn was loosely wrapped with another strip of the same material to hold the ring together.

Most of the pieces of worked wood are not distinctive or recognizable as parts of particular artifacts. A few are worthy of special mention, however. The fire-drill hearth from Room D is a flat piece of soft wood 3.5 cm. wide and 1.2 cm. thick and shows little deliberate shaping except for the characteristic burned depression along one side. The other hearths are round sticks about 1.2 cm. in diameter and have been used repeatedly. Both are broken. The wooden tube, possibly intended for a bead, is 4.6 cm. long and 1.1 cm. in diameter and was carefully cut. The hole through the center is 7 mm. in diameter and was apparently made by pushing out the pith. One roughly rectangular piece of thin wood 3.3 by 8.3 by 0.4 cm., broken at one end but cut off at the other, has several approximately straight and parallel lines drawn across it, apparently with charcoal. Another decorated rectangular piece of wood 18.3 cm. long and 0.3 cm. thick had apparently been carefully shaped, but all that is preserved is a strip less than 3 cm. wide split from one side. Near one end are six diagonal rows of dots averaging about 2 mm. in diameter which have been lightly burned into one surface.

The notched end of a broken reed arrow found at the site is 13.5 cm. long and 0.8 cm.

in diameter. Inside the notched end is a broken-off wooden plug, the outer end of which is 2 mm. farther in than the bottom of the notches. The reed is sinew-wrapped in a band 7 mm. wide just at the bottom of the notch. Three feathers had been attached with similar sinew bands 3 and 12 cm. from the end. The reed was identified as *Phragmites communis*.

The foreshaft is 15.5 cm. long and tapers to a point from a maximum diameter of 9 mm., at its base. A basal tang, most of which is broken off, but which was 6 mm. in diameter, had apparently been inserted into a reed arrow.

A cylindrical container (fig. 44, *b*), about 11 cm. in diameter and 14 cm. high, had been cut from the stem end of a cucurbita shell. It is unusual in that most gourd containers in the southwest are made from more nearly spherical gourds.

A slightly curved, split stick 18.5 cm. long and 0.9 cm. wide has a piece of light sinew securely tied to one end. The other end has been burned off so it is not possible to determine definitely whether the specimen had been a toy bow as its appearance suggests.

A stick 81 cm. long and 1 cm. in diameter had one end bent to form a hook with a 9-cm. diameter. The specimen looks like a light cane but shows only limited abrasion on the ends, both of which had obviously been carefully cut.

The cordage from this site is all two-ply, Z-twist and varies in size from 1 to 4 mm. Fibers used include juniper and yucca.

The fragment of feather cloth has a core of two-ply, Z-twist yucca cord around which split feathers were wrapped. Only one short section of this feather-wound cord was recovered, so nothing can be said as to how the cloth was made.

One of the pieces of hide thong was essentially round in cross section with a diameter of about 3 mm. The other was a thin flat strip about 6 mm. wide.

FREMONT RIVER DRAINAGE

The Fremont River, which joins with the Muddy River at Hanksville, Utah, to form the Dirty Devil River, drains some 2000 square miles of rather diverse country. The Fremont itself rises at an elevation of about 10,000 feet on the Fish Lake Mountains, which are part of the Wasatch range. After it leaves the mountains, the Fremont flows through a moderately broad, fertile valley with an elevation from 6000 to 7200 feet before it enters its narrow canyon through Capitol Reef, part of the Waterpocket Fold. From the Reef to its confluence with the Muddy, the valley of the Fremont broadens out and is flanked on either side by barren wasteland. Until after the arrival of white settlers, this lower part of the valley had a deep, rich alluvial fill that was heavily grassed. Now, erosion has cut so deep a channel for the stream that about the only vegetation on the remaining alluvial fill is that supported by irrigation.

Most of the tributaries of the Fremont River enter it from the south, rising at elevations up to 11,000 feet on the Aquarius Plateau (Boulder Mountain) or on the Henry Mountains. At the higher elevations, rainfall is sufficient to support heavy timber and many springs that provide conditions conducive to much wild life. The lower reaches of many of the tributaries have adequate alluvial fill (where not recently eroded out) to support primitive horticulture and the streams and springs provide water even where local rainfall is low. None of the tributaries, however, provides as favorable an environment as the section of the Fremont Valley that extends from just above the Waterpocket Fold near Fruita upstream to a few miles above Torrey where the elevation reaches about 6800 feet and the growing season is too short for dependable corn crops. At present this area is well suited for orchards, but the rich and broader upper part of the Fremont Valley is used primarily for hay growing.

The archaeology of the Fremont River drainage is best known from the report by Morss (1931), whose two summers' work there under the auspices of the Claflin-Emerson-Peabody Museum expedition provided the basis for his recognition and definition of the Fremont Culture. The additional work reported here, and the work of Gunnerson

(1957 a, pp. 80–86, 90–101) and Lister (1959 c) has not resulted in a really significant amount of new information regarding the archaeology of the Fremont drainage. The area was dominated by the Fremont Culture which is represented by open village sites, inhabited rock shelters, storage structures built in rock shelters, and panels of elaborate pictographs.

FL 11-1

This site, a small storage structure, is situated high in the canyon wall overlooking the Fremont River about 1.5 miles west of Torrey. A crevice under a slight overhang had been floored over with poles and the space above it enclosed with a wall of stone slabs and much adobe. The roof and back wall of the overhang served as the roof and back wall of the structure.

FL 11-2

This open village site is located about 1 mile north of Torrey, Utah, on the north edge of a flat, level bench about 0.5 mile wide which separates Sand Creek and Holt Draw. The valleys below are quite fertile and there are a number of springs near by. The ridge is strewn with small basalt boulders, some of which have been used as the lower portions, at least, of structure walls. Excavation by Roberts of one such structure (fig. 32B) at this site has been reported by Morss (1931, pp. 14–15), who designated it as Site No. 12. This is probably also the site described by Gunnerson (1957 a, pp. 99–100) as Site 42Wn17.

FL 12-1

For about 0.4 mile along the Fremont River just below the town of Fruita, there is an almost continuous pictograph panel containing perhaps 300 separate figures. The anthropomorphic figures are characterized by trapezoidal bodies, straight parallel lines for legs, and curved, horn-like headdresses. On some, a waist or hip area is delineated by horizontal lines forming a rectangle between the trapezoidal body and the legs. Ornaments on the body or around the neck also occur. Sheep or goats are depicted in many ways, but usually their cloven hoofs are shown.

FL 12-2

This site, located about 60 m. above site FL 12-1, contains the remains of a six-sided cist 1 m. in diameter, with the joints between the slabs sealed with adobe. The cist had been completely cleaned out previously. About 30 m. away on a promontory was found a 4-m. circle of rocks, each about 30 cm. in diameter, probably the remains of a structure. This, too, had been dug into previously.

FL 12-3

A rock shelter containing a small, neatly constructed storage room is located about 1 mile south of the Fremont River, about 2 miles downstream from Fruita. The structure consists of a curved wall enclosing a portion of a niche in a cliff, with bedrock providing both floor and ceiling as well as the rear wall. The front wall is supported by a curved pole about 5 cm. in diameter, which forms an arch with the ends resting on the shelter floor and the top leaned against the shelter ceiling. Against this arch were leaned vertical parallel poles heavily plastered with a mixture of adobe and cedar bark in which a few pieces of stone had been incorporated. The outer surface was plastered with adobe. At the top of the front of the wall is an opening 36 cm. wide which had served as a door. The maximum height of the wall (at the front) is 92 cm. and the maximum distance between the back and front walls is 1.2 m.

About 5 m. below this structure are the remains of what appears to have been one or more cists, now badly disturbed.

FL 12-4

The remains of several cists and a structure are located in two adjacent shelters on the right side of the Fremont River about 0.5 mile upstream from Fruita and about 60 m. above the river. The cists were simply bell-shaped pits dug into the floor of the shelter. The largest are about 1.2 m. deep, 90 cm. in diameter near the bottom, and 45 cm. in diameter at the top. The smallest is about 36 cm. deep and 30 cm. in maximum diameter and has an orifice 20 cm. in diameter. They may once have been fitted with stone slab covers. Corncobs were numerous in the shelters. The structure, built of stone slabs and blocks and plastered on the inside with adobe, had had a doorway at floor level.

SPECIMENS

Pottery sherds
Emery Gray	12
Emery Tooled	1
Corncobs	4

The tooled sherd, a portion of the rim of a large jar, is scored in a band 4.8 cm. wide extending from 1.2 cm. below the lip to where the neck joined the body of the vessel. The ten horizontal lines appeared to have been smoothly incised into the wet clay, while the nearly vertical lines were produced by a series of overlapping jabs of a fingernail or some similar tool.

The four corncobs have eight, ten, and twelve rows of kernels. One of the two twelve-rowed cobs has a stick inserted 4.5 cm. into its butt and extending out the same length.

FL 12-5: Deer Bone Cave

Deer Bone Cave, a rock shelter on the Fremont River 8 miles below Fruita, derives its name from a cache or burial of deer bones under grass and cedar bark in a carefully prepared, mud-lined depression in the floor of the shelter. Also in the shelter are three circular structures 1.2 to 2 m. in diameter, constructed of vertical stone slabs. The floor of the largest is slab-covered. The slabs on the north side of the middle-sized structure are leaned against two posts and the floor is covered with adobe. Roofs, partially preserved on two cists, had consisted of poles resting on top of the walls and supporting a second layer of poles laid at right angles and about 20 cm. apart. These, in turn, supported a layer of stone slabs which had probably been chinked with adobe.

SPECIMENS

Basketry fragments	3
Cedar bark brush (?)	1
Twisted sticks	2
Corncob on stick	1
Bone tubes	3
Modified bones	3
Unmodified bones	15
Modified horn	1
Chipped stone blade	1

The three basketry fragments, perhaps all from a single specimen, are coiled with a half-rod-and-bundle foundation. The rod is a nearly flat section of a twig, probably willow, and the bundle is a section of yucca fiber. The sewing material is probably willow bark. Very few of the stitches are split. The shapes of the fragments suggest that they are from a shallow bowl-shaped basket 20 to 30 cm. in diameter.

The brush consists of a bundle of cedar bark 2 by 3 cm. by 11 cm. long, tied together with two strips of juniper bark. One end of the bundle appears to be slightly charred. The other end is beveled to a point and is quite frayed and softened, apparently from use. Nothing adheres to the brush to provide a clue as to its use.

The two pieces of twisted sticks, probably squawbush, appear to be the results of "doodling" rather than any intentional fabrication.

The bone tubes, possibly beads, are the shafts of small rodent long bones from which both ends have been carefully cut. They measure 4.5 by 0.4, 3.3 by 0.3, and 1.9 by 0.3 cm. A straight section of rib with rounded ends is 6.6 cm. long and tapers from 2.1 to 1.5 cm. in width. The specimen is covered with very fine scratches and two grooves are incised across one face near the large end. Another specimen is the midsection of a mammal long bone 9.2 cm. long and 1.8 cm. in diameter, the end of which has been smoothly rounded. The entire specimen has been polished. Many lines from 3 to 14 mm. long have been incised transversely into the surface. The specimen had been split (probably accidentally) and only half was recovered. Another splinter of mammal long bone, 5.3 by 1.4 by 0.5 cm., is broken roughly at both ends, but it had been scraped on both surfaces to provide an essentially trapezoidal cross section. The unworked bones consist of 12 deer metatarsals and three rodent long bones.

The artifact made of mountain sheep horn (fig. 40, d) is 4.3 by 24 by 1.1 cm. and appears to have been a sickle, although weathering has all but obliterated the characteristic polish such a tool usually has.

The chipped stone blade (fig. 43, k), of red jasper, is 6.9 by 4.2 by 0.6 cm. It is roughly triangular in shape, with a convex base. The sides are concave near the base and convex near the point.

FL 12-6

This site is situated about 1 mile up a northern tributary canyon that enters the Fremont River at Site FL 12-5. It consists of a niche in the canyon wall, about 30 m. up a nearly vertical face from the canyon floor. Some sort of crude structure, probably for storage, had once been built in this small shelter, but has collapsed.

FL 12-7

About 0.5 mile farther up the canyon from FL 12-6 is a small niche in the canyon wall which contained a great deal of grass. The niche may have been used for storage, or its contents could represent some sort of nest.

FL 15-1

This site, a panel of well-preserved pictographs, extending along Temple Creek for about 0.3 mile, is located about 8 miles south of Fruita. The anthropomorphic figures have headdresses which suggest horns except that they sweep in a flat curve down around the body to the knees. A man with a bow and arrow is 20 cm. tall. There are sheep of many types and sizes, some alone, others in groups, and many showing action. One snake is over 6 m. long. Geometric designs include concentric circles and a crescent. The specimens, found by the children of a near-by rancher, were said to be from this site.

SPECIMENS
Pottery sherds
Escalante Gray 1
Emery Gray 1

The Emery Gray sherd is a neck fragment to which is attached a loop handle 2 cm. wide, 1.2 cm. thick, and 7 cm. long. The Escalante Gray sherd exhibits a knob that appears to be part of a handle which has been either broken or cut off. This knob, which has been partially smoothed, is 2.3 by 1.8 by 1.4 cm. long and has had a groove about 3 mm. wide and 2 mm. deep cut or ground around it after the vessel was fired.

FL 15-3

An open site characterized by a low mound was found on a sage flat along Tantalus Creek, about 2 miles above where it enters the Waterpocket Fold. Scattered stones, perhaps from structures, are concentrated in an area about 10 m. across and in one place they seem to form a circle. Sherds and chips can be found in an area about 100 m. across. Two metates were observed but not collected.

SPECIMENS
Pottery sherds
Emery Black-on-white 5
Emery Black-on-gray 1
Emery Gray 7
Tusayan Corrugated, Coombs Variety 1
Mancos Corrugated 1
Virgin Black-on-white 1
North Creek Black-on-gray 1
Stone
Blade and point fragments 4

The Emery Black-on-white sherds are decorated with Sosi-, Black Mesa-, and Dogoszhi-style designs and the Virgin and North Creek painted sherds with Sosi-style designs. Included among the Emery Gray sherds are a fragment of a handle and a sherd showing a mend hole.

Two of the point fragments are from slim triangular points with concave bases. A delicately serrated one of gray chalcedony had been about 3.1 by 1.2 cm., and one of red jasper had been about 4.1 by 1.4 cm. Another fragment is the base of a red jasper point that had two basal notches (leaving a small stem 5 mm. wide by 4 mm. long). The point had been 1.4 by about 2.5 cm. The fourth fragment is the basal portion of a large, yellow jasper, corner-notched blade that appears to have been triangular, about 4.4 by 10 cm., but only 6 mm. thick.

FL 16-1

On the left side of Temple Creek about 0.5 mile above the mouth of Sulfur Creek is a large rock shelter at the base of an imposing pink cliff. On a large rock in the shelter are at least twenty grooves about 1.2 cm. wide and 15 to 30 cm. long, and several broader grooves 8 to 10 cm. wide and 20 cm. long, which had probably been used for shaping or sharpening artifacts. The fill of the shelter had not been greatly disturbed.

SPECIMENS

Pottery sherds

Emery Gray	8
Emery Black-on-white	2
Emery Black-on-gray	2
Emery Tooled	2
Washington (?) Corrugated	5
Unidentified	1

Stone

Mano fragment	1
Serrated scraper	1
Point or blade fragments	2
Flakes or chips	8

The painted sherds are from bowls and show only straight lines of moderate width. Painted lines on one sherd are at right angles to one another and on another sherd the lines are parallel both to one another and to the rim. The tooled sherds are from the neck of a jar decorated with a very fine incised line parallel to the rim crossed by vertical parallel lines, 5 mm. apart, consisting of rows of fingernail jabs.

The mano fragment is approximately half a mano that was essentially rectangular with convex sides and ends. The two main surfaces are nearly parallel and only slightly convex. One surface has a maximum width of 5.8 cm. and the other of 6.4 cm. The mano had been about 16 cm. long and 2.9 cm. thick. The serrated scraper (fig. 43, *m*) is made from a thin gray chalcedony flake. On a curved edge, which is essentially an arc of a circle about 1.5 cm. in radius, are ten carefully chipped teeth about 2 mm. apart. The chipping was from one surface only so that, except for the teeth, the artifact resembles a very thin snub-nosed end scraper. On one side of this specimen is what appears to be an intentionally chipped graver point about 3 mm. long. The other two pieces of chipped stone artifacts are tips of blades or projectile points—one from a slim, very delicately chipped chalcedony point, the other from a much cruder quartzite blade. The flakes are mostly chalcedony, but one is black obsidian.

FL 16-2

There are several rock shelters, some of which have been occupied, in the lower 1 to 2 miles of Spring Gulch, which enters Temple Creek just above FL 16-1. In one of these

shelters on the right side of the canyon is a row of five anthropomorphic figures painted in red with white trimming. All have triangular or trapezoidal bodies with sharp square shoulders and elaborate headdresses consisting primarily of six to nine vertical lines. In addition, one has horns extending up from its headdress, another has two short lines pendant from its headdress, and a third apparently has some kind of necklace. The largest is 32 cm. tall and 19 cm. wide at the shoulders.

SPECIMENS

Pottery sherds

Emery Gray	3
Emery Black-on-white (?)	7

The black-on-white (?) sherds have a moderately well polished slip, but show no paint even though about an eighth of a bowl is represented. In one place on one sherd there is just a suggestion of three lines parallel to the rim as though organic paint might once have been there and burned off. This is probably a bowl that had been slipped but not decorated.

FL 16-4

A small storage structure was found under an overhang about 20 m. above the floor of a tributary canyon that enters Little Tantalus from the north. The overhang, about 1.2 m. high and 3 m. deep, could not be entered with equipment at hand so observations were made with the help of glasses. The structure, free standing, is about 1.3 m. high, 1.7 m. in diameter at the bottom, and shaped like a truncated cone. There is an opening about 35 by 25 cm. about halfway up the wall. Construction was apparently of nearly vertical slabs or billets of cedar, sloping in at the top and covered on the outside with a shell of adobe turtlebacks. The roof consists of poles, each about 8 cm. in diameter, which support a layer of much smaller parallel sticks.

The site was later entered by Morss (1931, p. 4) who called it Site 2 and provides a more detailed description.

SPECIMENS

Pottery sherds

Emery Gray	10
Tusayan White ware	1
North Creek Gray	1

Chipped stone
   Point or blade fragments   3
   Unmodified chips and flakes   9

The sherd of Tusayan White ware has a thin white slip on the inner surface, but no paint is present. One piece of chipped white quartzite is the square base of an unnotched blade 1.8 cm. wide that appears to have been relatively long and triangular. A worked piece of gray chalcedony is a section of what was originally a corner-notched blade 2.2 cm. wide and 4 to 5 cm. long.

MUDDY RIVER DRAINAGE

The Muddy River and its tributaries head on the Wasatch Mountains and drain a 40-mile-long section of their eastern slope from Ferron, Utah, south. The mountains, which are well wooded, with pine and aspen at high elevations and pinyon and juniper at low elevations, drop abruptly to Castle Valley, a smooth 60-mile-long strip of arid land averaging about 5 miles in width and lying nearly north–south, parallel to the mountains. To the east of Castle Valley is the San Rafael Swell, a beautiful but barren expanse of desert and fantastically shaped erosion remnants. Drainage is across, not along, Castle Valley, and out into the Swell; eventually the tributaries join the San Rafael River to the north or the Muddy River to the south. Where the streams leave the mountains and start to cross Castle Valley, at elevations of 6000 to 7000 feet, they have left alluvial deposits that could be farmed by means of irrigation from the clear spring-fed streams or even with flood water after the occasional summer "cloudbursts." Local precipitation, which averages about 8 inches per year in Castle Valley (Alter, 1941, p. 1147), is in itself inadequate for corn. In spite of the moderately high elevation, the shortest average growing season reported in Castle Valley is 119 days at Emery and Castle Dale (Alter, 1941, p. 1147). The area is so marginal and erosion so prevalent, however, that the amount of land under cultivation is now decreasing.

Archaeologically, Castle Valley is very rich and appears to have been the area where the Fremont population was most dense. Village sites are so numerous that as many as ten per mile have been observed along one side of a stream (Ivie Creek), a density that can probably be duplicated elsewhere in Castle Valley. The Claflin-Emerson expedition barely touched this area and can hardly be said to have even sampled it. Some idea of its richness was obtained from local informants, but since much of the valley could be reached by automobile, survey there was postponed and areas accessible only with horses were concentrated upon.

In Castle Valley, mostly in the drainage of the Muddy River, Gunnerson (1957 a, pp. 101–146) reported 75 sites, apparently just a sample. Excavation at seven Fremont sites in the area has been reported by Taylor (1955, 1957) and Gunnerson (1956 b, 1957 a, 1957 c, n.d.). In addition to Fremont sites, there are a few sites from which local collectors have recovered some very unusual artifacts, including figurines of non-Fremont styles (Gunnerson, 1957 d), a wide variety of eccentric chipped flints, bone harpoons, tiny carved bone ornaments, and an antler smoking pipe (Gunnerson, 1962 b). Another object recovered, apparently unique, is an unfired clay disk about 15 cm. in diameter and 3 cm. thick with many holes in one face to accommodate movable pegs (Gunnerson, 1959 a). Some of the sites in Castle Valley are suggestive of a Basketmaker-like occupation and at least one site has yielded fluted points (Gunnerson, 1956 a).

FL 4-1

On the west side of Rochester Creek at its junction with the Muddy River about 6 miles south of Emery, Utah, is a large square boulder, the east face of which is virtually covered with pictographs (fig. 25B). Some figures, such as a rhinoceros and an alligator, are very recent, but most elements appear to be of aboriginal authorship. The panel is dominated by a series of eight concentric arcs or a rainbow design which covers an area 1.2 m. long and 1 m. high. The remaining figures include geometric designs, animal forms, and anthropomorphic figures, some with horned headdresses. No evidence of habitation could be found near the site.

FL 4-4

A village site was found on the first bench on the south side of the Muddy River, just below the mouth of Ivie Creek, about 8 miles south of Emery. The lower parts of the walls of the structure, at least, had been constructed of basalt boulders or blocks, apparently set in adobe. Even though the site had been badly eroded, limited testing in one structure revealed a floor still covered with 15 cm. of fill. The floor consisted of a layer of thin flat stone slabs laid on a puddled adobe base. Structures appeared to be grouped around two or three central depressions.

Two other open village sites, FL 4-2 and FL 4-3, were seen just above this site on the south side of Ivie Creek, but they were not described in the notes and no collections were made at them.

SPECIMENS

Pottery sherds	
Emery Black-on-white	1
Emery Black-on-gray	13
Emery Tooled	1
Emery Gray	11
Chipped stone blade fragment	1
Chipped stone point	1

The painted sherds, all from bowls, are decorated primarily with parallel encircling lines. One bowl had had three parallel lines below the rim and three more circling the bottom. Between these sets was a band of large open squares, and in two corners of each a simple step element. One sherd has small triangles pendant from a line.

The tooled sherd was the vertical neck of a jar or bottle that had been decorated by scoring.

The blade fragment (fig. 43, *i*) was from a large tan chalcedony corner-notched (or stemmed) blade having a maximum width of 5.3 cm. The stem is 1.5 cm. long, 4.1 cm. wide at the end, constricting to 3.2 cm. The point, of similar material, is triangular with a straight base except for two small ears at the corners. It measures 2.4 by 1.5 cm.

FL 4-5

Many small storage structures were found on the south side of the Muddy, about 3.5 miles below the mouth of Ivie Creek. One of these, standing alone and well preserved, is 90 cm. in diameter with walls 15 cm. thick made of horizontal stone slabs and a few cottonwood poles laid in heavy adobe mortar and plastered on the outside with adobe. The roof was constructed of two layers of split poles covered with a layer of adobe 5 cm. thick. An opening 18 by 20 cm. had been left in the center of the roof. The floor is of stone slabs. On a lower ledge, about 16 m. long and 2 m. wide and protected by a slight overhang, is a row of eight more similar structures built one against another with some evidence that there once had been three more. In some, construction varied in that the lower part of the wall consisted of a single course of vertical stone slabs above which the succeeding courses were laid horizontally. All are more or less circular with diameters from 0.6 to 1.25 m. and still stand as high as 82 cm.

SPECIMENS

Pottery sherds	
Emery Gray	2
Unidentified Gray	17
Bone awl	1
Bone awl fragment	1
Cucurbita fragments	10

The unidentified sherds, apparently all from a single jar, have a polished black, but bumpy or undulating and pitted outer surface. This, in turn, was apparently decorated with fugitive red painted bands about 1.5 cm. wide and 2.5 cm. apart. The inner surface, also irregular and pitted, is covered with scraping marks. The paste is soft and tempered with sand derived from dark igneous rock. This pottery probably resembles Escalante Gray more than any other type.

One complete awl, made from a section of a mammal long bone, is 9.6 by 1.2 by 0.5 cm. It was smoothed and somewhat polished on all but part of the cancellous surface. The sides are nearly parallel for about two-thirds of its length, after which it tapers smoothly to a point. The awl fragment is just the point of what had apparently been another splinter awl.

FL 4-6

On the east side of the Muddy, just above FL 4-5, was found a site called a "lookout," presumably the remains of a stone structure built in the open on a point or ledge that commands a view of the valley.

FL 7-1

This village site about 300 m. north of Last Chance Creek and just below where it leaves the Coal Cliffs is on a broad level area covered with low brush. It may be Site 42Sv28 tested by Gunnerson (1957, pp. 105–106). In addition to material collected, several metates, one of the Utah type, were observed.

SPECIMENS

Pottery sherds	
Emery Black-on-white	6
Emery Black-on-gray	9
Emery Tooled	5
Emery Gray	14
Sevier Gray	1
Sosi Black-on-white	1
Tusayan Black-on-red	1
Tsegi Orange ware	1
North Creek Black-on-gray	1
North Creek Gray	1
Coombs Gray	3
Moenkopi (Coombs) Corrugated	2
Chipped Stone	
Points	2
Blade fragments	2

The design elements on the painted Emery sherds are assignable to Sosi and Black Mesa styles. The most common elements are single encircling lines of medium width or two or more such lines parallel to one another. Also present are wedge-shaped or triangular elements, curved lines (possibly parts of spirals), rounded-in corners between right-angle lines, and dots in contiguous squares. All painted sherds are from bowls.

All the tooled sherds are from jars. Three sherds, all from necks of jars, have scored designs with the lines essentially horizontal and vertical. Another neck sherd has vertical incised lines about 2 mm. apart. The other tooled sherd is from the shoulder just below the neck of a jar and is decorated with vertical rows of deep punctations, perhaps made with a fingernail, about 6 mm. apart. The bands between the grooves so produced are rounded on top and about 2 mm. high. The resulting decoration superficially resembles corrugation. Two of the Emery Gray rim sherds are large enough to suggest vessel shapes: a low-rimmed, flaring jar and a tall, straight-rimmed bottle or pitcher. Also included are two loop handles, 1.5 to 2 cm. in diameter, at least one of which had extended to the lip of the vessel.

One very nicely chipped point of nearly white chalcedony (fig. 43, b) is triangular with straight sides and a concave base and measures 4.9 by 1.3 by 0.4 cm. A second triangular point, of the same material but slightly scalene and much cruder, is 3.0 by 2.0 by 0.5 cm. The base of a square-based blade of similar material (fig. 43, j) is 3.3 cm. wide and has only slightly converging straight sides. Originally, it was probably 10 to 12 cm. long and narrowed rather abruptly near the point. The other chipped stone artifact is just the tip of a blade made from a nearly white opaque flint.

DESOLATION CANYON

The Green River, which drains the entire Uinta Basin as well as a large area to the north, has had to cut a deep gorge through the 9000-feet-high Book Cliffs that form the Basin's southern edge. The river drops from an elevation of about 4900 feet where it comes out of Split Mountain in the foothills of the Uinta Mountains on the north side of the Uinta Basin to about 4200 feet where it emerges from the Book Cliffs south of the basin. At both of these places, the Green flows in very shallow broad valleys flanked by broad level terrain only slightly higher than the river. Desolation Canyon, the river's entrenchment, separates the East and West Tavaputs Plateaus, of which the Book Cliffs form the southern face or escarpment. Since the plateaus are highest on the south, most of the drainage is to the north. A few moderately large tributaries, such as Range Creek and Nine Mile Canyon, flow into Desolation Canyon from the West Tavaputs. Smaller canyons, such as those of Florence Creek and Chandler Creek, enter it from the East Tavaputs. Even smaller watercourses, most of them dry, have been incised into the very steep Book Cliffs and drain to the south. Today the Book Cliffs provide a formidable barrier, especially to vehicles; no roads cross the Book Cliffs proper and Desolation Canyon is so narrow and rough that a road along it is infeasible. There is no evidence, however, that the Book Cliffs served as a significant barrier in aboriginal times. Sites are known from three widely spaced points along the foot of the Book Cliffs—near Cisco, Thompson, and Price (Wormington, 1955; Gunnerson, 1957 a, pp. 73–77).

Moreover, the Claflin-Emerson expedition located a number of archaeological sites along Desolation Canyon and in the lower reaches of its minor tributaries, as well as numerous sites in some of the larger tributaries. Published references to archaeological sites in Desolation Canyon are very few. Gaumer (1937, 1939) describes two and mentions others without giving their locations, even roughly.

ET 5-1

On the west bank of the Green River, 2.5 miles above the mouth of Jack Canyon, is a circular wall on a small shoulder 10 m. above the valley floor. The room outlined by the wall is 2.1 m. in diameter and the wall itself, now only 1.05 m. high at the highest part, is composed of thin rectangular slabs, in rough courses, chinked with adobe and small fragments of rock. The rocks were not set in adobe mortar; the adobe was used to fill the crevices between the rocks after they were laid in place. The 20 cm. of fill inside the room consisted of earth and pieces of adobe. No charcoal was found.

ET 5-2

Three small storage structures and possibly a dwelling were found on the west side of the canyon of the Green River about 3 miles below its confluence with Jack Canyon. The small structures are on ledges under slight overhangs, two about 8 m. above the canyon floor, the third about 17 m. higher and so situated that during rain storms water pours down in front of it. All three are difficult of access. One of the structures is rectangular, 1 by 0.75 m., and is constructed of thin pieces of shale roughly coursed in a great abundance of adobe. A few slender poles parallel to the cliff had apparently been part of the roof. The second structure, consisting of a semicircular

wall 2.5 m. long and 1.35 m. high, is constructed of rough, uncoursed slabs set in much adobe. Poles near by were probably from the roof. The third structure is about the same size as the second, but contains no adobe in its walls.

The possible dwelling, nearly demolished, consists of a roughly circular stone wall about 3 to 3.6 m. in diameter and of moderately large stones, apparently constructed without adobe. It is on a shoulder about 6 m. above the canyon floor.

PR 8-1

A small structure was found under an overhang 7 m. above the valley floor, about 0.25 mile up a side canyon that enters the Green River about 0.25 mile below Rock Creek. The main structure, built in a corner, is 1.0 by 2.2 m. and 1.3 m. high. The front wall, supported by a log, both ends of which were wedged in place, is constructed of stone slabs and logs laid in adobe. The inner surface was not completely plastered and cracks had been filled with adobe of a different color at some time after the original construction. The roof, supported by poles most of which run parallel to the cliff, is of stone and adobe. A circular opening through the roof is surrounded by a collar made of a bundle of withes, bound together at intervals and also bound to the main roof beams. The collar had been plastered with adobe, but there is no depression in the lip to accept a cover.

A second structure adjacent to the main structure encloses an area 1.8 by 0.9 m. The wall, in places still 75 cm. high, incorporates two natural rock projections.

SPECIMENS

Corncobs	8
Sticks, worked	X

Nine of the cobs and all the sticks were inside the cist. The sticks are not portions of identifiable artifacts. Most if not all of the cobs are from ears which had been picked green.

PR 8-2

Two small semicircular structures on a protected ledge about 20 m. above the canyon floor are located on the north side of Rock

Creek, about 0.1 mile above its mouth. Both are of moderately large sandstone slabs laid in courses with adobe mortar and they have one wall in common. One structure, built in a corner, encloses an area 82 by 84 cm., and the adjoining structure encloses an area 75 by 95 cm. Both are about 83 cm. high.

SPECIMENS

Pottery sherds	
Uinta Gray	13
Cucurbita fragment	1
Flint chip	1
Corncob	1

PR 8-3

On the south side of Rock House Canyon, 0.5 mile from the Green River, there is a small structure situated on a ledge 15 m. above the canyon floor. The structure consists of a semi-circular wall, built in a corner and enclosing an area 1.5 by 1.2 m. The wall, poorly preserved, was constructed of poles 1 to 3 cm. in diameter and 2 to 3 cm. apart, set vertically in a base of adobe and plastered with adobe to form a wall about 10 cm. thick. Larger poles up to 15 cm. in diameter, found just outside the room, were probably once part of the roof. A flat stone slab, 3 cm. thick and chipped to a rough oval 40 by 55 cm., presumably had served as a cover for the structure's entrance.

On the cliff just east of the structure are two groups of painted triangles 6 to 7 cm. high. Each group consists of six horizontal rows of eight to fourteen triangles, alternately red and yellow, and one group has an additional two rows of yellow triangles.

PR 8-4

On the north side of Jack Canyon, about 100 m. below the upper forks, pictographs were found on the back wall of a rock shelter almost at the level of the canyon floor. The pictographs included six circles painted in red and overlaid with white, four hands in red, and several sheep in white. A man, a sheep, and an anchor-like figure had been pecked into the wall.

SPECIMENS

Corncobs	2

PR 12-21

On the south side of Bear Canyon, about 0.4 mile from its mouth, is a rock shelter 25 m. above the canyon floor containing remnants of a small two-room structure. This structure, little of which is preserved, had been constructed of crude stone and adobe masonry and had probably had a roof supported by poles, a few of which were found in the shelter. Two roughly round, thin sandstone slabs, each about 50 cm. in diameter, were found in the shelter and had probably been covers for roof openings to the two rooms. The entire structure had apparently been about 2 m. long, 1 m. wide, and 1 m. high, with each room essentially square.

PR 12-22

A rock shelter containing pictographs was found on the valley floor on the west side of the Green River about 2 miles above the mouth of Chandler Creek. The pictographs include a person 35 cm. tall with arms extended to the side, elbows bent 90°, feet apart, and knees slightly bent. Above the head are two curved lines, probably horns. The figure is painted in red and surrounded with a vague yellow line. A second anthropomorphic figure, now very indistinct, is 30 cm. tall and painted in red. Five yellow triangles and red and yellow lines complete the panel.

RANGE CREEK CANYON

Range Creek heads at an elevation of almost 11,000 feet 25 miles east of Price, Utah, and, in its 30-mile length, drops to 4500 feet where it joins the Green River some 15 miles before the latter emerges from the Book Cliffs. The gradient in the lower half of the canyon, where the archaeological sites were found, is not unduly great, and sandy alluvial fill suitable for aboriginal farming is common. Limited agriculture is still practiced with the aid of irrigation from the unfailing, spring-fed creek. The canyon walls do not provide really large overhangs or shelters, but there are numerous small ones adequate for storage structures and even dwellings. The tributaries of Range Creek Canyon are few and small, and the area surrounding it is high and rough on all sides, so that the canyon seems isolated. The walls of Range Creek Canyon are not vertical but rise in a series of steps or ledges, giving the impression of a steep-sided valley rather than a deep canyon.

In spite of this seeming isolation, however, the survey reported here and subsequent work (Leh, 1936; Morss, 1954, pp. 3–7; Gunnerson, 1957, pp. 69–73) has shown that archaeological sites are moderately abundant. There is nothing to suggest that any of the Range Creek sites are of other than Fremont authorship.

PR 12-1

The remains of a small structure were found on a narrow ledge on the north side of Range Creek Canyon, about 10 m. above the canyon floor. Projecting from the cliff face are two sections of wall 80 cm. apart and about 50 cm. high, which apparently had been the end walls of a structure. Construction was of chunks of roughly coursed stone, alternating with lumps of adobe.

Below this structure, near the canyon floor, is a group of pictographs including a white zigzag line 50 cm. long, a pecked cross with a forked bottom 15 cm. high, straight red and yellow lines, and a red circle partially filled in.

PR 12-2

On the south side of Range Creek, 4 miles below Gooseberry Creek, are the remains of two small structures on a ledge about 25 m. above the canyon floor. Rocks, adobe, poles, and logs, five of which are still standing vertically in place, appear to be from a structure that had covered a triangular ledge 1.5 by 1.6 by 2 m. A near-by, but inaccessible, structure of adobe containing a few rocks and small poles is about 60 by 60 cm.

Pictographs just above the talus slope included a globular-bodied man, sheep, serpents with sheep front parts, a rainbow-like design, and a spiked spiral.

SPECIMENS

Pottery sherds	
Uinta Gray	2
Blade fragment	1

The blade fragment was from a beautifully chipped, square-based blade, at least 4 cm. wide and only 0.6 cm. thick, made from light pink flint. All three specimens were collected at the base of the cliff.

PR 12-3

A rock shelter showing some evidence of occupation was found on the west side of Range Creek about 4 miles below Gooseberry Creek. The shelter, at the top of a steep slope and about 50 m. above the canyon floor, was about 15 m. long, 5 m. wide, and 6 m. high. Under 15 cm. of sand and stones fallen from the roof was found an occupation level, just above which three sherds were collected.

SPECIMENS

Pottery sherds	
Emery Gray	2
Uinta Gray	1
Digging stick	1

The digging stick is T-shaped, slightly curved, and 56 cm. long, with a transverse handle 14 cm. long. The stick tapers gradually to a point from a maximum diameter of 3 cm. near the handle.

PR 12-4

The remains of four small structures were found on a ledge under a moderately large overhang on the south side of Range Creek, 4.5 miles below Gooseberry Creek. Three of the structures are contiguous and about 8 m. above the valley floor. Construction was primarily of stone slabs laid in, and plastered with, adobe. A few large vertical slabs had been incorporated into the lower part of one wall. The cliff had served as the back wall for all three structures and the front walls were almost completely gone, although enough remained of one to indicate a rounded corner. The floors were approximately 1 by 0.75 m., 1.3 by 1.2 m., and 1.3 by 0.8 m. Roofs had been supported by horizontal poles, two of which remained parallel to the cliff across the end rooms. Poles projecting from the ledge may also have been part of these structures.

The fourth structure, about 3 m. above and to one side of the first three, had also had walls of slab and adobe masonry and was 1 by 1.25 m.

PR 12-5

A log platform was found in a crevice in the wall of Range Creek Canyon, 4.5 miles below Gooseberry Creek. The platform consisted of about ten poles, supported by a ledge at one end and by two logs across the crevice at the other. It had probably been used for storage.

PR 12-6

On the west wall of Range Creek about 6 miles below Gooseberry Creek and 40 m. above the canyon floor is a ledge upon which there are three well-preserved small structures and traces of a fourth. The ledge is under an overhang that faces south across a wide section of canyon bottom, with the stream running on the far side. The back wall of the overhang serves as the rear wall of all the structures. The front walls, semicircular and constructed of small to medium-sized stone slabs laid in adobe mortar, are partially plastered both inside and outside. The three best-preserved structures are contiguous and were apparently built consecutively, each utilizing a portion of the wall of the previous one. The earliest and largest room has a floor 1.56 m. (along the cliff) by 1.27 m. Since the bedrock floor slopes, the wall is highest (1.2 m.) at the front.

The middle and best-preserved structure is 70 cm. wide along the cliff and 1.65 m. from front to back, with a maximum height (at the front) of 1.15 m. Much of the roof is still intact. Parallel to the back of the shelter and resting on the end walls are two horizontal poles which, along with the front wall, support eight poles perpendicular to the back of the shelter. The poles, all straight and trimmed, are from 3 to 8 cm. in diameter and are lashed together with withes where they cross. On top of the eight poles is a mat of sticks 1 to 2 cm. in diameter and about 2 cm. apart, woven together with withes that are about 8 mm. in diameter and spaced 8 to 10 cm. apart. This mat, in places two layers thick, is covered with a layer of adobe 2 to 5 cm. thick, which in turn is covered with additional sticks. The heavy elements of the mat were perpendicular to the eight poles which supported it, and the sticks on top of the adobe were at right angles to the heavy ele-ments of the mat. Entrance to the structure had apparently been through a hole in the roof. A stone slab about 62 cm. in diameter and 5 cm. thick found on the roof had probably served as a cover for the entrance.

The third structure, built in part against the second, was of similar construction, but no part of the roof remained. The fourth structure, smaller than any of the others and almost completely destroyed, is about 1 m. farther along the cliff.

Above the structures are some pictographs consisting of two sets of four concentric circles alternating red and white. The outside circle is 13 cm. in diameter and red in each case. There is also a red triangle 8 cm. high surrounding a white triangle.

SPECIMENS

Corncobs	8
Twisted withes and sticks	X
Bone fragment	1

PR 12-7

A very crude stone wall was found on a small knoll about 6 m. high in Range Creek Canyon, about 7 miles below Gooseberry Creek. The wall, of rounded rocks irregularly piled, has a maximum height of 60 cm. and encloses a rough oval, 2.5 by 4 m., which conforms to the outline of the top of the knoll.

PR 12-8

On the west side of Range Creek about 5 miles above its mouth is an open site on the edge of an elevation about 13 m. above the valley floor. A crude stone circle about 4 m. in diameter and 30 cm. high is probably part of a structure. This wall, made of irregular stones, has a gap, possibly a doorway, in the southeast side.

PR 12-9

A rock shelter showing some evidence of occupation is located on the east side of Range Creek Canyon, about 6 m. above the valley floor and about 4.5 miles above the mouth of the canyon. The shelter is 13 m. long and 2.5 m. deep. On its back wall are a sinuous pecked line 40 cm. long and a red arc opening down, possibly the remains of a circle 75 cm. in diameter.

SPECIMENS

Pottery sherds
Emery Gray 1
North Creek (?) Gray 1
Hammerstone 1

The hammerstone is a flat pebble that shows battering from use on both ends.

PR 12-10

Across the canyon from PR 12-9, on the point of a ridge about 13 m. above the valley floor, is a crude circle of rocks similar to those at PR 12-7 and PR 12-8.

PR 12-11

A rock shelter containing some pictographs and the remains of two structures is located on the east side of Range Creek Canyon, about 13 m. above the canyon floor and about 4.1 miles above its mouth. The best-preserved structure is about 1.5 m. square and still stands 45 to 75 cm. high. Three walls had been constructed by piling up stone slabs without the use of adobe. The fourth wall consists of two large vertical stone slabs. The second structure is too fragmentary to reveal its original size or shape. A little detritus was found in the thin fill of the shelter.

Six human figures 60 to 85 cm. high are painted on the shelter wall in a variety of combinations of red, white, brown, green, and blue.

PR 12-12

About 4 miles above the mouth of Range Creek Canyon and about 20 m. up its sloping northwest wall is a crude oval structure standing in the open. The wall, which encloses an area about 5 by 4 m., is 50 to 60 cm. high and is made of irregular rocks roughly coursed. There is a gap, presumably an entrance, in the southwest side.

PR 12-13

Directly opposite PR 12-12 is a rock shelter containing several logs, presumably once part of a small structure. A horizontal log across the front of the shelter serves as a retaining wall. Behind it, set in the sand and rock which it retains, is a vertical pole extending to the shelter roof 1.8 m. above. A third pole, apparently a brace, has one end resting in a fork of the vertical pole and the other end set in the rubble behind the retaining log. Several other poles and logs are scattered about the shelter.

SPECIMENS

Pottery sherds
Emery Gray 3

These specimens were picked up on a rock pile at the base of the cliff.

PR 12-14

On the northeast side of Range Creek Canyon 2.25 miles above its mouth and 15 m. above the canyon floor a curved wall, 80 to 90 cm. high, had been constructed across the front of a V-shaped niche in the cliff face to form an essentially triangular room with sides 1.3, 1.5, and 1.6 m. long. The lower portion of the wall consists of three vertical stone slabs chinked with adobe and the upper part is of coursed slab and adobe masonry. Enough of the roof remains to show that it once consisted of poles supported at one end by the cliff and at the other by the masonry wall. On the poles was a twined mat with sticks 1 cm. in diameter forming the warp and withes forming the weft. Over the mat was a layer of adobe plaster about 5 cm. thick. The bare ledge had served as a floor for the structure.

PR 12-15

A small structure was found on a ledge 20 m. up the right wall of Range Creek Canyon, about 2.25 miles from its mouth. Access to the ledge, protected by an overhang, can be gained only from above. The structure, built against the back wall of the shelter, is trapezoidal, with sides from 50 to 70 cm. long, the longest side at the front. Three of the walls consist of thin stone slabs set on edge and chinked with adobe. They stand 55 cm. high. The top had apparently been made of two stone slabs, one of which is still in place.

PR 12-16

Two stone walls are located on the opposite rims of a point or ledge on the south side of, and 35 m. above, Range Creek, 2 miles from its mouth. One section is rather carefully laid, with small rocks filling the interstices. Behind and about 1 m. above the walls is a small rock shelter.

PR 12-17

On the south side of Range Creek Canyon, 2 miles from its mouth, is a ledge under an overhang about 30 m. above the canyon floor. At one end of the 5-by-2-m. ledge are two sections of a wall, 60 cm. high. The two sections, neither of which touches the cliff, join at a 60° angle. One section is 0.6 m. long, the other is 1 m. long. The wall contains large stone blocks at the bottom and smaller stones laid horizontally in the upper part. No adobe is present. Another wall, 80 cm. high, extends for 2.5 m. along the front of the shelter. It is much cruder and appears to be a retaining wall, since the area behind it was filled with sand and loose adobe. Numerous sticks from 1 to 6 cm. in diameter and up to 3 m. long, possibly from structures, were found on the ledge.

PR 12-18

A cleft in one side of a rock shelter located 20 m. up the northwest side of Range Creek Canyon, 1.9 miles from its mouth, has been crudely walled up to a height of 30 to 60 cm. with large rocks.

PR 12-19

This site extends for about 30 m. under an overhang at the top of a talus slope about 8 m. above and on the west side of Range Creek about 1 mile from its mouth. Three semicircular structures, each about 6 m. across where it joins the cliff face and 3 m. deep, are from 0.3 to 1 m. high. The best preserved is constructed of large stone blocks laid in regular courses with adobe mortar. A doorway 30 to 45 cm. wide is near the middle of the wall. Part of this structure was excavated, revealing an adobe floor 3 to 5 cm. thick on top of which was debris containing pieces of burned adobe, probably from a roof. Under the structure was a layer of debris 60 cm. thick which contained three layers of grass, possibly representing occupation levels.

SPECIMENS

Pottery sherds	
Emery Gray	5
Uinta Gray	1
Chips and flakes	2
Bone fragments	X
Red pigment	1
Fire drill hearth	1
Cord	2
Sticks and fiber	X
Corncobs	3

The Uinta Gray sherd is part of a handle. A stick, oval in cross section and 1.8 cm. wide, had been used as a hearth for fire drills 1.1 and 0.6 cm. in diameter. A notch had been cut from the edge of the stick into each of the two depressions.

One piece of fiber cord 2 mm. in diameter is two-ply, Z-twist. The other cord is about the same size but appears to be two-ply, S-twist, each of the two elements being two-ply, Z-twist cords. Both of the component cords are of yucca fiber.

The pigment is a lump of red ocher (?) about 7 mm. in diameter.

PR 12-20

A storage cist and a masonry structure were found on different ledges, 13 and 30 m. up the north wall of Range Creek Canyon, about 1 mile above its mouth. Both are under overhangs and are difficult of access. The cist is an oval pit, 1.3 by 0.8 m. and 0.75 m. deep, lined with stone slabs set on edge in adobe and covered with poles 6 to 9 cm. in diameter. These, in turn, were covered with smaller sticks which were intertwined with and tied to the poles with withes and covered with 2 to 8 cm. of adobe. A circular hole through the middle of the top is surrounded by a collar made from a bundle of withes and plastered with adobe. A circular stone slab cover 45 cm. in diameter was set in a depression in the collar. Rocks had been piled around the cist, perhaps for camouflage. When it was opened, it was found to be about one-third full of unidentified grass seed.

The masonry structure, protected by an overhang, is rectangular, 2.1 m. long, 0.5 to 0.85 m. wide, and 0.8 to 1.1 m. high. A partition perpendicular to the long wall divides the structure into two rooms of unequal size. Walls are constructed of stone slabs, many of them quite irregular, laid in adobe mortar. The front wall has as its base a log 12 cm. in diameter. The roof over the smaller room is almost completely gone, but much of the rest is well preserved. Two horizontal poles parallel to the back of the shelter span the entire structure; a third is supported at one end by the partition. Two or three poles cross these at right angles and are tied to them with withes. This framework supports a mat that has sticks 1 cm. in diameter and 2 to 3 cm. apart for warp, and withes 10 to 20 cm. apart for weft. The roof was covered with a layer of adobe 5 to 7 cm. thick. An opening roughly circular and fitted with a slab cover about 40 cm. in diameter had been left through the middle of the roof.

SPECIMENS

Pottery sherds	
Emery Gray	3
Grass seed	X
Twisted withes	X
Corncob	1

NINE MILE CANYON

The area in eastern Utah north of the Book Cliffs which, on the basis of present knowledge, has the greatest concentration of archaeological sites is Nine Mile Canyon, also known as Minnie Maude Creek. This creek rises at an elevation of about 9000 feet 20 miles north of Price, Utah, and flows essentially straight east to join the Green River in Desolation Canyon, 60 miles north of the town of Green River. The mouth of the creek is at an elevation of 4700 feet, but most of the archaeological sites are at elevations between 4800 and 6400 feet. The main canyon, although less than a quarter of a mile wide, has a great deal of excellent farm land that is irrigated from the creek. Argyle Canyon, the largest tributary, has limited amounts of tillable land and the others, most of which are dry, have virtually none. At present the number of ranches in Nine Mile is decreasing, but at one time it supported perhaps two dozen.

The walls are high and nearly sheer along much of Nine Mile, but the canyon can be entered without much difficulty via some of its tributaries, and early in the present century the main road into the Uinta Basin followed the central portion of Nine Mile.

To the south and west of this canyon, the country is high plateau land. It is well forested for the most part, but also provides summer range for cattle. To the north, after one emerges from the canyon, the land is very barren and slopes gradually down to the northeast toward the Duchesne River.

Sites in Nine Mile Canyon have received and are still receiving the attention of many amateur collectors and relic hunters. Fortunately, some of the archaeology of this relatively rich area has been reported in the literature. Part of the work done by the Claflin-Emerson expedition was reported by Morss (1931, pp. 28–30, 40–41). Our best information on open sites comes from the excavations of Gillin (1938), which also supplied wood for tree-ring dating (Schulman, 1948; Ferguson, 1949). Still other reports are by Beckwith (1931, 1932), Reagan (1931 a; 1931 b; 1931 d, pp. 127–128; 1933), and Gunnerson (1957, pp. 67–68). The earliest description of archaeological sites in Nine Mile Canyon is apparently that by Montgomery (1894, pp. 335–340).

PR 3-1

On the north wall of Argyle Canyon about 1 mile from its mouth is the ruin of a small structure on a ledge about 30 m. above the canyon floor. It appears to have been constructed of stone slabs laid with thin layers of adobe mortar.

Near by are several small panels of simple geometric pictographs.

PR 3-2

About 3 miles above the mouth of Argyle Canyon, on a narrow sandstone outcrop about 50 m. up the cliff on the north side, are the remains of what was probably a low, rough wall.

PR 3-3

Directly across Argyle Canyon from PR 3-2 is an open site consisting of the remains of a room located on a bench on the south side of the canyon about 50 m. above its floor. The room is about 4 m. in diameter, and the wall still stands to a height of over 1 m.

in one place. Much fallen stone, both inside and outside the room, indicates that the wall was once higher. Construction was of large stone slabs with smaller stones inserted between them. The bottom course of the wall consists mainly of large irregular boulders. No evidence of adobe mortar could be found.

PR 3-4

Five small structures were found on ledges about 30 m. above the canyon floor on the west side of the mouth of Trail Canyon. One of the structures is at the top of the talus slope and directly below the others. One of the four upper rooms, the only room not in complete ruin, had straight parallel end walls 1 m. long, 1.5 m. apart, and perpendicular to the cliff, which served as the back wall. Wall construction was of stone slabs laid in adobe mortar and the roof was of stone slabs supported by poles, which rested on the walls. In one place the wall extended above the level of the roof, suggesting that there had been a second story.

PR 3-5

A two-room structure, now partially in ruin, is located about 50 m. up a draw that enters Nine Mile Canyon about 1 mile below the mouth of Trail Canyon. It is situated about 30 m. above the canyon floor under an overhang on a ledge that can be reached only from above. The structure had been about 5 m. long and 1.2 m. high. Walls are constructed of small stone slabs laid in courses in adobe mortar. Pine poles 3 to 4 m. long rest on the partition and end walls and support stone slabs that form the roof. One of the rooms contains what appears to be a shelf made of sticks.

PR 4-1

About 1.5 miles above the mouth of Bull Canyon a crude wall was found on an open bench on the west side of the canyon about 25 m. above its floor. The wall, which is semicircular, follows the edge of a point. It is 4.3 m. long, 80 cm. high in the middle, and 55 cm. high at the ends, which are 1.6 m. apart. A near-by rock pile may be the remains of another wall.

PR 4-2

A rock shelter containing what appears to be a retaining wall is located on the north wall of Nine Mile Canyon 250 m. upstream from the mouth of Bull Canyon. The floor of the shelter, 13 m. above the bottom of the canyon, is about 3 by 5 m. and is within 86 cm. of the ceiling at the rear. The slightly curved retaining wall of stone slabs, now about 70 cm. high and 1.52 m. long, may once have extended all the way across the front of the shelter. Small test pits, however, revealed only sterile fill.

On the ceiling are pictographs painted in red, white, and yellow. One figure, 18 cm. long, is a four-toed quadruped with a stubby erect tail and either long ears or horns. Another red quadruped 15 cm. long looks vaguely like a moose. Of three sheep, all over 30 cm. long and painted in white, two have horns. Three small red animals may represent dogs, and other figures apparently represent men, some in the style of "stick men." Geometric designs, especially zigzag lines and rows of dots in red, yellow, and white, are very common.

PR 4-3

A roughly coursed stone wall 4 m. long and 1 m. high was found on the edge of a bench on the north side of Nine Mile Canyon, 1.2 miles below the mouth of Bull Canyon.

PR 4-4

At the mouth of a small canyon on the south side of Nine Mile about 0.2 mile below the mouth of Bull Canyon are eight small structures, five about 30 m. above the canyon floor and three about 25 m. above it. All are of stone and adobe masonry; all are on ledges under overhangs; no two are contiguous; and only one is nearly complete. This one, which lacks only part of its roof, consists of a semicircular wall built in front of a hollow in the back wall of the shelter. The wall, 50 cm. high and 15 cm. thick, encloses an area 60 cm. in diameter. Irregularities in the cliff wall behind the structure had been smoothed off with adobe plaster. A few variations in construction were noted in some of the other structures. One had a wall that included some large blocks of stone, another wall was predominantly adobe, and a large vertical slab formed part of yet another wall.

PR 4-5

An open site composed of nine to twelve rooms is located on a ridge situated between Nine Mile Canyon and the mouth of a side canyon which enters it from the south about 0.3 mile below Bull Canyon. The ridge or plateau, about 40 m. long, 15 m. wide, and 40 m. above the canyon floor, can be reached by climbing a steep slope. The structures, which extend for the full length of the plateau, are apparently all circular, and from about 1 to 4 m. in diameter. Most of the rooms have walls still standing to a maximum height of at least 1 m., sometimes 3 m., and most have much fallen rock around and in them. Construction is of rectangular slabs of varying sizes, chinked with smaller stones. No evidence of adobe was found.

One room had a northwest-facing floor-level doorway 54 cm. wide and 60 cm. high, with a stone slab lintel 78 by 28 by 6 cm. The walls thickened to 0.8 m. on one side of the doorway and to 1.5 m. on the other.

SPECIMENS

Pottery sherds	
Uinta Gray	7
Emery Gray	1
Tusayan (?) Corrugated	1
Mancos (?) Black-on-white	1
Mancos (?) Corrugated	1
Stone chips	X

The sherd of Emery Gray had been broken and the edges partly ground to form a disk about 2 cm. in diameter. The painted sherd was decorated with very irregular vertical lines on the inside and the thinned lip had been painted also.

PR 4-6

In the north wall of Nine Mile Canyon, 60 m. above its floor and 0.6 mile below the mouth of Bull Canyon, there is an oval ledge 5 by 2.8 m. that is about half covered by an overhang 3 m. above it. A portion of a wall that probably once extended nearly across the entire shelter still stands 2.1 m. high. The area behind the wall had been leveled by filling with adobe to within about 90 cm. of the top of the remaining wall fragment. (At the front of the room the adobe floor rises

to within 55 cm. of the top of the wall.) Wall construction is of roughly coursed stone slabs laid in adobe mortar.

In one corner of the room so formed are the remains of a small storage room 0.85 by 1 m. and 1.1 m. high (inside measurements). It had been either rectangular or quadrant-shaped and had been constructed of roughly coursed stone slabs laid in and plastered with an abundance of adobe mortar. The floor was of adobe and slightly basin-shaped. It had had a roof made of two layers of sticks about 1.5 cm. in diameter and 5 to 10 cm. apart. The layers were laid at right angles and covered with a layer of adobe which was topped with a layer of stone slabs, chinked and plastered with adobe. A circular stone slab 60 cm. in diameter and 2 to 4 cm. thick was found in the shelter and had probably been a cover for this small structure.

SPECIMENS

Cord	2
Arrowshaft fragment (?)	1
Twisted withes	5
Cornhusk	X
Corncob	1
Bone fragments	2
Hide fragment	1

Both pieces of cord are two-ply, Z-twist. One piece, 2 mm. in diameter, is of yucca fiber; the other, 3 mm. in diameter, is of juniper bark. The fragment of hide is an irregular strip of soft buckskin about 5 mm. wide. The cornhusk had been tied in three knots. A stick about 6 mm. in diameter with the bark still on it is wrapped with a few turns of sinew near one end, which had been roughly cut off. The other end of the specimen, which may be part of an arrow, is broken.

PR 4-7

In a crevice 40 m. northeast of and about 25 m. above PR 4-6 are two small structures. One consists of a wall 1.3 m. high enclosing a portion of the crevice 1 m. wide at the top of the wall and 55 cm. wide at the bottom. Construction is of irregular stone slabs laid in adobe mortar. Just below this structure is a cist 85 cm. in diameter and 1 m. deep, made of six vertical stone slabs that average about 80 by 25 by 2 cm. The bottom of the cist is the bottom of the crevice.

PR 4-8

Two inaccessible structures, one built on top of the other, are located in a southeast-facing shelter in a sheer wall 8 m. above the top of a talus slope on the north side of, and 70 m. above, the floor of Nine Mile Canyon, about 0.6 mile below the mouth of Bull Canyon. The front wall of the lower structure, over 1 m. long and about 1 m. high, is constructed of rocks, slabs, and adobe and appears to be supported, at least in part, by two or three horizontal logs about 15 cm. in diameter. Four vertical poles 4 m. long and 8 cm. in diameter are incorporated in the wall. The roof is formed by logs 6 to 8 cm. in diameter running perpendicular to the cliff wall.

The roof of the lower structure forms the floor of the upper structure (or structures). A semicircular 80-cm.-high wall of coursed slabs and adobe had been built against the cliff face. In front of this there appears to have been another wall, only the ends of which remain.

PR 4-11: Nordell's Fort

The best-preserved structure in the region, a "fort" or tower (fig. 33A) built on the end of a high, steep-sided ridge, is located on the south side of Nine Mile Canyon about 0.5 mile above the mouth of Bull Canyon. The site has been described previously by Gunnerson (1957 a, p. 68) and given the number 42Dc5. The structure, built on bedrock, conforms to the shape of the end of the point, which it completely occupies. It is essentially rectangular with rounded corners and measures 6.2 by 5.75 m. The wall has a maximum height of 2.24 m. and a thickness of 40 to 68 cm. It is carefully constructed of a double row of dry-laid stone slabs chinked with smaller stones. There is a floor-level doorway 54 cm. wide and 64 cm. high, with a two-piece stone lintel, through the southwest side of the room, making it accessible from the ridge upon which it is built.

About 16 m. southwest of the main structure where the ridge joins the canyon wall are some stone slabs, in places two or three courses high, suggesting another structure about 2 by 4 m.

SPECIMENS

Scrap of worked bone	1
Bone fragments	X

PR 4-12

A crude coursed stone wall is located on top of a pinnacle 30 m. high on the west side of Mack Canyon, about 100 m. above its confluence with Nine Mile Canyon. The east face of the pinnacle is almost sheer, but access can be gained by climbing a steep slope behind the structure.

PR 4-13

A small structure (fig. 33B) was found in an east-facing overhang in the left wall of Nine Mile Canyon, about 25 m. east of the mouth of Frank's Canyon, and about 30 m. above the canyon floor. The remaining wall of this structure, of coursed stone and adobe masonry, is 2.4 m. long and from 0.6 to 1.8 m. high. Differences in construction suggest that additions had been made to the original wall.

SPECIMENS

Pottery sherds	
Emery Gray	8
Stone chips and flakes	4

All specimens were collected on the slope below the site.

PR 4-14

An open site consisting of four structures is located on a 30-by-10-m. ridge about 300 m. up Frank's Canyon from its mouth and from 15 to 30 m. above the canyon floor. All structures are represented by crude stone walls, one of which is about 1 m. high. There is a circular wall 1.5 to 1.75 m. in diameter. Another, the best preserved of the four, is rectangular with no evidence of a south wall. The third, semicircular, is also open to the south. The fourth structure is 1.5 m. wide and has an opening to the west.

PR 4-15

There is an open site with at least three structures on a low bench jutting into Nine Mile Canyon from the south about 1 mile above the mouth of Bull Canyon. Approach to the bench, the lowest point of which is about 15 m. above the canyon floor, is up one of two steep slopes.

One rectangular room 4.65 by 5.15 m. is represented by a north wall of thick horizontal stone slabs laid two courses high and a west wall of two large slabs standing on end, the largest about 1 m. high. Test excavations revealed ash and charcoal from 12 to 39 cm. deep within this structure and, at 23 cm., two heavily burned stone-slab-paved "hearths," one about 46 cm. in diameter, the other about 81 by 52 cm. These could have been part of one large paved area, since a previous excavation between them had disturbed both.

A somewhat scattered circle of rocks suggested a second structure about 3.3 m. in diameter. Excavation within it revealed only charcoal. A metate fragment was found directly outside the circle.

At the edge of the bench on a minor projection is a pile of rocks that may represent a third structure, but original size and shape could not be determined.

In a cleft in the cliff 1.8 m. below this third possible structure were found traces of adobe and two stones set in adobe, apparently the remains of a small storage room.

SPECIMENS

Metate fragment	1
Mano (?)	1
Chips	3

The metate fragment, of light gray sandstone, is from a well-made specimen with a trough about 3 cm. deep. It appears to have been well finished except for the bottom (outside) which was left rough. An elongate cobble of the same material may have been used as a mano, but shows no modification except for possible abrasion on one surface.

PR 4-16

Test pits were dug in a rock shelter at the level of the canyon floor on the north side of Nine Mile Canyon 0.8 mile above the mouth of Bull Canyon. Nothing was found except a little charcoal and ash 20 to 27 cm. below the surface.

PR 4-17

An open site that showed some evidence of stone structures was located on a bench on the south side of Nine Mile Canyon, about 0.2 mile below Frank's Canyon.

PR 4-18

A small storage structure with three rooms was observed on the east side of Desborough Canyon, about 60 m. from its mouth and 15 m. above the canyon floor. The front wall, 3 to 4 m. long and about 1 m. high, is of stone-and-adobe masonry plastered with adobe on the outside and supported at one end by a pole.

PR 4-19

The remains of five small structures are situated about 6 m. above the canyon floor under a slight overhang in the side of a bench that extends into Nine Mile Canyon from the north about 1 mile above Frank's Canyon. The only structure even partially preserved consists of a semicircular wall about 1 m. in diameter and 1.2 m. high made of stone slabs and adobe mortar. The others were probably similar.

PR 4-20

The remains of four small structures were found under an overhang about 3 m. long in the north wall of Nine Mile Canyon, just below the mouth of Desborough Canyon and about 30 m. above the canyon floor. The shape of all four had apparently been dictated by expediency in that naturally occurring niches had been walled up as simply as possible. In one case, a corner had been partially closed in by leaning a slab 75 by 55 cm. from the floor to the ceiling of a niche and sealing the edges with adobe. Other similarly placed slabs had probably been used to finish enclosing an area about 0.65 by 1 m., which was 25 cm. below the level of the surrounding part of the ledge.

A second structure, enclosing an area about 0.55 by 1.0 m., was also built around two sides of a hole 25 cm. deep. A corner in the cliff formed two walls, and slabs leaned against these and sealed in place with adobe had completed the enclosure. Two other large slabs formed most of the roof.

Traces of adobe showed the location of

another structure, about 0.9 by 1.25 m., which had been built in front of a concavity in the back wall of the shelter. Similar evidence indicated a fourth structure along the cliff which had apparently been 1.3 m. long.

SPECIMENS

Pottery sherds	
Emery Gray	13
Chipped blade fragment	1
Chips	2

These specimens were found on the slope below the site.

PR 4-21

At least two structures appear to be represented by scattered stones on top of the bench in the side of which Site PR 4-19 is located. In only one of these, a circular structure 3.35 m. in diameter, were the stones still sufficiently in place to indicate original size or shape.

SPECIMENS

Pottery sherds	
Uinta Gray	1
Moenkopi Corrugated	1

PR 4-22

On the same bench and about 0.2 mile southwest of PR 4-21 are the remains of another stone structure in the open overlooking the valley floor about 100 m. below.

PR 4-23

On the south side of Nine Mile Canyon about 30 m. above the floor, and just below the mouth of Pinnacle Canyon, is an open site with three probable structures, all represented by wall remnants. Two of these, 4.15 and 1.2 m. in diameter, appear to have been circular. The third, about 20 m. higher up the cliff, consists of a wall 60 cm. high and 4.15 m. long that extends from an overhang. Results of limited testing in the three structures were negative.

SPECIMENS

Pottery sherd	
Snake Valley Gray	1

PR 4-24

A small structure is located about 11 m. above the floor of Nine Mile Canyon in its north wall, about 30 m. east of the mouth of Devil's Canyon. The structure, 1.3 m. in diameter and, at present, 1.5 m. high, is constructed of five courses of stone alternating with layers of adobe mortar.

PR 4-25

The most extensive site (fig. 11) along Nine Mile Canyon is on a butte at the end of the ridge that forms the divide between Nine Mile and Devil's canyons at their junction. On three sides of the butte there is a nearly sheer drop of about 100 m. to the canyon floors below. Between the butte and the canyon wall proper there is a saddle about 50 m. high which can be reached by climbing up a steep talus slope from Devil's Canyon. The butte becomes progressively smaller toward the top, leaving a series of ledges, some of which are accessible only from above. The lowest ledge, about 10 m. above the saddle, can be gained only by a not-too-difficult climb up a chimney. A relatively easy trail leads from this ledge to the top of the butte.

At the top of the chimney are walls that can be interpreted only as defensive. The main wall is built across the trail, so that anyone wishing to ascend the butte must go through a doorway. This wall, 7 m. long and standing 1.7 m. high, is crudely built of very large stone blocks. The doorway, 86 cm. wide and 94 cm. high, is spanned by an immense stone lintel (1.1 by 0.67 by 0.14 m.) supported at one end by the wall and at the other end by a ledge.

On a moderately wide ledge about 5 m. above the top of the chimney are several walls perpendicular to the cliff face, obviously parts of structures. Excavation within these rooms revealed detritus-rich fill, in places up to 35 cm. thick, resting on bedrock.

On a narrow ledge under a slight overhang on the west side of the butte and about 6 m. below its top are three small semicircular storage structures built of a combination of vertical stone slabs and small horizontal slabs set in adobe mortar. One of these structures, which has a roof of horizontal stone slabs covered with adobe, has an outside diameter of 1 m. and an inside height of 42 cm. Near by, two similar structures that share one wall

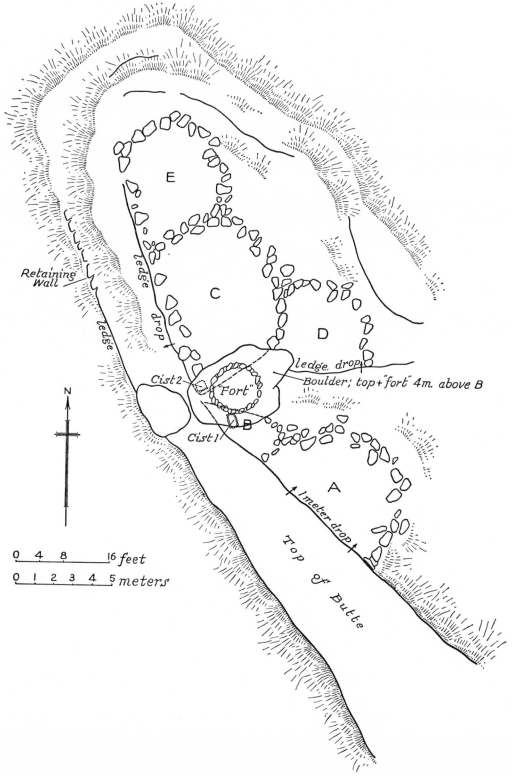

Retaining
Wall

ledge

ledge drop

E

C

D

Cist 2

"Fort"

ledge drop

Boulder; top+"fort" 4m. above B

B

Cist 1

A

1 meter drop

Top of Butte

N

0 4 8   16 feet
0 1 2 3 4 5 meters

Fig. 11. Plan of Site PR 4-25.

extend from the floor to the roof of the small overhang which contains them. They are 65 cm. high and measure 1.57 by 1.25 and 1.1 by 0.97 m., respectively.

On the next lower ledge on the west side is another fragment of a wall and about 10 m. lower still, on an apparently inaccessible ledge, is another small stone-and-adobe structure. Other ledges also show traces of structures.

Almost at the top of the butte on its southeast side are two contiguous semicircular rooms (A and B) constructed of a combination of vertical and horizontal slabs. The walls, in no place exceeding 60 cm. in height, enclose areas 7.4 by 4.75 and 4.5 by 2 m., respectively. The latter area is partially under an overhang which also shelters a slab-lined cist (Cist 1) 45 by 75 cm. and 49 cm. deep. The cist had apparently been covered with sticks and adobe, much of which was found in its fill along with other detritus.

On the other side of the summit are three more semicircular contiguous structures (Rooms C, D and E), now represented only by low stone-slab-and-rock walls. The approximate measurements of these structures are 7.7 by 6, 4.6 by 4.35, and 5 by 5.65 m., respectively. In Room E, under a slight overhang, there are the remains of a slab-lined cist at least 1 m. wide that had been sealed with adobe. An ashy hearth area was also found in this room 8 to 10 cm. above bedrock and 23 cm. below the top of the fill.

On top of the large boulder that caps the butte is a circular wall 2.67 m. in diameter and still standing 63 cm. high. Scattered stones attest to a considerably greater original height.

On the saddle, and hence not within the area protected by the defensive wall, is at least one and probably many structures built in the open. The one obvious structure is represented by a stone circle standing two to three courses high.

SPECIMENS	Room E	Cist 1	Lower Ledge	Slope below Site
Pottery sherds				
Emery Gray	3	–	–	51
Uinta Gray	–	1	–	13
Uinta Tooled	–	–	1	–
Sevier Gray	–	–	–	1
Unidentified gray	–	–	–	3
Emery Tooled	–	–	–	2
Mancos (?) Black-on-white	–	–	–	1
Mano	–	–	1	–
Retouched flake	–	–	–	1
Chips and flakes	–	–	16	4
Awl (?) fragment	–	–	1	–
Bone fragments	–	1	X	–
Sticks and reeds	–	X	X	–
Corncobs	–	3	3	–
Cornhusk	–	3	1	–
Cucurbita fragments	–	–	2	–
Cedar bark	–	–	X	–

A few of the sherds deserve special mention. The Uinta Tooled sherd is part of a strap handle 2 cm. wide and 1.2 cm. thick. Numerous punctations in the outer side had been made with a round tool about 1.5 mm. in diameter. One of the Emery Gray sherds is a fragment of a slightly larger undecorated handle. The Emery Tooled sherds are decorated with vertical (?) parallel incised lines 0.7 to 1.2 cm. apart. Between and perpendicular to these lines are rows of slightly curved punctations, possibly made with a fingernail to produce a pattern somewhat suggestive of indented corrugation. The painted sherd has a Dogoszhi-style decoration on the outer surface. The unidentified plain gray sherds are tempered with coarse, somewhat angular sand but otherwise are not unlike Uinta Gray sherds.

The mano is especially large, having a 20-by-8-cm. grinding surface (convex in both directions) and a thickness of 10.5 cm. This specimen is of white sandstone, finished on all surfaces, and is roughly rectangular, with rounded edges and corners.

PR 4-26

The remains of three small structures were observed on the south side of Nine Mile Canyon, about 80 m. above the canyon floor and about 0.5 mile below the mouth of Cottonwood Canyon. The structures are in a nearly sheer section of canyon wall and appear to be inaccessible.

PR 4-27

This site includes pictographs as well as a variety of structures situated both in the open and under overhangs. It is located on the north side of Nine Mile Canyon about 60 m. above the floor, and about 0.5 mile above the mouth of Cottonwood Canyon. There are six structures on an open bench and two of these are represented by circular free-standing stone walls with outside diameters of 3.75 and 6.5 m. The other four, built against a cliff, are semicircular, with the cliff forming the straight wall. The measurements of these structures are 7 by 6 m., 2 by 0.7 m., 4.2 by 2.8 m., and 5.4 by ? m., the first measurement being that of the wall formed by the cliff. The amount of fallen stone around the open structures suggests that the stone portions of these walls had been higher than those at many of the sites in the area. Also in the open is a cist about 60 cm. deep and 40 to 50 cm. in diameter. When the cist was cleaned out, a stone slab, presumably its cover, was found in it.

A small storage room was found in a niche about 4 m. above the bench upon which the open structures were built; it is about 1 m. in diameter and constructed of alternate layers of stone and adobe with one vertical slab incorporated in the wall. A vertical cleft in the cliff about 12 to 15 m. above the bench contained a platform of logs, apparently the floor of another structure, upon which a little detritus was found.

SPECIMENS

Pottery sherds	
Emery Gray	24
Emery Tooled	1
Emery Corrugated	1
Uinta Gray	8
Manos	2
Cord	1
Corncobs	16
Cornhusk	X
Corn kernels	X
Cedar bark	X

Each mano has one essentially rectangular grinding surface that is convex lengthwise and, to a limited extent, crosswise as well, and each is of sandstone. The better-made one is finished all over, has slight depressions on both sides that provide a better grip, and a convex upper surface. It measures 15.7 by 6.7 cm. and has a maximum thickness of 6.1 cm. The other specimen is 17.7 by 6.9 by 5.2

cm. and has a natural smooth depression on one side which could serve as a thumb grip.

The cord, two-ply, Z-twist and 3 mm. in diameter, is made of juniper bark.

PR 4-28

A rock shelter with a southern exposure offering exceedingly good protection against the elements is located about 4 miles up Dry Canyon from its mouth. The shelter, which has a floor about 5 by 25 m. and a ceiling 2.5 m. high, is situated behind a pile of fallen rock and earth about 25 m. above the floor of the canyon. Two piles of rocks within the shelter are probably the remains of structures. Testing revealed a little detritus to a depth of 67 cm., where bedrock was encountered. Occupation, however, had apparently not been intensive.

SPECIMENS

Mat fragment	1
Cord	1
Corncobs	5
Cornhusk	X
Cucurbita fragment	1
Twisted sticks	2

A fragment of a very frayed twined mat was recovered. Each warp element apparently consisted of two bulrush (*scirpus*) stems and the weft elements (single-ply, Z-spun of juniper bark) were about 3 cm. apart. The cord, two-ply, Z-twist, was about 2 mm. in diameter and also made of juniper bark.

PR 4-29

Two small storage structures are situated on ledges on the west side of Dry Canyon about 2.5 m. above the canyon floor and about 1 mile above the canyon mouth. One structure, 75 cm. in diameter and 60 cm. high, consists of alternate layers of stone and adobe with an adobe-and-stone roof supported on poles. Through the roof is a hole surrounded by an adobe collar and fitted with a stone slab cover 30 cm. in diameter.

The other structure, about the same size, is built almost entirely of adobe turtlebacks, each 3 to 6 cm. thick, 12 to 15 cm. long, and 7 to 8 cm. wide. A few rocks are included in the base of the wall. The roof is missing.

PR 4-30

A large rock shelter well suited for occu-

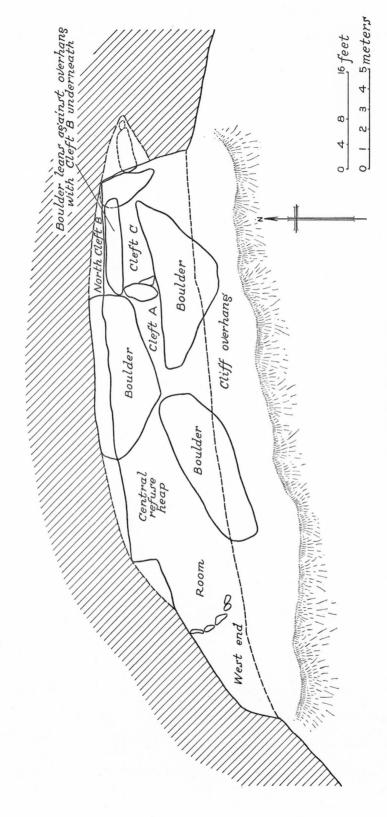

Boulder leans against overhang
with Cleft B underneath

North Cleft B

Cleft C

Cleft A

Boulder

Boulder

Cliff overhang

Boulder

Central
refuse
heap

Boulder

Room

West end

0   4   8   16 feet

0   1   2   3   4   5 meters

N

Fig. 12. Plan of Site PR 4-31.

pation is located about 1.5 miles up Cottonwood Canyon from its mouth. Testing revealed, about 60 cm. below the shelter floor, a thin layer of ash and charcoal upon which a mano was found. Occupation had apparently been very limited.

SPECIMENS

Mano   1

This mano, of sandstone, is 18 by 7 cm. by 5.5 cm. thick, has a grinding surface that is convex in both directions, and is essentially rectangular with convex sides and ends. One of the edges is slightly convex lengthwise and may also have been used for grinding. The upper surface has been shaped to a limited extent.

PR 4-31: Rasmussen Cave

Extensive excavation was carried out in a rock shelter with a southeast exposure located across Nine Mile Canyon from the mouth of Dry Canyon. The shelter, 10 to 15 m. up a rock-strewn slope from the canyon floor, is 28.8 m. long and has a maximum width of 6.5 m. Within the shelter (figs. 12, 34A) are many large angular boulders or blocks, fallen from the ceiling, which divide the shelter into areas of varying sizes. The largest areas (west and central) had been lived in and contained, in addition to refuse, occupation levels and the remains of a structure. To the east are three narrow clefts between fallen boulders which had been filled with rubbish. This site, also visited by Morss (1931, p. 29) and designated by him as Site No. 31, had previously been subjected to a great deal of indiscriminate digging, especially in the central part, by people in search of "mummies," three to eight of which had allegedly been found. A great deal of very interesting material was said to have been found in this site about a month prior to the excavation herein reported, but the fate of this collection, excavated by two individuals from Myton, Utah, according to Reagan (1933, pp. 57–58), is unknown. The Claflin-Emerson excavations at this site produced evidence of two distinct cultures. The earlier was represented by a Basketmaker II–like burial and the later by detritus and part of a structure, probably of Fremont affiliation. These two complexes and their as-

sociated artifacts will be discussed separately.

FREMONT COMPONENT

There was no evidence of disturbance at the far west end of the shelter, that is, beyond the possible structure. Excavation here produced four figurine fragments 45 cm. below the surface and a flint blade and an ear of dent corn between 45 and 60 cm. below the surface.

The structure was represented only by its west wall, the remainder presumably having been destroyed by "mummy hunters." The wall, consisting of vertical stone slabs, extended about 40 to 45 cm. below the modern surface. A charcoal-hearth layer and a section of floor or occupation level were found about 35 to 45 cm. below the surface. Detritus at this level included one sherd, bone fragments, stone chips, withes, cord, and cornhusk. A restorable olla, possibly associated with the structure, was found between 45 and 60 cm. deep. Below what had probably been the limits of the structure was a layer of detritus-rich fill, in places as much as 65 cm. thick, resting on bedrock. Charcoal and corncobs were found all through this lower layer, but most of the artifacts, including two metates, were in a level near its midpoint that was especially rich in charcoal.

The central area, to the east of the structure and concealed from the outside by a large boulder, is the largest rock-free area in the shelter and contained a great deal of refuse. Here the upper 80 cm. of fill had been repeatedly dug through, making the stratigraphic position of artifacts recovered meaningless. However, living surfaces, the upper one possibly deliberately prepared of earth, were found at depths of 0.8 and 1.23 m. Artifacts and detritus were associated with both surfaces, but below the lower one detritus consisted of a little charcoal and a few flint chips to a depth of 1.7 m., where the fill became sterile. The lower portion of the fill extended under the edge of a large boulder, but the temporal relationship between the refuse deposit and the falling of the boulder could not be determined.

Clefts B and C in the shelter were quite small, but both yielded specimens from undisturbed deposits, apparently Fremont.

Part of the fill in Cleft A had been removed previously by persons unknown, but they had stopped just a few centimeters short of encountering the lower part of a skeleton, the upper part of which was still covered by about 1 m. of refuse. The most significant objects found in the refuse above the skeleton were a burned figurine (found in some burned refuse) and a figurine head, both from 60 to 90 cm. above the skeleton and in no way associated with it. A little detritus had apparently sifted down around the burial from the refuse which accumulated above it, perhaps with the help of rodent activity.

Specimens (Fremont component)	Below room, 35 cm.	45-60 cm.	70 cm.	85-115 cm.	Center, 80 cm.	123 cm.	Cleft A, 0-20 cm.	30-50 cm.	50-80 cm.	near burial	Cleft B	Cleft C	West end	Site general
Pottery, Emery Gray	1	1	–	–	–	–	–	–	–	–	–	–	–	–
Figurines & fragments	–	–	–	–	–	–	2	–	–	–	2	8	6	1
Clay cone	–	–	–	–	–	–	–	–	–	–	–	–	–	–
Clay blobs	5	–	–	–	–	–	–	–	–	–	–	–	–	6
Adobe samples	7	–	–	–	–	–	–	–	–	–	–	–	–	–
Stone points	–	–	1	–	–	–	–	–	–	–	–	–	–	–
Blades & fragments	–	–	–	–	1	1	–	–	–	–	–	–	–	–
Crude blade	–	–	–	–	–	–	–	–	–	–	–	–	1	–
Scraper	–	1	–	–	–	–	–	–	–	–	–	–	–	–
Manos	–	–	–	–	–	–	–	–	–	–	–	–	–	3
Flakes & chips	–	–	–	1	–	2	–	–	–	–	–	–	–	–
Concretions	–	–	–	–	–	–	–	–	–	–	–	–	–	2
Asphaltum chunk	–	–	–	–	–	–	–	–	–	–	–	–	–	1
Bone awl fragment	–	–	–	–	–	–	–	–	1	–	–	–	–	–
Bone bead	–	–	–	–	–	–	–	–	–	–	–	1	–	–
Worked antler	–	–	–	–	–	–	–	1	–	–	–	–	–	–
Bone fragments	24	–	2	6	9	6	–	–	8	15	1	1	1	2
Hide fragments	–	–	–	–	–	1	–	–	–	?	–	–	–	–
Fur cloth fragments	–	–	–	–	–	–	–	–	1	?	–	–	–	–
Cord fragments	1	–	–	1	–	–	–	–	1	?	1	–	–	–
Reed tube	1	–	–	–	–	–	–	–	–	–	–	–	–	–
Reed mat fragments	–	–	–	–	–	–	1	–	–	–	–	–	–	1
Basket fragments	–	–	–	–	–	–	–	–	1	–	–	–	–	2
Basketry material	–	–	–	–	–	–	–	–	–	X	–	–	–	–
Digging stick	–	–	–	–	–	–	–	–	–	–	–	–	–	1
Misc. worked wood	–	–	–	–	1	–	–	–	–	–	–	–	–	3
Unworked plant	–	–	2	–	2	1	–	2	–	3	–	–	–	4
Cucurbita fragments	–	–	–	–	–	–	–	–	2	–	–	–	–	–
Corncobs	–	–	2	5	4	1	–	–	–	15	–	–	–	13
Cobs on sticks	–	–	–	2	–	–	–	–	–	–	–	–	–	–
Ears of corn	–	–	1	6	–	–	–	–	–	–	–	–	–	–

Pottery from this site was restricted to one restorable vessel (fig. 44, *a*) about 60 per cent complete, and one sherd which had probably not been part of the vessel, even though they were both Emery Gray. The vessel is a flat-bottomed olla 20 cm. high, with a maximum diameter of 21 cm. about 9 cm. above the bottom. The rim is flaring, about 2 cm. high, and has a maximum outside diameter at the lip of 17.5 cm. The diameter of the orifice is 14.3 cm. One essentially circular handle 1.9 cm. wide extends from the lip to a point on the shoulder about 2 cm. below its junction with the rim. The lip is rounded and 5 mm. thick. The vessel wall varies from 3 to 6 mm., the thickest part being the rim. The surface is buff to black, smooth and partially polished.

Fragments of unfired clay figurines in the Fremont style were quite abundant in the upper portion of the cave fill. The better specimens have been illustrated and discussed by Morss (1954, pp. 15–16, fig. 14). Two of the figurines are nearly complete. One of these, from the disturbed central area, is only 3.6 cm. long, 1.7 cm. wide, and 1.3 cm. thick, and roughly elliptical in outline. Its only features are at one end and consist of a median ridge pinched up to form a nose, on either side of which was applied a round pellet about 7 mm. in diameter, with a small hole punched in the center. The other nearly complete specimen, from Cleft B, is more characteristic of Fremont figurines. It is 6.5 cm. long and has a maximum width of 3 cm. at the head end and a maximum thickness at the breasts of 2.1 cm. Facial features are also represented by a pinched median ridge for the nose, flanked by applied and punched pellets for eyes. Hair or a head ornament is represented by a row of round pellets, each about 5 mm. across, which extends along both sides and across the top of the head. Breasts are in prominent relief slightly below the center of the figurine. The lower part, narrower than the head, is featureless.

The third nearly complete figurine was found in a burned area in the top layer in Cleft A and was blackened. The portion remaining is roughly an inverted trapezoid 6.3 cm. long with rounded corners. The break is along the short (2.7 cm.) side where a "skirt" had probably been attached. This figurine is unusually thin, 1.5 cm. at the nose, the thickest place, and has a maximum width of 4.9 cm. The nose is a pinched-up median ridge and the eyes, located almost at the top of the head, are pellets 7 mm. in diameter with a round punctation in the middle. Part of a narrow strip of appliquéd clay remains on one side of the chest and appears to have extended up the side of the head. Two small bumps not far below the tip of the nose probably represent breasts.

Five fragments are from the lower or body portions of figurines. No representation of feet or legs is present on any of these. Two have appliquéd decorations suggestive of belts. In one case, a row of round pellets, each about 6 mm. in diameter, crosses the front at a point where the figurine narrows to 2.2 cm. in width. Below the belt, the specimen expands to a width of 3.4 cm. and a thickness of 2.1 cm. The other belted figurine has an appliquéd and punched band 7 mm. wide crossing it where it is 1.8 cm. across. Below this belt the specimen narrows gradually to a square end 1.3 cm. wide.

The other three figurine termini have skirts or aprons. The most elaborate, from the west end of the shelter, has a "belt" 8 mm. wide around the specimen where it constricts to a width of 2 cm. The belt is painted black, contrasting with the body above, which is painted red. Below the belt is an apron consisting of vertical strips of clay, each 3 mm. wide, over which is draped another band of clay decorated with very fine punctations and red paint. This specimen is widest (2.8 cm.) very near the bottom.

What appears to be about the bottom half of another apron had originally been about 6 cm. wide and 1.6 cm. thick. It is covered with vertical strips of clay, each 6 mm. wide, over which are scattered nine tear-drop-shaped pellets of clay, points up, each about 1.4 by 0.6 cm. This specimen is from Cleft B. The third apron, from Cleft C, consists of a horizontal strip below which are vertical clay strips, each about 4 mm. wide, covering the lower 2.7 cm. of a specimen 3.8 cm. wide. Other figurine fragments are either small or undistinctive.

A crude unfired conical clay object 5.5 cm. long and 3.6 cm. in greatest diameter appears to have been attached to some sort of vessel as a leg or handle. It may, however, be just a piece of clay which had been held in one fist while a finger was pushed into the end.

Several blobs of clay from 3.5 to 5.5 cm. in diameter have one flat side and a roughly rounded opposite side as if balls of clay had been thrown forcibly against a flat rock. None, however, was found adhering to any such surface.

The only projectile point small enough to have been used on an arrow is rather crudely made and has a rounded stem (fig. 43, f). This point, 3.5 by 1.2 cm., 5 mm. thick, and made of brown chalcedony, was found in disturbed fill. Another point, similar to those found with the burial, came from the 70-cm. level under the structure. This point, of dark gray quartzite, 4.6 by 2.3 cm., is relatively thin and of good workmanship.

The blade from the 123-cm. level in the center of the cave is of gray chert, is a pointed oval, and measures 5.7 by 3.0 by 0.7 cm. (fig. 43, *l*). The one crude blade found is of tan chert, almond-shaped, and chipped entirely by percussion. It measures 6.8 by 4.4 by 1.7 cm. The scraper is a nearly circular flake about 5 cm. in diameter which has a thin unifacially chipped scraping edge about halfway around it on the end opposite the bulb of percussion. The material is tan chalcedony.

Two of the three manos found were just chunks of sandstone of convenient size that had been used. The third, which is fragmentary, is triangular in cross section and 6 cm. thick, and had had an essentially flat rectangular grinding surface, 5 by about 15 cm.

The only significant bone artifact from the site, other than those found with the burial, is a cylindrical bone bead with rounded ends which was made from a section of a mammal long bone. The bead, 2.3 cm. long and 1.3 cm. in diameter, is moderately well finished.

The pieces of fur cloth are all very fragmentary, but some idea of the range of variation can be gained from them. The only piece in which warp and weft are still together has warp elements made by twisting together two narrow strips of hide, each about 1 to 2 mm. wide. The weft consists of strips of buckskin 5 to 7 mm. wide. Construction is by twining, with the warp elements about 1 cm. apart and the weft about 2 cm. apart. Other loose strands appear to be from this type of fur cloth. A second type, represented by only one strand, has a core of two-ply, Z-twist, S-spun cord of yucca fiber around which was wrapped a strip of hide from 2 to 5 mm. wide.

All the miscellaneous pieces of cord from this site are two-ply, Z-twist, S-spun, and most are well made. Diameters vary from 2 to 4 mm. and the fiber was primarily juniper bark, although some of the pieces were of yucca fiber and a few were mixed juniper and Indian hemp. The only pieces that are not well made are of juniper bark and were found in Cleft B.

A section of reed (*phragmites communis*) 5.4 cm. long and 1.1 cm. in diameter has been carefully cut at both ends but shows no further modification or evidence of use.

The best example of twined rush matting was found in a disturbed area. The width of the flattened rushes that form the warp is 5 mm. and the distance between the cords that form the weft is 2.5 cm. At the edge, the rushes have been doubled back on themselves around some sort of cord that is now missing. No loose ends of rushes could be found in the 20-cm.-wide strip of mat preserved, except, of course, along broken edges. The weft had progressed back and forth across the piece and was twisted on itself at the edge to provide the spacing between weft elements. A hole in the mat had been crudely mended with flattened grass stems. The warp of the mat is bulrush (*scirpus*) and both juniper and Indian hemp fiber cord were used for the weft.

The other mat fragment, also twined, is somewhat coarser with warp elements about 8 mm. wide and weft elements about 4.5 cm. apart. It is made of rushes (*scirpus*) and cord consisting of Indian hemp (*Apocynum*) fiber.

The largest piece of basketry recovered is the bottom (14 cm. in diameter) of a coiled basket, found in Cleft A. The foundation is a half-rod and bundle, probably of squawbush and yucca, respectively. It is tightly sewed with thin strips of squawbush with about 3 stitches per cm. The stitches are noninterlocking and most of them are split. The basket bottom had apparently been sewed back onto the rest of the basket with a coarse cord after it had broken away. The rods are about 5 mm. wide and 2 mm. thick, while the stitching material is about 2 mm. wide. The bundle is quite thin. There are about 2 coils per cm. Two small fragments, possibly from the same basket, are of essentially the same construction as the first, but are somewhat finer and more neatly woven.

A bundle of about 200 willow wands, carefully debarked, was found tied together with a strip of willow bark. The stems, up to 70 cm. long and 4 mm. in diameter, had apparently been gathered and cached for future basket making.

The digging stick, a nearly straight piece

of wood 62 cm. long and 3 cm. in maximum diameter, tapers gently to a rounded point at one end and is roughly broken off at the other. The tapered portion shows much polish, presumably from use.

Two pieces of stick which have been roughly pointed at one end but modified in no other way show polish, probably from use, on the points. They are 22 by 0.8 cm. and 18 by 0.6 cm., respectively.

A piece of soft wood is interesting in that it has designs lightly burned into both surfaces. The piece is roughly rectangular, 5.9 cm. long, 1.9 cm. wide, and 3 mm. thick, and does not seem to be either deliberately shaped or broken from a larger decorated artifact. On one side three chevrons and three zigzag lines cross the specimen. On the other side it is crossed by three straight lines, three straight lines broken in the middle, one zigzag line, a row of three large dots, and two rows of about ten small dots. The lines are about 2 mm. wide. This specimen is from a disturbed area in the site.

BASKETMAKER-LIKE BURIAL

The individual was lying on his left side in a flexed position (fig. 34B) on the refuse-free bottom of a crevice (Cleft A) with his head partially under a slight overhang formed by one of the boulders. The skeleton is described in Appendix III. The body had been covered with grass, but not with earth, and refuse had accumulated above it. Many objects (fig. 41) were apparently associated with the body. In front of the face were an animal tooth grooved for suspension and three spear foreshafts, two with stone points in place. There was a pair of moccasins over the head and a bundle consisting of a pair of buckskin leggings was under the head. Also found beneath the head was an extra moccasin tied with a piece of cedar bark. It was probably a medicine bundle, since it contained red paint pigment in a small buckskin pouch, a serrated bone artifact, a hafted blade (now missing), the wooden portions of four spear foreshafts and a piece of worked horn (possibly a flaker). Behind the skeleton were an atlatl, two broken spearshafts, a hafted bone flaker, a flint drill, and five chipped blades. There was a skin bag or legging under the

skeleton and a bone awl in front of the abdominal region. Also possibly associated were a piece of fur cloth and miscellaneous pieces of cordage including a tump line and some fragments of hide. There is little evidence to associate the individual with the occupation of the shelter, which he obviously predated. The artifacts buried with this man closely resemble what could be expected in a Basketmaker II burial except for the hide moccasins and leggings. This burial is probably assignable to the Uncompahgre complex or to the Basketmaker culture of the Anasazi area.

Since no habitation sites reported from Nine Mile Canyon or adjacent areas appear to have the same cultural affiliation as the burial, it is possible that the individual died and was buried far from home. Nothing associated with him would be out of place for a man to have been carrying on a hunting or exploring trip.

SPECIMENS (with burial)

Stone points	2
Stone blades	5
Stone drill	1
Bone awl	1
Serrated bone artifact	1
Tooth pendant	1
Worked horn	1
Flaker, hafted	1
Spearshaft	1
Spear foreshaft	1
Atlatl	1
Moccasins	3
Leggings	2
Buckskin bag of paint	1
Hide fragments	X?
Cord fragments	X?
Fur cloth fragments	X?
Tump line	1?
Grass	X

The two points from the burial, both hafted on spear foreshafts, are triangular with extreme corner notching that leaves a stem with nearly parallel (slightly diverging) sides. The points are 6.0 by 2.0 cm. and 4.2 by 2.6 cm. and are of reddish and dark brown chalcedony, respectively.

Four of the five blades associated with the burial are essentially triangular, with both sides and the base slightly convex, and show good workmanship. Two of the blades are symmetrical and unnotched, 8.1 by 2.6 by 0.5 cm. and 5.1 by 2.4 by 0.4 cm. The other two are asymmetrical in that one has only a single corner notch while the other has one large and one small corner notch. These measure 6.0 by 2.6 by 0.5 cm. and 5.9 by 2.6 by 0.6 cm., respectively. All four are of jasper, the smallest red and the others dark brown. The fifth blade from the burial, much thicker and cruder, is of tan jasper. It is oval, 6.3 cm. long, 2.2 cm. wide, and 1.3 cm. thick.

The only drill from the site, of very dark brown jasper, has an expanding base with side notches. Its over-all length is 5.4 cm.; the bit is 2.9 by 0.8 cm.

The one complete awl found with the burial is L-shaped, was made from the spine portion of a scapula, probably deer, and is 15.5 cm. long.

A serrated bone artifact, possibly a flesher, was probably made from a nearly flat section of scapula scraped down on both surfaces until it is only about 2 mm. thick. It is trapezoidal, 13.6 cm. long, 3.5 cm. wide at one end, and 6 cm. wide at the other end, into which were cut 15 notches 1 to 2 mm. deep and about 2 mm. wide. This serrated edge is not much sharper than the other edges, but it does seem to show a little more wear. This bone artifact, the function of which is unknown, somewhat resembles horn artifacts from Lovelock Cave (Loud and Harrington, 1929, plate 15, g) and White Dog Cave (Guernsey and Kidder, 19, plate 17, i) and a fragment of a bone "pendant" from Hells Midden (Lister, 1951, fig. 29, b).

A section of horn, possibly designed for use as a flaker, had been carefully worked to a cylinder with an elliptical cross section and at least one rounded end. (The other end has been eaten away by insects.) The portion remaining is 6.6 cm. long, 2 cm. wide, and 1.3 cm. thick.

A canine tooth of a bear (?) has a groove 2 mm. wide and 1 mm. deep cut around it 5 mm. from the root end, presumably so that the specimen could be suspended for an ornament.

An unusual specimen, probably a flaker, has a bone tip hafted on a wooden shaft 96 cm. long and 1.2 cm. in diameter. One end tapers to a rounded point, the other is flattened on one side to accommodate a flat bone tip which is bound in place with sinew. The bone tip,

triangular and 6.3 cm. long, 1.2 cm. wide and 0.4 cm. thick, is rounded on the wide end, which projects 1.2 cm. beyond the end of the wooden shaft. Also held by the same sinew binding is a strip of buckskin 0.5 cm. wide which extends to the end of the bone point where it is sewed to a roughly triangular piece of soft buckskin about 6 by 8 cm.

The shaft is wrapped with two-ply cedar-bark cord for about 1.5 cm., starting 8 cm. from the bone tip. At 30 cm. and again at 65 cm. from this same end, the shaft is wrapped with sinew for distances of 2 cm. and 1.5 cm., respectively. Protruding from under each of these sinew wrappings is a short piece of buckskin about 5 mm. wide which had perhaps been attached to something else. Three light-colored bands around the shaft at distances of 28, 41, and 84 cm. from the bone tip appear to represent other places where the shaft had been wrapped with some material, probably sinew. The shaft has been carefully smoothed over all of its surface except where a large splinter was broken out near the bone tip, but the spiral tool marks were not entirely obliterated by smoothing. This specimen is similar to one from White Dog Cave reported by Guernsey and Kidder (1921, pp. 96–97).

A portion of a spearshaft, probably almost complete, was associated with the burial. The part recovered is 1.51 m. long and has a maximum diameter of 1.3 cm. at one end and 0.9 cm. at the other where it is broken off. The shaft, now somewhat bent, is of solid wood and shows very careful workmanship. It has a uniform taper for its entire length and the surface is not only smoothed but polished. The large end, which is wrapped with sinew for a distance of 3.4 cm., has a tapering hole with a maximum diameter of 0.8 cm. drilled into it to a depth of 2.6 cm. Without doubt, the hole was to accept the foreshaft. A section of the shaft 17 cm. long, starting 7.5 cm. from the small (broken) end, is red and appears to have been so painted. A band of sinew 3 mm. wide is wrapped around the shaft 8 cm. from the broken end.

Seven wooden spear foreshafts, all of the same design but only two with stone points attached, were found with the burial. The foreshafts varied from 11.2 to 12.8 cm. in length and from 0.9 to 1.0 cm. in diameter. About 4 cm. of one end of each was ground to a blunt point and no effort was made to obliterate the spiral tool marks. Into the other end was cut a cleft 2 to 3 mm. wide and 1.0 to 1.2 cm. deep for the insertion of the base of a stone point. The point was held in place by a sinew wrapping which not only surrounded the stem of the point but also extended up the foreshaft for about 7 mm. The stems of the points are a little wider than the foreshafts and have their maximum widths at their bases rather than where they attach to the blades.

The atlatl from the site is quite well preserved and lacks only the finger loops. It is made from a slightly curved piece of wood 55 cm. long, 1.7 to 2.2 cm. wide, and 0.6 to 0.9 cm. thick. The spur that engages the dart is 2.4 cm. from one end and was left as a projection into a groove 8 cm. long, 9 mm. wide, and 5 mm. deep that had been carved on the inner surface. The weight is an elongate egg-shaped white pebble 6.0 by 2.4 by 2.0 cm., with one flat side which is bound against the outside of the atlatl with sinew and rawhide so that its center is 21.5 cm. from the spur end. A strip of deer hide 1.5 cm. wide with the hair left on had been bound with sinew to the outside of the atlatl 2 cm. from the end of the weight. The remaining portion of the strip is now only 11 cm. long, but hairs stuck to the atlatl suggest that the strip originally extended nearly to the spur end. The hide appears to have been attached only at one end, so that it would have fluttered like a streamer. A broad and a narrow groove, contiguous to each other, had been cut into each edge of the handle end, starting 6.5 cm. from the end and extending for a combined length of 3 cm. Pitch in this area shows that something, presumably finger loops, had been attached here.

The moccasin and the sole that were found at the head of the skeleton appear to have been a pair and to have differed slightly in construction from the third moccasin which served as a container for small objects.

The better-preserved one of the pair is constructed of a single piece of hide folded to form both sole and upper. The fold is along the outer edge of the foot and the two parts are sewn together along the inner side of the foot and across both ends. A piece had been cut out to permit the foot to be inserted. The edge of the sole had been turned up slightly where it attaches to the upper, and added thickness of sole had been obtained by sewing four strips of hide across the bottom of the moccasin. These strips are apparently not patches because there are no holes through the inner sole. A cord had been passed through probably four pairs of closely spaced holes to tighten the moccasin around the ankle. Additional pieces of thinner, softer hide had been sewed around the opening to increase the height, probably to ankle height but perhaps even higher. A strip of this thinner hide 40 cm. long and up to 5 cm. wide appears to have been used as a tie around the ankle. All the hide had had the hair removed and had been incorporated into the moccasin with the hair side out. Sewing was done with two-ply, Z-twist fiber cord. The soles of the moccasins are about 24 by 10 cm. The better-preserved moccasin contained grass, possibly a pad.

The odd moccasin that served as a pouch had a stiff sole with the hair out and was turned up slightly all around the edge. The upper is in two pieces, one piece covering the instep, the other surrounding the heel and providing a flap to be wrapped around the ankle. The piece covering the instep turns under where it joins the sole so that only the edge of the sole is exposed, whereas the heel piece turns out and the edges of both the sole and the upper are here exposed. The two pieces of the upper were sewed together on either side to a height of about 4 cm., with the heel portion outside of the instep portion. A row of holes around the heel about 3 to 5 cm. above the sole had obviously once contained a cord or thong for securing the moccasin to the foot. There is no indication as to how the flap was secured around the ankle. This flap, now 20 cm. high at the highest point, may be incomplete.

Two extra pieces of rawhide have been attached to the bottom of the sole and nearly cover it, but do not overlap and do not extend to the edge. Both pieces are rounded, the larger one under the toes, ball of the foot, and arch, the smaller one under the heel. These appear to be part of the original construction rather than patches, since there are no holes under the front piece. In the middle of the heel piece, however, there is a hole extending through both layers. The sole of the moccasin is 11 by 25 cm.

Most of one legging, the top of a second, and a portion of possibly a third were recovered. The two definite leggings, probably a pair, are from under the head of the skeleton. Except for a small additional piece which is attached near the top and presumably served to attach the leggings to a waist belt, each legging was made of a single piece of rawhide with a seam up the back of the leg. This seam was sewed with sinew in a simple whipping stitch. The leggings had been at least 70 cm. long, 20 cm. wide at the top, and 12 cm. wide near the bottom. There is nothing to suggest that the leggings had been attached to moccasins.

The other possible legging, found under the pelvis of the skeleton, had had the fur or hair left on and was sewed with a two-ply, Z-twist plant fiber cord. It is wide enough (13 cm.) to have been from the lower part of a legging, but it could also have been part of a bag. The preserved portion is 37 cm. long.

The small leather pouch, made by folding a piece of rawhide and sewing it across the bottom and up one side, is about 6 cm. wide and 20 cm. high. It was found inside the moccasin bundle and contained about one ounce of hematite, including one large piece with facets worn on it and many smaller pieces. The top of the bag had been doubled over and a juniper-bark cord tied twice around it. The cord is two-ply, Z-twist and about 1 mm. in diameter.

A large section of a tump strap or burden strap made of juniper-bark cord was possibly associated with the burial. It consisted of a flat portion 2.5 cm. wide, 3 mm. thick, and at least 35 cm. long, made of ten parallel cords, each two-ply, Z-twist, S-spun, sewed together with a similar cord having a smaller diameter. The ten cords were probably in actuality all one continuous piece, doubled back and forth on itself spirally with a loop left in each end. However, only one end has survived. At this end, the cords pass through what is essentially an eye splice at the end of a three-ply, Z-twist, S-spun cord. This cord has a diameter

of 8 mm. to within about 30 cm. of the end, where it starts to thin and where it is doubled back on itself. The thin end is worked into the thicker part of the cord for a distance of 30 cm. to form a very neat and serviceable "splice." The cord is not untwisted as is the end in a regular splice, however. The end of the heavy cord is broken, so it is not possible to determine how long it was originally, but three other pieces of what appears to be the same heavy cord are 0.4, 0.75, and 1.4 m. long. At one end of each of the two longest pieces is a simple overhand knot. Since there is no evidence of a loop splice on any of the loose pieces of cord, it seems likely that at least 30 cm. are missing from even the longest, which suggests that each end cord was at least 1.7 m. long and that the entire specimen had been at least 3.75 m. long.

PR 4-32

The remains of what was probably a structure built in the open are located on a bench on the north side of Nine Mile Canyon about 25 m. above the floor and 0.6 mile above the mouth of Devil's Canyon. In the cliff above the bench are two small structures.

SPECIMENS

Pottery sherds	
Emery Gray	11
Emery Tooled	3
Uinta Gray	4
Chips	3

The tooled sherds, representing at least two vessels, appear to show a deliberate attempt to imitate the appearance of indented corrugation. Two of the sherds have thin horizontal incised lines about 5 mm. apart which have been partially obliterated by broad, smooth, vertical grooves about 1 cm. apart, apparently made by pinching the wet clay. The other sherd has thin horizontal incised lines about 8 mm. apart with vertical fingernail (?) punctations between them. One of the first two sherds has a lip that is nearly square and thickened toward the outside. The last sherd described has a simple rounded lip and appears to be from a bottle. All of the specimens were collected from the float below the site.

FLORENCE AND CHANDLER CREEKS

Florence and Chandler Creeks, each only about 12 miles long, flow through deep narrow canyons to enter the Green River from the east in Desolation Canyon about 5 and 12 miles above the mouth of Range Creek, respectively. The divide between Hill Creek to the east and Florence and Chandler creeks to the west lies on the 8000-to-9000-feet-high East Tavaputs Plateau. The steepness of the canyons, even along their watercourse, makes the climb from the plateau into Florence and Chandler canyons or out again an arduous task. Entrance from the Green River is much easier, which may in part account for the greater concentrations of sites near the creek mouths. Also, it is in this portion of the canyons that alluvial fill is found, enough so that until a few years ago a ranch existed at the mouth of Florence Creek Canyon. The only previous description of sites in these two canyons appears to be that by Reagan (1934).

ET 9-4

Two small structures were found on a narrow ledge on the north side of Florence Creek about 4 miles above its mouth and about 6 or 7 m. above the canyon floor. One structure, of adobe turtlebacks, had been crushed by stone slabs that had fallen on it. It had been supported in part by a cedar pole projecting from the ledge. Six other cedar poles, presumably part of the roof, protruded from the rubble. About 16 m. away was a semicircular wall of stone slabs and adobe laid in courses. This wall, which contained more adobe than stone, had apparently extended from the floor to the ceiling of the shelter.

On the back wall of the shelter about 3 m. above the floor are a number of pictographs. A solid yellow circle about 60 cm. in diameter is nearly surrounded by a brown-red spiral and has a crescent of the same color in its center. Below it are three solid red circles, each about 8 cm. in diameter. Also present are a square-shouldered man, 1 m. tall with long curving horns, and a pecked sheep.

ET 9-5

On the north side of Florence Creek Canyon 3.5 miles above its mouth is a semicircular stone-and-adobe structure built on a ledge 5 m. above the canyon floor in front of a concavity in the cliff face. The wall, supported in part on poles extending out from the ledge, is canted in toward the top and now stands to a maximum height of 75 cm. The room formed is 1.90 by 1.35 m. No evidence of a roof is preserved.

ET 9-6

A two-story structure containing four small rooms is located on a ledge about 10 m. above the canyon floor on the north side of Florence Creek 2 miles above its mouth. The lower level consists of a semicircular outside wall 1.05 m. high, enclosing an area 2 by 3 m., and a partition perpendicular to the cliff that forms the back wall. The roof is supported by poles parallel to the cliff. Entrance to the rooms is through a central opening in the roof. The ends of the roof poles that were cut to make the opening are supported by cross poles tied with withes to uncut poles. The opening is surrounded by a collar made of about 25 withes that had been tied in a bundle about 10 cm. in diameter.

The upper rooms, enclosed by semicircular walls, cover the back one-half of the lower rooms and block about one-third of the entrance to them.

Except for a few stones in the base of the wall of the lower room, construction is entirely of adobe turtlebacks. The roof poles, 15 in number, project 7 to 25 cm. beyond the wall. Part of the lower wall is missing, permitting observation of construction detail.

ET 9-7

Two or possibly three small rooms, one above another, had been built in a cleft in the north wall of Florence Canyon, 1.5 miles above its mouth. Each room is about 1 m. wide and from 0.6 to 1 m. deep. One floor beam is supported by a forked pole which had been built into the wall below. Cedar poles appear to be remnants of a roof. The walls had been constructed of adobe turtlebacks.

ET 9-8

Two small structures about 10 m. apart

are on a ledge about 40 m. above the canyon floor on the north wall of Chandler Canyon, about 4.5 miles from its mouth. One room, beehive-shaped and 1.5 m. wide, is built of coursed stone-and-adobe masonry and at the rear extends to the ceiling of the shelter. It is roofed with adobe turtlebacks supported on cedar poles. A doorway, the top of which has collapsed, is 0.8 to 1 m. wide. The second room is very similar to the first and a third room may be represented by a pile of wood and stone.

ET 9-9

There are four small ruined structures in a rock shelter in the east wall of a side canyon that enters Chandler Canyon from the north about 4.5 miles above its mouth. The rock shelter, about 20 by 5 m. in size and 50 m. above the canyon floor, contains a natural shelf about 1 m. high and 2 m. wide, upon which the structures were built. Each structure was about 1 by 2 m. and the walls had apparently been about 1.2 m. high and 0.6 to 1 m. thick. Construction was of uncoursed stone and adobe with no evidence of wood.

ET 9-10

At the mouth of a side canyon 4.5 miles up Chandler Canyon from its mouth is another cluster of 4 small structures in a rock shelter about 15 m. above the canyon floor. The best-constructed one, semicircular and built against the cliff, has a maximum diameter of 1.6 m. at its bedrock floor, is 56 cm. across its top, and is 77 cm. high. Wall construction is of flat stone slabs laid in adobe. The roof had apparently been supported by a triangle of three poles resting on the walls. The second structure, also semicircular and of stone and adobe but more crudely built, is 50 cm. high and 1.1 m. in greatest diameter across the top. The roof had apparently been supported by a square of four poles. The other two structures were similar to those described.

HILL AND WILLOW CREEKS

On the east side of the Green River, due east of Nine Mile Canyon, are Willow Creek and its major tributary, Hill, along which there are many archaeological sites. These two creeks rise very close together at the top of the Book Cliffs, at an elevation of 9000 feet, and flow essentially straight north to join each other less than 10 miles before Willow Creek enters the Green River at a point 16 miles above the mouth of Nine Mile Canyon. In its 60-mile course, Willow Creek loses about 4200 feet of elevation.

The upper portions of both Willow and Hill are deep and narrow, but farther down they widen until they look more like steep-sided valleys than canyons. At the mouth of Willow Creek, the surrounding terrain is nearly barren and relatively flat. The middle sections of the canyons have had deep, rich alluvial fill, but at present this is being rapidly scoured out, with consequent loss of what was good farm land until perhaps A.D. 1900.

For the most part the area on either side of and between Hill and Willow Creeks is a plateau that slopes down to the north. Stands of pinyon and juniper are heavy and numerous and at higher elevations there are large stands of quaking aspens. This plateau, the East High Tavaputs, is now a very rewarding area for deer hunters. Good springs are common along both canyons and their numerous tributaries. In spite of the high elevation, foot travel along and between the various canyons is not difficult, and automobile roads have been built even to the upper reaches of Hill and Willow Creeks.

Archaeological reconnaissance in the East Tavaputs has been previously reported by Reagan (1931 c, 1934) and by Gunnerson (1957 a, pp. 61–67). Tree-ring dates for specimens of wood from this area have been reported by Schulman (1948). Probably the first archaeologist to report sites in this area was Fewkes (1917 a, 1917 b), who gives excellent descriptions of the more spectacular sites along Hill Creek.

ET 6-1

In a rock shelter about 20 m. above, and on the east side of, Hill Creek, about 2 miles above its confluence with Horsecorn Canyon, is a low (30 to 60 cm.) wall partially enclosing a semicircular area about 4 by 5 m. The wall is composed of loosely piled stone slabs. A little fire-reddened earth and small pieces of charcoal were found within the wall on the bedrock floor of the shelter. A few charred cedar logs on top of the shallow fill may have been from a roof.

ET 6-2

Very close to ET 6-1, on the east bank of, and about 25 m. above Hill Creek is a rock shelter with a nearly level floor about 25 m. long and from 0.5 to 1.5 m. wide. Two crudely built uncoursed walls (fig. 35A), neither of which had apparently reached the roof, had been built in the shelter about 15 m. apart. One wall is from 0.8 to 1.4 m. high and encloses an area about 1 by 5 m. The other wall, from 0.3 to 1.5 m. high, cuts off an area 0.3 to 1 m. wide. Test pits failed to reveal any additional evidence of habitation or use.

ET 6-3

Evidence of occupation was found under an overhang about 50 m. up a side canyon that joins Hill Creek about 0.5 mile above the mouth of Horsecorn Canyon. The site, which was not visible from Hill Creek Canyon, contains a cist (fig. 35B) constructed of vertical stone slabs chinked with adobe, adobe turtlebacks, and poles plastered with adobe. The inside dimensions of the cist were 1.27 by 0.87 m. It had probably been about 1 m. deep, with bedrock serving as the floor. At the time the cist was built, the top of the fill was about 40 cm. above bedrock. An additional 40 cm. of fill had accumulated since then. Corncobs were found in the upper 47 cm. and charcoal was found to a depth of 54 cm., where a hearth was uncovered.

SPECIMENS

Unworked sticks	5
Charcoal	X
Knotted rush	1
Corncobs	30

ET 6-4: Pinnacle Rock

This site (figs. 13, 38A) is on a flat-topped promontory jutting westward from the east wall of Hill Creek Canyon at the south side of the mouth of Tom's Canyon. About 25 m. above the canyon floor and at the foot of

a 6-m.-high mushroom-shaped formation that gives the site its name, are three circular stone walls 3, 4, and 4 m. in diameter. The highest remaining wall is 50 cm. high. Charcoal and ash were found in the fill inside all three structures. Charred cedar poles, a mano, and a metate fragment were found in one. Scattered stones suggest other possible walls. Sections of rough stone walls up to 75 cm. high on top of the pedestal suggest that a wall had once surrounded its 7.3-by-2.4-m. top and that a cross wall might also have existed. Partial excavation of this probable structure revealed one hearth on bedrock, as well as charcoal, ashes, and burned bone in the fill.

SPECIMENS

Mano	1
Metate fragment	1
Sticks	X
Bone fragments	X

The mano, of Uinta quartzite, was well finished on all surfaces. It has an elliptical grinding surface that is curved (convex) lengthwise. The top is convex in both directions, but primarily crosswise. It is 14.4 cm. long, 6.9 cm. wide, and 5.0 cm. thick.

The metate, about one-half of which was collected, had been neatly shaped from a slab of gray quartzite and could have been used with the mano described above. The metate is 22 cm. wide and 5 cm. thick and had been 40 to 50 cm. long. The trough-shaped depression is 17 cm. wide and 3 cm. deep.

ET 6-7: Long Mesa, Fortification Rock

This site (figs. 14, 36A, B) consists of five masonry structures on top of a small isolated mesa in Hill Creek Canyon at the mouth of Horsecorn Canyon. The top of this 100-m.-long, narrow mesa can be reached only by climbing a steep slope at the south end. At about the mid-point a stone wall had been built across the mesa, presumably to protect the structures, which are all on the north half.

The first structure is circular, 1.3 m. in diameter, and divided into two rooms by a partition. The outside wall, which stands to a maximum height of 2 m., is 0.4 to 1 m. thick and composed of stone blocks (pried from the top of the mesa) up to 1.0 by 0.6 by 0.3 m. The structure has an entrance 65 cm. wide

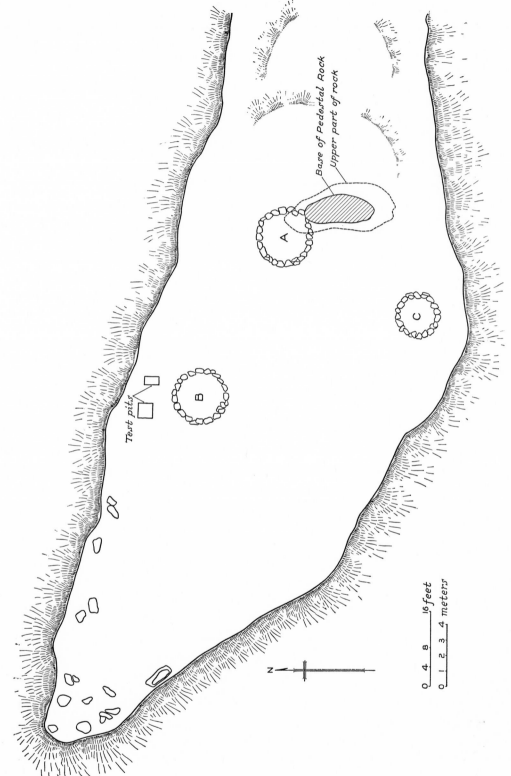

Base of Pedestal Rock
Upper part of rock

A

C

B

Test pits

N

0   4   8   16 feet
0   1   2   3   4 meters

FIG. 13. Plan of Site ET 6-4.

through its northeast side. Excavation revealed that bedrock, in which there was a hearth depression in the middle of the structure, had served as a living surface. The lower 30 cm. of fill in the room contained many artifacts as well as ash and charcoal, including sections of poles 7 to 15 cm. in diameter, apparently the remains of a burned roof. The partition wall, built on top of this 30-cm.-thick detritus layer, indicates that the structure was rebuilt.

The second structure, which was not excavated, is slightly to the northeast of the first and of similar construction, although smaller stone slabs were used. It is nearly circular, with diameters of 5.1 and 4.6 m. A third structure just to the northeast of the second is a nearly circular room with diameters of 6.1 and 5.7 m. To it is attached a rectangular room about 4.8 by 2.5 m. A gap of 1.9 m. in the southeast wall of the latter probably served as an entrance. The walls of this structure, which had been built on bedrock, are about 40 cm. thick. Partial excavation of the 30-cm.-thick fill in this structure produced a few artifacts.

Additional evidence of occupation, or at least cultural detritus, was found in and just in front of a rock shelter about halfway to the top and near the north end of this mesa. Some of this detritus could be refuse from the structures directly above.

This site has been described previously by Fewkes (1917 b, pp. 27–28) and by Gunnerson (1957 a, p. 67), who assigned it number 42Un120. Five dendrochronological dates between A.D. 957 and A.D. 1073 have been reported for this site by Schulman (1948) and Smiley (1951, site 85a), and Schulman (1951) reported one date of A.D. 1042.

SPECIMENS

Pottery sherds	
Emery Gray	1
Emery Black-on-gray	1
Uinta Gray	4
Mancos (?) Corrugated	1
Ground stone	
Manos	2
Metate fragment	1
Spindle whorl	1
Shaft smoother	1
Hammerstones	4
Chipped stone	
Point	1
Small blade	1
Drill	1
Scraper	1
Blade fragment	1
Bone	
Awls and fragments	3
Fragments	X
Plant material	
Corncobs	20
Beans and pod	3
Worked stick	1
Cornhusks	3

The best mano is well made and finished all over. The grinding surface is rocker-shaped (convex lengthwise) and elliptical in outline. The upper surface is convex in both directions so that the ends are quite thin. It is 15 by 6.5 cm. and 4.5 cm. thick. The other mano, less well made, appears to have been of the same general shape but a little larger; about one-third of it is missing. The metate fragment appears to have been from a rectangular metate with a trough at least 6 cm. deep. It was well finished except for the bottom (outside), which was left rough.

Stone spindle whorls are unusual in eastern Utah and the one from this site is very well made. It is of gray-tan lightweight shale, is almost a perfect circle 6.8 cm. in diameter, and has a uniform thickness of 0.7 cm. except for the edge, which is uniformly thinned. The hole, 5 mm. in diameter, is well centered and slightly biconical. The surfaces are smooth, almost polished. Woodbury (1954, p. 186) suggests that such spindle whorls might have been a Hohokam or Mexican trait.

Arrowshaft smoothers made of sandstone are also uncommon in eastern Utah. The fragment from this site is nicely made of coarse red sandstone. The specimen is essentially half of a slightly tapering cylinder. It has a maximum width of 3.9 cm. and a maximum thickness of 2.1 cm. The groove is about 7 mm. wide and 1.5 mm. deep.

The hammerstones vary in size. The largest one, which weighs about 5 lbs., may have served as an anvil.

Except for the drill, the chipped stone artifacts are not very impressive. The drill (silicified chalk?) is well chipped, has a point triangular in cross section, and is 3 cm. long, with a maximum "diameter" of 0.7 cm. (fig. 43, a). It has an expanding base to serve as a handle.

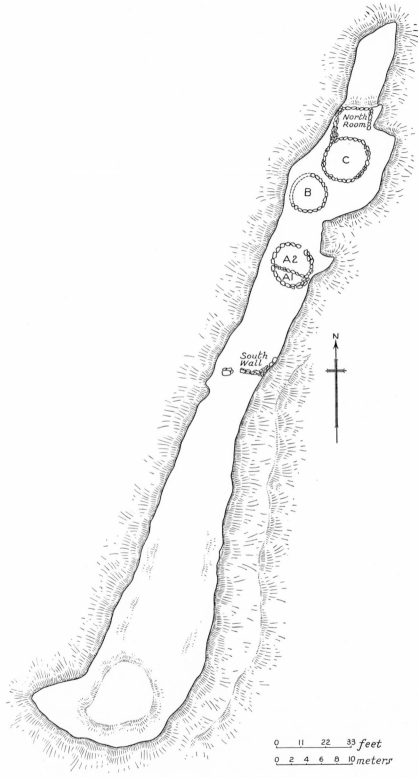

North
Room

C

B

A2
A1

South
Wall

N

| 0 | 11 | 22 | 33 | feet |

| 0 | 2 | 4 | 6 | 8 | 10 | meters |

FIG. 14. Plan of Site ET 6-7.

The projectile point is crudely chipped white chalcedony, is lenticular in outline, and measures 2.4 by 1.1 by 0.5 cm. The blade is of crudely chipped black chert, is irregular in outline, and measures 3.9 by 1.9 by 0.6 cm. A flake has scraping edges, one straight and one convex, chipped along two sides.

The one complete bone awl and two tips are all poorly preserved, but have obviously been made from splinters of mammal long bones. The complete one is 18 cm. long. One possible awl butt had the articulation left on the bone. A bone tube, possibly a bead, is 4.5 cm. long and 0.8 cm. in diameter and was made from the shaft of a long bone from a small mammal. The cut ends have been smoothed, but little other modification is evident.

The worked plant material consists of one piece of cut stick whose use remains undetermined.

Three beans, identified as *Phaseolus vulgaris*, and the pod that presumably contained them were found in the rock shelter under the edge of the mesa. Corncobs were found both in this shelter and in a midden area near the south wall on top of the mesa.

ET 6-8

About 90 m. up the north wall of Horsecorn Canyon, just where it enters Hill Creek Canyon, is a structure in a rock shelter that can be entered only by clinbing up the talus slope, then up the cliff to a point above, from which one can drop to the ledge forming the floor of the shelter, which is about 10 by 4 m. and 1.3 m. high. A nearly straight wall, 3 m. long and 40 to 50 cm. thick, extends from floor to ceiling, walling off a portion of the shelter. Construction is of irregular pieces of stone without adobe. A door 1 m. high and from 30 to 58 cm. wide is located near one end of the wall.

ET 6-9

The remains of several stone structures are located on top of a point which projects into Horsecorn Canyon about a mile above its mouth. The point, which is about 50 m. long and 50 m. high, extends from the south side of the canyon at a sharp bend. Near the east end of the point is a wall 2 m. long, made of rounded chunks of sandstone laid in courses. It is still standing 1.2 m. high. No traces of adobe were found in the wall. On a ledge about 6 m. below the top of the point is a circular wall about 1.5 m. high and 2 m. long.

ET 6-10

Three small structures, probably granaries, were found on a narrow ledge under an overhang on the left bank of Horsecorn Canyon, about 0.25 mile above its mouth. The ledge is from 0.6 to 2 m. wide, about 65 m. long, and situated about 55 m. above the canyon floor.

All three structures were made of thin alternate layers of sandstone slabs and adobe in about equal amounts, and in each case the cliff face formed the back wall. The first room, 1.75 m. long with a maximum inside width of 1 m., had a wall 75 cm. high which incorporated a large boulder. Stick-impressed adobe and sticks of a size comparable to that of the impressions found within the room were probably from a pole-and-adobe roof. The second room, 20 m. from the first, was 1.27 by 1.37 m. on the inside. Built against this room, but not sharing a wall with it, was a third room, 1.2 by 1.3 m.

SPECIMENS

Pottery sherds	
Uinta Gray	7
Corrugated black-on-white	
(listed in catalog but missing)	1
Cord	1
Corncob	1
Sticks	X

The piece of cord, two-ply, Z-twist, is of milkweed or Indian hemp.

ET 6-11

The ruins of a stone structure occupy an eminence about 30 m. above the floor of Hill Creek Canyon, about 1 mile below the mouth of Horsecorn Canyon. Directly across Hill Creek is a fragment of wall, probably the remains of another similar structure.

ET 6-12

Two masonry structures are located on top of two pinnacles about 20 m. apart on the left bank of Hill Creek, about 1 mile above the mouth of West Squaw Canyon. The pinnacles, in turn, are situated on a point about

50 m. above the floor of Hill Creek Canyon. On one pinnacle is a semicircular wall about 8 m. long that abuts a rock ledge of about the same height (1 m.) to form a room. Wall construction is apparently of dry-laid stones, progressively smaller from bottom to top. At the base of this pinnacle are the remains of what appears to have been a circular room about 2.5 m. in diameter, with one section of dry-laid masonry wall still standing 60 cm. high.

The top of the second pinnacle is completely covered by a two-room 6-by-12-m. structure. The walls, which are about 45 cm. thick and still stand from 0.6 to 1.3 m. high, are constructed of relatively uniform, flat, thin stone slabs. On the southeast is a doorway 0.6 m. wide and 1.3 m. high. The stones were so laid as to make smooth sides for the doorway, but no lintel had been used. A large stone slab had served as a sill. On a ledge just below the door and extending into a crack in the bedrock were two walls that appear to have been built to buttress the wall above. There are remains of what was possibly another room about 3 m. in diameter at the end of the point.

ET 6-13

The most spectacular structure along Hill Creek Canyon is a wall built across a point at the north side of the mouth of West Squaw Canyon about 65 m. above the canyon floor. The wall is 1.4 to 1.6 m. thick, about 8 m. long, and, at one point, 6 m. high. It is situated about 10 m. from the end of the point and cuts off the only possible approach to the end. Just inside the wall is a solid bench 1.7 to 2 m. high and 2 to 3 m. wide, which is, in fact, just a thickening of the lower part of the wall. All construction is of rather large stone slabs—thin in the upper part of the wall and thicker toward the base. A doorway about 1.2 m. wide is located in the approximate center of the wall at the height of the bench. It is not possible to determine whether this wall was built as such, or whether at one time it was part of a room, the rest of which has since collapsed over the edge of the point.

This site was described previously by Gunnerson (1957 a, p. 65) who assigned it the number 42Un105, and by Fewkes (1917 b, pp. 24–26).

ET 6-14

On a butte just across the mouth of West Squaw Canyon from ET 6-13 is a similar but less impressive structure. A masonry wall 9.2 m. long extends entirely across the point, cutting off the end just north of the only point of easy access. The wall is now 0.7 to 1.8 m. high, and 1.4 m. from the east end of the wall there is a doorway 80 cm. wide. Just north of the wall and built against it is a quadrant-shaped room whose two straight walls are 2.6 and 3.5 m. long (on the inside) and 40 to 50 cm. thick. The walls are carefully made from stone slabs of nearly uniform thickness laid in courses that are kept fairly uniform by the insertion of smaller stones. A few ashes were found in the fill of the west half of the structure, the only portion excavated. A half-dozen stone slabs found at the south end of the butte may have been part of another small structure.

ET 6-15

Pictographs of deer, buffalo (?), and several unidentified animals are pecked on the face of a gray sandstone ledge about 27 miles below the head of Willow Creek. The panel faces south-southwest and is about 1.5 m. above the canyon floor.

ET 6-16

In a shallow rock shelter about 30 miles below the head of Willow Creek was found an irregular 6-m.-long row of rocks that follows the curve of the bedrock floor. The shelter, which is about 6 m. up a sandstone ledge from the canyon floor, faces the east. It is about 15 m. long, 1.2 to 1.8 m. wide, and about 1 m. high.

ET 6-17

A pictograph panel about 1.2 m. square was found about 30 miles below the head of Willow Creek under an overhang on the east side of the canyon. Figures included three red-and-white cross-shaped men, one man in white, an animal head (buffalo?), two red crosses, one blue cross-like figure, and one red man with blue marks.

ET 6-18

A stone wall was found on a mushroom-shaped formation on top of a point in a U-bend of Willow Creek canyon about 40 miles below its head. This site, which is about 100 m. above the canyon floor, could have served as a lookout.

SPECIMENS

Chipped stone	
Small blade	1
Blade or point fragment	1
Modified flakes	2
Chips and flakes	X
Hammerstone	1

The small blade, triangular with a convex base, is 2.7 by 2.3 by 0.6 cm. This blade and most of the flakes are brown jasper, but two worked items are gray and brown chalcedony. The hammerstone is a small nodule of petrified wood and shows much battering.

ET 6-19

A small structure was discovered under a slight overhang in the north wall of Big Water Canyon, which enters Willow Creek Canyon about 40 miles below its head. The overhang, about 6 by 2 m., is 80 m. above the canyon floor. The cliff face formed the back wall of the room, now represented only by the two end walls, which are 2 m. apart and project 75 cm. from the cliff, and by three poles that span the tops of the walls and support a covering of flat stone slabs. The front wall is completely missing. The walls are composed of flat stone slabs and adobe in nearly equal amounts and laid in alternating courses. The three cedar poles, from 5 to 12 cm. in diameter, were also set in adobe and traces of adobe on the floor and roof slabs suggest that the roof had been sealed with that material.

ET 6-20

This site, a pictograph panel, is located about 45 miles below the head of Willow Creek on a southwest-facing cliff at the level of the canyon floor. Two figures had been produced by pecking. One was rather amorphous; the other, a trapezoidal-bodied anthropomorph, was about 50 cm. high.

ET 6-21

Another pictograph panel was found about 30 m. up the west wall of Willow Creek Can-

yon about 0.5 mile below ET 6-20. Figures included a white 16-point star enclosed by a red circle about 3 m. in diameter, and a white trapezoidal-bodied anthropomorph.

ET 6-22

About 25 m. up the west wall of Willow Creek Canyon some 48 miles below its head are various painted designs, including red serrated lines, a white serrated line, and six figures (possibly anthropomorphic), five white and one red and white. There is also one solid yellow circle with spokes or rays extending from it.

ET 6-23

Two small structures were found about 150 m. up a side canyon that enters Hill Creek Canyon about 3.5 miles below the mouth of Horsecorn Canyon. One structure is about 50 m. above the canyon floor, the other about 11 m. lower. The higher structure is on a small ledge under a slight overhang at the top of a nearly vertical section of cliff that extends upward for about 6 m. Below this structure is a step of stone and adobe from which it can be reached. The structure itself is a semicircular wall, about 20 cm. thick, enclosing an area 1.7 by 0.85 m. It is constructed of stone slabs and adobe in alternate layers, each about 4 cm. thick. The floor and back wall of the room are bedrock. The roof had probably consisted of rock slabs (one of which remains) covered with adobe.

The lower structure was of the same general construction, but may have been more nearly rectangular, with a floor 1.28 by 1.1 m. Pieces of stick-impressed adobe about 10 cm. thick, presumably part of the roof, were found in the room.

SPECIMENS

Bone awl fragment	1

ET 6-24

A cleft in the north wall of a small canyon that enters Hill Creek Canyon from the west about 6 miles below the mouth of Horsecorn Canyon probably contained a small structure at one time. The cleft, about 25 m. above the canyon floor, was plugged with a mass of fallen rock forming a floor about 40 by 80 cm.

About 1.5 m. above this floor, the cleft expands to about 2 by 4 m. Chunks of adobe, including two turtlebacks, were found in the detritus on the floor and daubs of adobe were found stuck to the wall to a height of about 1 m. above the floor.

SPECIMENS

Corncobs	3
Corn kernels	X
Bone and fragment	2

ET 6-26: Rock House, Eight Mile Ruin

The most extensive group of open structures (figs. 15, 37A, B) in the area, known locally as "Rock House," is on the west rim of Hill Creek Canyon, immediately south of a side canyon, about 11 miles below the mouth of Horsecorn Canyon. Some of the walls were built so close to the canyon rim, which is about 65 m. above the canyon floor, that they have fallen into the canyon as the rim has broken away. Altogether, there are the remains of about 9 masonry rooms with walls still standing from 0.3 to 2.25 m. high and varying in thickness from 0.2 to 1.0 m. Except in the one small isolated structure, no evidence of adobe mortar or plaster was found. Limited excavation in the rooms produced very few artifacts. This site has been described previously by Gunnerson (1957a, p. 64) under the number 42Un104, and by Fewkes (1917 b, pp. 28–29), who called it "Eight Mile Ruin."

SPECIMENS

Pottery sherd	
Emery Gray	1
Chipped blade fragment	1
Disk bead	1
Corncob fragments	X
Bone fragments	X

The disk bead, made of a dark brown shale (?), is 1.1 cm. in diameter, tapers from 2 to 3 mm. in thickness, and has a slightly off center biconical hole 2 mm. in diameter. The cob fragments are from the surface; the other artifacts from Structure E.

ET 9-1

A rock shelter with a southern exposure was found about 3 m. above the floor of Hill Creek Canyon, about 20 miles above its confluence

with Horsecorn Canyon. Only a section 7 by 20 m. at one end of the shelter would afford protection since water runs through the other end during rains. There is a large spring about 150 m. away.

Two shallow metates or milling slabs with depressions of 29 by 14 by 1 cm. and 16 by 9 by 0.5 cm. were observed. Except for a few irregularly placed small pits surrounding the depression in the former, they showed no other evidence of modification.

ET 9-2

On the west side of Hill Creek Canyon about 20 miles above the mouth of Horsecorn Canyon is a rock shelter situated between two small springs. It is not obvious from the canyon floor 50 m. below. Only a part of the shelter about 24 by 5 m. remains dry during a rain. Small amounts of charcoal and ash were found on the shelter floor and some shallow grooves, possibly natural, were noted on a fallen boulder.

SPECIMENS

Pottery sherd	
Emery Gray	1
Chipped point fragment	1
Flakes and chips	X
Bone fragments	X

The point fragment and the chips are all of nearly white chalcedony.

ET 9-3

About 300 m. up a canyon that enters Hill Creek on the west side about 19 miles above its confluence with Horsecorn is a shelter (about 22 by 10 m.) containing many fallen sandstone slabs. Two of these have depressions, 39 by 12 by 1.5 cm. and 20 by 9 by 0.5 cm., worn into them.

ET 10-1

A 45-by-15-m. rock shelter, on the west side of Willow Creek 15 m. above the canyon floor and about 10 miles below its head, may have been occupied. One sandstone slab with a shallow depression worn in it may have been a milling slab.

ET 10-3

On the north wall of Pioche Canyon about

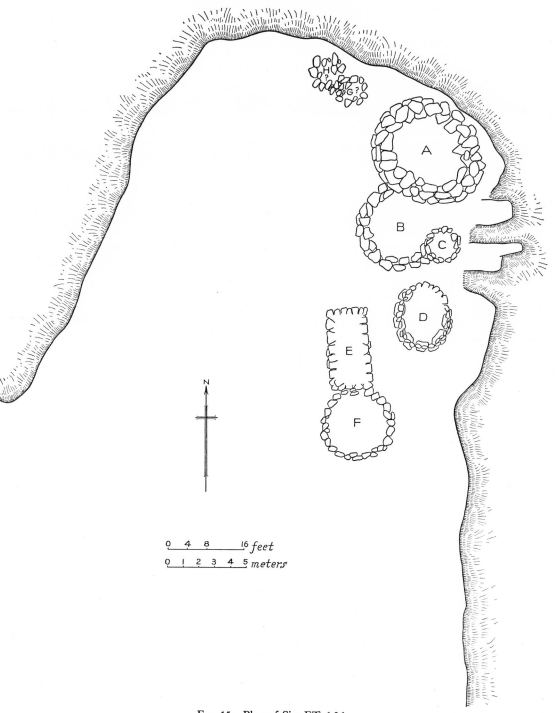

Fɪɢ. 15. Plan of Site ET 6-26.

0.5 mile from its mouth and about 2 m. above the canyon floor are some pecked pictographs, now very faint, consisting of simple curvilinear designs.

ET 10-4

On the east wall of Willow Creek Canyon, about 20 miles below its head and 15 m. above the canyon floor, are pecked pictographs of a mountain sheep 24 cm. long and a deer 51 cm. long.

PR 10-5

On the same side of Willow Creek Canyon as PR 10-4 and 0.5 mile below it are some pictographs about 12 m. above the canyon floor that can be reached with the help of some worn toeholds in the cliff. The painted figures, protected by an overhang, consist of a faint yellow deer, 44 cm. long, and two red and yellow anthropomorphic figures with outspread arms and practically no suggestion of legs, each 1.07 m. long. One apparently has two curved horns and is holding a semicircle about the same size as the horns in each hand.

ET 10-6

About 0.25 mile below ET 10-5 and 4 m. above the canyon floor are four pictographs painted in red. Two of them are too dim and amorphous to be identified. The third, 28 cm. long, is probably a sheep or goat and the fourth is a circle 19 cm. in diameter with 37 radiating lines, each about 2 cm. long.

ET 10-7

Pictographs were found on a large boulder at the base of the west wall of Willow Creek Canyon, about 22 miles below its head. The figures, all pecked, include a mountain sheep 20 cm. long, a man 26 cm. high with a bow and arrow, a snake 37 cm. long, and two figures 22 and 46 cm. tall which may be anthropomorphic. Both of these have possible bows and one has a circular body. There are also several other figures more difficult to characterize.

UINTA MOUNTAIN FOOTHILLS

The northern edge of the Uinta Basin is clearly delimited by the high rugged east–west range of the Uinta Mountains, which join the Wasatch Mountains on the west and high plateau country to the east. The Uintas are high enough to hold snow all summer in most years and to provide the source for many small streams that drain down into the Uinta Basin and eventually join the Green River, which flows diagonally across the Basin from northeast to southwest. The Green, with a few major tributaries, also drains a large area in northwestern Colorado and southwestern Wyoming.

The Uinta Basin is very barren except along the watercourses. Present settlements hug the foothills at elevations of 5000 to 6000 feet, where streams can be tapped for both culinary and irrigation water to supplement the sparse (6 to 9 inches) annual precipitation. This settlement pattern also characterized the area a thousand years ago. The high mountains near by, with their abundance of game and variety of plants and trees, would have provided the aboriginal inhabitants with a ready source for many materials. The geological formations are such that numerous small rock shelters occur in the lower portions of the canyons, where rich alluvial fill is also frequently found. Moreover, the larger streams have alluvial terraces along them after they emerge from the foothills.

In spite of the many published references to sites along the northern edge of the Uinta Basin, the archaeology of the area is still not well understood. Reagan has provided a number of descriptive reports (Reagan, 1931 d, 1931 e, 1931 f, 1931 g, 1931 h) plus some briefer articles which at least mention the archaeology of the area. Steward (1933 a, pp. 32–34) excavated at four open sites north of Fort Duchesne, and Gunnerson (1957 a, pp. 39–52, 1957 b) limited his work almost exclusively to reconnaissance. Just to the north of the Uinta Basin in the canyon of the Yampa River, the University of Colorado excavated two important sites, Hells Midden and Mantle's Cave (Burgh and Scoggin, 1948; Burgh, 1950; Schulman, 1950; and Lister, 1951). Baldwin

(1947) had earlier conducted a reconnaissance in the same general area.

U 16-1 TO U 16-7: SOUTH MYTON BENCH

For at least 2 miles along the south edge of Myton Bench where it slopes off to Pleasant Valley there are many large boulders, some large enough to provide overhangs which could offer shelter from the elements. Evidence of sparse occupation, probably over a long time span, can be found among the boulders, but in few places has this been intensive enough to justify assigning site numbers to restricted areas. Limited testing in promising spots produced a few artifacts and traces of charcoal in the upper 15 cm. of fill, but very little below that. The area has apparently long been subjected to wind and water erosion.

At each of three places, U 16-1, -4 and -7, the shelter afforded by the boulders was apparently supplemented by the construction of a crude rock wall, but not enough remained to indicate the nature of the structures (if such had existed). Within the partial enclosure so formed at U 16-4 was an area about 75 cm. in diameter containing ash and charcoal. It may have been a hearth, but no further suggestion of construction could be found.

Under an overhang at U 16-2 and buried 2 to 12 cm. deep was found a layer of grass, presumably a bed. It was 1.2 m. long, up to 60 cm. wide, and up to 1.5 cm. thick. A few artifacts were found near by.

Pictographs on the northeast and south sides of a large boulder (U 16-6) include sheep, eight buffalo, and line figures.

SPECIMENS	U 16-1	U 16-2	U 16-3–7
Pottery sherds			
Uinta Gray	–	1	16
Emery Gray	–	–	7
"Paiute"	–	–	3
Projectile points	–	–	3
Point fragments	–	1	1
Blades	–	1	6
Blade fragments	–	–	18
Choppers	4	1	37
Chopper fragments	6	–	11
Pebble tools	–	–	2
Graver	–	–	1
Milling slab (?) fragment	–	–	1
Chips and flakes	–	–	X
Fire-spalled rock	1	–	–
Bone fragments	2	–	–

Included among the Uinta Gray sherds from U 16-3–7 are four handle fragments. The occurrence of Paiute sherds at this site extends the geographical range of this distinctive fingernail-indented, heavily sand-tempered type.

The chipped stone artifacts from this area are of special interest in that they are predominantly crude percussion-flaked choppers and blades (fig. 42). The type referred to as choppers could probably as well be called cores or core tools. They are bifacially chipped and are generally about one and one-half times as long as they are wide, with one end tending to be more pointed than the other. Some are nearly discoidal. The thickness, on an average, is about half the width. Length varies from 5 to 12 cm., with the smaller choppers tending to be better made and grading into what have been called blades. Most of the larger choppers and some of the smaller ones show the cortex on one or both sides. The most common material is white-to-tan chert, although chalcedony and quartzite were also used. The two pebble tools consist of long thin pebbles that have had a cutting or chopping edge chipped along the broad end and a little way along the side. They belong at the smaller end of the size range of the choppers. The chopper fragments are all from relatively small tools.

The blades are distinguishable from the choppers in that they are thinner and more carefully made and, in most cases, show some pressure retouching. The range in outline is from almost triangular to pointed oval. Bases are from slightly convex to rounded. The maximum width, which occurs near the base, varies from 2.5 to 5 cm. Thickness varies from 0.5 to 1 cm. and there is little correlation between thickness and width. The blade from U 16-2 is a pointed oval 4.0 by 1.8 by 0.6 cm.

What appears to be the base of a moderately large blade had been rechipped from one face to form a graver point about 2 cm. wide and 1.5 cm. long.

The points, which seem out of place with most of the other stone artifacts, are well made. One (fig. 43, c), triangular with a slightly concave base and side notches, is 1.7 by 3.2 cm. Another (fig. 43, *e*), triangular with convex sides and base and corner notches, is 1.4 by 3.3 cm. The third, which lacks the tip, has been 1.4 by about 4.6 cm. It is unnotched and has a square, slightly constricted base. Maximum width occurs about one-third of the way from the base. The second point is of agate, the other two of chert.

A fragment of what appears to have been a 3-cm.-thick sandstone milling slab has been finished on the grinding surface and the edges have been rounded. The bottom was left unfinished.

U 11-1

What had apparently been a camp site is located in a clearing surrounded by cedar trees on the first bench about 25 m. above, and 0.4 mile east of Rock Creek. Sparse detritus was found over an area roughly 25 m. in diameter, but the only suggestion of a structure was seven small rocks in a line 75 cm. long.

SPECIMENS
Pottery sherds	
Uinta Gray	146
Points	2
Point or blade fragments	5
Small "choppers"	2
Bone fragments	X
Hammerstone	1

Two of the sherds were pot handles which extended from the lip of the vessel to a point on the shoulder just below its junction with the neck. One was 2.4 by 1.1 cm. and 6 cm. long; the other 1.6 by 1.2 cm. by 5 cm. long.

One of the points, triangular with slightly convex sides (fig. 43, *d*), a concave base and basal and side notches, was very nicely made of gray chert. It measures 2.7 by 1.6 by 0.2 cm. The other point, its tip missing, had been about the same size, but had a straight base and side notches and was less well made.

One of the blade fragments, most of the base of a lanceolate specimen, seems out of place in the assemblage. It appears to have had a broad notch removed from the base, leaving two ears. Its maximum width of 2.2 cm. occurs about 2 cm. from the base. It is lenticular in cross section with a maximum thickness of 5 mm. It has moderately good parallel flaking, but no evidence of basal grinding. The

material is a tan chert with many very small brown spots in it.

Another basal fragment shows corner and basal notching on what was probably a triangular blade. It is crudely chipped from black chert and has a maximum width of 2.4 cm.

The small "choppers" resemble those from U 16-1–7 except that they are very small— 5.0 by 2.6 by 1.4 cm. and 3.6 by 2.5 by 1.4 cm. One is made of nearly white chalcedony, the other of brown jasper. These crude little almond-shaped artifacts are not out of place at Fremont sites, however.

A 6-1: Well Cave

A partially dry cave located about 0.25 mile north of the junction of Dry Fork and Ashley Creeks was investigated. The small entrance, about 25 m. above the valley floor, can be reached by climbing about 4 m. up a chimney from the top of the talus slope. Another opening to the cave overlooks Ashley Valley but is inaccessible. Only a portion of the cave about 5 by 15 m. had a floor level enough for occupation and part of this was dampened by water coming in through a crack. In the occupied portion of the cave there were 2 to 3 m. of fill, mostly sand, but so much digging had been done previously and the fill was so loose that it was usually impossible to determine whether pits were being dug in disturbed or undisturbed portions, and no definite stratigraphy could be ascertained.

At the north end of the cave were the remains of a large cist, said to have been coffin-shaped originally. It was constructed of large (up to 30 by 60 cm.) stone slabs set on edge in adobe mortar. A second cist, perhaps the earliest evidence of occupation in the cave, was found covered by 1.3 m. of fill near the middle of, and against the east wall of, the cave. The floor and front walls of the cist were single stone slabs and the end walls, built on the floor slab, were entirely of lumps of adobe, each about 10 by 10 by 7 cm. The cist was nearly square, about 1 m. on a side, and the highest point (on the front wall) was 30 cm. above the floor. In it were found pieces of adobe, two stone slabs about 15 by 30 by 3 cm., and two corncobs. Apparently a little water ran into the cist after it was abandoned.

Most of the evidence found in the cave suggests that its main function was storage. In addition to the cists, two baskets of corn appeared to have been buried deliberately. One, covered by a second basket, contained both ears and shelled corn. The other, covered with a piece of buffalo hide, contained shelled corn and three squash seeds. A few other ears of corn, as well as pieces of stick-impressed adobe and a little additional detritus, were found in the cave. A pile of fifteen or twenty poles from 1.2 to 1.7 m. long and about 5 cm. in diameter was found on the surface. Their function was not obvious.

SPECIMENS

Baskets and parts	5
Cord	1
Cucurbita fragments	X
Corn ears	10
Corncobs	19
Corn kernels	X
Cornhusk	X
Hide	1
Adobe	X
Reed tube	1

All the baskets and fragments recovered from this site are coiled. One basket (fig. 44, d) that contained corn when found has a foundation consisting of grass, probably *Phragmites communis*, which had been lightly twisted into a bundle about 8 mm. in diameter. Sewing was done with strips of bark, probably squawbush, 3 to 4 mm. wide. Interlocking stitches spaced about 1 cm. apart were used. This well-preserved basket is 14 cm. high and has a maximum diameter of 20 cm. about 8 cm. above the bottom. At this point, it begins to constrict abruptly to a vertical neck 2 cm. high and 6 cm. in inside diameter. The lip was finished with a simple whipping stitch that entirely covers it. This basket was covered with an irregular piece of buffalo (?) hide, tanned with the hair on. A second basket (fig. 44, e) appears to have been of the same general shape, but about 30 cm. in maximum diameter. It has a neck 4 cm. high and 10 cm. in inside diameter. This basket, however, had a foundation consisting of a twisted bundle of juniper bark about 8 mm. in diameter, and it was sewed with strips of willow bark. The stitches are interlocking and spaced about 6 mm. apart.

Another piece of basketry (fig. 44, c), found inverted over the neck of the larger bottle-shaped basket, is a nearly complete coiled bowl 16 cm. in diameter and 8 cm. high. This has a half-rod-and-bundle foundation (squawbush (?) and yucca, respectively) with rods about 4 mm. wide and 1.5 mm. thick. It is sewed with strips of squawbush (?) bark 2 mm. wide in noninterlocking stitches that are very rarely split. Sewing is so finely and tightly done (4 stitches per cm.) that virtually none of the foundation is visible. The lip of the basket is finished with a simple whipping stitch.

Two fragments, possibly from the same basket, appear to be parts of a shallow bowl (or bowls) at least 20 cm. in diameter. These specimens are coiled with a half-rod foundation and interlocking stitches. There are many interstices through which light can be seen, but there are few places where the foundation is visible between the stitches, which are never split. The half-rods are 4 mm. wide and 1.5 mm. thick, the stitches are 2 to 3 mm. wide, and both are probably squawbush. There are two stitches and three coils per cm.

Two other very small basket fragments have a half-rod-and-bundle foundation with noninterlocking stitches. The rods and stitching are probably both squawbush and the bundle is yucca.

The single piece of cord, two-ply, Z-twist, is 2.5 mm. in diameter and made of yucca fiber.

The reed tube, probably of phragmites, is 4.5 cm. long and 0.5 cm. in outside diameter. Both ends have been carefully cut off. A small notch has been cut in one side, about 5 mm. from an end.

Two of the pieces of adobe show impressions of sections of coiled baskets, another, the impression of a section of a twined rush mat, and the fourth, the impression of what looks like a corncob.

A 6-2

A rock shelter 19.5 m. long is located on the west side of, and about 30 m. above, Ashley Creek, about 2 miles above its junction with Dry Fork Creek. Although there had already been extensive digging at the site, the remains of three cists were recognizable. A pit with a maximum diameter of 1.4 m. had been dug into the shale floor of the shelter and plastered with adobe on the inside. Around the mouth of the pit, which was 1.05 m. in diameter, a wall of horizontal stone slabs had been laid in adobe mortar. The second cist had been cut into a sloping part of the floor and plastered; the front part was enclosed with three large vertical stone slabs. A third cist, also partially cut into the shale, had been completely demolished.

In front of the cave in a large sandstone boulder were several grooves from 10 to 15 cm. wide and 20 to 30 cm. long.

SPECIMENS

Cord	1
Corncobs	3
Cornhusk	1

The cord, made of juniper bark, is two-ply, Z-twist and 4 mm. in diameter.

A 6-3

A rock shelter about 5 miles north of Vernal shows some evidence of occupation. This north-facing shelter on the valley floor is 10 by 25 m. and 5 m. high. One storage cist, the top of which was at a possible occupation level about 15 cm. below the present surface, was 1.19 by 0.45 m. and 1.17 m. deep and thinly plastered with adobe. Scattered specks of charcoal were found in the upper 30 cm. of the sandy shelter fill, but very little detritus or other evidence of occupation was found. A thin layer of carbonized seeds was found in the bottom of the cist.

A 6-5

Two test pits were dug in a rock shelter located about 5 miles north of Vernal. The shelter, about 8 m. long and 3 m. high, was at the level of the valley floor and is reputed to have been used by bandits at the turn of the century. One possible cist, an unlined pit about 80 cm. deep and 75 to 100 cm. across, was encountered about 50 cm. below the surface. Several lenses of charcoal and ash and a layer of cedar bark were found between 0.3 and 1 m. below the surface. Very little detritus was recovered.

SPECIMENS

Corncob	1
Corn shank	2
Bone fragments	X

A 6-6

On the east side of Dry Fork Canyon about 1.2 miles above its mouth and about 10 m. above the canyon floor is a 30-m.-long shelter that has been extensively dug out by a local collector. Included in the material that he recovered are a skeleton, a bark blanket, dew-claw moccasins, corncobs, gourd storage vessels containing corn, a buckskin bag, and a woven bark bag containing squash (?) seeds. A cist that had been uncovered but left in place is about 50 cm. in diameter and 70 cm. deep. It consists of six or seven stone slabs set on end without the use of adobe. Limited testing by the Peabody Museum party produced very few artifacts.

SPECIMENS

Corncobs	6
Cucurbita fragments	X
Bone fragment	1
Hair	X
Adobe chunk	1
Digging stick	1

The piece of adobe contains an impression of what appears to be a coarsely coiled basket.

The digging stick (fig. 40, *a*) is 42 cm. long and tapers gradually to a use-polished point from a maximum diameter of 1.8 cm. A handle 7 cm. long and at about a right angle to the shaft is formed by a piece of the trunk of which the shaft is a branch.

A 6-7

About 50 m. above the mouth of a small draw that enters Spring Creek near its mouth, and 15 m. above the canyon floor, is a small structure in an overhang with a southeast exposure. The structure, 94 cm. in diameter on the inside and still standing to a height of 15 cm., is very neatly constructed of small stone slabs and adobe turtlebacks laid in courses, with the adobe layers the thicker.

A 7-1

An open site with evidence of structures was found on the first bench on the west side of and 50 m. above Brush Creek, about 12 miles east of Vernal. The main structure, 9 m. square, is outlined by a single course of small boulders, but scattered similar rocks found on the site had apparently also been part of the wall. A test trench within the square revealed, at a depth of 22 cm., a use surface characterized by a layer 2 to 5 cm. thick containing ash and charcoal. What was apparently a stone-slab-lined hearth 1.1 m. in diameter was found in the middle of the room at this level. Test pits through the use surface and under the wall stones revealed undisturbed earth. Two stone circles, 2 to 3 m. in diameter and presumably the bases of walls of other structures, were found to the northwest and southeast of the main structure.

SPECIMENS

Pottery sherds
Uinta Gray	17
Small crude blades	3
Large blade fragment	1
Graver	1
Flakes	4
Metate fragment	1
Mano fragment	1

One of the sherds is a fragment of a handle. The crude blades are more or less almond-shaped. The smallest is 3.2 by 1.6 by 0.8 cm., the largest is 4.3 by 2.7 by 1.3 cm., and the third is almost the size of the largest. The blade fragment is from a much larger and much better made specimen. The graver has a small point carefully chipped on a discoidal piece of obsidian about 1.5 cm. in diameter.

About half of what appears to be a mano was recovered. The grinding surface is slightly keeled, with each of the two facets about 4 cm. wide and convex lengthwise. The top is rounded and finished all over. The portion recovered has a maximum thickness of 8.5 cm. and a width nearly as great. Originally it had been about 22 cm. long. The metate fragment shows careful shaping both inside and out, and was probably basin-shaped, although it was too small for determination of the shape to be certain. Both the mano and metate are of Uinta quartzite.

A 7-2

Another open site with structures is located about 1.5 miles downstream from A 7-1 on a bench 30 m. above Brush Creek. The largest structure, 6.5 m. square, is outlined with small boulders or cobbles. A test pit in the middle disclosed a stone-lined hearth at a depth of 15 cm., under which the fill was undisturbed and sterile. Attached to the southeast side of this room was apparently a second room or structure of undetermined size. Indefinite outlines of what are probably two rectangular structures, neither more than 2.5 m. across, were noted 70 m. northeast of the square structure. A test pit in one of these disclosed nothing of significance.

SPECIMENS

Pottery sherds
Uinta Gray	1
Point or blade fragments	3
Flakes and chips	11
Used flake	1

A curved flake of petrified wood, 8 by 3 cm., shows evidence of use as a cutting tool.

A 9-1

North and east of Fort Duchesne on low benches near the Uinta River are a number of sites characterized by low mounds, lumps of hard-fired stick-impressed adobe, potsherds, and worked flint.

Excavation at A 9-1 revealed a mound composed mostly of burned adobe, apparently the remains of burned jacal structures, over a rather indefinite use surface about 3 by 4 m. and 20 to 40 cm. below the surface of the mound. On the east, probably the direction in which the structure fell when it burned, the thick layer of adobe chunks extended about 1 m. beyond the edge of the use surface. Test pits through the floor revealed undisturbed earth.

The chunks of hard-fired adobe show impressions of sticks or poles up to about 5 cm. in diameter and reeds (?) as small as 3 mm. in diameter. Some impressions are at right angles to one another and most pieces of adobe have one flat side, roughly parallel to the long axis of the poles. One set of three contiguous impressions, each about 5 mm. across, appears to be from cords or withes which had lashed together two large poles where they crossed. This adobe is apparently the plaster from a wattle-and-daub or jacal structure.

SPECIMENS

Pottery sherds	
Uinta Gray	29
Emery Gray	2
Stick-impressed adobe	X
Blade fragment	1
Flake	1
Point	1
Metate	1

Included among the Uinta Gray sherds were four handle fragments.

The point, very crude, was 1.4 cm. wide and 0.7 cm. thick and had been about 3 cm. long. It has a square stem 6 mm. wide and 5 mm. long.

A broken metate was found when reassembled to be 44 by 30 cm., 4 cm. thick at the middle, and 7 cm. thick at the edge.

A 9-2

An open site (figs. 16, 38B) located on a rock promontory at the end of a low ridge about 1 mile west of A 9-1 was also excavated. Here a living surface was found 10 to 20 cm. below the surface but, when cleared, it was found to be devoid of both artifacts and post holes. This living area, situated in a depression between two sections of ledge, was protected on a third side by a very crude wall of large rocks, now mostly fallen. The floor of this area was not level but sloped up toward the sections of ledge.

In the more-or-less flat horizontal surface of the sandstone which forms the ridge are 28 round holes. The largest is 40 cm. in diameter and 35 cm. deep; the smallest, 8 cm. in diameter and 4 cm. deep. Most of them, however, are 10 to 20 cm. in diameter and 8 to 20 cm. deep. The holes are all within an area 5 by 13 m. but, for the most part, they form no discernible pattern. Five medium-sized holes form a straight line 1.7 m. long, at the ends of which are one and two holes suggesting the beginning of a square or rectangle. The function of such holes, which occur sporadically either alone or in groups from the Kaiparowits Plateau to the foothills of the Uinta Mountains, is unknown.

SPECIMENS

Pottery sherds	
Emery Gray	2
Point (?)	1
Flake	1

The point is very crude and asymmetric. It was made from a flake of white chalcedony with a triangular cross section with a minimum of retouching, predominantly from one side. There are two notches, probably intentional, near the base. The specimen is 3.2 by 1.5 by 0.5 cm.

A 9-3

Another open site, east of Fort Duchesne, was also characterized by a low mound and an abundance of burned, stick-impressed adobe. From 5 to 15 cm. below the surface of the mound and under the burned adobe a lightly burned living surface was found. Extending out of it about 5 cm. was the charred butt of a post about 5 cm. in diameter, which was set 12 cm. into the earth. Possible post holes were also observed. A pit of undeterminable shape, but about 70 cm. in diameter and extending to bedrock 1.35 m. below, was cleaned out. It contained mostly earth with some charcoal, a dozen cobbles, a metate fragment, and a charred corncob. A trench dug across the middle of the structure failed to reveal a hearth, but it did show that burned adobe was more abundant near the middle than at the edges, suggesting either that the structure collapsed inward toward the center or that the walls contained little or no adobe.

SPECIMENS

Pottery sherds	
Uinta Gray	2
Stick-impressed adobe	X

The adobe, fired hard, shows impressions of sticks or poles up to about 3.5 cm. in diameter. One piece shows roughly square-bottomed grooves about 5 mm. wide crossing the pole impressions. The square impressions are probably from thongs or withes used to lash the poles together to form the framework for a jacal, or wattle-and-daub, structure.

A 12-1

About 75 m. up a side canyon from Jones' Hole is an easily accessible, low rock shelter or cave with a northwest exposure. It is 10 m. deep, 1 to 2 m. high, and 1 to 2 m. wide. Stick-impressed adobe, poles, and willow withes in the middle of the cave suggest that there was once a structure there. Other pieces of adobe, perhaps from a hearth, had been

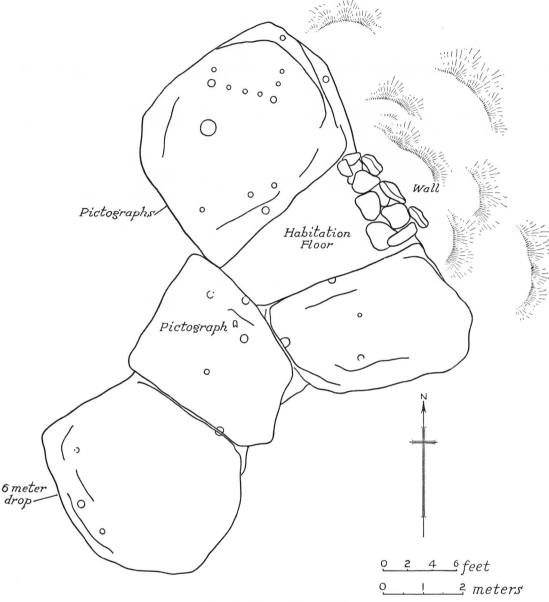

FIG. 16. Plan of Site A 9-2.

burned and much of the sandy fill in the cave was blackened, perhaps from fire. Detritus was not especially abundant, but was found to a depth of 1.1 m. in what might have been a refuse dump at the west side of the mouth of the cave.

SPECIMENS

Pottery sherds
  Uinta Gray   6

Cucurbita fragment	1
Twisted withes	5
Corncobs	6

All the sherds appear to be from one jar which had been about 20 cm. in diameter with an orifice about half that. The rim, markedly flaring, is 2.5 cm. high. The body was probably a slightly flattened sphere.

TABLE 1: DISTRIBUTION OF SPECIMENS FROM SITES REPORTED IN THIS PAPER.

POTTERY

Coombs Gray
FL 7-1

Emery Black-on-gray

ET 6-7	FL 4-4	FL 7-1	FL 15-3	FL 16-1
SR 12-5	SR 16-3	SR 16-4		

Emery Black-on-white

FL 4-4	FL 7-1	FL 15-3	FL 16-1	FL 16-2?
SR 16-3	SR 16-4	SR 16-5?		

Emery Corrugated

PR 4-27	SR 12-5	SR 16-5?

Emery Gray

A 9-1	A 9-2	E 11-6	E 12-6	ET 6-7
ET 6-26	ET 9-2	FL 4-4	FL 4-5	FL 7-1
FL 12-4	FL 15-1	FL 15-3	FL 16-1	FL 16-2
FL 16-4	H 3-8	LS 9-1	LS 13-14	PR 4-5
PR 4-13	PR 4-20	PR 4-25	PR 4-27	PR 4-31
PR 4-32	PR 12-3	PR 12-9	PR 12-13	PR 12-19
PR 12-20	SR 10-1	SR 10-4	SR 12-1	SR 12-5
SR 15-2	SR 16-1?	SR 16-3	SR 16-4	SR 16-5
SR 16-7	SR 16-8	SR 16-10	U 16-3-7	

Emery Tooled

FL 4-4	FL 7-1	FL 12-4	FL 16-1	PR 4-25
PR 4-27	PR 4-32	SR 12-5	SR 16-3	SR 16-5
SR 16-8				

Escalante Gray

E 11-6	FL 15-1	SR 12-5?

Flagstaff Black-on-white
H 3-8   H 9-3

Gallup Black-on-white
LS 13-3

Garfield Black-on-gray
SR 16-3

Jeddito Black-on-yellow
E 12-4   H 6-3

Lino Gray
LS 13-14?

Mancos Black-on-white

LS 9-1	LS 13-3	LS 13-4	LS 13-5	LS 13-6
LS 13-7	LS 13-14	LS 14-1	LS 14-11	PR 4-5?
PR 4-25?	SR 12-5	SR 16-8?		

Mancos Black-on-white Corrugated
H 6-3?   H 7-2?   LS 13-4

Table 1 (continued)

Mancos Corrugated

ET 6-7?	FL 15-3	H 3-7	H 6-3	H 7-2
LS 9-1	LS 13-1	LS 13-2	LS 13-3	LS 13-4
LS 13-5	LS 13-7	LS 13-8	LS 13-13	LS 13-14
LS 14-8	LS 14-11	PR 4-5?	SR 12-1	SR 12-5
SR 16-1	SR 16-3	SR 16-9		

McElmo Black-on-white

H 7-1	H 7-2	H 7-3	LS 9-1	LS 13-1
LS 13-2	LS 13-3	LS 13-4	LS 13-5	LS 13-6
LS 13-7	LS 13-8	LS 13-12	LS 13-13	LS 13-14
LS 13-15	LS 14-1	LS 14-8	LS 14-11	SR 12-1
SR 16-1	SR 16-3	SR 16-9		

Mesa Verde Corrugated

H 3-8?	LS 13-1	LS 13-14	SR 16-3

Middleton Black-on-red

E 12-6

Middleton Red

E 12-6

Moenkopi Corrugated

E 11-6	E 12-3	E 12-6	FL 7-1	H 3-8
H 7-2	H 9-3	PR 4-21	SR 16-3	

North Creek Black-on-gray

E 11-6	FL 7-1	FL 15-3	SR 12-5?

North Creek Corrugated

E 11-1-3	E 11-6

North Creek Gray

E 11-6	E 12-4	E 12-6	E 12-7	FL 7-1
FL 16-4	H 6-3	H 9-3	PR 12-9?	SR 12-1?
SR 12-5?	SR 15-2?	SR 16-3	SR 16-7	

"Paiute"

U 16-3-7

Sevier Gray

FL 7-1	PR 4-25	SR 15-2

"Shoshoni" ware

SR 12-5?

Snake Valley Black-on-gray

SR 10-4?

Snake Valley Gray

PR 4-23

Sosi Black-on-white

FL 7-1	LS 13-5

Tsegi Orange ware, misc.

H 3-8	FL 7-1	LS 13-7

TABLE 1 (continued)

Tsegi Red-on-orange
  SR 12-5

Tusayan Black-on-red
  H 3-8   FL 7-1

Tusayan Corrugated
  FL 15-3   H 3-6   H 6-3   LS 13-1   PR 4-5?
  SR 16-3   SR 16-7   SR 16-10

Tusayan White ware, misc.
  E 12-6   FL 16-4   SR 16-4

Uinta Gray
  A 7-1   A 7-2   A 9-1   A 9-3   A 12-1
  ET 6-7   ET 6-10   PR 4-5   PR 4-21   PR 4-25
  PR 4-27   PR 4-32   PR 8-2   PR 12-2   PR 12-3
  PR 12-19   U 11-1   U 16-3-7

Uinta Tooled
  PR 4-25

Virgin Black-on-white
  E 12-4   E 12-6   FL 15-3

Washington Corrugated
  E 11-6   E 12-6   FL 16-1?

Unidentified
  FL 4-5   FL 16-1   LS 9-1   LS 14-1   PR 4-25
  SR 12-1   SR 12-5   SR 16-5   SR 16-6   SR 16-10

Worked sherds
  LS 14-11   PR 4-5   SR 12-5   SR 16-3   SR 16-4

CLAY (OTHER THAN POTTERY)

Adobe
  A 6-1   A 6-6   A 9-1   A 9-3   PR 4-31

Clay objects, misc.
  PR 4-31

Figurines and fragments
  PR 4-31   SR 12-5   SR 16-10

STONE

Abraders and sharpeners
  SR 12-5

Asphaltum
  PR 4-31

Atlatl weights
  PR 4-31   SR 16-10?

TABLE 1 (continued)

Bead
ET 6-26

Blades

ET 6-7	ET 6-18	FL 12-5	H 3-8	LS 13-14
LS 14-1	PR 4-31	SR 12-5	SR 16-1	SR 16-6
SR 16-9	U 16-2	U 16-3-7		

Blades, crude

A 7-1	PR 4-31

Blade and point fragments

A 7-1	A 7-2	A 9-1	E 12-4	ET 6-7
ET 6-18	ET 6-26	ET 9-2	FL 4-4	FL 7-1
FL 15-3	FL 16-1	FL 16-4	H 3-8	LS 9-1
PR 4-20	PR 4-31	PR 12-2	SR 12-1	SR 12-5
SR 16-1	SR 16-4	SR 16-5	SR 16-8	U 11-1
U 16-2	U 16-3-7			

Choppers

SR 12-5	U 11-1	U 16-1	U 16-2	U 16-3-7

Concretions
PR 4-31

Drills

ET 6-7	H 3-8	PR 4-31	SR 12-1

Flakes, modified

ET 6-18	PR 4-25	SR 16-6	SR 16-8

Flakes and chips

A 7-1	A 7-2	A 9-1	A 9-2	ET 6-18
ET 9-2	FL 16-1	FL 16-4	H 3-6	LS 13-14
PR 4-5	PR 4-13	PR 4-15	PR 4-20	PR 4-25
PR 4-31	PR 4-32	PR 8-2	PR 12-19	SR 16-3
U 16-3-7				

Gravers

A 7-1	SR 12-5	U 16-3-7

Hammerstones

ET 6-7	ET 6-18	PR 12-9	SR 12-5	SR 16-10
U 11-1				

Manos

A 7-1	ET 6-4	ET 6-7	FL 16-1	PR 4-15?
PR 4-25	PR 4-27	PR 4-30	PR 4-31	

Metates and milling slabs

A 7-1	A 9-1	ET 6-4	ET 6-7	LS 14-8
PR 4-15	U 16-3-7			

Pebble tools
U 16-3-7

Pigment

PR 4-31	PR 12-19	SR 12-5	SR 16-6

TABLE 1 (continued)

Points

A 9-1	A 9-2?	E 12-6	ET 6-7	FL 4-4
FL 7-1	LS 9-1	LS 13-14	PR 4-31	SR 10-4
SR 12-1	SR 12-5	SR 16-10	U 11-1	U 16-3-7

Scrapers

ET 6-7	PR 4-31	SR 12-5	SR 16-5	SR 16-6
SR 16-10				

Serrated scrapers or "saws"

FL 16-1

Shaft smoothers

ET 6-7

Spindle whorls

ET 6-7

Worked stone, misc.

SR 10-1	SR 12-5	SR 16-6	U 16-3-7

BONE, ANTLER, HORN AND SHELL

Awls

ET 6-7	ET 6-23	FL 4-5	H 3-8	PR 4-25?
PR 4-31	SR 12-5			

Beads and tubes

FL 12-5	PR 4-31	SR 12-5	SR 10-1

Flakers

PR 4-31	SR 12-5	SR 16-4?

Flesher (?)

PR 4-31

Gaming pieces

SR 12-5

Pendant, bone

SR 12-5

Shell

SR 10-1	SR 12-1	SR 16-10

Skeleton, human (see also Appendix III)

PR 4-31

Sickles, horn

FL 12-5	LS 13-1?	SR 12-5

Tooth, modified

PR 4-31

Bone, antler, and horn, misc.

A 6-5	A 6-6	ET 6-4	ET 6-7	ET 6-24
ET 6-26	ET 9-2	FL 12-5	H 3-8	PR 4-6
PR 4-11	PR 4-25	PR 4-31	PR 12-6	PR 12-19
SR 10-1	SR 10-4	SR 12-5	SR 15-2	SR 16-4
SR 16-6	SR 16-12	U 11-1	U 16-1	

TABLE 1 (continued)

HIDE, HAIR AND FEATHERS

Bag
PR 4-31

Feather cloth
SR 12-5   SR 16-6

Fur cloth
PR 4-31   SR 16-12

Hair
A 6-6

Leggings
PR 4-31

Moccasins
H 3-4   PR 4-31

Pad (umbilical?)
SR 16-6

Hide pieces, misc.

A 6-1	PR 4-6	PR 4-31	SR 10-1	SR 12-5
SR 15-5	SR 16-6			

PLANT MATERIAL (see also Appendix II)

Animal figure, split twig
SR 16-6

Anvils or hearths (for fire drill)

LS 13-1	PR 12-19	SR 12-5

Arrowshafts and fragments

PR 4-6?	SR 12-5

Atlatl
PR 4-31

Bag
SR 16-6

Basketry

A 6-1	FL 12-5	PR 4-31	SR 12-5	SR 16-6

Beans
ET 6-7

Cord

A 6-1	A 6-2	ET 6-10	LS 14-11	PR 4-6
PR 4-27	PR 4-28	PR 4-31	PR 12-19	SR 12-5
SR 16-6	SR 16-10			

Cucurbita fragments

A 6-1	A 6-6	A 12-1	FL 4-5	H 9-3
LS 14-11	PR 4-25	PR 4-28	PR 4-31	PR 8-2
SR 12-5	SR 16-10			

TABLE 1 (continued)

Digging sticks
A 6-6 PR 4-31 PR 12-3

Foreshafts, spear
PR 4-31

Gum
SR 16-6 SR 16-10

Innersoles
PR 4-31 SR 12-5 SR 16-6

Maize (see also Appendix I)

A 6-1	A 6-2	A 6-5	A 6-6	A 12-1
ET 6-3	ET 6-7	ET 6-10	ET 6-24	ET 6-26
FL 12-4	FL 12-5	H 7-2	LS 14-11	PR 4-6
PR 4-25	PR 4-27	PR 4-28	PR 4-31	PR 8-1
PR 8-2	PR 8-4	PR 12-6	PR 12-19	PR 12-20
SR 16-6				

Matting

E 12-7	LS 14-8	LS 14-11	PR 4-28	PR 4-31
SR 10-1	SR 12-5			

Quids
SR 15-2 SR 16-10

Ring "pot rests"
LS 13-1? LS 14-11 SR 12-5

Sandals
LS 14-11 SR 12-5 SR 16-6

Sickle?, wooden
SR 16-6

Spearshafts
PR 4-31

Tubes, reed
A 6-1 PR 4-31 SR 12-5

Tump line
PR 4-31

Wood (with burned decoration)
PR 4-31 SR 12-5

Plant material, misc.

A 12-1	ET 6-3	ET 6-4	ET 6-7	ET 6-10
FL 12-5	LS 14-11	PR 4-6	PR 4-25	PR 4-27
PR 4-28	PR 4-31	PR 8-1	PR 12-6	PR 12-19
PR 12-20	SR 12-5	SR 16-6	SR 16-10	

PART III

A FUNCTIONAL SYNTHESIS
OF THE
FREMONT CULTURE

A FUNCTIONAL SYNTHESIS
OF THE
FREMONT CULTURE

IN presenting this synthesis of the Fremont culture, an attempt has been made to consider all the information available. The discussion is based to a large extent on published information, but the previously unpublished data presented in this volume have provided additional details that have in turn led to modifications of ideas previously advanced. Some of these modifications are essentially slight changes of emphasis. Others are definite refinements of interpretation and significant extensions of hypotheses. A certain amount of pure speculation is involved but a deliberate effort has been made to differentiate among observations, interpretations, and speculations. When traits mentioned are characteristic of the Fremont culture and are found at several sites, documentation is frequently omitted, but when traits are rare, or their associations with the Fremont culture are dubious, it has been so indicated and documentation has been included.

The organization of this section has followed to a large extent that devised by Murdock and others (1950) in their "Outline of Cultural Materials." There has, however, been some revision of order and no close adherence to Murdock's levels of classification.

The "Outline of Cultural Materials" was followed in an attempt to provide the archaeological data, and the implications drawn from them, with much of the vital, dynamic feel that can be conveyed in a well-written ethnography. The archaeological data are, after all, the result of activities of living people. In the case of the Fremont material, we are apparently dealing with a vigorous, enthusiastic, frontier culture. To describe it in terms of numerous static traits would not portray any of this spirit. Since detailed descriptions are essential to an archaeological report, many are presented in this synthesis of the Fremont culture and many more, in far greater detail, have been presented in the descriptions of the sites. Table 1 is a guide to the description and distribution of specimens. Many facets of a culture are forever lost to the archaeologist so, by comparison with an ethnography written on the basis of full knowledge of a living group, the present summary is not too much more than the dry material-culture skeleton of the once living culture. Other systems of the culture are known to have existed—they had to; but for the most part they must be inferred on a functional basis and the inferences supported by limited indirect evidence. An anatomist knows that muscles had to be present to move the bones of a skeleton, and he can identify on the bones the areas to which the muscles were once attached. By comparisons with similar living animals the anatomist can shrewdly reconstruct much of an animal represented only by the skeleton. However, since cultures are subject to all sorts of vagaries of change, the archaeologist needs to exert great caution in his reconstructions.

For the most part, a comparison of Fremont traits with similar traits found elsewhere will not be included with these functional descriptions. Rather, external comparisons and resulting interpretations will be discussed later in this volume.

GEOGRAPHY

The area where remains of the Fremont culture predominate, here called the Fremont area, is essentially an oval about 200 miles long and 100 miles wide. It is bounded on the west by the Wasatch Mountains, on the north by the Uinta Mountains, on the south by rough terrain south of the drainage of the Fremont River, on the southeast by the canyon country near the Colorado River, and on the northeast by a line more or less parallel to and just east of the Utah-Colorado state line. Beyond these boundaries in all directions (except possibly west) is to be found sparse evidence showing or suggesting Fremont occupation or use. Limited evidence of the Fremont culture has been found a short distance south of the Colorado River in eastern Utah and western Colorado and in the Escalante drainage, both areas where other complexes are better represented. And a little Fremont material has been found in canyons well into the Uinta Mountains and as far north as southern Wyoming.

The entire Fremont area is drained by the Colorado River, and most of it by two tributaries, the Green River and the Dirty Devil River. Much of this area is either bare rock or not too well stabilized sand. Soil, where present, is thin and poorly developed, but the paucity of rainfall has left what nutrient it contained unleached. The richest land is found in the tributary canyons, although in the past hundred years much of this alluvial fill has been eroded out.

Along the streams grow various deciduous trees such as willow and cottonwood, as well as other plants that need abundant moisture. On the terraces back from the watercourses the vegetation is dominated by shrubs such as saltbush, greasewood, rabbitbrush, squawbush, and yucca. Even farther from the streams, where plants have access only to local precipitation, shadscale and saltbush occur. On mesas and rolling hills, at somewhat higher elevations, there are pinyon and juniper, and at still higher elevations, where the rainfall is greater and more effective, quaking aspen and ponderosa pine occur. Since in many parts of the Fremont area elevation can in-

crease several thousand feet within a few miles, a variety of life zones with their various resources are available to the inhabitants.

Nearly all Fremont sites are at elevations between 5000 and 7000 feet, but in the northern half of the region few if any sites are at elevations above 6000 feet. The average annual growing season throughout the Fremont area is 100 to 160 days and the average annual precipitation is 6 to 10 inches, with about 65 per cent falling during the warm season. Since the relative humidity is generally very low, the rate of evaporation is high. The precarious conditions for horticulture suggested by these statistics are slightly ameliorated by the fact that most Fremont settlements are situated either in relatively deep valleys or along the foothills of the mountains. Alter (1941, p. 1158), in discussing the climate of Utah, points out that most of Utah's

". . . farming lands are near the mountains, which have a very important influence in preventing frost or freezing temperatures. On cold, clear nights the coldest air usually forms, or accumulates by radiation and drainage, on the valley-bottoms, while the gravitational movement of the cooling air on the mountain slopes serves to mix and unify the temperature of the air near the ground over the foothill and bench lands, thus retarding frost formation and freezing temperatures. . . . A difference of 2 weeks is often noted in the same valley between the bottom lands and the adjacent farming lands at the foot of the mountains."

Water, however, appears to have been the environmental factor most critical for Fremont farmers. Throughout the Fremont area there is relatively little land that would have received adequate natural subirrigation, and in most areas where Fremont sites are found no such land is apparent. Thus, farming would have depended heavily upon some sort of irrigation or utilization of runoff.

THE PEOPLE

Estimates of the Fremont population are at best highly conjectural. The Fremont people occupied about 20,000 square miles of territory, but only a small percentage of it was usable for farming and it is in such restricted areas that evidence of intensive occupation occurs. A few of the most favorable areas, such as Ivie Creek, Nine Mile Canyon and

Ferron Creek, could each have had populations of a few hundred at the time of maximum population. Since areas showing intensive occupation are not numerous, a total peak Fremont population of a few thousand, probably no more than 10,000, appears to be a reasonable estimate.

Unfortunately, the amount of human skeletal material from Fremont sites is small. Gillin (1938, pp. 24–25) excavated one Fremont burial and Wormington (1955, pp. 36–43) excavated four, one of them double. Four other partial skeletons, probably Fremont but not collected under controlled conditions, have been described by Gunnerson (1957 a, pp. 30–36). Some but not all of the skulls show lambdoidal flattening, presumably induced by cultural practices. There is also considerable somatological variation in this small sample, even within the individuals from the Turner-Look Site (Eric Reed, *in*: Wormington, 1955, pp. 38–45) but, in general, all the Fremont individuals seem to have been within the range represented by the Anasazi population.

FOOD QUEST

ANIMALS HUNTED

The Fremont people depended upon foodstuffs secured by hunting and gathering as well as upon what they raised. The animals best represented in collections of identified bones from excavated Fremont sites are mountain sheep and rabbits. The composite list (below) of animals represented at the Turner-Look, Old Woman, and Snake Rock sites (Wormington, 1955; Taylor, 1957; Gunnerson, n.d.) shows a great deal of variety, with few animals being reported from only one site. It is not certain, of course, that all of these animals were eaten. Some might have been used for other purposes. The following list, somewhat inconsistent as to nomenclature because of its composite nature, presents the fauna in approximately the order of frequency, starting with the most numerous.

Bighorn sheep (*Ovis canadensis*)
Rabbits
    jack rabbit (*Lepus townsendi*)
    cottontail (*Sylvilagus nuttalli*)
    snowshoe hare (*Lepus americanus*)
Deer (*Odocoileus hemionus*)
Elk (*Cervus canadensia*)
Paririe dog (*Cynomys parvidens ?*)
Marmot
Ground squirrel (*Citellus variegatus*)
               (*Citellus beldingi*)
               (*Citellus lateralis*)
Gopher
Buffalo (*Bison bison*)
Wood rat
Badger
Coyote
Beaver
Chipmunk
Grouse (*Denragopus* sp.)
Golden Eagle
Bear ? (*Ursus*)

Rock shelters in Castle Park, along the Yampa River, have yielded evidence of a number of species not represented by bones at village sites farther south: white-footed mouse, wolf, red fox, possibly striped skunk, and unidentified specimens of birds and fish (Burgh and Scoggin, 1948, *passim*).

A large quantity of crushed or ground grasshoppers found in a cist pit in Mantle's Cave strongly suggested that grasshoppers had been intentionally caught, ground and stored. Most were adult and all that could be identified were of the genus *Melanoplus*. (Jones *in*: Burgh and Scoggin, 1948, p. 98).

PLANTS GATHERED

The longest list of identified wild plant materials that probably served as food comes from Mantle's Cave (Jones, *in*: Burgh and Scoggin, 1948, pp. 94–97). Included are seeds of Indian Millet (*Oryzopsis hymenoides*), pinyon nuts, bulbs of probably two species of lilies, seeds of wild sunflowers, seeds of goosefoot (*Chenopodium* sp.), and seeds of Utah Juniper. Seeds and fruit of other unidentified species that may or may not have served as food were also recovered.

Pine nuts, probably the most important wild plant food gathered, have been found at several Fremont sites. Throughout the Fremont area, many small sites, often yielding only a few chips or sherds and sometimes a mano or metate, are found in areas now thickly covered with pinyon and juniper trees. These small sites, sometimes several miles from known villages or farmable land, may have been occupied by Fremont people while they were gathering pine nuts. The best alternative explanation is that they were hunting camps. In any case, they probably relate to hunting and/or gathering activities that took the people away from their permanent villages.

HUNTING IMPLEMENTS

Animals were presumably hunted with the bow and arrow and caught with snares and small nets. Other methods were probably also used, but no definite evidence for such has been found. The chipped stone blades of a size suitable for spearpoints were probably used as knives instead. The snares recovered by Morss (1931, p. 70) consist of slightly tapered two-ply cords about 2 to 3 m. long with a slip knot at one or both ends. Most of the snares from Mantle's Cave are similar, but four were found each having a wooden tube to which one end of the cord was tied and through which the cord passed. "The wooden tube may have served only to provide a free-running noose, or it may have served as a trigger when the snare was set" (Burgh and Scoggin, 1948, p. 59).

The Fremont net reported by Morss (1931, pp. 70–71) is hemispherical, about 30 cm. in diameter, and considered by him too small for catching rabbits. The list of fauna represented at Fremont sites, however, includes smaller animals, such as prairie dogs and ground squirrels, which could probably have been caught with such a net. Two nets of comparable size, but with a somewhat larger mesh, were found at Mantle's Cave (Burgh and Scoggin, 1948, p. 60). One of these has a drawstring laced through the top so that it could have served as a trap. The net reported by Morss has a piece of heavier cord attached to the top that could also have been a drawstring. All of these nets could, however, have been used as carrying nets.

Fish bones and fishhooks were found at Mantle's Cave. The hooks are composite, made of a bone barb lashed to a wood shaft, and attached to cords about 3 m. long. Two of the hooks were attached to either end of one such cord (Burgh and Scoggin, 1948, p. 41). Morss (1954, p. 18) was told that bone fishhooks had been found in the Fremont River area, but it was impossible for him to verify the statement.

HORTICULTURE

Various lines of evidence show that horticulture played an important role, if not the most important role in Fremont subsistence. Nearly all Fremont sites are located near tillable land, and most are near land that could be easily irrigated. Numerous storage structures of a wide variety of types are found in the Fremont area. And the settlements indicate a sedentary or at least seasonally sedentary way of life.

PLANTS CULTIVATED

More significant, however, is the direct evidence of maize, beans, and squash. Maize remains are by far the most common, but this may be due in large part to the fact that maize produces residue that is not only easily identifiable but is more apt to be preserved, either through desiccation or charring, than beans or squash.

As can be seen in the detailed study of the maize from Fremont sites presented in Appendix I, and from the more general discussion of maize presented by Galinat and Gunnerson (1963), Fremont maize is basically like other contemporary Southwestern maize, with slight modifications probably due to local natural selection. The preponderance of Fremont maize is Fremont Dent, a moderately well stabilized race that is now considered a blending of Chapalote, teosinte, and Maíz de Ocho. There is some variation in the relative strength of the three ingredients from ear to ear, and Maíz de Ocho occasionally reasserted itself in nearly pure form. This assertion could have resulted from the deliberate selection of such ears for seed or it could represent a combination of chance selection influenced by local climatic conditions. That care went into the selection and storage of seed is suggested by several finds of a few well-preserved choice ears of maize sometimes obviously cached with special pains. One such ear of nearly pure Maíz de Ocho from Morss's Site 37 strongly suggests that ears of this race were not deliberately avoided for seed, although most ears that seem to have been saved for seed were Fremont Dent.

In the past it has been suggested that Fremont maize included a large increment of a central Mexican pyramidal race (*Zapalote Chico*) that was missing in the intervening areas. On the basis of maize from widely distributed Fremont sites, Galinat and Gunnerson (1963) concluded that the few ears from Fremont sites which do have a slight resemblance to Zapalote Chico represent, in all probability, nothing other than a variation of Fremont Dent, which, like most nonscientifically hybridized maize, is somewhat variable.

There is direct though limited evidence of the cultivation of beans and cucurbita at Fremont sites. Beans have been reported from several sites visited by Morss in the Fremont drainage (Morss, 1931, p. 58), from Yampa Canyon (Burgh and Scoggin, 1948), from the Emery Site (42Em47) excavated by Gunnerson (1957 a, p. 127), and from Site ET 6-7 described in this report. Morss (1931, p. 58) found a buckskin bag containing about three pounds of beans along with about a half pound of squash seed and some shelled corn at Site 27 on Oak Creek, south of Fruita, Utah. This bag of assorted seed strongly suggests a cache that was being held for future planting. The beans range from light to dark red and vary in size. White beans were collected by Morss (1931, p. 59) from another site.

The evidence of cucurbita found by Morss in the Fremont River drainage is augmented by the present report, which shows that cucurbita were grown over all the rest of the Fremont area. The number of species grown is not certain; perhaps there was only one.

Cucurbita were not only eaten, but the shells were probably dried after they were cleaned out and used as containers as elsewhere in the Southwest. The only specimen in the Claflin-Emerson collections that had been utilized for a container is from Site SR 12-5 in Barrier Canyon. However, this site contained a Mesa Verde and probably an earlier occupation as well as a Fremont occupation; therefore, it is not certain to which of the occupations the container should be attributed.

Horticultural Implements

Horticultural implements used by the Fremont people were very simple. The digging stick, made from a single piece of wood about 0.5 m. long was apparently the principal tool. Often digging sticks were made from branches that had joined larger branches in such a manner that a section of the latter could be left attached to form a short T- or L-shaped handle. In cross section the points were round rather than flat, and there is no evidence that blades or points of other material such as bone, antler, or stone were ever attached to digging sticks.

Three wooden shovels of probable Fremont manufacture reported from Nine Mile Canyon (Gunnerson, 1962 c) are very similar to one of probable Virgin manufacture from the Escalante River drainage (Gunnerson, 1959 c, pp. 96–97). One of the Nine Mile specimens is made from a single piece of wood and the other two have blades that had been lashed or bound to straight handles. The specimens vary in length from about 0.7 to 1.0 m., while the blades vary in width from 10 to 23 cm. and are between 15 and 21 cm. long. These shovels are all made from cottonwood except for one maple handle. There is nothing about the specimens to associate them with definitely horticultural activities, but such a use seems likely. No diagnostic artifacts were found with these shovels, but two coiled basketry fragments presumably associated with them, one with a half-rod-and-bundle foundation and the other with a bundle foundation, are not out of place in a Fremont site.

Gillin (1938, p. 27) found one slate tool that he called a hoe at Sky House. It is comparable in both outline and size to the blade portions of the two-piece wooden shovels just described, which are also said to be from Nine Mile Canyon.

Irrigation

There is evidence to indicate that prehistoric people practiced ditch irrigation in at least three areas heavily settled by Fremont people. Since there is no evidence of other prehistoric horticultural inhabitants in any of these areas, it is safe to assume that the Fremont people constructed these irrigation systems. Morss (1931, p. 7) was told of and shown a portion of an aboriginal irrigation ditch along Pleasant Creek, south of Fruita, Utah. Reagan (1931 f) described irrigation ditches along Brush Creek northeast of Vernal, Utah, that were said to have been found by early settlers and later partially reused by recent farmers. And Gunnerson (1957 a, p. 134) was told that early settlers found irrigation ditches west of Ferron, Utah, along Ferron Creek just before it leaves its canyon. Thus, there seems to be little question but that the Fremont people diverted water from small streams and conducted it via ditches, perhaps for several miles, to their fields. Since reports of such irrigation ditches come from both ends and the middle of the Fremont area, the trait was probably known to all the Fremont people and practiced wherever the requisite conditions prevailed.

The proximity of mountains to farm land makes available additional water in the form of springs from which water could be diverted or carried. Also, rain that falls on the steep slopes of the foothills often flows in a broad sheet across the more nearly level areas before eventually entering established watercourses. The author has seen automobile traffic stopped on the highway south of Ferron, Utah, until such a sheet, about a foot deep and several hundred yards wide, drained across the paving after a local cloudburst. Planting could have been and probably was done in areas where such water resources could be utilized.

FOOD STORAGE

Much effort apparently went into the building of small structures, presumably granaries, in protected niches and rock shelters throughout the Fremont area. Some of these were built in nearly inaccessible places; others were so situated that they could not be seen from any point where a person would be expected to go, and still others were camouflaged, intentionally or unintentionally, by building them of stone and adobe the color of their surroundings.

Observations made on really well preserved storage structures suggest that they were constructed well enough to be at least rodent-proof and perhaps even insect-proof. Evidence of repairing or patching, sometimes even of filling cracks, can be seen. Openings that gave access to the contents were probably all so designed that they could be sealed with stone and adobe. In some of the smaller granaries, the openings were only large enough for an arm.

The reasons for the dispersion of storage structures are not clear from the data available. Some have been found several miles from the nearest known village, while others are very close. To some extent this may reflect local conditions, since not all villages situated close to good farm land are also close to cliffs affording small shelters suitable for such storage structures. On the other hand, villages may once have existed near by that have since been destroyed by erosion or cultivation and it seems obvious that the sparse coverage of the area by archaeologists has left many sites undiscovered. If the purpose was merely protection from the weather, then why were

nearly inaccessible locations selected? Perhaps in areas where storage structures are found in such locations they were built in the more accessible niches, too, but have been completely destroyed by vandals of the past century. If it was necessary to make granaries inconspicuous to provide protection against theft, it would seem unwise to store valuable food at a great distance from habitations where the approach of a larceny-bent neighbor, from either near or far, could go undetected. Also, anyone specifically looking for these small storage structures could identify most of them from a distance in spite of their camouflage.

In any case, the smallness of most of the storage structures in rock shelters suggests that they were used by a family rather than a community. Thus, there is a good chance that the idiosyncrasies of the builders had much to do with the selection of storage sites and the shapes of the structures, and that probably all the factors discussed above played a part in the choice. In general, however, storage chambers in rock shelters appear to be poorly located to provide maximum security against a determined raid of people intent upon looting. The dispersal could be a safeguard against complete loss in case one cache was either destroyed or stolen.

Small caches of maize and sometimes other seeds have been found in rock shelters that often show little or no evidence of occupation or use. The small amount of grain, a bundle of a few ears of maize or a basket or skin bag of loose seeds, suggests that this material was probably seed rather than food grain. Some of the best specimens are from such finds, and may represent small emergency caches of seed that were forgotten, or never needed, or not reclaimed for any one of many other possible reasons.

Within the villages, provision for storage apparently consisted of either rows of small, contiguous, rectangular rooms or separate rooms built on the surface of the ground, traits common elsewhere in the Southwest. Some rooms interpreted as storage chambers have been found attached to habitation structures. From the limited amount of excavation at Fremont villages, however, no consistent pattern has yet emerged so far as the relative positions of these storage structures and habitations are concerned. Since many of the reported surface storage rooms in villages are constructed of adobe (Taylor, 1957, p. 29; Gunnerson, 1957 a, p. 135), their presence would not be obvious without excavation and many sites known only from surface survey may have had such structures even though they have not been noted.

Still another type of structure, the "towers" or "forts" found on high eminences difficult of access may also have served for storage. The almost complete lack of diagnostic features and artifacts associated with these sites makes functional interpretation speculative. Since, however, storage rooms are commonly without specialized features, such a function seems the most likely. Ethnographic evidence of the construction of granaries on top of isolated rock formations is found in much of northern Mexico (Hernandez, 1949), and granaries resembling even more closely these structures in the Fremont area were observed and photographed in the Tarahumara country of northern Mexico by Dr. Campbell Pennington (personal communication).

If the Fremont towers did serve as storage rooms, their relatively large size would suggest some sort of communal storage rather than individual family enterprises. It is conceivable that worsening climatic conditions made crop failures more frequent, or that increased population resulted in the cultivation of progressively more marginal land. Since there was apparently much dependence upon irrigation, a fair crop might have been produced in one valley while in the next there was a crop failure. Or villages located at intervals along the same stream may have found themselves competing for water rights. Such conditions might have led to intervillage hostility and raids and a more determined effort to protect the increasingly more precious store of food. The towers in question are so situated that they could be defended by a few people, and often there are smaller, less well built rooms near by that could have served as shelters for such guards. The lack of datable material from these towers makes it impossible to prove that they were built late within the time span of the Fremont culture, but the extreme paucity of artifacts at such sites as Rock House (ET 6-26), where there is the greatest likelihood of detritus, precludes their having been occupied for any significant length of time. Within the Fremont area, towers are most numerous in the canyons of the Tavaputs Plateau, which is just slightly north of the middle of the Fremont area. At the present time, if one excludes the results of large-scale irrigation projects along the foothills of the Uinta Mountains, some of the canyons in the Tavaputs Plateau area appear to have the most dependable supply of water in the Fremont area. It is possible that a similar situation existed near the end of the Fremont occupation and that the Tavaputs Plateau might have served briefly as a last refuge for a horticultural way of life. But even in the Tavaputs Plateau area there is now inadequate water in drought years. For example, during 1931 when the Claflin-Emerson expedition was working in the Hill and Willow Creek areas, there were disputes over water rights and it was necessary to have a watermaster to supervise distribution of irrigation water (J. O. Brew, personal communication).

FOOD PREPARATION

Little evidence exists regarding the manner in which the Fremont people prepared their food. There is no doubt that maize was ground with manos and metates, which are common at Fremont sites and which occur in a variety of forms, ranging from deep basins and open-ended troughs to shallow milling slabs. The most distinctive is the so-called Utah-type metate, which has, in addition to a large deep trough, a much smaller shallow depression at one end that may have served either as a mano rest or as a place where corn was cracked by pounding prior to grinding. Usually metates were not shaped on the bottoms or edges, although a few were. The shallow milling slabs, which sometimes occur with the deeper metates, do not differ from ones found in much older archaeological complexes. These may have served a special purpose, such as the grinding or crushing of wild seeds which continued to contribute to the diet of the people. In at least two instances a basin metate and a milling slab have been found buried face to face. Wormington (1955, p. 28) found such a pair in a house at the Turner-Look Site and Robert Thorne (personal communication) found a similar pair near Jensen, Utah.

Manos also vary greatly. The simplest are cobblestones of convenient size that have been used but in no other way modified. Some suggest a much-flattened sphere or even a disk in their over-all shape. Most manos, however, are two to three times as long as they are wide and tend to be a little wider at the middle than near the ends, which are somewhat rounded. The grinding surfaces vary from nearly flat to strongly convex, some being shaped like a section of a cylinder. Still others have two facets which meet to form a keel. Some manos have been used on only one face, others on two; some show little attempt to finish the nongrinding surfaces while others are well finished all over. A few manos resemble a loaf of bread in shape. One distinctive form, found mainly in the Uinta Basin, has a concave upper surface more or less matching the convex lower surface so that the specimens are of essentially uniform thickness for their entire length. A few manos have small depressions in their edges, apparently to provide a better grip for the fingers. Manos are made from a wide variety of stone, including quartzite, sandstone, and basalt, and rarely exceed 20 cm. in length.

Throughout the Fremont area, holes that may have been used in some way for the preparation of food are found pecked or ground into bedrock outcrops. The holes are circular, with a depth slightly greater than their diameter, and the largest have a capacity of about five gallons. Large holes are sometimes surrounded by small holes. Since the holes are not well placed to receive runoff water, they are probably not reservoirs. None of the suggestions advanced as to the function of these large holes, such as bedrock mortars, or containers for cooking with hot rocks, or storage pits, seem too reasonable. On the other hand, no nonculinary use seems any more likely. Groups of small holes that form more or less geometric patterns are found at some sites. These probably did not serve the same purpose as the large holes.

Cooking was apparently commonly done in pottery vessels, which are well represented, at least by sherds, at Fremont sites. Sherds of unpainted vessels, especially from excavations, are often heavily covered with soot, as if they had been used over open fires. Hearths have been found both inside and outside houses, and it seems likely that cooking was not confined to one location or the other.

Charring on the insides of basketry trays found at Mantle's Cave (Burgh and Scoggin, 1948) suggests that they had been used for parching or popping seeds.

Some of the corncobs found show that the kernels were cut off while the corn was green, so green corn was probably prepared and eaten in some manner. Moreover, other cobs are strongly bowed, apparently from uneven drying after they were discarded—another indication that the kernels were removed while still green.

DRUGS AND NARCOTICS

The only evidence for the use of drugs or narcotics by the Fremont people is smoking pipes. Two elbow pipes were found at Snake Rock (Gunnerson, 1957 a, fig. 7) and fragments of stone and pottery objects from the Turner-Look Site were tentatively identified as parts of pipes by Wormington (1955, pp. 65–66). Both Morss (1931, pp. 51–52) and

Taylor (1957, p. 55) describe and illustrate tubular pottery pipes, and Burgh and Scoggin (1948, pp. 53–54) describe and illustrate a tubular stone pipe from Hells Midden. The

Fremont people apparently made tubular pipes from both stone and pottery, but elbow pipes only from pottery.

AMUSEMENT

Many Fremont sites have yielded flat rectangular pieces of bone, some of which have distinctive marks engraved and/or painted on one side. These bone objects, as well as pottery or stone disks about 2 cm. in diameter sometimes found with them, have been interpreted as gaming pieces. The pottery disks are frequently from painted or tooled sherds, and thus would have been easy to identify.

The bone rectangles and the pottery or stone disks could have been used together in a game like one still played by the Hopis (Gunnerson, n.d.), in which rectangular dice (now made from cane instead of bone) are thrown, and counters are moved on a course for a number of spaces determined by the way the dice fall. Now the counters are dis-

tinctive stones or other small objects, but the sherd or stone disks found at Fremont sites would be ideally suited for such use. Wormington (1955, p. 93) reported that similar gaming devices were used by the Cheyenne.

The stone balls found at Fremont sites range from golf-ball to tennis-ball size. Similar balls are kicked in a game played by the Pima (Russell, 1908, pp. 172–173). The balls from the Fremont area have presumably been found associated with patterns of small pits pecked into the surface of nearly level bedrock (Wormington, 1955, p. 93; Gunnerson, 1957 a, p. 25). This association suggests some sort of game like marbles in which the balls would be rolled into the pits.

WEAVING AND CORDAGE

Little direct evidence of weaving has been found at Fremont sites except in Castle Park. Here six small pieces of very fine twilled cloth (over three, under one) were found at Hells Midden (Lister, 1951, pp. 34–36). The specimens, of an unidentified fiber, but not cotton, were so small that it was impossible to determine whether the material had been loom-woven or braided.

No evidence of cotton has yet been found at Fremont sites and it is assumed that it was not grown, perhaps because of climatic restrictions. Nor have such woven items as tightly twined bags and sandals, found elsewhere in the Southwest, been recovered. Even twill mats are missing, although twined reed mats with a number of variations in the selvage are fairly common.

Pieces of cord have been found in many sites, but they show little variation in spinning.

Nearly all are two-ply, Z-twist, S-spun. Two specimens of three-ply cord were found in Mantle's Cave (Burgh and Scoggin, 1948, pp. 58, 60). One was a snare and the other was a bowstring made of sinew. Cords vary in weight from light string to light rope. Those apparently intended for use as snares often taper from one end to the other. Materials from which cords are made include yucca, juniper, and apocynum.

The only artifacts found that appear to be definitely associated with the processing of fiber are spindle whorls, perforated disks usually made from pottery sherds. One unusual spindle whorl from Site ET 6-7 is nicely made from dark gray-tan shale and may represent a trade item from the Hohokam area. A possible spindle whorl of coiled basketry was found in Marigold's Cave (Lister, 1951, p. 36).

BASKETRY

The Fremont people made good baskets. By far the most common technique employed was close coiling with a half-rod-and-bundle

foundation sewed with a simple noninterlocking stitch such as is shown by Morris and Burgh (1941) in their figure 3 h. Although split stitches and interlocking stitches are not uncommon in baskets of this type, they appear to be accidental and never occur consistently in any one specimen. The half-rods are either squawbush or willow and the stiching material appears to be the bark of the same material in each case. The bundle is always yucca. The rods are stripped of their bark and some appear to have been scraped. Decoration is rare, but occasionally darker stitching material was included to provide simple geometric designs.

Baskets of this construction are usually broad, relatively shallow bowls. Morss (1931, p. 73), however, found a large carrying basket "24 inches in diameter and 18 inches high" made with a half-rod-and-bundle technique. At Mantle's Cave (Burgh and Scoggin, 1948), this technique was represented in a conical carrying basket with a black woven-in zigzag design, in a tray charred on the inside, presumably from parching or popping grain, and in a globular basket.

A second close-coiled technique has a single half-rod foundation without a bundle and with simple interlocking stitches. This technique is like that shown by Morris and Burgh (1941) in their figure 2 a, except that they illustrate it with a one-rod foundation rather than a half-rod foundation. As Morris and Burgh (1941, p. 7) suspected, re-examination disclosed that the baskets described by Morss (1931, p. 73) as having a two-rod foundation are actually of this single-rod type. Fragments of an especially thin and well-made basket of this type from Morss's Site 11 appear to be from a pitch-covered water bottle.

Baskets with a single half-rod foundation and interlocking stitches from Mantle's Cave include a fragment of a globular basket the rim of which is decorated with a false braid, a complete globular basket, a fragment of a probable parching tray, two miniature bowls, and an unusual small dipper.

Another variation, represented by one specimen from the Old Woman Site (Taylor, 1957, p. 46), was coiled with a foundation consisting of a full rod surrounded by a bundle of yucca leaves. It was rather loosely sewed with noninterlocking stitches. The more common half-rod-and-bundle basketry was also recovered at this site.

Two-half-rod-and-bundle foundation, stacked basketry with noninterlocking simple stitches is represented by at least one Fremont specimen. This, a bottom from a basket that had been repaired with a leather thong, was illustrated by Morss (1931, plate 39 d), who classified it as a rod-and-bundle foundation specimen.

One example of basketry with a two-half-rod stacked foundation and simple, interlocking stitches was reported by Burgh and Scoggin (1948, p. 58) from Mantle's Cave. The stitches are widely spaced so that the foundation rods are exposed between them.

A few Fremont baskets were coiled with a bundle foundation. Both cedar bark and long narrow grassy leaves were used for the bundles. The sewing was done with strips of tough bark (squawbush or willow) and the stitches were widely spaced and interlocking. The two baskets from Site A 6-1 with bundle foundations were somewhat flattened spheres with markedly constricting necks. One was found covered with a small coiled basket and another, containing corn, was covered with a piece of buffalo hide. A very similar specimen, said to be from Nine Mile Canyon, is reported by Gunnerson (1962 c). Morris and Burgh (1941) do not report this particular technique.

The only known specimens of twined basketry from a Fremont site are from Morss's Site 36 and are previously unreported. Three fragments, probably all from a single basket of undetermined shape, were recovered. The warp elements are full rods about 3 mm. in diameter and the weft elements are thin strips of bark about 3 mm. wide. The technique employed is that described by Mason (1904, p. 234) as "diagonal twined weaving" with the weft element going over two and then under two warp elements and advancing one warp element on each successive row. Between each pair of warp elements, the two weft elements that are being used together cross over one another but they are not twisted around one another. In other words, the outer surface of any one particular weft element always shows on one surface of the finished basket and the inner surface of the weft element always shows on the other surface of the finished basket. The basket was as tightly woven as possible; that is, the pairs of weft elements touched one another. The general size, shape, and weight suggest that these fragments could be from a large conical carrying basket for which such a weave is very common among many historic groups in the Great Basin.

Morss (1931, p. 71) reports a twined coarse bag or limp basket made entirely of cedar bark. He thinks it likely that this once served as a covering for a pottery jar. Its coarseness would preclude its effective use as a container for such material as shelled corn, although ears of corn could have been stored in it. Considering the coarse nature of the raw material, this bag or basket is well made. Its shape is very suggestive of the coiled baskets with a bundle foundation.

Bone awls and pointed sticks may have been used in the making of baskets.

LEATHER

The Fremont people were obviously accomplished in the preparation of hides. There is no direct evidence of the methods used, but the fact that pieces of buckskin are still very soft and pliable shows that they were well tanned. Buckskin provided the material for small bags and was probably also used for clothing. Other hides, such as those used in moccasins, had been prepared so that they were harder and tougher. Moreover, the hair was left on. With regard to the Fremont moccasins, one very interesting detail is that hide from the legs had been specifically selected and cut in such a way that the dew claws projected from the sole, presumably to serve as hob nails. Still another specialized use of skin was in the manufacture of furcloth, presumably in the form of robes.

Except for bone awls and chipped stone knives, tools that would have been especially useful in preparing and processing hides have not been identified as such. Snub-nosed end scrapers and side scrapers are virtually absent from the Fremont complex. Probably some of the less distinctive stone tools or artifacts called blades or knives served as scrapers.

CERAMICS

Fremont pottery was constructed by coiling and thinned by scraping. Ground sherds have been found that were probably used to scrape the pottery during thinning. The outer surfaces of the vessels were carefully smoothed and often partially polished, presumably with smooth pebbles, which are sometimes found at Fremont sites. Only rarely were the coils left unobliterated to form the distinctive corrugated exterior so common throughout much of the Anasazi area, but Fremont ware exhibits a variety of other approaches to decoration, as well as several vessel shapes (Gunnerson, 1956 c). In fact, its distinctiveness makes it the most diagnostic of common Fremont artifacts.

All Fremont pottery is gray (fired in a reducing atmosphere) and it is all tempered with crushed rock. Wormington (1955) named the ware in general Turner Gray and distinguished two varieties, "Variety I" and "Variety II," on the basis of the kind of rock that was crushed for tempering. The most common of these, tempered with crushed igneous rock, was Wormington's "Variety II." Gunnerson has since called it "Emery Variety" after Emery County, which is within the area where it is most common. It is usually called simply "Emery Gray" when it is undecorated and, when decorated, "Emery Tooled," "Emery Black-on-white," or "Emery Black-on-gray," depending on the nature of the decoration. Painted vessels of this variety have also been called "Ivie Creek Black-on-white" by Lister and others (1960).

Wormington's "Variety I" is an inferior ware because it was tempered with crushed calcite, which decomposes under even moderate firing temperatures. It was apparently made only where igneous rock was unavailable, particularly in the Uinta Basin. Again, for simplicity, this variety has been given the name "Uinta." Undecorated sherds are designated as "Uinta Gray" and sherds decorated with surface manipulations as "Uinta Tooled." Thus far, no painted calcite-tempered sherds have been reported. The name is doubly appropriate because this is obviously the pottery called "Uintah Gray" by Steward (1936, pp. 18–19) and its area of distribution is essentially limited to the Uinta Basin.

The feature of Fremont pottery that is most distinctive upon gross examination is the common use of surface manipulation for decoration. Embellishment is achieved by incising, punching, pinching, or applying small pellets or strips of clay, all prior to firing the vessel. Frequently combinations of these techniques are employed. Decoration is usually restricted to the rims, necks, shoulders, and handles of vessels. Very rarely is a decorated lip found.

The most common motif achieved by tooling is a right-angle scoring produced by incised horizontal and vertical lines, or incised horizontal lines and punctated vertical lines, or incised horizontal lines crossed by vertical lines made by pinching. The last approach, especially, and to some extent the other two, produce an effect somewhat resembling indented or pinched corrugation. A few sherds here, as in western Utah, show what appears to be a deliberate imitation of corrugation and, as mentioned before, a few Fremont sherds are actually corrugated.

Sherds decorated by punctation show that a variety of tools were used. The most common is the fingernail, but tools with circular ends, such as small twigs, and straight sharp implements, such as flint chips, were apparently also used. Punctations usually fill areas, either in parallel rows or more or less at random, but they also occur in single lines or narrow bands. Small round punctations sometimes occur in the middle of or at one edge of applied pellets, which in turn are found in rows encircling the neck of a vessel or extending vertically down from the lip.

Painted designs are found on the outsides of ollas, pitchers, and bottles and on the insides of bowls. The paint usually contained carbon pigment, but iron paint was also used. The surface to be painted was sometimes covered with a good thick white slip. Some of the unslipped surfaces had been smoothed well enough to float small clay particles to the surface; in such cases it was difficult to determine whether or not a thin slip had been applied. Painted sherds with a slipped surface are here classified as black-on-white and those without a slip as black-on-gray. Design styles do not seem to vary with the presence or absence of a slip. Decoration is almost always geometric, with straight lines more common than curved. Most design elements can be classified as Sosi, Dogoszhi, or, more commonly, Black Mesa, while the general design layout most closely resembles the last. These various elements, along with dots, are combined in several different ways. Encircling lines constitute the most characteristic design motif.

Fugitive red pigment is sometimes found on the outsides of excavated specimens.

Reworked potsherds are fairly common at Fremont sites. Sherds were carefully ground down to disks from about 1.2 to 5 cm. in diameter and were sometimes perforated in the center by drilling. The largest perforated disks were probably used for spindle whorls. The smaller ones were probably ornaments and the small unperforated disks may have been counters or "men" used in some game.

Other reworked sherds with one or more nearly straight or somewhat curved ground edges probably served as scraping tools in the manufacture of pottery. Unmodified sherds may have served as paint dishes. Modified sherds from painted or tooled vessels are more common than those from plain gray vessels, while, in contrast, unworked plain gray sherds are much more abundant than unworked sherds that exhibit decoration.

Fremont pottery, especially of the Emery varieties, shows a great deal of variation in vessel shape. Globular jars are apparently most common. These had a number of rim forms, varying from vertical or slightly flaring through strongly flaring to recurved. Rims join the body either in smooth curves or sharp angles and vary in height from about 1 cm. to about 10 cm. Single handles extending from the lip to the rim–shoulder junction are commonly found on globular vessels. Probably next most common are bowls, usually approximately thirds of spheres. Other bowls had essentially vertical rims and a few had constricted orifices (seed bowls). Other vessel forms include large pitchers with tall vertical necks on flat-bottomed globular bodies of slightly greater diameter, small pitchers which grade into small globular vessels, and water bottles with globular bodies and small vertical necks. The pitchers have handles but the bottles do not. The recurved rims on globular vessels sometimes reach such proportions that the vessel has a compound silhouette suggestive of a globular vessel on top of a slightly larger one. Pottery ladles occur, but are not common.

Some vessels have unusual shapes. A small pitcher illustrated by Morss (1931, plate 23 c) has 11 nodes pushed out along the vessel's equator. One sherd from Snake Rock (Gunnerson, n.d.) could be from a stirrup-spout or some other complex vessel, or it could be from a badly warped pot. A small vessel in a private collection from a Fremont site is shaped like an animal head and another vessel in the same collection has a flat lid to which is attached a snake looped up to form a handle. A shoulder in the neck of the vessel is designed to accommodate the lid (Gunnerson, 1962 b).

EXPLOITATIVE ACTIVITIES

The Fremont people made use of a wide variety of mineral resources. Chipped stone implements were fabricated from chalcedony, jasper, flint, fine-grained quartzite, and, occasionally, obsidian. No attempt has been made to locate the sources of these materials, although one possible quarry site has been reported by Gunnerson (1957 a, p. 108). Ground stone artifacts, specifically manos, metates, and balls, were made from basalt, sandstone, and quartzite, especially the distinctive Uinta quartzite. There are local variations that obviously correspond to material available. Quartzite originating in the Uinta Mountains and carried as boulders by the Green River was commonly used in the northern part of the Fremont area, where basalt does not occur either naturally or in the form of artifacts. On the other hand, basalt was the usual material in Castle Valley and in the Fremont River drainage where volcanic action has left much of the countryside strewn with basalt boulders. Sandstone is available throughout the Fremont area and was used for large artifacts.

Small ground stone artifacts, especially ornaments and disks, were made from a variety of soft, fine-grained stone such as hematite, lignite, alabaster, turquoise, and shale. It is not certain which of these materials are available locally and which were traded for, either as raw material or as finished products.

Structures were built of whatever stone was available. The most suitable material was sandstone, which often occurs as thin layers or slabs, or in thicker deposits that split into slabs of convenient thickness. Basalt boulders and, to a lesser extent, boulders of other stone were used in structures, but required mortar (adobe) to hold them in place. Adobe clay was frequently used in conjunction with wood or stone or by itself for the walls and roofs. Floors were usually plastered with adobe.

The ceramic industry also utilized a variety of minerals. Clay, of course, was the major ingredient and was probably selected with care. Clay for the slip on pottery would have been even more carefully chosen. Igneous rock, available almost everywhere except in the Uinta Basin, was utilized in crushed form for tempering material. Where it was not available, calcite was crushed and used for temper. Pottery was sometimes painted with a black mineral pigment and sometimes covered on the outside with a fugitive red pigment, presumably hematite.

Mineral pigment, especially red, was extensively used on pictographs, and pigments of various colors were used to decorate figurines and probably other objects as well.

Gilsonite, an asphalt-like petroleum product that occurs in the Uinta Basin, was collected and used to coat baskets, presumably to waterproof them. It probably also served as an adhesive in the mounting of chipped stone points and blades and in other manufacturing processes.

PROCESSING OF BASIC MATERIALS

BONE

Evidence of bone-working techniques is provided by the appearance of completed bone artifacts, incompleted artifacts, and scraps of material from the process of manufacture, as well as by tools that could have been used for bone working. Bone was apparently cut by grinding or incising a groove deep enough to permit the piece to be broken, after which the rough edges were ground or scraped smooth. Long bones of mammals were sometimes split so that splinters of bone suitable for the manufacture of awls resulted. Narrow grooves that could have been used for grinding bone artifacts are found in sandstone bedrock or large boulders, and sometimes in smaller pieces of sandstone. Holes could have been drilled through or into bone with the stone drills that are found. Grooves in bone, either for cutting or decoration, were probably made with chipped stone knives, gravers, or "saws," sometimes called "serrated scrapers." One bone artifact from the multicomponent Site SR 12-5 (and thus not necessarily of Fremont manufacture) is decorated with circular grooves that were apparently ground with some sort of thin-walled hollow tube and an abrasive, probably sand.

Wood

Woodworking techniques probably paralleled those of bone working. In addition, a few other methods were employed. Ground stone axes are apparently absent in the Fremont area and the heaviest cutting or chopping tools are roughly chipped crude blades or "choppers." Trees were probably felled by first charring them around their bases and then by chopping out the charcoal, perhaps with the crude choppers. A chisel-shaped antler artifact from the Emery Site (Gunnerson, 1957 a, fig. 8 ee) may have been a wordworking tool. Grooved sandstone abraders, such as the specimen found at Site ET 6-7, had probably been used in pairs to smooth wooden arrowshafts. Such tools are not common at Fremont sites, but they have been reported before (Morss, 1931, p. 55). By drawing a shaft back and forth between a pair of such abraders held with their grooves directly opposite each other, one could achieve a nearly uniform diameter for the shaft.

Stone

Stone was worked by chipping, pecking, and grinding. Both percussion and pressure were used in making chipped stone artifacts. A few small crude blades or choppers, usually almond-shaped, were apparently made exclusively by percussion, but most of the chipped stone tools, such as projectile points and blades, were finished by pressure flaking. Hammerstones, more or less spherical and 5 or 6 cm. in diameter, are found at Fremont sites and could have been used for percussion flaking and for detaching large flakes to be worked by pressure flaking. Artifacts definitely identified as flakers have not been reported for the Fremont culture, but a number of bone and antler artifacts found could have served such a function.

Hammerstones were probably used for shaping metates, manos, and stone balls, all of which occur at Fremont sites. Additional smoothing could have been accomplished by grinding with sandstone. Some of these ground stone artifacts show very careful workmanship: many of the stone balls are nearly perfect spheres and a few are well polished.

In sandstone bedrock and large boulders throughout the Fremont area are found broad grooves that have been called axe sharpeners. Such a function seems highly improbable in view of the complete absence of ground stone axes in the area. However, these grooves may have resulted from the shaping of manos, which do occur in abundance at Fremont sites and are often well finished. Even some of the depressions in bedrock that have been considered bedrock metates, primarily because a small depression suggestive of "Utah type" metates is found at the end of a larger depression, may have been used for shaping manos. These paired depressions, about the same size as and vaguely suggestive of the print of a shoe with a heel, are much smaller than metates and usually occur in groups (Morss, 1931, plate 11 c; Gunnerson, 1957 a, p. 25). The long depression could have been used for shaping the grinding surfaces of manos and the circular depression for shaping the ends.

ARCHITECTURE

Information on Fremont architecture comes chiefly from a few sources. Gillin (1938) and

Steward (1933 a) describe several structures they excavated in Nine Mile Canyon and the

Uinta Basin, respectively. Wormington (1955) includes good descriptions of structures at the somewhat anomalous Turner-Look Site and Taylor (1957) provides detailed information on a variety of architectural styles from two Fremont sites near Emery, Utah. Data obtained mostly from Castle Valley, but from elsewhere in the Fremont area as well, are reported by Gunnerson (1957 a, 1957 c, n.d., and in this report). Various other references provide corroborative information, especially on small storage structures.

Fremont architecture is noted for its diversity, even within a site. Structures were built in the open and under rock shelters, on the surface of the ground and in pits. Building techniques included dry-laid masonry, stone slabs laid in adobe, vertical stone slabs, boulders laid in or chinked with adobe, adobe and poles (jacal), adobe, adobe turtlebacks, and adobe-plaster-lined pits. Rooms were both round and rectangular and built singly or as parts of small multi-roomed structures.

PITHOUSES

The most common Fremont habitation was probably the pithouse. These varied from perhaps 0.3 m. to 1.5 m. in depth and were from 3 to 8 m. across. Pithouses range from nearly square to nearly round. Limited excavation at Snake Rock near Emery, Utah (Gunnerson, n.d.), uncovered all or parts of five pithouses that were partially overlapping and thus related stratigraphically, as well as a sixth, isolated one. Artifacts associated with the five stratified structures gave no indication of change through time, but there were differences in the construction of the pithouses. The oldest pithouse, which had been dug into the virgin earth of the site, was only partially excavated. It had apparently been nearly square; its pit was the deepest and had the thickest lining, composed of moderately large boulders and adobe. Subsequent pithouses were all smaller, nearly round, and progressively shallower with thinner pit linings. The most recent of the series had been dug almost entirely into refuse accumulated in and around previous pithouses. Its walls and floor were plastered with adobe and the only rock in the wall was a large boulder that had been too heavy to move.

All the pithouses excavated at Snake Rock had a central, circular, adobe-rimmed fireplace, and in all but the most recent of the five stratified pithouses the bottom of the fireplace was paved with stone slabs. No post holes were found in the isolated pithouse, which was only about 3 m. in diameter, but in all the rest where enough excavating had been done to uncover them, four post holes were found symmetrically spaced around the fireplace and about halfway between it and the wall. In at least one house where the post butts were well enough preserved to make such an observation possible, the posts had been set upside down in the holes. This was shown by the angle at which the branch stubs joined the trunk.

At the Emery Site (Gunnerson, 1957 a, p. 127), an interesting variation was noted in an especially large pithouse. In addition to posts set in conventional holes, two posts had been set in broad shallow basins and adobe filled in around the butts. It is probable that additional posts were needed to support a sagging roof after the house was built and that the basins were dug to permit the bases of the posts to be slid into place while their tops were against roof beams.

Details of roof construction were preserved in one burned pithouse at Snake Rock. The stone-and-adobe lining of the pit had not been brought quite to the surface of the ground. It was surrounded on the outside by a narrow shelf of earth slightly lower than the top of the pit lining. Evidence was found showing that poles had been shallowly set in this ledge of earth and had probably sloped up so as to be supported at their other end by some kind of central framework supported by the four center posts. Charred roof material showed that these poles had been covered with a coarse mat that supported a layer of plant material, including cornhusks and corncobs. The plant material, in turn, was covered with a layer of adobe.

No evidence of antechambers or entrances through the walls has been found in Fremont pithouses. The probability that entrance was through a hole in the roof is supported by the discovery of a circular stone slab, presumably a "hatch cover," on the floor of the pithouse partially excavated at the Emery Site by Gunnerson (1957 a, p. 127). No ventilators and deflectors have been reported for Fremont pithouses. Pithouse floors are usually covered with adobe. Cists or bins are sometimes found in pithouses, either above or below the floor level. In one pithouse at the Old Woman Site (Taylor, 1957) several distinctive clay figurines were found in a subfloor cist, and an amateur found another similar cache of even better preserved clay figurines and carved bone effigy pendants in a cist under the floor of a pithouse at Site 42Em4 near Ferron, Utah (Gunnerson, 1962 b). Partitions have not been found in Fremont pithouses.

Another variant of the Fremont pithouse pattern was represented by the isolated structure excavated at Snake Rock (Gunnerson, 1957 c, n.d.). A pit about 3 m. in diameter and a little less than 1 m. deep had been excavated and the floor thinly plastered with adobe. On the surface of the ground surrounding the pit, a wall of boulders and adobe had been constructed, perhaps two or three courses high. There was a fireplace in the center of the floor, but no post holes were found. Presumably the house had been roofed either by spanning the encircling boulder structure with rafters or by cribbing. The only surface evidence of the structure was a boulder ring about 4 m. in diameter, and during excavation many boulders that had apparently fallen from the wall into the pit were removed. Such boulder rings, presumably wall bases surrounding pithouses, are often seen at Fremont sites.

Pithouses in which the walls of the pit were lined with vertical stone slabs have been reported from Nine Mile Canyon (Gillin, 1938) and Ferron Creek Canyon (Gunnerson, 1957 a, p. 138). Erosion and vandalism had destroyed most of the details of construction at the small houses on Ferron Creek (42Em7), but House B at NM 17 was covered by a low mound and many details were preserved. The spaces between the slabs lining the pit were filled with adobe, and a capping of smaller horizontal slabs was found on top of the vertical slabs for part of the circumference. Between the central adobe-rimmed fireplace and the wall were two post holes and it was thought that two more (to complete a square pattern) had probably once existed.

The roof had apparently been composed of successive layers of heavy poles, light poles, straw (possibly a mat), interlaced willow stems, adobe, and scattered stones. As Gillin (1938, p. 9) points out, these slab-lined houses are reminiscent of Basketmaker houses in the Four Corners area. They are also suggestive of somewhat later open-site structures in the Virgin area (Steward, 1941 a, p. 288; Schroeder, 1955; Gunnerson, 1959 c, p. 32) as well as of Basketmaker structures in rock shelters in the same area (Nusbaum, 1922; Judd, 1926, p. 92).

SURFACE STRUCTURES

Structures built on ground level in the open are made of stone masonry, coursed adobe, and jacal. The circular to nearly circular surface structures found thus far show evidence of only the first two materials, but square or rectangular structures of all three materials have been reported.

The best-preserved masonry structures are Rock House (ET 6-26) and Nordell's Fort (PR 4-11) along Hill Creek and Nine Mile Canyon, respectively. The scarcity of artifacts at both these sites makes their assignment to Fremont tentative, but the complete lack of evidence of other archaeological complexes in the area where masonry exists strongly supports their Fremont authorship. Fewkes commented on the paucity of artifacts at the Hill Creek "towers" in 1917; one Fremont sherd was found at Rock House by a Claflin-Emerson party, and Gunnerson found a few flint chips.

A number of observations can be made regarding Fremont masonry structures on the basis not only of these few well-preserved structures of uncertain association, but of less spectacular finds at sites known to be Fremont. The stone slabs used were apparently never carefully dressed, although some attention was paid to the selection of slabs, and some rough shaping may have been done. A few dressed stones, including a rectangular one especially well dressed, were found along Ivie Creek at Site 42Sv9 (Gunnerson, 1957 a, p. 117) and may have been from a structure. On the other hand, they may have served some special purpose. Some of the masonry structures were dry-laid and probably plastered or chinked with adobe. In others the stones were apparently laid in adobe mortar. Little or no effort was made to maintain courses, and sometimes only one surface of a wall was kept at all even or smooth. Wormington (1955) found vaulted or canted masonry walls at the Turner-Look Site, but this trait appears uncommon elsewhere except in small storage structures in rock shelters.

Floors within masonry structures were often covered with a layer of adobe or, less commonly, paved with flat stones. The hearths, which usually occupy the centers of dwellings, were surrounded with adobe rims and were sometimes floored with small stone slabs. Post holes sometimes occur in the floors of masonry surface structures and, where they have been found, they usually form either a centrally situated square or a portion of a square that suggests other undetected post holes. Internal support posts were probably used when the width of the structure was too great to be spanned with the timbers available.

Some masonry surface rooms have small, rectangular ground-level doorways with stone lintels. Others show no evidence of openings through the wall and were probably entered through the roof. A number of structures have been reported at Fremont sites in which some of the walls, usually three, were masonry, while the remaining wall, presumably of some perishable material, was missing (Wormington, 1955; Taylor, 1957; this paper, *passim*).

Some structures seem to have had a foundation made of stone slabs, blocks, or boulders, which presumably once supported a wall of less durable material, perhaps adobe. Such a stone foundation would resist erosion by surface water far better than would adobe walls built directly on the ground. There is always the possibility, however, that what appears to be a stone foundation for a perishable wall is just the lower courses of a masonry wall, the rest of which was removed for reuse.

Structures with adobe walls have been reported at a number of Fremont sites (Gillin, 1938; Wormington, 1955; Taylor, 1957; Gunnerson, 1957 a). Construction consisted of laying up courses of stiff but still plastic adobe loaves or "turtlebacks" and finally smoothing the surfaces to more or less obliterate the joints. The individual loaves are somewhat concave on the bottom and convex on top, have a width equal to the thickness of the wall, are a little thinner than they are wide, and are definitely longer than they are wide. Adobe walls were probably used more commonly in small storage structures than in dwellings, but the sample is too small for certainty. Small adobe structures apparently never had posts to support the roof, but larger ones did.

Occasionally room-size areas are found outlined with concentrations of small gravel at Fremont sites. It is thought that these outlines may represent structures that were built of adobe containing a little gravel and that rain melted them down after they were abandoned. Careful excavation might reveal fireplaces or post holes that would help verify such an interpretation.

Jacal structures are also widely distributed in the Fremont area, having been reported from the Old Woman Site on Ivie Creek (Taylor, 1957) and from sites along the northern edge of the Uinta Basin (Gunnerson, 1957 a, pp. 41–42, and this report). In addition to vertical poles set in a shallow wall trench, the small structure at Site 42Un66 (Gunnerson, 1957 a) had a more substantial post just inside the wall in each corner. At Site A 9-3 (this report) post holes were also observed. At the Old Woman Site, where the lower portions of jacal walls were well preserved, vertical poles and light horizontal withes were found incorporated in the wall, but no additional posts were found. Hard-fired, stick-impressed adobe has been found at many sites and could be from either jacal structures or from pole-and-adobe roofs of structures made primarily of some other material.

SHELTERED STRUCTURES

Small structures and cists in rock shelters and niches are numerous and vary with regard to design and material. Occasionally structures in rock shelters are large enough to be entered, but there is no evidence that the Fremont people built substantial stone and/or adobe houses or dwelling rooms in rock shelters or caves. Rock shelters were inhabited, but wherever indications of possible domestic structures have been found (Morss, 1931, pp. 18–20; Burgh, 1950) they appear to have been of rather flimsy construction. It is quite possible that occupation of rock shelters was uncommon and only temporary when practiced. Habitation structures within them may have been little more than brush screens or windbreaks supported by a few poles. Thus, what was thought to be roof material at Site SR 12-5 in Barrier Canyon might have been such a screen that fell onto an occupation surface. This would account for the lack of evidence of walls.

Storage structures, or "granaries," as they are often called, are usually constructed of pieces of more-or-less flat stone laid in an abundance of adobe mortar. Less commonly, they are dry-laid and plastered with adobe. Ordinarily, little or no effort was made to maintain courses and, if the stones were shaped at all, it was only roughly. The simplest construction consisted of walling up a niche of convenient size so that bedrock served as floor, ceiling, and all the walls but one. Only slightly more elaborate was the building of a curved wall, or two or three more-or-less straight walls from floor to ceiling of a low rock shelter, the back of which formed the back wall of the structure. In rock shelters with higher ceilings, similar structures were sometimes built except that, when the walls had been completed to the desired height, a roof was often constructed of stone and adobe that rested on a coarse mat supported by poles laid on the tops of the walls.

A more distinctive type of stone-and-adobe storage structure is free standing and shaped like a truncated cone. In these, bedrock formed only the floor.

Several kinds of material were used in storage structures. Walls were sometimes built of adobe turtlebacks or loaves as in a well-preserved example in Ferron Canyon (Gunnerson, 1957 a, p. 140). Poles were sometimes incorporated into adobe or stone-and-adobe walls, presumably to give them greater support, and cedar bark was sometimes mixed with the adobe. One unusual variant consisted of a stack of hoops, made by bending light poles, which had been plastered over with adobe.

Access to the contents of these small storage structures was either through the roof, where the structures were not built to the ceiling of the shelter, or through the wall, well above floor level. Openings were probably always fitted with stone slab doors or covers that could be sealed in place with adobe. In a few instances, such slabs have been found associated with the structures. Some doorways still have adobe or stick-and-adobe jambs in place, and a few roof openings are still surrounded with adobe rims to accept a cover. Lintels are either sticks or stone slabs. The builders apparently attempted to keep storage structures rodent- and perhaps insect-proof. Partial rebuilding or patching and sealing of cracks is sometimes obvious where adobe of different colors was used.

The second major type of storage facility in rock shelters is cists that have been excavated into the fill of the shelter. Some of these are holes lined with vertical slabs, the interstices being chinked with adobe. Others, where the fill of the shelter was firm enough, were unlined and sometimes were undercut or bottle-shaped. Cists were apparently covered with stone slabs that in some cases were supported by a cribbed roof built over the cist. In other cases the cover apparently rested directly on the fill. Occasionally what appear to be small slab-lined cists are found in the open, but the function of these is uncertain.

CEREMONIAL STRUCTURES

The only features that suggest themselves as ceremonial structures at Fremont sites can be best called small open plazas. On top of a small hill at the edge of the Old Woman Site, a rectangle about 20 feet on a side was outlined by a low rock wall (Taylor, 1957). At the near-by Snake Rock Site, an area that capped the ridge appeared to have been cleared of rocks. From the Turner-Look Site, Wormington (1955) reports five large "monoliths" deliberately set in a row. Near them were two arcs of smaller stones, all of which may have served as a ceremonial complex.

SETTLEMENT PATTERN

Fremont villages were never large, although they were frequently close together. The largest villages probably contained no more than a dozen rooms in use at any one time.

More characteristic were clusters of three to six rooms, and some sites appear to have consisted of a single room. Along favorable valleys such as that of Ivie Creek, occupation was intensive. Ten sites per mile were found on the one side of Ivie Creek that was checked.

Open Fremont habitation sites are almost always on some sort of elevation. A slight knoll, ridge, or terrace remnant served when no more formidable elevation was near suitable farm land. Therefore, on any elevation about 20 or 30 feet high near farmable land within the Fremont area, one can expect to find evidence of a habitation site. The reasons for selecting an elevation as a dwelling site are not entirely clear, but a number of possible reasons can be advanced. Such locations would provide good drainage, an especially desirable feature when the structures were pithouses. Also, the elevations would not be as good for cultivation as the lower areas, which could be irrigated or which would be favored with runoff water from rains. The advantages might, however, have been primarily psychological. The Fremont people may have valued particular, identifiable locations, or sites from which they could command a wider view of the surrounding territory. The last consideration would be especially reasonable for people settling a new frontier where they would be surrounded by, and interested in, the unknown.

Some sites in Castle Valley and even more along Hill Creek and Minnie Maude Creek (Nine Mile Canyon) are situated on high ridges or eminences difficult of access. A few such sites show almost certain evidence of fortification. Most Fremont sites, however, were not especially well located with regard to defense, and there appears to be a high negative correlation between amount of detritus at a site and difficulty of access. It has already been suggested in this paper that the fortified and least accessible sites were built late in the period of Fremont occupation and were either not lived in for a significantly long period, or served as defensible communal storage structures or possibly as retreats in time of attack.

Some Fremont people chose to live in rock shelters, but such sites appear to have accounted for a relatively small percentage of the total population. The evidence indicating that Fremont people actually lived in rock shelters suggests that such occupation was probably temporary or intermittent, possibly associated with hunting trips or other travel. However, rock shelters were used for storage extensively throughout the Fremont area, and even though there are often no diagnostic artifacts associated with such sites, there is little doubt that most of the small storage structures or granaries built in shelters were constructed by Fremont people. The presence of numerous small structures, often not over a meter high, has given rise to legends that they were once inhabited by little people called Moquis, and the structures are commonly called "Moqui houses."

TOOLS

WEAPONS

The weapon used in both warfare and hunting seems to have been chiefly the bow and arrow. Large chipped stone blades are found that could have been spearpoints but were more probably knife blades. Chipped stone points suitable for use on arrows show considerable variation (fig. 43, *b-f, n-t*), but nearly all are basically triangular with the length two to four times the maximum width. All three sides of a few unnotched points are essentially straight, but points with concave bases are more common. In one distinctive variation (fig. 43, *s*), a broad trapezoidal section has been removed from the base, leaving two small ears projecting in line with the sides of the points. Side-notched points with straight, concave, or slightly convex bases are also common. Such notches are very close to the base. Projectile points of a third major variety (fig. 43, *e, f, n*) have had large corner notches removed, leaving a stem that usually constricts slightly where it joins the blade. The two sides of the corner notches meet at a right angle only rarely and never at an obtuse angle.

Morss (1931, p. 61) recovered several arrow parts which suggest that Fremont arrows were characteristically made of cane with a notched plug inserted in the base to accept the string. Hardwood foreshafts were found at several sites. One was notched to hold a projectile point and was wrapped with sinew just below this notch. The other end still had traces of resin on it. Another foreshaft had a blunt point. One cane shaft and one wooden foreshaft had been decorated with paint. The portion of a reed arrow and the wood fore-shaft found at Site 12-5 in Barrier Canyon and reported herein may have been of Fremont manufacture, but it might also represent Mesa Verde workmanship. Three feathers had been attached to the base of the arrow with sinew. If the one specimen from Site PR 4-6 is part of an arrow, which is doubtful, it would have been a very crude one.

Apparently no specimens identified as parts of Fremont bows have been reported, but Burgh and Scoggin (1948, p. 60) found a three-ply sinew bowstring from a bow about 53 inches long which may be Fremont, and Morss (1954, p. 18) reports a two-ply sinew bowstring 42 inches long from the Fremont area.

For hunting, the Fremont people used both snares and nets in addition to arrows (Morss, 1931). These do not appear to differ from similar devices found elsewhere in the Southwest. It is perhaps surprising that more snares and nets have not been found at Fremont sites, since the Fremont people were probably more dependent upon hunting than were the Pueblo peoples in general. Fishhooks have been reported from a site in the Fremont River drainage (Morss, 1954, p. 18) and from Castle Park (Burgh and Scoggin, 1948, p. 41).

CUTTING TOOLS

Cutting tools are represented primarily by chipped stone blades (fig. 43 g–l, u–w), some of which are shaped like projectile points and differ from them primarily by being larger. However, there is no exact duplication in forms. Unnotched blades usually have either straight or convex bases and convex sides which are nearly parallel toward the base. Other blades are essentially pointed ovals or teardrop-shaped. Occasionally a large un-notched (or notched) blade has concave sides except near the base, so that there is discontinuity in the curve of the sides. This condition may be the result of resharpening hafted blades without taking them out of their hafts.

Notched blades are usually triangular with straight to convex bases and convex sides. For the most part, the notches are in the sides near the base, but some blades are corner-notched. Blades with nearly parallel-sided stems are rarely found. Notched blades were rarely 10 cm. in length, while unnotched specimens were sometimes longer.

In addition to chipped stone blades manufactured according to set patterns, there are flakes with suitable sharp edges that show evidence of use. Occasionally the edges of a flake show limited retouching, presumably to form a stronger or more efficient cutting tool.

Flakes with serrated edges (fig. 43, m), usually chipped from only one surface, have been called "saws," or "serrated scrapers" and would probably have been effective for cutting bone or wood. Except for the serrations, they seldom show any additional modification.

Scrapers made on either the ends or sides of thick flakes are so rare as to be virtually missing from the Fremont assemblage.

Chipped stone knife blades were at least sometimes hafted in wooden handles. Morss (1931, p. 62) recovered two handles, one flat, the other round in cross section. They were 3¾ inches and 5 inches long, respectively. Notches had been cut in one end of each and the round handle had been wrapped just below the notch. One blade of possible Fremont manufacture from Site 12-5 has some black material that looks like pitch or gilsonite adhering to its base. This substance had probably helped secure the blade to the handle. Burgh and Scoggin (1948, fig. 19d) illustrate a hafted stone knife from Castle Park.

Cutting tools made of material other than chipped stone are not common, perhaps because of poor preservation of perishable materials at most sites. Sickles made from sections of mountain sheep horn cannot yet be assigned to the Fremont culture with assurance. The well-preserved sickle from Site SR 12-5 in Barrier Canyon could have been from either the Fremont or the Mesa Verde occupation, or from a possible earlier occupation. The specimen of worked horn from Site FL 12-2, probably a Fremont site, is too poorly preserved to be definitely identified as a sickle. Although Morss (1931, pp. 59–60) found worked horn, he did not recover any specimens even resembling sickles.

Notched bone tools showing much wear have been reported by Wormington (1955) and Burgh and Scoggin (1948). Two possible uses have been suggested—to separate animal tendons into sinew, and to strip the fiber out of yucca leaves.

Perforating Tools

Perforating tools known to have been used by the Fremont people include bone awls and chipped stone drills. Awls, commonly found at Fremont sites, are usually portions of long bones of mammals about the size of deer or sheep, although other bones were sometimes used. The simplest awls are splinters of bone that have been sharpened at one end. More commonly, however, the entire splinter was at least superficially smoothed, and sometimes the shank of an awl was worked to a uniform circular or elliptical cross section and very nicely finished. All or part of an articular end was sometimes left on the section of bone chosen for an awl, presumably to serve as handle. Again, the amount of care and effort used in finishing such awls varied greatly. Other less common awls were made from pieces of ribs or scapulae of mammals and from bird bones. The L-shaped awl, the kind found with the burial at Site PR 4-31 and at many early sites in western North America, does not appear to be included among Fremont types. Bone awls were probably used by the Fremont people in the sewing of hide objects and the manufacture of coiled baskets.

Chipped stone drills (fig. 43, *a*) are not abundant at Fremont sites and appear to be restricted to two general types. The most common has an expanding base that seldom shows any deliberate shaping and a tapering bit, usually diamond-shaped or lenticular in cross section. The second type has an expanding base that resembles the base of a notched blade. These drills could, in fact, have been made from blades, perhaps ones from which the tips had been broken. It is not known whether either type of drill was hafted. The notches on the second type suggest that they were. Some artifacts, such as beads and pendants, have had holes drilled through them that are much smaller than any drills yet found at Fremont sites. The tool used for this fine work has not been identified, although the tips of some chipped stone artifacts classified as projectile points are small enough to have served such a function.

Abrading Tools

Abrading tools used by the Fremont people were apparently all of sandstone. Grooved "shaft polishers" are occasionally found, usually as single items, but a matched pair was found at Castle Park (Burgh and Scoggin, 1948) and another pair at Site 34 (Morss, 1931, p. 55). Their use is discussed under woodworking. Narrow grooves are commonly found in sandstone bedrock or in very large fallen blocks and sometimes in smaller pieces of sandstone. These would have served very nicely for shaping bone artifacts such as awls and gaming pieces. Larger grooves in sandstone, generally called "ax sharpeners," were more probably used for shaping manos as discussed under stoneworking.

Milling Devices

Manos and metates and, less commonly, mortars and pestles, were probably used for grinding a variety of seeds and grains and such other materials as pigment, pottery tempering material, and pottery clay. Some of the holes found in bedrock may have been mortars.

Pounding Tools

Pounding tools were unspecialized among the Fremont people; neither grooved mauls nor polished grooved axes have been found at Fremont sites. The most characteristic pounding tools are simple hammerstones, usually a piece of tough rock of a size convenient to hold in the hand. These show no modification except for a great deal of battering from use. Chipped stone disks 4 to 7 cm. in diameter show dulled edges and may have served some special pounding function. The stone balls found at Fremont sites might have been hide-covered and mounted on handles to serve as clubs, but there are no clues to support such an idea.

Firemaking Equipment

Fire was apparently made by means of some

sort of fire drill. A number of pieces of wood that had served as hearths or anvils for fire drills have been found. These have a notch cut into the edge, presumably to accommodate the tinder, and a hemispherical depression worn into the top so that the notch would lead into it. These pieces of wood are simply sticks 1 to 3 cm. in diameter, and they generally contain more than one depression. However, the depressions are not always of the same diameter. No fire drills have been identified, so it is not known whether they were simply twirled by hand or whether a bow was used.

DRESS AND ADORNMENT

CLOTHING

Not a great deal is known about the clothing of the Fremont people but, for the most part, it appears to have resembled that of the Pueblo people farther south, with the exception that hide was more commonly utilized in the Fremont area. This is especially evident in footwear since moccasins of a distinctive style, the Fremont moccasin described in detail by Morss (1931, pp. 63–68), were apparently worn to the complete exclusion of plant-fiber sandals.

Morss has suggested that this may represent a necessary adaptation to the colder winters encountered in the Fremont area. The style of the Fremont moccasin shows no close relation to any other known moccasin tradition.

Sandals are still unreported from a definite Fremont context. At Site SR 12-5 in Barrier Canyon, a sandal was found, but since there had also been a Mesa Verde occupation it seems more probable that the sandal had come from it.

Still another style of hide footwear, the Yampa moccasin found in Castle Park, resembles a sandal even more closely (Burgh and Scoggin, 1948, p. 63). This style, apparently not found elsewhere, consists of a hide sole to which a second piece of hide was attached to cover the front third of the foot. A narrow strap that passed behind the heel was also attached to the sole and was tied to the upper with a thong that passed on either side of the ankle.

While the Fremont people themselves presumably wore the "Fremont moccasin" and their Basketmaker predecessors, if adequately represented by the Rasmussen Cave burial, also wore skin moccasins, some inhabitants of the area, at some time, probably wore sandals. Carved in a horizontal outcrop of bedrock at "the box" of Ferron Creek about five miles east of Ferron, Utah, are the outlines of several pairs of sandals. Some represent sandals of adults; some, those of children. Some are carved side by side; some represent a series of steps. In one case a pair of child's sandals are depicted beside those of an adult.

Fremont figurines sometimes appear to represent individuals wearing small twined aprons or skirts. Morss (1931, pp. 71–72) recovered several mats, each less than 30 cm. square, that could be such garments. The best-preserved consist of a pair (Morss, 1931, plate 41, a) tied together at two adjacent corners by means of cords over which the reeds forming the warp elements are doubled. This cord would have served as a waistband. Each of the two "mats" has a short piece of cord tied to it just below and to one side of the center at points directly opposite each other. Perhaps these passed between the wearer's legs to prevent the fore and aft aprons from flapping. Morss considers the possibility that these are skirts or aprons, but rules it out because the pair found together would fit only a person with a 24-inch waist. Although this is a rather small waist, it certainly is not impossibly small, especially for children and young people, and other interpretations of the mats seem less likely.

A number of Fremont sites have yielded either fragments of rabbit-skin robes or strands of rabbit-fur string that are presumably from such robes (Morss, 1931; Burgh and Scoggin, 1948, p. 66; and this report). Three basic techniques of manufacture are represented. Some of the strings are just a strip of twisted hide; others consist of two strips of hide twisted together; and still others consist of a strip of hide wound around a plant-fiber cord. Where portions of fur cloth are preserved, the warp elements, composed of the fur string, are held together by twining. Plant-fiber cord serves as the weft elements. Feather cloth, in which plant-fiber cords are wrapped with split feathers, is apparently represented only by two pieces of string found at Morss's Site 11 and in Mantle's Cave (Burgh and Scoggin, 1948, p. 66). Fragments of feather cordage from Site SR 12-5 could be from the Fremont, the Mesa Verde, or a possibly earlier occupation. A charred mass of what appeared to be part of either a fur or a feather robe was found at Snake Rock (Gunnerson, n.d.), but it was not possible to identify the material.

Fragments of both rawhide and well-tanned leather have been found at a number of Fremont sites. Some of these appear to be scraps left from the manufacture of hide objects. Others that show sewing appear to be remnants of skin garments. Some of these nondescript pieces seem to have been mended. With subzero temperatures expectable throughout the Fremont area and temperatures as low as −40° F recorded at some places (Alter, 1941), the warmth of hide clothing would be welcome.

ADORNMENT

To judge by figurines and pictographs, the Fremont people valued ornaments. Some of the figurines show especially elaborate necklaces and pendants. And most ornaments found at archaeological sites could appropriately be worn suspended from the neck. Materials include stone, bone, tooth, shell, and possibly plant material and pottery. Small perforated stone disks, presumably beads, and nearly rectangular stone beads or pendants have been reported from a number of Fremont sites (Morss, 1931, p. 60; Burgh and Scoggin, 1948, p. 40; Wormington, 1955, p. 62; Gunnerson, 1957 a, p. 25). The stone used, all moderately soft, includes turquoise, alabaster (?), shale, lignite, and hematite. It is not known whether all the stone ornaments were made by the Fremont people or whether some were traded for.

Bone beads, or at least artifacts probably used as beads, are of several general types (Morss, 1931; Wormington, 1955; Gunnerson, 1957 a). The simplest are mid-sections, 1 to 12 cm. long, of long bones of birds or small mammals. The cut ends are smoothed and the surface is sometimes scraped or decorated with incising. Pieces cut from larger bones and perforated are either ground to form disks or left square. It may be that the square beads (Morss, 1931, p. 60) were to have been ground to a disk shape, but were never completed. They are rather rough and were found in association with a grooved section of bone that appeared to represent a beginning step in the manufacture of beads. Other bone ornaments more properly classified as pendants are flat pieces, rectangular to oval in outline and perforated near one end. A deer metatarsal found at Site SR 10-1 had been cut and ground to form essentially a truncated cone and a hole had been drilled through it. Still another type of bone bead is represented by a specimen from Site ET 4-31 made from a section of long bone extensively scraped down to a shape resembling that of a wooden barrel.

Several dozen burned elk teeth, perforated for suspension, were found at the Emery Site by two young collectors who showed them to Gunnerson (1957 a, p. 22). An imitation elk tooth carved from bone and similarly perforated was found at a near-by site (Snake Rock). Thus, elk teeth were apparently prized so highly by the Fremont people that they were imitated in bone as they were by Indians of the Plains in historic times. The use of perforated elk teeth in the Great Basin in historic times is attested by several collected from the Bannock in 1896 and now on display at the Peabody Museum, Harvard University (Catalogue No. 49719). A Paiute dress decorated with more than 60 elk teeth is also on exhibition at the Peabody Museum (Catalogue No. 51057). The dress was collected in Utah in 1876 by Major Powell.

The most spectacular ornament recovered from a site yielding Fremont material is the flicker-feather-and-ermine-fur headdress from Mantle's Cave (Burgh and Scoggin, 1948, pp. 38–40; Hewes, 1952). This elaborate specimen, probably for ceremonial use, was found in a pouch made from the hide of a deer's face and scalp. The pouch also contained a bundle of feathers, a piece of rawhide shaped like a butterfly and decorated with small lignite beads, a chipped stone blade, two polished dome-like stone objects, two pieces of worked antler, one kernel of corn, one bean, and several miscellaneous items. Morss (1954,

p. 18) describes a less elaborate but similar specimen from a cist on Temple Creek in the Fremont drainage.

Mantle's Cave yielded another headdress consisting of the hide from the crown of a deer scalp with the ears attached and stiffened with feather quills. The hide had been tanned after the hair was removed, and the eye holes were sewn shut (Burgh and Scoggin, 1948, pp. 41–42). This headdress was found associated with a pair of Fremont moccasins. A similar deer-skin headdress was observed by Morss (1954, p. 18) in a private collection in Torrey, Utah.

Another unusual ornament reported from Mantle's Cave, but not from other Fremont sites, is a pendant of fiber cordage and rabbit fur (Burgh and Scoggin, 1948, p. 42).

As Morss (1954, pp. 4–5) has pointed out, the hair style of the female figurines in the Pillings group is like that on a skull from a Pueblo I burial found in Segi Canyon. Guernsey (1931) illustrates the skull in Plate 12, and describes the mode of hairdressing on p. 94 as follows: "The long hair was gathered into two heavy bobs, which were wrapped with a cord about the thickness of a lead pencil made up of heavy strands of fine fibre string. This cord wraps both bobs, crossing from right to left at the nape of the neck." Also on p. 94 Guernsey illustrates two pictographs that show the same method of hairdressing. One was found on the back wall of Cave 1, from which the skull was recovered, and one was from a small cave in the same vicinity. Thus there is reason to believe that Fremont women dressed their hair in a style practiced in Pueblo I times in northeastern Arizona, or at least knew of the style.

Morss interprets the pubic covering on the males among the Pillings figurines as breech-cloths, except for one kilt, and those on the females as aprons. He points out that these items of dress bear no resemblance to the simple Basketmaker III aprons of loose cord found by Guernsey in caves in Segi Canyon. However, the pubic coverings on the pair of wooden figurines from near Ferron, Utah (Gunnerson, 1957 d), resemble the Segi specimens (Guernsey, 1931, plate 53) very strongly.

EXCHANGE

The Fremont people had limited trade relations in various directions. Pottery appears to have been the most common import, but even trade pottery is not common at most sites. In the southern half of the Fremont area, the trade sherds are predominantly from the Virgin and Kayenta cultures to the south. Nearly all the Mesa Verde trade sherds have come from Fremont sites along the southeastern edge of the area, where Turner-Look has yielded more than any other purely Fremont site. The presence of Mesa Verde sherds at a few sites, particularly SR 12-5 in Barrier Canyon, appears to have been the result of actual Mesa Verde occupation. Throughout the Fremont area, one finds sherds from various parts of Utah west of the Wasatch Mountains, where Sevier, the culture most like Fremont, is found.

Olivella shells from the Pacific coast have been found at several Fremont sites. This is not surprising since these shells are commonly found over much of the Southwest at sites representing a wide range of dates. The occurrence of Olivella shells in Utah archaeological sites has been discussed by Malouf (1939, 1940) and Taylor (1957, pp. 108–112).

Turquoise, found sporadically at Fremont sites, was probably traded into the area either as raw material or as finished ornaments, since no deposits of turquoise are known to occur within the area occupied by the Fremont people.

A stone disk spindle whorl found at Site ET 6-7 appears out of place in a Fremont context since it is a unique occurrence and is so well made that it does not appear to be an experimental attempt. Woodbury (1954, p. 186) has suggested that stone spindle whorls are a Hohokam or Mexican trait, so perhaps the Fremont specimen is of such an origin.

SOCIAL STRUCTURE

The smallness of Fremont villages suggests that the basic social group was no larger than an extended family. Houses, predominantly one-roomed, were also small and could not have accommodated more than one nuclear family. The usual pattern is for several such houses to occur at a single site, although some sites may have consisted of only one structure. Since villages are often less than 0.1 mile apart, however, a family living in such an isolated house would not be remote from neighbors.

Evidence for social groups larger than extended families can also be found. The clustering of many small villages along a single stream suggests that some social interaction took place between communities. Although irrigation systems were not really large, they appear to have been much too large to represent the work of an individual or even an extended family. Moreover, the regulation and allocation of water in this semiarid region, as well as the construction and maintenance of the ditches, would have necessitated some sort of social and/or political organization that would have involved perhaps as many as fifty households in some areas.

As yet, there is no evidence of specialized ceremonial structures at Fremont sites comparable to kivas. At some sites there does appear to be one pithouse a little larger than average that could have served as a meeting place or club house in addition to being a dwelling, a pattern reported by Steward (1933 c) for the Owens Valley Paiute. Possible dance plazas at some villages are large enough to have accommodated the members of a few villages, but the interpretation of these areas as dance plazas is speculative. It is suggested in the section on religion that some of the extensive pictograph panels, which usually occur in large natural amphitheaters remote from population concentrations, might have been the scene of religious activities involving many people.

The gathering activities of the Fremont people would for the most part have been most effective if carried out by small groups. No wild food occurred in sufficient abundance to justify the cooperation or attention of many people. Possibly such animals as antelope and rabbits were hunted communally by the Fremont people, but there is no archaeological evidence to support such an interpretation. Even if such activities did take place, they would not necessarily have entailed a permanent organization.

One last line of evidence suggesting possible large-group cooperative activity may be reflected in large, defensible structures, thought to have been storage facilities, that are too large for the use of a single family.

There is as yet very little evidence to suggest much social stratification or the presence of specialists. The best pictographs, the execution of which would have been time-consuming, appear to have been the work of a few skilled artists, possibly religious practitioners. The occurrence of caches of figurines in cists in houses that are otherwise undistinctive may identify them as residences of other religious specialists. The paucity of Fremont burials thus far found does not permit any speculations regarding possible status differentiation in burials.

BURIAL CUSTOMS

The best information regarding Fremont burial practices is from the Turner-Look Village Site (Wormington, 1955). Here four burials, one of them double, were found within a restricted area. Individuals were interred partly flexed, lying on their sides with very few nonperishable artifacts accompanying them. One grave was partly lined with rocks and a rectangular stone slab covered the torsos of both bodies in the double (adult-child) burial. Many of the bones from one burial were missing, which may account for at least some of the bones found scattered through the village.

Amateurs have uncovered human skeletal material at several Fremont village sites in the vicinity of Ferron, Utah (Gunnerson, 1957 a, p. 30). Pottery vessels may have been associated with some of these at the Emery Site. Gillin (1938, p. 24) found a skeleton in a cist just outside a burned house in Nine Mile Canyon. Moreover, a burned beam from the house was found lying over part of the burial, and charred tissue adhering to one knee suggests that the body was interred just prior to the burning of the house, at which time a burning beam fell on the inch-thick layer of dirt covering that part of the skeleton. Perhaps the firing of the house was customary procedure after a death, although the evidence from Turner-Look does not support such an interpretation.

The Fremont people may also have buried their dead in caves or rock shelters. Here again the information comes from local collectors, who have found portions of partially mummified bodies near Ferron, Utah, and a skeleton at Site A 6-6 near Vernal, Utah.

ART

Pictographs

It was in pictographs that the artistic ability of the Fremont people appears to have found its highest expression, and in quantity, quality, and variety the pictographs of the Fremont area are unrivaled in North America. Because they are so numerous and so well executed, a thorough study of the pictographs in this area would be a lengthy project. In this paper, only a cursory discussion can be presented that will supplement to some extent the initial statement made by Morss (1931, pp. 34–43) and the outline of the general relationships of these pictographs contained in the distributional study of pictographs in California and adjoining areas prepared by Steward (1929.)

In general, of course, it is difficult to relate any one pictograph to a particular culture. And some of the pictographs in the Fremont area —figures of horsemen, wagons, and railroad trains—are obviously not Fremont. Moreover, many of the figures, such as common wild animals and simple anthropomorphic and geometric designs, have a wide distribution throughout western North America. Some of the panels, especially in the southeastern part of the Fremont area, may be of Basketmaker authorship, but the fact that the major aboriginal occupation in this area was Fremont increases the chances that the pictographs there originated with the Fremont people. And the very fact that most of the simpler elements appear to have a long duration in time as well as broad geographical distribution makes it reasonable to assume that the Fremont people participated in the tradition of depicting simple zoomorphic, anthropomorphic and geometric designs on rock surfaces by painting and pecking or cutting.

But it is not necessary to depend on such general evidence to link some of the rock art to the Fremont people. A number of more specific styles of anthropomorphic pictographs are probably unique to the Fremont culture since their distribution appears to be restricted to the Fremont area. These all have basically trapezoidal bodies, are all shown in front view, and are all stiffly posed. Usually, little emphasis is placed on arms and legs, which sometimes are not indicated at all. The generalized description thus far would not differentiate the figures in the Fremont area from some with a much wider distribution. The differences consist in various details. One style, pecked into the rock surface, shows a great deal of ornamentation, especially in the form of headdresses, necklaces, and chest ornaments. Sometimes a skirt, breechcloth, or apron appears to be represented. Facial features, especially eyes and mouth, are often depicted in a simple manner. Occasionally lines extending down from the eyes suggest tears or face paint. The faces, especially on the larger figures where more detail was possible, suggest masks, and this effect is emphasized on many by the almost complete lack of constriction at the neck. A few of these figures in the northern part of the Fremont area are shown holding in one hand what has been interpreted as either a mask or a trophy head. Others appear to be holding snakes. Hands with fingers and feet with toes are depicted on some figures, but limbs are entirely missing on others. Pecked anthropomorphic figures vary in size from a few inches tall to what Morss describes as heroic or large. The best examples of figures in the latter style come from the vicinity of Fruita, Utah (Morss, 1931), and Vernal, Utah (Beckwith, 1935; Reagan, 1931 e), although they are commonly found over most if not all of the Fremont area.

A second style of pictograph that seems to be restricted to the Fremont area shows large (sometimes life-size or larger), highly decorated anthropomorphic figures painted primarily in red, but with details occasionally executed in white or bluish-gray. Decoration consisting of straight lines, zigzag lines, rows of dots, and sometimes animals frequently covers all or a major portion of the figure. This treatment is suggestive of a decorated robe or possibly body paint rather than of necklaces or other similar ornaments. Headdresses are rare and simple, and facial features are often missing or restricted to two blank circles for eyes. Faces are often covered with lines and dots as are the bodies. Bodies are trapezoidal, heads are slightly rounded squares with little or no constriction for the neck, and arms and legs are missing. By far the most numerous and best preserved figures of this style are at the Great Gallery in Barrier Canyon (Site SR 12-4).

These most distinctive pictographs—stiff, unrealistic, awe-inspiring and in no sense mundane—are usually so well executed that they appear to be the work of a specialist, perhaps some sort of religious practitioner. Furthermore, many of the figures at a single site share enough distinctive characteristics to suggest that they were the work of a single artist. The great amount of work required to produce these paintings or carvings would suggest that the role of artist was a time-consuming although not necessarily a full-time one.

Somewhat simplified forms of the elaborate painted figures are found associated with them at the Great Gallery and are also found elsewhere in the Fremont area. One variety is painted solid red except that two large blank spaces are sometimes left for eyes, giving the figures a ghostly appearance accentuated by the rounder shoulders and more attenuated body. In another variation the bodies are of essentially the same shape and proportions as the elaborate painted figures, but are filled in solidly with red paint. These solid red figures also often have either two curved horns, suggesting bison horns, or one vertical "horn" that projects straight up from the center of the head. A one-horned and a two-horned figure sometimes occur together in either pecked or painted form. In this connection it is interesting to note that a "one-horn" and a "two-horn" kachina patrol Hopi villages together at night to keep unauthorized people from getting close to ceremonies that are under way (Hopi informant, personal communication).

Indeed, the kachina-like appearance of many

of the more elaborate and better-executed pictographs in the Fremont area has struck many people. The pictographs could be a graphic expression of a religion having much in common with that of the Hopi, which also involved murals (Smith, 1952), although the Fremont pictographs are crude by comparison.

Pictographs representing the humpbacked flute player are found as far north as the Yampa River (Burgh and Scoggin, 1948) and sporadically in the rest of the Fremont area, as well as over much of the Southwest. It is generally agreed that this figure is a depiction of Kokopeli, who still figures prominently in Hopi religion.

Another style of anthropomorphic figure found in some of the pictograph panels in the Fremont area shows a circular area interpreted as either a shield or a body from which limbs and a head usually project. Wormington (1955, p. 160) points out similarities between these figures and ones to the north in Wyoming and Montana and considers the resemblance an indication of Plains influence. However, attention should be called to pictographs of this type in northeastern Arizona (Guernsey, 1931, plates 22, 37), where various other parallels to traits found in the Fremont area occur.

In addition to distributional evidence, there is one very specific link between pictographs and the Fremont culture. Some of the pictographs resemble the more elaborate Fremont clay figurines, and other pictographs unquestionably represent them. The general similarities are most obvious in the trapezoidal outline of the body, the lack of or slight indication of arms and legs, and the ornamentation of the head or chest. One small panel of pictographs in Barrier Canyon (fig. 31A), however, shows a row of seven small figures, alternately carved in the rock and painted in red, that depict the same type of figures represented by Fremont figurines such as those from Range Creek, Ferron, and the Old Woman Site.

FIGURINES

Nearly all the figurines found at Fremont sites are of unfired clay, although some have been baked accidentally in the burning of houses. These figurines vary greatly with regard to size, shape, and amount of detail represented, but among them are the most elaborate yet discovered north of Mexico.

Wherever these elaborate or "classic" Fremont figurines have been found associated, both males and females have been represented, possibly as pairs. The first such group discovered, the Pillings figurines, was found by a rancher in a rock shelter on a tributary of Range Creek Canyon (Morss, 1954). Then a small cist under the floor of a house at the Old Woman Site in Ivie Creek Canyon yielded a second group that had been preserved by accidental firing when the structure burned. Among these elaborate figurines was a small, very simple one (Taylor, 1957; Morss, 1957).

Next, a collector recovered several well-preserved figurines from a sealed cist in a pithouse near Ferron, Utah. In the same cache were several carved bone figurines with holes to permit their suspension from a carved bone bar (Gunnerson, 1962 b). Fragments of other flat, somewhat ornate figurines have been recovered here and there in the Fremont area, but none seems to have been as ornate as those in the groups enumerated above.

Morss (1954), in a detailed study of the Fremont figurines known as of 1954, states that Fremont clay figurines are related to Basketmaker III figurines of northern Arizona in "material, subject matter, and general technique," and his numerous illustrations permit the reader to observe the similarities that caused Morss to assign both the Basketmaker III and the simpler Fremont figurines to a "northern tradition." The elaboration of such Fremont figurines as the Pillings group he attributes to the influence of a "southern tradition" that had penetrated as far north as the Flagstaff area by the close of the eleventh century. Although it seems logical that the more elaborate Fremont figurines should be later, there is as yet no evidence to distinguish them chronologically from the simpler ones, which are also more numerous. Rather, there is evidence to show that they were contemporaneous. Therefore, the possibility suggests itself that different types of figurines were used to represent different beings or were used for different purposes.

A very simple stone figurine found at Sky House in Nine Mile Canyon by Gillin (1938, fig. 24) somewhat resembles a specimen found in Castle Valley near Ferron. The collector

who found it also discovered three well-preserved wooden figurines in Ferron Canyon. One, representing a pregnant female, was found wrapped in a mat in a rock crevice. It does not resemble any other figurine from the Southwest known to the present author. The other two wooden figurines, a male and a female, were found together in a walled-up crevice in a split boulder, along with a large quantity of shredded cedar bark. In the general approach to the carving, they resemble a wooden "doll" found by Guernsey in a Basketmaker II context in northeastern Arizona (Guernsey, 1931, p. 72, plate 51, f). Moreover, the Utah specimens had been stained to a dark color; the Arizona specimen had been painted red. The Utah figurines wear pubic coverings that resemble Basketmaker III aprons, also found by Guernsey in northeastern Arizona (Guernsey, 1931, plate 53). However, the wooden pair from near Ferron, like the "classic" Fremont clay figurines, are thin, flattish, and meant to be viewed from the front. All of these figurines from near Ferron have been illustrated by Gunnerson (1957 d, 1962 b).

In view of other similarities, it is not surprising that the figurine tradition of the Fremont people was shared with the Sevier culture west of the Wasatch, where it exhibits somewhat different traits. Morss (1954) has discussed the relationship of Fremont clay figurines not only to those of Sevier, but to those of the entire Southwest. It might be added that several of the Hopi kachina dolls collected in the late 1800's and now in the Peabody Museum bear a striking resemblance to the Fremont figurines in having a virtually featureless body without limbs but a more carefully executed and ornamented head.

POTTERY

The Fremont people decorated some of their pottery by manipulating the surface either with the fingers or with simple tools, or by painting decorations on the outsides of jars and pitchers and on the insides of bowls. Designs are almost always geometric, with straight lines predominating over curved lines, but apparently zoomorphic designs were sometimes painted on. Possible Fremont specimens in a private collection (Gunnerson, 1962 b) include a small paint (?) vessel in the form of an animal head, a handle on a pot lid in the form of a snake, and a small animal effigy on a pottery pipe.

While incision, punctation, and pinching were used to decorate both pottery and figurines, the form of decoration that serves to relate them most conspicuously is the "coffee-bean appliqué," which was used on both.

RELIGION

The kiva, focal point of San Juan Anasazi religious practices, has not yet been reported from the Fremont area. In fact, excavation has revealed few structures there large enough to accommodate more than a small number of people. The absence of kivas suggests that Fremont religious life differed from and may not have been as highly organized as that of the San Juan Anasazi, just as the settlement pattern suggests a looser political organization.

In the absence of a trait such as the kiva, from which many other traits of the religious complex, and even its general pattern, might be inferred, it is necessary to draw what inferences one can from traits in Fremont that are known to be connected with religious practices elsewhere. While the creation of the pictographs in the Fremont area probably represents a religious act, the pictographs, once created, may or may not have been sacred. Morever, the anthropomorphic pictographs strongly suggest religious practices similar to the modern Pueblo Kachina cult. This supposition is further strengthened by the presence in the Fremont area of pictographs of the humpbacked flute player, who figured in the religion of the prehistoric Anasazi people and that of the modern Hopi, to whom he is known as "Kokopeli." The occurrence of paired pictographs that may have some connection with the paired "one-horn" and "two-horn" Hopi kachinas has already been mentioned.

With regard to the zoomorphic pictographs, one can guess that the snakes were thought to be associated with rain, and that pictographs of anthropomorphs holding snakes represented a ceremony comparable to the snake rituals of the historic Pueblos, best known from that performed by the Hopi. The horned animals may have been depicted to insure success in hunting sheep, which appear to have provided the major part of the Fremont meat diet.

In speculating on the function of Fremont figurines, Morss (1954) reviews the uses to which figurines have been put in various parts of the world. His own hypothesis concerning the Fremont specimens is entirely consistent with the picture of the Fremont culture that this paper strives to present.

"There is another hypothesis which may be speculatively advanced for the consideration of those who like a strong dash of economic determinism in their culturology, although its actual merits are difficult to evaluate. According to this hypothesis the advent of agriculture, by increasing the productivity of labor, including child labor in the production of food, creates a demand for children and greatly enhances the importance of the ancient increase cult. Pioneer settlers run to large families. In this view the apparent decline in gynecomorphic figurines after the Ubaid period in Mesopotamia, after Ticomán in central Mexico, after the Sedentary Period in southern Arizona, and after Basket Maker III in northern Arizona (where, however, effigies of food animals continued to be common) might in each case be due to the restoration of the pressure of population upon the means of subsistence at the existing level of technology; while the persisting emphasis on figurines in western Mexico as compared with the Valley of Mexico, in the Nothern Periphery as compared with the San Juan, and possibly in the Indus Valley as compared with Mesopotamia, might be ascribed to the persistence of easier conditions in newly developed frontier areas. Just as polygamy temporarily found favorable conditions in pioneer Utah in the mid-nineteenth century, the increase cult flourished in pioneer Utah of the ninth to eleventh centuries. The interest in the cult evinced by both the Sinagua and the Anasazi settlers in the area of the Sunset Crater ash-fall of course fits neatly into the theory, since the ash-fall virtually created thousands of acres of arable lands which cried for hands to work them."

(Morss, 1954, pp. 61–62)

Since it is the more elaborate figurines that resemble the anthropomorphic pictographs, another of Morss's (1954, p. 62) suggestions has relevance:

"The small, crude, female figurine, seemingly adapted to private, if not actually secret, magical practices, presents in general a marked contrast to the large, masculine, hieratic, masked figures to be seen on the canyon walls; but the addition of her male companion and the development of specific indicia of two personalities, as seen in the Pillings and Kanosh pairs, suggests that more advanced concepts reflected in the masked dancer cult of the petroglyphs have influenced the primitive figurine cult."

However, since the crude figurines and the elaborate ones may be contemporaneous, the suggestion made in this paper under the discussion of figurines may provide an explanation. Perhaps the crude figures were used for increase rites by the Fremont people, while the elaborate paired ones were made to represent characters in a pantheon of deities whose pairing, like that of modern Hopi supernaturals, had little or no direct sexual significance.

The fact that Fremont figurines were sometimes kept in sealed cists in houses suggests three possibilities: (1) that religious ceremonies were conducted on the household level; (2) that the houses were those of specialized religious practitioners; (3) that the figurines represented the villagers themselves, and were in the keeping of some important person (see Morss (1954, p. 63)).

Moreover, the sealing of clay figurines in cists suggests an esoteric element in Fremont religion. The wooden figurines from Ferron

Canyon had obviously been hidden away, but it is not yet certain that these are Fremont.

While the most elaborate and extensive groups of pictographs seem to occur well away from open villages, they are often in locations where the setting is spacious and impressive. Such locations would have been suitable for the gathering of either large or small groups of people and the holding of public religious ceremonies. And it has already been suggested that the areas outlined by rocks in or near Fremont villages were dance plazas. Thus Fremont religion may have had a well-developed esoteric aspect.

In fact, the large, elaborate remote pictograph panels may have been the foci of Fremont religion. Such outdoor religious centers, not specifically associated with any particular village, are reminiscent of religious camp meetings that were so common in many areas of the United States, especially at the time that the areas were being settled and before more formalized and stable religious congregations were organized and churches built. The camp meetings provided an opportunity for the sparse, scattered frontier population to come together for social as well as religious purposes, and ceremonies at pictograph-dominated centers could have done the same for the Fremont people.

SUMMARY

In brief, the Fremont culture can be characterized as basically Puebloan. Subsistence was based on corn, bean, and squash horticulture, practiced with the aid of irrigation and supplemented by hunting and gathering activities. The people lived in small villages comprising both pit and surface houses. Rock shelters were sometimes occupied, but were more often used for storage. Storage structures were also built on the surface of the ground within villages and on high isolated points. Building materials included stone, adobe, jacal, and various combinations of these. The most distinctive Fremont structure is the pithouse, which was generally nearly round, with an adobe-rimmed central fireplace, four roof-support posts, wall lining of adobe or adobe and stone, but without ventilators, entrance passages, antechambers, benches, or partitions.

The Fremont ceramic assemblage is distinctive in that the pottery is tempered with crushed rock and is predominantly a plain, sometimes polished, gray ware. Corrugation is rare, but other surface manipulation is common. Painted designs occur on both slipped and unslipped surfaces.

Other distinctive Fremont artifacts include elaborate clay figurines and dew-claw moccasins. Within the area occupied by the Fremont people are many unusually well executed pictographs that are probably of Fremont authorship.

The rest of the traits attributed to the Fremont culture are of little diagnostic value, since they occur in one or more of the surrounding areas, although not necessarily on the same horizon or with the same emphasis. Within the Fremont complex are to be found many traits which lost popularity throughout most of the Southwest but which were retained by the Fremont people. This retentive or additive character of the Fremont culture has resulted in a great deal of variability, often as great within a site as between sites. This variability is especially remarkable when considered in the light of the approximately two and one-half centuries which apparently encompass the entire span of the Fremont culture.

Thus, while few individual Fremont traits are not reported from elsewhere in the Anasazi area, the Fremont assemblage, when considered as a whole, is distinctive.

PART IV

FREMONT CULTURE DYNAMICS

FREMONT CULTURE DYNAMICS

I N attempting to reconstruct culture history from the evidence provided by archaeological data, the anthropologist must ask the four standard journalistic questions: "who," "what," "when," and "where." If he concerns himself with culture dynamics, he will also ask "how," and "why."

In the case of the Fremont culture, the first four questions could not be answered in the order preferred by the journalist, corresponding in general to the anthropologist's "direct historical approach." As is true of most prehistoric complexes, information on the "what" and "where" accumulated first, although more work must be done before even these questions can be answered in the detail that is desirable. The preceding portions of this paper have contributed new data on the nature and areal distribution of the Fremont culture and in Part III these data were integrated with what was already known in a functional synthesis. Fortunately, dendrochronology and cross dating by means of trade sherds have furnished an answer to the "when" for several Fremont sites and even population centers.

The answers to the remaining questions are more difficult. The identity of the people who lived at Fremont sites, the mechanisms by which Fremont became a distinctive complex and the reasons for its development (and, later, its termination) cannot be inferred entirely from the archaeological data; increasingly, as one progresses from a consideration of pots to a consideration of people, collateral data from other branches of anthropology must be used to achieve synthesis.

It was pointed out in the history of trans-Colorado archaeology that several authors have speculated on the who, how, and why of the Fremont culture. The part of this report that follows will present a synthesis that the author considers more comprehensive and internally consistent than those offered in the past. Moreover, it seems more reasonable in the light of what is known of culture process among historic groups. Because dating is crucial to the validity of this synthesis, however, the information on which the present dates for Fremont is based will be discussed in some detail.

AGE OF THE FREMONT CULTURE

Our best evidence for the age of the Fremont culture comes from dendrochronological studies in Nine Mile Canyon and Hill Creek Canyon, which are situated just north of the middle of the Fremont area. These dates, released originally by Schulman (1948, 1951) and Ferguson (1949), have been summarized by Smiley (1951). A single tentative date has been published for Castle Park (Schulman, 1950). The most important of these dates are tabulated below. Where there are several dates from one structure, and none is a bark date, only the most recent is included in the tabulation.

Site	Outer Ring Date, A. D.	Comments
NINE MILE CANYON		
Sky House	1090	possibly plus five or more
Upper Sky House	1011	probably plus many more
Four Name House	1151	bark date, probably from the structure; other much later specimens below site
Olger Ranch Ruin	1065	bark date

167

Site	Outer Ring Date, A. D.	Comments
Nine Mile X	951	possibly plus five or more
Nine Mile X	915	probably plus many more
Nine Mile X	1145	probably plus a few more
Nine Mile Area (Site PR 8-2 of this report)	924	probably plus many more
HILL CREEK CANYON		
Long Mesa (Site ET 6-7)	1073	probably plus many more
Ruin No. 2	1000	
CASTLE PARK (YAMPA RIVER)		
Marigold's Cave	690+	Rings after 610 very crowded, "cutting date" tentatively estimated at A.D. 750 ± 50

Twelve samples from Sky House, reported by Gillin (1938), have been dated. The outside rings ranged from A.D. 768 with many rings probably missing to A.D. 1090 with possibly five or more rings missing. Nine of the twelve specimens, all with rings missing, dated after A.D. 1000. The only specimen from Upper Sky House, Site NM 10 of Gillin (1938), was dated at A.D. 1011 plus probably many more. One specimen found below Four Name House, a small storage structure about 6.5 miles down canyon from Sky House, gave a bark date of A.D. 1151. It was judged to have been from the structure. Four other specimens, all poles found below the structure, gave dates after A.D. 1750 and were probably placed there recently by people trying to gain access to the site, which cannot be reached without some sort of ladder. The Olger Ranch Ruin, located about 1.5 miles down canyon from Sky House, is dated at A.D. 1065, fortunately a bark date, by a single specimen. It is not clear from the literature just how many sites are represented by the samples identified as "Nine Mile X." The sample identified as "Nine Mile Area" is from Site PR 8-2, located near the mouth of Rock Creek, a western tributary that enters the Green River about 20 miles below the mouth of Nine Mile Canyon. The site, which contains a small storage structure, is described in this report.

In Hill Creek Canyon, about 8 miles east of the mouth of Nine Mile Canyon, two sites have been dated by dendrochronology. Five specimens from Long Mesa, Site ET 6-7 of this report, have dates ranging from A.D. 957 with probably many rings missing to A.D. 1073 with probably many rings missing. Hill Creek Ruin No. 2, located on a promontory a few hundred yards below Long Mesa, is dated by one specimen with no comment as to the nature of the outer surface.

The one date from Castle Park is from a house in Marigold's Cave described by Burgh (1950). The ring history of this specimen could be followed to A.D. 610, but after that the rings were so crowded that they could only be counted (not measured) to determine an outside date of A.D. 690+. With regard to this specimen, Schulman (1950, p. 18) states, "The bark or cutting date of the Marigold timber may be estimated, somewhat conditionally, at A.D. 750 ± 50. The outer part of one sector of this irregularly charred cross section seems to be nearly complete, but growth was so slow that only a few millimeters of burnt-off radius could represent a hundred rings or more. Thus, in the absence of dated companion beams, the estimated correction to bark date for the Marigold beam must be considered quite tentative."

Since the deviation of this date from those for all other dated Fremont sites is probably due largely to the condition of the specimen, no interpretations should be based on it. In any case, it is unsafe to date the Fremont occupation of the Castle Park area on the basis of one specimen, since the timber may have been long dead when it was used.

Even if one ignores the missing rings, all the Fremont sites dated by dendrochronology fall between A.D. 915 and A.D. 1151 except for the highly tentative estimated cutting date for the sample from Marigold's Cave. Furthermore, the only samples on which bark was present date after A.D. 1065. Since a bark date marks the actual year in which the tree was cut or died, it normally dates the time that a structure was built or, possibly, repaired, unless a beam was collected dead or was reused. Morss (1954, p. 17), following O'Bryan (1949), points out that lack of axes would have made the felling of dead trees more attractive to the Fremont people since these could be felled by charring more easily than could living trees. He also astutely reasons that the absence of axes would make the use of down timber and the reuse of timbers highly desirable, and points out that the apparent recent use of poles with outside dates in the 1700's in an attempt to enter Four Name House supports the feasibility of using long-dead timbers in this particular area.

In any case, a structure could not have been abandoned prior to the most recent tree ring found in one of its constituent timbers and thus any such tree-ring date would place a limit on the maximum age of the structure, but not on its minimum age. From this reasoning, it follows that the structures in Hill Creek and Nine Mile Canyon for which we have tree-ring dates all postdate A.D. 915 and are probably even more recent. And we have no evidence that any was occupied more than a few years after A.D. 1151. Thus, on the basis of tree rings, we have no evidence to extend the span of the Fremont culture beyond the two centuries between A.D. 950 and A.D. 1151 with any degree of certainty. To be sure, our total number of dates is small and two areas from which the specimens came are close together. Fortunately, however, they are more or less centrally located and thus presumably more representative than if they were from an edge of the area.

Our second-best line of evidence for dating the Fremont culture comes from the designs found on painted Fremont pottery and the dates assigned to trade sherds found at Fremont sites. The elements found on Fremont pottery are predominantly of three styles: Black Mesa, Sosi, and Dogoszhi, which have been dated by Colton (1955) at *ca.* 900–*ca.* 1100, *ca.* 1070–*ca.* 1150, and *ca.* 1070–*ca.* 1150, respectively. While it is possible that these styles of decoration were first used by Fremont people and later spread south, it is far more probable that the spread was in the other direction and that the designs were not used in the Fremont area before they were introduced in the Virgin and Kayenta regions.

Trade sherds reported from Fremont sites by various workers (Wormington, 1955; Gunnerson, 1957a; Taylor, 1957) include types that are reasonably well dated by Colton (1955, 1956) and Abel (1955). Among these are the following:

Tusayan Polychrome	A.D. 1150–1300
Tusayan Black-on-red	1050–1150
Middleton Black-on-red	1050–1131
Deadman's Black-on-red	750–1050
Mancos Black-on-white	950–1150

On the basis of the dates assigned to these trade sherds, one must assume that the Fremont culture persisted from before A.D. 1050 until after A.D. 1150. All of these dates, however, are approximate and may be modified as additional work is done.

The finding of Fremont pottery at the Coombs Site just south of the Fremont area provides us with still another check on the age of the Fremont culture. Lister and Lister (1961, p. 6) conclude that settlement of the Coombs Site began during the latter part of the 11th century and probably lasted for 50 to 100 years, perhaps reaching its maximum about A.D. 1100. In any case, the dated ceramics from the Coombs Site would place its occupation within the A.D. 1075 to A.D. 1275 period (Lister and Lister, 1961, p. 4).

Since the Fremont culture seems to have existed for at least 250 years and had a wide geographical distribution, not all Fremont sites could be of the same age. Therefore, it is reasonable to expect some differences in artifact assemblages. But the Fremont culture, along with its postulated ancestor, the Virgin branch, are apparently both characterized by an additive orientation with retention of earlier traits; hence, it may be that the only evidence for earliness will be the absence of late traits. And the dating of sites by the absence of traits is unsafe, especially when little or no excavation has been done and the sample of artifacts, as well as the amount of other data, is small. One can guess that the earliest Fremont sites do not have black-on-white (slipped) or corrugated pottery, but even these traits could have been present early in Fremont history if the slip came from the Mesa Verde branch and corrugation from either Kayenta or Mesa Verde.

It seems significant that our various lines of evidence regarding dates for the Fremont culture are consistent with one another. When all the evidence is considered together, the span of the Fremont culture can not be compressed to include any less than the period *ca.* A.D. 950–1150 and the latter date could more reasonably be placed significantly later, at least as late as A.D. 1200. There is less to suggest that the beginning of Fremont was earlier than A.D. 950, although it is always possible that additional work may produce a series of datable beams that will extend the span of Fremont in that direction.

ORIGIN OF THE FREMONT CULTURE

There are two logical possibilities with regard to the origin of the Fremont culture. It could have developed *in situ* from a Desert culture base with the addition of Anasazi traits, a theory championed by Rudy (1953), Jennings and Norbeck (1955), and Wormington (1955). The second possibility, that the Fremont culture represents a movement of people with a Puebloan culture into the area, is developed here.

The same general thesis was advanced earlier by Steward, but the points of origin and the mechanisms of culture change that he favored differ radically from those suggested in this paper.

As for the first possibility, the *in situ* transition from Desert culture to Fremont has nowhere been demonstrated archaeologically. Moreover, the manifestations of the Fremont culture are remarkably similar throughout its time span, suggesting that this Puebloan complex entered the area after it was already developed, and as a unit. Such a phenomenon is more likely to be effected by a migrating population than by diffusion, especially when the complex exhibits the internal variability discovered in the Fremont culture. Nor is there any need to look to the Desert culture for the "early" traits in Fremont, since they are all present in the Virgin culture. In short, Fremont is probably no more directly derived from Desert culture than is Mesa Verde or Kayenta.

While it seems unlikely that the Fremont area was entirely uninhabited just before the Fremont occupation, the sites there that cannot be assigned to Fremont are usually so undistinctive that they cannot be assigned to any other culture, nor do they, in themselves, furnish the basis for establishing a new complex. Perhaps the Basketmaker or Basketmaker-like occupations represented at sites in the Waterhole Flat area and by the burial in Rasmussen Cave in Nine Mile survived until the beginning of the Fremont culture. The prehorticultural, nonceramic occupation at Hells Midden (Lister, 1951), which appears to have given way abruptly to the Fremont culture there, is probably related to the Uncompahgre complex (Wormington and Lister, 1956) and/or these Basketmaker-like remains. Some traits in the Fremont complex may reflect contact with an indigenous, pre-Fremont population. However, it is to the Puebloan cultures that one must look for Fremont's nearest relatives.

FREMONT RELATIONSHIPS

Across the Wasatch Mountains west of the Fremont area was the Sevier culture (also called Puebloid or Sevier-Fremont) which resembles Fremont closely and does not seem to predate it. Sevier gives every indication of having developed parallel to the Fremont culture and from the same ancestor. Hence, much of what is said with regard to Fremont applies also to Sevier, with some notable exceptions.

To the south and southeast of the Fremont area were the Mesa Verde and Kayenta branches of Anasazi, or San Juan Anasazi as they are called collectively. For most Fremont traits one can find specific counterparts in the Anasazi culture at the same or earlier times, and only a few traits which made their appearance in Anasazi culture before or during Pueblo II are lacking in the Fremont culture. Differences for the most part are ones of quantity or relative importance. The most spectacular trait found at some Developmental Pueblo sites, but missing at Fremont sites, is the large multiroom pueblo. Nowhere in the Fremont area is there to be found evidence of large concentrations of population at single sites. Thus far there have been no kivas reported from controlled excavations, but the small amount of excavation completed may account for this lack. Turkeys, also, are thus far unreported. Stone axes are apparently missing in the Fremont complex, but these are also scarce in Developmental Pueblo complexes. Corrugated pottery was known to the Fremont people as a trade item and they made a very little locally, but they apparently chose to make more than 99 per cent of their utility ware plain, or plain with tooled decorations.

Yet direct comparison with Anasazi of the Four Corners area made the Fremont culture seem an anomaly of late Developmental Pueblo times; for in Fremont, Basketmaker traits such as plain utility ware, pithouses, and clay figurines, nearly extinct in the Four Corners area in Pueblo times, occurred together with Pueblo traits. This situation led Steward to the conclusion that a culture ancestral to the complexes of the "Northern Periphery," and showing the same blend of Basketmaker and Pueblo traits, must exist somewhere between the San Juan area and the "Northern Periphery." It has already been mentioned that he searched specifically for an archaeological complex having the requisite traits, only to decide that the region east of Kanab was not related to the "Northern Periphery," and that the source of "Northern Periphery" culture should be sought in western Colorado or extreme eastern Utah, then an archaeologically unknown area (Steward, 1941 a, pp. 281–2, 355).

A review of the results of Steward's work east of Kanab plus additional information from the northern drainages of Glen Canyon (Lister, 1958 a; Gunnerson, 1959 c) revealed that sites as far east as those in the Escalante drainage could be at least tentatively assigned to the Virgin branch of the Anasazi. Furthermore, this work, along with information from the Zion Park area west of Kanab (Schroeder, 1955), strongly suggested that the Virgin branch contained at a relatively late time a complex of early and late traits from which the Pueblo traits in Fremont could have been derived (Gunnerson, 1960 a).

We now have additional evidence regarding the Virgin branch (Shutler, 1961) as well as the new information on the Fremont culture presented in this paper. Neither contribution has changed the over-all picture significantly and both have provided new details that support the author's previous generalizations (Gunnerson, 1960 a, 1962 a).

The Virgin branch, in brief, is thought to include the Pueblo sites in the northern drainages of the Colorado River from the Escalante River drainage on the east to, and including, the Muddy River on the west. This branch appears to have developed independently, but with strong Kayenta influence, from a Basketmaker level to a Classic Pueblo level. However, a few traits which characterize the better known branches of Anasazi, especially in the Pueblo I stage, are lacking in the Virgin branch, although some of the differences may only reflect the unevenness of the data. Throughout its development, the Virgin culture retained most of its earlier traits when new traits were added to the complex. Thus, at about A.D. 950, the Virgin people were using a wide variety of materials and styles in their architecture. Structures were both semisubterranean and above ground. Rooms were both isolated and contiguous. Walls were of horizontally laid stones, stone slabs set on edge, adobe, stone and adobe, or jacal. Storage cists were still built, and both open sites and rock shelters were utilized. Pithouses, however, lacked ventilators, antechambers, and passage entrances. Kivas had apparently not yet been introduced, but there may have been benches around the insides of pithouses by this time. Fireplaces in dwellings were central and rimmed with adobe, and floors of structures were sometimes paved with stone slabs.

At about A.D. 950, Virgin utility pottery was still smooth plain gray ware, although corrugation was soon to make its appearance. The Pueblo I neck banding, however, was never accepted and even trade pieces are rare. On painted pottery, the designs were applied with organic (carbon) paint to unslipped surfaces, but the use of a slip started soon afterward in the eastern half of the Virgin area. Designs retained old elements similar to those used on Lino Black-on-gray and Black Mesa style decoration had recently been adopted. When Sosi and Dogoszhi styles of decoration later became popular throughout the Anasazi area, the Virgin potters adopted them also.

Morever, at about A.D. 950, the Virgin people were living in small villages and engaging in an economy that combined farming with hunting and gathering. Thus, at the time that the Fremont culture seems to have started, there was a complex very similar to it in the Virgin area. The similarity becomes even more obvious when Fremont is compared to its various neighbors in more detail.

A few Fremont ceramic traits may belong to only the later part of the culture, but much more excavation of the sites that can be closely dated will be needed before one can be certain. Present evidence suggests that the use of a thick white slip did not enter the Virgin area until late Pueblo II times, so it may also be late in Fremont. Lister and Lister (1961), in their thorough discussion of Anasazi pottery, graphically demonstrate that not all Anasazi ceramic traits are confined within the same boundaries. They suggest convincingly that the use of a slip in Virgin pottery was introduced from either Fremont or Mesa Verde.

Up to this time, the only evidence for Mesa Verde–Fremont contact has been the presence of Mesa Verde trade sherds at a few Fremont sites. The results of the Claflin-Emerson expeditions reported here, however, indicate that Mesa Verde sites interfinger with those of the Fremont culture in the southeastern part of the Fremont area. Therefore, it now seems even more probable that the Fremont people did acquire the use of a slip, along with the use of crushed rock tempering and the occasional use of iron pigment, from the Mesa Verde people. Since the use of a slip in the Mesa Verde area appears to have started at about the same time that the Fremont cul-

ture began, we cannot assume that slipped Fremont pottery is late. Shutler (1961) found so few slipped (Virgin Black-on-white) sherds at Virgin sites in southern Nevada that he concluded they were trade sherds from farther east in the Virgin area. His experience supports the Listers' suggestion that this trait entered the Virgin area from the east.

No obvious origin for tooled decoration, one of Fremont's most characteristic traits, can be found outside the Fremont culture. Very similar tooling does occur on pottery at Sevier sites in western Utah, but it is no more reasonable to derive Fremont tooling from Sevier tooling than vice versa. Tooled pottery (O'Leary Tooled and Honani Tooled) was made in the Kayenta area in early Pueblo II times, but it was very rare. Moreover, Schroeder (1955) mentions a few sherds of a type he calls North Creek Tooled from the Virgin area. Similarities to the Virgin and Kayenta tooled types are not specific enough, however, to establish either as ancestral to Fremont or Sevier tooling.

Incised and punctate decoration, often in conjunction with corrugation, is sometimes found at Pueblo II Mesa Verde sites, but it is not common (Brew, 1946; Abel, 1955). Elsewhere in the Southwest tooling occasionally occurs during Fremont times, as well as before and after, but similarities to Fremont are not especially marked. Haury (1936) described three types, Alma Scored, Alma Incised, and Alma Punched, for the Mogollon area. On the northeastern periphery of the Southwest incised pottery (Taos Incised) occurs with a preponderance of plain gray ware and limited amounts of corrugated pottery and painted sherds of a Pueblo II or III age (Gunnerson, 1959 e). Although this archaeological development in northeastern New Mexico appears to have paralleled the Fremont development in some ways, there are no obvious cultural relationships between the two.

Thus, Fremont tooled ware probably represents independent invention. Some Fremont potter who was unaware of the techniques involved in corrugated pottery may have seen it and attempted to imitate it. There is a superficial resemblance between much of the tooled pottery and corrugated pottery, and a few Fremont and Sevier specimens almost certainly show deliberate imitation of corrugation. Meighan *et al.* (1956) have even suggested a type, "Snake Valley False Corrugated." The addition of fillets and blobs of clay to pottery in the Fremont and Sevier areas may represent a transference of decorative techniques used on figurines.

A few other comments on similarities and differences between the pottery of eastern and western Utah are in order. The rarity in western Utah of pottery with designs painted on a slipped surface (Rudy, 1953) helps support the suggestion that the use of a slip spread from the Mesa Verde area. The designs on painted bowls from western Utah (Steward, 1936; Rudy, 1953; Meighan *et al.*, 1956), where enough of the vessel is present to permit visualization of the over-all pattern, resemble closely those found on Fremont pottery. Designs are predominantly of Black Mesa style with the same few basic elements and the same characteristic variations being the most popular. Sosi and Dogoszhi elements are also present in both areas. The spread of crushed rock temper into the part of Utah west of the Wasatch Mountains, if its presence there does represent such a spread, was more extensive than the spread of the use of a slip. Crushed igneous rock temper is found in Sevier Gray and related types (Rudy, 1953) of the east-central part of western Utah, the part directly across the Wasatch Mountains from that part of the Fremont area where the pottery is tempered with crushed igneous rock. The tempering in these two areas, however, is distinctly different. To the west and north of the area where Sevier Gray occurs, the two main types are Snake Valley Gray and Great Salt Lake Gray, respectively. Both are sand-tempered. Thus there was apparently continued contact between the Virgin and Sevier areas, whereas contact between the Fremont and Virgin areas after the beginning of the Fremont culture seems to have been greatly reduced. This situation probably explains why Anderson (1963) found greater similarity between Sevier and Virgin plain gray pottery than between Fremont and Virgin plain gray pottery.

In much of Utah west of the Wasatch Mountains, especially in the areas where Snake Valley Gray and Sevier Gray predominate, corrugated pottery is common. At Paragonah, for example, corrugated pottery constitutes about one-fourth of the utility ware, whereas corrugated wares rarely account for even one per cent of the total sherd count at Fremont sites from which there is a significantly large sample. Much of the western Utah corrugated pottery is finely made, being characterized by, among other things, a high number of coils per inch (Rudy, 1953). The introduction of corrugated pottery into western Utah probably reflects a relatively late movement of Virgin traits, which probably also included the use of ventilators in pithouses such as those found at Paragonah (Meighan *et al.*, 1956), Marysvale (Gillin, 1941), and Kanosh (Steward, 1933 a).

For some as yet unexplained reason, the Fremont people appear to have almost completely rejected the technique of corrugation even though it was being practiced on three sides of them. Perhaps it is significant that more corrugated sherds occur at the southernmost peripheral Fremont sites than elsewhere (Gunnerson, 1957 a), since these sites are close to Virgin, Kayenta, and Mesa Verde sites, all of which would have an abundance of corrugated pottery. The analysis of the Claflin-Emerson expedition's collections from the Waterhole Flat–Lower Dirty Devil River area suggests, however, that a re-examination of the corrugated sherds reported by Gunnerson (1957 a) from the southern part of the Fremont area would disclose that many should be reidentified as Mesa Verde and that the few small sherds that were thought to be from neck-banded vessels are more probably from plain corrugated vessels with wide coils.

Another interesting practice that continued throughout all or at least most of the history of the Virgin, Fremont, and Sevier cultures was the application of a fugitive red paint or pigment to the outsides of many pottery vessels after they were fired, a trait that was also common at the Coombs Site. Although this trait was common at an earlier date in the San Juan, it decreased greatly in popularity during Pueblo II times just when it appears to have been accepted north of the Colorado River.

Fremont basketry, as noted before, shows considerable variety in techniques used, as does Southwestern basketry in general. Fremont basketry differs from that of most Southwestern cultures, however, in that it is predominantly close-coiled with a half-rod-and-bundle foundation, whereas this technique is rare in the Four Corners area, according to Morris and Burgh (1941, p. 9). The use of a half-rod-and-bundle technique, however, appears to have been very popular north of the Colorado River, since it is characteristic of the Uncompahgre complex (Wormington and Lister, 1956) and was the most common basketry technique found at Danger Cave (Rudy, 1957, p. 257), where single-rod foundations without a bundle were also common. Rudy, in discussing the rod-and-bundle foundation, shows its distribution to be predominantly northern as far as the Southwest is concerned.

At the Alvey site in the Escalante drainage, where the cultural material appeared to be chiefly of Virgin branch affiliation, 41 specimens of basketry large enough for identification of technique were recovered. Of these, 34 had either a single-rod or a split-rod foundation. Most had a half-rod-and-bundle foundation; a few had a rod-and-bundle foundation, and a few had a rod or half-rod as a core in a bundle. Other techniques represented included two-rods-and-bundle, two-half-rods, and two-rods. There was one specimen of spaced coiling and one of twined twilling with a coiled two-rod-foundation rim (Gunnerson, 1959 c, pp. 97–106). It was not possible to determine in a number of specimens whether the rod had been split or not. Most of the stitching was uninterlocking, although a few specimens had partially interlocking stitches. It is interesting that the one specimen from the lowest (preceramic) level at the Alvey Site had a one-rod-and-bundle foundation, and that the greatest variety of techniques was found in the uppermost level.

Our sample of basketry from other Virgin sites helps support a Virgin origin for the half-rod foundation. Judd (1926, p. 148) reports four "Cliff-dweller" baskets from Cottonwood Canyon just east of Kanab, Utah, two of which had a single-rod foundation and two a single-rod-and-bundle foundation. Whether the rods were whole or split is not indicated. Schroeder (1955, p. 156), however, reports only three specimens from the Zion Park area; two had a two-rod foundation and the third had a bundle foundation. In the

upper level of Pine Park Shelter, which contained a mixed Paiute-Virgin assemblage, Rudy (1954 b, p. 21) found only three specimens of basketry—two twined and one coiled with a half-rod foundation. Shutler (1961) reports specimens from southern Nevada, including ones with a single-rod-and-bundle foundation, a bundle foundation, a two-rod foundation and a two-rod-and-bundle foundation, but it is not possible to be certain as to the cultural or temporal placement of these few specimens.

Wheeler (1942, p. 17) reports twined basketry in the upper (Paiute ?) level at Etna Cave in southern Nevada and one piece in the Pueblo detritus, with coiled basketry occurring throughout. Of the 30 specimens of coiled basketry, 22 had a single-rod-and-bundle foundation, three had a two-rod-and-bundle foundation, and one had a single-rod-surrounded-by-fiber foundation.

On an earlier time level, however, we find that of the 30 basketry specimens found by Nusbaum (1922, pp. 90–97) at the Basketmaker II Cave du Pont, 25 were of the common and widespread two-rod-and-bundle type. One specimen had a foundation consisting of a single rod surrounded by a sheath or bundle of fibers, a technique noted in a few specimens from both Virgin and Fremont sites.

Thus, preponderance of half-rod-and-bundle foundation in coiled Fremont basketry is probably another trait derived from the Virgin branch, where it was apparently the dominant type in at least the eastern part of the area when the Fremont culture began. The possibility that this trait was derived from the Uncompahgre complex or Desert culture cannot be ruled out. It seems more likely, however, that the half-rod technique was popular for a long time north of the Colorado River and that any relationship between its occurrence in the Desert culture in general and the Virgin-Fremont continuum predates the beginning of the Fremont culture.

In considering other traits, we find that many were shared by Fremont and Virgin, although most of them are not restricted to these two complexes. With regard to chipped stone artifacts, virtually all the Virgin types illustrated by Shutler (1961) and Schroeder

(1955) are found in Fremont, and the converse is also true. With regard to projectile points in particular, however, specimens of Shutler's (1961, p. 36) Group H "Stem narrower than blade, tapering, pointed base, sharp-oblique tangs (pl. 65, *i-p, u-w*)" are relatively rare at Fremont sites as compared to the Virgin sites of southern Nevada, and Paragonah (Meighan *et al.*, 1956). Such points could be another trait that gained late popularity in Virgin and Sevier, but failed to spread to the Fremont area. That is, it may be part of the suggested late corrugated pottery–ventilator complex. The most common projectile points from Fremont sites are triangular and have no notches, small side notches, or large corner notches that leave an expanding stem. All these types occur also in western Utah and in the Virgin branch.

Chipped blades, either notched or unnotched and presumably used as knives, are found in both Fremont and Virgin. Some of the smaller ones do not differ significantly from Basketmaker dart or spear points. Drills with expanding bases are found in these two complexes, but the type is so widespread that they are of no diagnostic significance. Artifacts classified as small, crude choppers occur in both complexes, as do chipped stone disks, ground stone disks, and ground stone balls. The wide variety of manos, metates, and milling stones is very similar in both complexes, with nearly all the specific types, including the distinctive "Utah" type, being shared.

Four stone mortars were found at Virgin sites in southern Nevada (Shutler, 1961). Mortars have not been reported from Fremont sites, although one was found by a collector near Ferron, Utah, an area where there are many Fremont villages. Steward (1936, pp. 49–50) describes a number of pestles from western Utah. Woodbury (1954, p. 118), in discussing the distribution of mortars, found that they had wide geographical and sporadic temporal distribution in the Southwest and Great Basin, but that they were never very common in the Southwest and were most plentiful in the San Juan drainage in Basketmaker III times. In the Jeddito area, a few appear in Pueblo III times, but they are more common in Pueblo IV times, possibly representing a reintroduction from the Hohokam area. The abundance of mortars and pestles (13 each) at the Coombs Site (Lister *et al.*, 1960, 1961) is hard to explain.

Turquoise was mined by the Virgin people, who also fabricated ornaments from it, and they may have been the source of the few turquoise specimens found at Fremont sites. Other ornaments made of various kinds of stone, bone, and shell are common to both cultures.

Tubular pipes made from both clay and stone and elbow pipes made from clay are found in Fremont sites (Morss, 1931; Wormington, 1955; Gunnerson, 1957 a). In the Sevier area, tubular and elbow pipes of both stone and clay are found (Steward, 1936; Gillin, 1941) but elbow pipes have apparently not yet been reported from Virgin sites. The clay elbow pipes in the Fremont and Sevier areas are of the same type, with a conical to hemispherical bowl meeting the stem at an obtuse angle. They look as if they could have developed from the tubular pipes that have a conical bowl in line with the mouthpiece, which is perforated with a much smaller hole. Since elbow pipes are relatively rare in the Southwest, their presence in Sevier and Fremont could represent an entirely local development. Perhaps future work will show some connection between these and elbow pipes elsewhere in the Southwest, in Gallina (Hibben, 1938, p. 135), for example, but at present a local development seems more probable.

Only one T-shaped or "monitor" stone pipe is reported from the Sevier area and that, apparently deliberately "killed," was near a burial in a house at Paragonah (Meighan *et al.*, 1956, p. 66). No pipes of this type have been reported from either Virgin or Fremont sites.

In the Virgin branch the use of clay figurines continued even into the latest phase. While no Virgin figurine yet reported is as elaborate as the diagnostic Fremont figurines, the similarities are very striking and none would be out of place in a Fremont collection. And some Virgin figurines among those illustrated by Shutler (1961) resemble the classic Fremont figurines more closely than do some of the less distinctive Fremont figurines. The southern Nevada figurines also resemble very closely specimens from western Utah illustrated by Steward (1936, figs. 8–10).

The rather common occurrence at Fremont sites of perforated pottery disks, assumed to have been used as spindle whorls, may be one point of difference between the Fremont and Virgin cultures, since such specimens were apparently not included in the collections reported by Schroeder (1955) and Shutler (1961). Rudy and Stirland (1950, p. 46) found part of only one possible sherd whorl at one of their latest sites. They are apparently rare in the Sevier culture of western Utah, although Gillin (1941, plates VII, VIII) illustrates what are probably parts of three sherd spindle whorls and Green (1961, p. 46) reports five from near Provo. Haury (1945 a, p. 119), in discussing the distribution and variations in spindle whorls, says that the variety made from sherds occurs almost everywhere in the Southwest and as early as the Sweetwater Phase at Snaketown, but that they did not become common in the San Juan area until about Pueblo III times. This suggests that sherd spindle whorls were probably an addition, possibly quite late, to the Fremont culture after it had become established in eastern Utah. Another possibility is that sherd spindle whorls were introduced early into the Fremont culture from some point south of the Anasazi area. The occurrence at Site ET 6-7 of a shale disk spindle whorl of a type that Woodbury (1954, p. 186) considers to be Hohokam or Mexican suggests that both sherd and stone whorls might have come to the Fremont area from southern Arizona. The one stone disk spindle whorl reported by Woodbury, however, is from the surface of the Pueblo III-IV site of Kokopnyama in the Awatovi area, and hence is altogether too late to provide a possible link for the Fremont specimens. Steward (1936, pp. 53–54) did describe two possible stone spindle whorls, one of schist and the other of a hard granitic rock, from near Provo, Utah. Thus the problem of Fremont and Sevier spindle whorls is still open.

Small bone gaming pieces or dice, usually rectangular with rounded ends and made from sections of mammal long bones, are common at Fremont, Sevier, and Virgin sites, but appear to be less common in the San Juan area. Morris (1939, p. 213) found only two such specimens in the La Plata area and feels that they are more common in earlier than later times. Brew (1946, p. 244) found them at only one site at Alkali Ridge, that assignable to Pueblo I. There were, however, eight from this single site. The use of these bone objects, presumably in some sort of game, may be an early pan-Pueblo trait that survived with greater vigor north of the Colorado River than elsewhere in the Pueblo area.

One trait generally considered diagnostic of the Fremont culture is the distinctive dew-claw Fremont moccasin, best known from specimens from the Fremont drainage reported by Morss (1931) but also reported by Burgh and Scoggin (1948) from Mantle's Cave in the extreme northeast corner of the Fremont area. The Fremont people appear to have used hide footgear to the complete exclusion of the fiber sandal found throughout most of the Southwest. As yet there is no certain evidence that the Virgin people used the Fremont moccasin, or any footgear other than the sandal, but there is a possibility that they did.

One specifically Fremont moccasin, complete with dew claws, was found at Etna Cave in southern Nevada (Wheeler, 1942, p. 30; 1938). The cave had apparently contained a Paiute occupation; three Virgin occupations (Pueblo II, Basketmaker III, and an earlier prepottery occupation); and a still earlier occupation. The Fremont moccasin was found in a pit considered to belong to the Pueblo II occupation. A total of 59 sandals and fragments were found at the cave, in marked contrast to the single moccasin, making its presence difficult to interpret. Here, it would seem to be either a minority type of Virgin footwear that became the dominant type in the Fremont area or a "trade" item from Fremont.

One pair of Fremont moccasins was found in the top level of the Alvey site, a stratified rock shelter located on a tributary of the Escalante River (Gunnerson, 1959 c, p. 83). This site did not contain any other artifacts diagnostic of the Fremont culture. The pottery from the top level was predominantly Tusayan Corrugated (variety undetermined) and North Creek Gray plus a number of painted types. The occupation of this level is either primarily Virgin with Kayenta trade material or a double (Virgin-Kayenta) occupation. Thus, at this site, there is a suggestion that the Fremont moccasin might have been used by Virgin people on this their northeastern frontier, but the nature of the find and its associations suggest a date well after the beginning of the Fremont culture.

Another find of the characteristic Fremont moccasins is reported from just south of the Colorado River in western Colorado by Huscher and Huscher (1943, p. 67). This is outside the main area of Fremont occupation, but very close to it. Still another occurrence outside the Fremont area is represented by a pair of Fremont moccasins found in either Grand Gulch, in southeastern Utah, or Poncho House, on the Chinle in northeastern Arizona. These are now in the American Museum of Natural History (Morss, 1954, p. 14).

The only other moccasins similar to the Fremont style from outside the Fremont area are those from Lovelock Cave (Loud and Harrington, 1929) in western Nevada, a site that contained a great deal of probably Northern Paiute or Paviotso material. The precise temporal or cultural position of the Fremont-like moccasins at this site is not determinable, however.

The single moccasin found in a cave in Nevada near Wendover, Utah (Rudy, 1953, pp. 29, 157), is made from a single oval piece of buffalo hide that was brought up around the foot and laced together across the top. Its simplicity, the lack of conformity to basic moccasin styles, and the fact that it was manufactured from hide with the hair left on align it with the Fremont style, rather than with the Promontory style, as suggested by Rudy. This specimen does not, however, have the characteristic dew-claw hobnails or the ankle flap found on Fremont moccasins. Unfortunately, nothing very diagnostic was found in the nonceramic assemblage from this site.

It was pointed out earlier that moccasins have been found sporadically in earlier sites in the Southwest, but none show enough similarity to the Fremont (or Yampa) style to suggest ancestry. The Fremont moccasin is more probably an adaptation to a colder climate and it has been previously suggested that it is essentially a covered sandal (Loud and Harrington, 1929, p. 173; Morss, 1931, p. 68). The Yampa moccasin (Burgh and Scoggin, 1948, plate 15), which looks even more like a sandal made of hide, would have been a better summer than winter foot covering. There is virtually no chance of a relationship between the Fremont and the very different Promontory moccasins reported by Steward (1937 b), which were probably left by late Plains Apache hunters who presumably followed the bison from the Plains into the area north of the Great Salt Lake (Gunnerson, 1956 d).

We have seen that a few traits shared by some of the sites in the Sevier area and some of the late sites in the Virgin area are missing or very rare at Fremont sites. The most conspicuous of these are corrugated pottery, ventilators in pit structures, and projectile points with small pointed stems. These traits were probably either very rare or not present in the Virgin culture at the time that the Fremont and Sevier cultures split off, and entered the Virgin area later. It seems most probable that their presence at sites such as Paragonah (Meighan et al., 1956), Marysvale (Gillin, 1941), and Kanosh (Steward, 1933 a) represents a late spread of these traits, perhaps together, from the Virgin area into the southern half of the Sevier area, but not into the Fremont area and probably not into the northern part of Utah west of the Wasatch Mountains. There is as yet no evidence that the kiva proper and large, multiroomed structures ever entered either the Fremont or Sevier areas, and they apparently never became very common even in the Virgin area.

Three other Virgin traits not yet definitely reported from Fremont sites are cotton, turkeys, and dogs. It is likely that cotton and turkeys were not raised by the Fremont people and any attempts to do so would doubtless have been unsuccessful because of the rigors of the environment. Doyle (1941, p. 350) gives the climatic conditions for successful commercial cultivation of cotton as an annual mean temperature of 60° or, under special conditions, 50° F; a frostless season of 180–200 days; and a minimum rainfall of 20 inches per year, with suitable distribution. There is probably no single spot within the Fremont area where conditions would approach these minimum requirements. Even most of the San Juan and Virgin areas would be very marginal for the growing of cotton. Although turkeys are now raised in many places in Utah, they require a great deal of special care and they apparently are not native to any part of the Fremont and Sevier areas.

It seems probable that the Fremont people did have dogs. The absence of dog remains at Fremont sites may reflect the fact that dogs were not eaten. In such case their bones would not have been added to the village detritus. Dogs are known from the Virgin branch primarily from dog burials or the burial of dogs with people (Shutler, 1961). Since relatively few human burials have been reported from Fremont sites, it is not too surprising that dog burials (if such exist in Fremont) have not been found.

ROUTES CONNECTING THE VIRGIN AND FREMONT AREAS

The route by which the Fremont culture would have spread from the Virgin area into eastern Utah cannot be definitely established, but there are few logical choices. The natural barriers that separate the Virgin, Sevier, and Fremont areas are not formidable, but nevertheless they represent cultural boundaries. The Fremont and Sevier areas are separated by the Wasatch Mountains, a range running north–south through the middle of Utah. Pairs of streams that head close together and flow down opposite sides of the Wasatch provide a number of passes, several of which serve as the routes of modern highways. Even the lowest passes, however, are too high for horticulture to have been practiced at their summits, so a strip 20 miles or more wide separates the areas utilized for permanent villages by the Fremont and Sevier people. The divide between the southern edge of the area of internal drainage of western Utah and the area drained by the northern tributaries of the Virgin River coincides closely with the boundary between the Virgin and Sevier cultures. This physiographic feature is less well defined than the Wasatch Mountains and a few of the passes through it are both lower and farther south than those through the Wasatch, but even so, there does not appear to have been any unbroken string of horticultural villages between the two areas.

The boundary between the southern edge of the Fremont area and the northeastern edge (or end) of the Virgin area does not correspond to a natural feature as marked and easily defined as the other two. The sites in the drainage of the Escalante River are predominantly of Virgin affiliation, but a few appear to represent either Fremont or an archaeological complex transitional between Virgin and Fremont. In this area, there is also evidence at a few sites of a Kayenta or strongly Kayenta-influenced occupation. To the north of the Escalante drainage, the next major western tributary of the Colorado River is the Dirty Devil River, the two main branches of which are the Fremont and the Muddy. Except for the lower reaches of the Dirty Devil, this drainage was dominated by the Fremont culture. Between the Escalante drainage and the Dirty Devil drainage is a large rough area that contained few archaeological sites and those present apparently did not represent a permanent occupation. The area immediately north of the lower portion of the Escalante River is so rough and barren that it would have served as an effective barrier even to foot travel. Farther up the Escalante River, however, there are a number of tributaries entering it from the north that head on the south and east slopes of Boulder Mountain, which is an eastward projection of the Wasatch Plateau. Heading on the northern and eastern slopes of Boulder Mountain are many spring-fed tributaries of the Fremont River. Travel by foot would have been relatively easy up the tributaries of the Escalante River to the eastern slopes of Boulder Mountain and then down the tributaries of the Fremont River. Boulder Mountain, lush and pleasant by contrast to the near-desert conditions immediately to the south and east, would have been (and still is) attractive to hunters at medium to high elevations, and to farmers at medium elevations.

Moreover, in the Escalante drainage and on the Kaiparowits Plateau just to the south of the Escalante River are many sites, almost all of which date from essentially Pueblo II times and appear to have their strongest cultural ties with the Virgin branch (Gunnerson, 1959 c, 1959 d). In many ways these sites resemble sites of the Fremont culture more strongly than do Virgin sites farther west. Some of the plain gray pottery from sites in the Escalante drainage identified as Turner Gray (Suhm, 1959) should probably be assigned to a new type, "Escalante Gray," suggested by Gunnerson (1959 c), who identified the tempering material as probably sand derived from igneous rock. This sand resembles the crushed igneous rock with which Fremont (Emery series) pottery is tempered. And "Escalante Gray" pottery lacks the tooling characteristic of Fremont pottery. Collections from the Kaiparowits Plateau contained both Escalante Gray and North Creek Gray with the two types grading into each other. Furthermore, some of the North Creek Gray sherds appeared to be tempered with crushed sandstone rather than with the traditional sand.

For some reason, there seems to have been a great deal of experimentation or variability in pottery making, especially in the choice of tempering material, in this area. It is perhaps most noticeable in the large collections from the Coombs Site (Lister, Ambler and Lister, 1960; Lister and Lister, 1961). Here, at a site considered basically Kayenta, crushed igneous rock was substituted for the traditional sand temper in the manufacture of much of the pottery assigned to local varieties of Kayenta. Tempering material identified as igneous sand was found mixed with crushed igneous rock in some of the pottery, and crushed sherd tempering was found in other locally made pottery. Trade pottery from many areas, including Kayenta, Mesa Verde, and Chaco, as well as the closer Virgin, Fremont, and Sevier cultures, was found at the Coombs Site. With such far-flung connections it is not surprising that diverse traditions should be reflected here. Furthermore, the Escalante drainage is probably closer to more different divisions of Anasazi than is any other area so small. Although no site has produced the information necessary to demonstrate it, the Escalante drainage was probably also a cultural crossroad during early Pueblo II times, prior to the Kayenta thrust into the area represented by the Davis Kiva Site and the Coombs Site.

The role that the Escalante drainage played in the history of the Fremont culture cannot be determined until much more excavation has been completed in several areas. There appears to be no question that the Fremont culture is in some way involved with this area. Some of the sites in the Escalante drainage and on the Kaiparowits Plateau may be the Virgin sites out of which the Fremont culture evolved and thus may be transitional between Virgin and Fremont. One possible route for the postulated movement of people from the Virgin area into the Fremont area, therefore, would have been from the Escalante drainage around the eastern side of Boulder Mountain (Aquarius Plateau) and down various tributaries of the Fremont River and then north across the rest of the Fremont area.

The proto-Fremont people could also have left the Virgin area by going north and east from the Virgin River, perhaps from near St. George or Kanab, Utah, to the upper Sevier River and across the Wasatch Mountains by any one of several easy passes that would have taken them into the southwestern part of the Fremont area, from which dispersal could have taken place. Although there is altogether too little evidence strongly to support one route over the other, the route via the Escalante drainage seems more probable at the moment.

CAUSE OF THE PUEBLO II EXPANSION

It has become more and more apparent that there was a marked expansion of the area occupied by people with Anasazi Pueblo culture during Pueblo II (*ca.* A.D. 900–1100) times, and concomitant with this geographical expansion there seems to have been an increase in population. This expansion was most extensive in the Fremont and Sevier areas, which together compose a region about half as large as all the rest of the Anasazi area.

One explanation of the cause of the Pueblo II expansion is increased rainfall. But recent studies of climatic changes in the Southwest (Schulman, 1956; Smiley, 1958) do not reveal significantly higher precipitation during the A.D. 900–1100 period.

Recently, Galinat and Gunnerson (1963) re-examined the problem of the history of maize in the Southwest while preparing Appendix I of this paper. They concluded that the single element most responsible for the Pueblo II expansion was probably the introduction of a new eight-rowed race of maize, Maíz de Ocho, into the Southwest about A.D. 700.

This, when crossed with the previous maize, which was predominantly a mixture of Chapalote and teosinte, apparently resulted in a significantly increased yield of grain that was much easier to mill and that was well suited to a far greater range of environments, especially to higher latitudes or elevations. Its ability to thrive at higher elevations and latitudes was due to the fact that an ancestor of the new eight-rowed maize had evolved at high elevations in South America, from where it had apparently spread quite rapidly to northern Mexico and the Southwest, appearing there about A.D. 700.

Prior to about A.D. 900, successful maize horticulture, the hallmark of the Pueblo culture, had apparently been confined to the area south of 38° north latitude, with possibly a few exceptions.

The introduction of a new, abundant, easily prepared food could have resulted in an increase in population. Since this same food could be grown satisfactorily over a much larger area than had been possible for previous maize, it could have permitted the population to expand geographically without significantly changing the pattern of its culture. In the case of the Fremont people, this expansion would have been into an area that appears previously to have supported only a very sparse population, so that their entry would probably not have met strong resistance. It is not yet possible to say whether the indigenous population was annihilated, displaced, or absorbed.

Predecessors of the Fremont People

Gunnerson (1960 a) has suggested that some of the distinctive flavor of the Fremont culture may be the result of influence from a sparse indigenous population that was occupying the Fremont area when the Fremont people arrived. Prior to about A.D. 950, this area had apparently never been inhabited by horticultural people, but had supported a scattered hunting and gathering population for several thousand years. To the west of the Wasatch Mountains were the Desert culture people, represented by a 10,000-year-long occupation at Danger Cave (Jennings, 1957) and by similar but undated occupations at other caves near the Great Salt Lake, such as

Black Rock and Deadman Caves (Smith, 1952; Steward, 1937 b). East of the Wasatch Mountains, in the area eventually to be occupied by the Fremont culture, there is a percussion-flaked stone tradition that may be very early. Probably following this, and extending until the beginning of Fremont times, was what appears to have been a local variation of the Desert culture to which the name "Uncompahgre complex" was applied by Wormington and Lister (1956). In addition to sites on the Uncompahgre Plateau, after which the complex takes its name, it or some complex closely akin to it is represented at many sites on the LaSal Mountains (Hunt, 1953), in the lower levels of Hells Midden (Lister, 1951), possibly by part of the material in Mantle's Cave (Burgh and Scoggin, 1948), at sites in the High East Tavaputs (Grosscup, 1962), and probably at a few of the non-ceramic sites reported on the basis of survey by Gunnerson (1957 a). Lister and Wormington suggested a possible relationship between the Uncompahgre complex and the Basketmaker II phase of the Four Corners area. Such a connection might be supported by the pre-Fremont burial at Site PR 4-31 in Nine Mile Canyon, herein reported. The material accompanying this skeleton is strongly reminiscent of the Basketmaker II complex except that it included hide moccasins and leggings, a very practical adaptation to the colder conditions encountered this far north. No occupation sites attributable to this Basketmaker-like complex have been found, so we do not know whether the man in tailored skin clothing lived as well as died here. The hide clothing, apparently well-made to a well-established pattern rather than the result of "field expediency" does much to exclude the possibility that he was a wanderer from the San Juan or Virgin rivers. Since very little perishable Uncompahgre material has been recovered, it is not possible to compare all the items found with him with traits of the Uncompahgre complex. Two of his possessions, the atlatl weights and L-shaped awls, which could be expected to have been found at Uncompahgre sites, have apparently not been found, although the amount of excavation has not been large and their absence may only reflect the small sample. Until a great deal of additional work has been done to clarify the situation, it seems safe to assume that the Rasmussen Cave burial and the Uncompahgre complex are in some way related to the Basketmaker II phase farther south, and to each other.

In any case, and no matter what name is applied to it, there was an earlier sparse hunting and gathering occupation that apparently persisted until the Fremont people moved in to dominate the area. It seems probable that this earlier complex had some influence upon the Fremont culture, although so little is known about it that the influence is difficult to demonstrate.

THE FATE OF THE FREMONT CULTURE

Although the most recent piece of wood dating a Fremont house had a bark date of A.D. 1151, the terminal date for Fremont was rounded off arbitrarily at A.D. 1200 for several reasons. First, there is no reason to believe that the A.D. 1151 house was the last to be built. Moreover, A.D. 1200 is compatible with the A.D. 1150–1300 date for Tusayan Polychrome (Colton, 1956), which is occasionally found at Fremont sites. It is possible that the terminal date for Fremont might vary nearly 50 years one way or the other from A.D. 1200, but it is highly improbable that the variation is any greater than that.

Also, the terminal date of A.D. 1200 corresponds closely to the beginning of the great drought of A.D. 1215–1299 in the Southwest (Schulman, 1956, p. 69). Since the Fremont area is precariously marginal as far as precipitation is concerned, it is reasonable to suppose that reductions in moisture so slight that they would not be obvious in the tree-ring record could affect farming adversely. Throughout the duration of the Fremont culture, there were occasional dry years or runs of a few years with below-average rainfall. The worst drought was from about A.D. 1262 to about A.D. 1310, however, when there was almost continuous subnormal rainfall according to the tree-ring record (Schulman, 1948). A somewhat less severe drought appears to have occurred between about A.D. 1150 and A.D. 1166. It could be that this relatively minor drought was actually disastrous and that the Fremont culture came to an end during this period, especially since the evidence that suggests it lasted longer is not direct. In any case, drought was probably the major or initial cause for the disintegration of the Fremont culture. As conditions worsened, there may well have been competition for the land with the most dependable source of irrigation water, as well as changes in the methods of storing the increasingly more precious corn. The possibility that some of the structures built in the most defensively situated places were constructed late for the protection of corn has already been discussed.

Termination dates for the Virgin and Sevier cultures are largely extensions of dating in the Kayenta and Fremont areas since there are no direct tree-ring dates for Virgin and Sevier sites of this period. As mentioned earlier, Colton, Schroeder, and Shutler assign a terminal date of about A.D. 1150 to the Virgin branch, but since a few Tusayan Polychrome sherds were found by Rudy and Stirland in Washington County, Utah, this date should probably be extended slightly. Shutler (1961, p. 69) feels that there was a population decrease during his last phase, which started about A.D. 1100. Such a decrease in population and a nearly complete evacuation of the area by about A.D. 1150 could reflect the presence of drought in the western part of the Virgin area somewhat earlier than in the Fremont area.

On the basis of similarities in culture and environment, it seems reasonable to assume that the Sevier culture came to an end approximately when the Virgin and Fremont cultures did. Certainly there is no evidence to the contrary. Rudy (1953, p. 170) concluded that the Puebloid (Sevier) occupation of western Utah was brought to an end by drought conditions that coincided with those in the Fremont area, and that the Sevier culture could not have survived the severest part of the drought that lasted from about A.D. 1270 to 1295 in the Nine Mile Canyon area. He would appear to be safe in setting a terminal date no later than A.D. 1270.

When a horticultural life became impossible in the area that they occupied, the Fremont people had to: (1) move elsewhere in order to continue to farm, (2) die out, or (3) change the subsistence base of their culture. If all the Fremont people had moved out of their former territory and continued their old way of life elsewhere, recognizable Fremont sites dating from after A.D. 1200 should have been found by now, but they have not been. If they had moved out and joined some existing group such as the Hopi (at that time Kayenta), one could expect to find Fremont traits at the host sites, but such have not been reported. Furthermore, it is hard to imagine that a few thousand Fremont refugees from a drought would be welcome at other villages that were also feeling the effects of the same drought. To be sure, there are a number of specific similarities between the Fremont culture and the Hopi culture but these could reflect a common heritage and diffusion of ideas before A.D. 1200. It is not at all unlikely that a few Fremont people would have been able to attach themselves to one of the Kayenta villages and introduce some of their ideas, but there is no evidence that a large number of Fremont people consummated such an unlikely merger.

In times of food shortages and malnutrition, there is generally a population decline, or at least a slowing of the rate of increase. But people in general, unless they are badly demoralized (and there is no evidence that the Fremont people were) will go to almost any lengths to keep from starving to death. It is very difficult to visualize the Fremont people simply giving up and dying out when they could no longer raise crops. Theirs was a relatively young and vigorous culture based on a subsistence pattern that included hunting and gathering as well as farming. The additive nature of their culture and of the ancestral Virgin culture had never allowed them to become overly specialized and to lose their nonfarming subsistence techniques. It is highly probable that they utilized these techniques to survive under changed climatic conditions.

The fate of the two cultures most closely related to Fremont presents a similar problem. Rudy (1953, p. 169), unable to find any evidence to suggest that the Puebloid (Sevier) people moved to another area after their horticultural way of life came to an end in western Utah, concluded that they probably changed the base of their economy.

The fate of the Virgin branch is equally uncertain. During Pueblo II times there was an increase of the Virgin branch population in the Walhalla Glades area (Hall, 1942) and on the Kaiparowits Plateau (Gunnerson, 1959 d), probably part of the same expansion that resulted in the Fremont culture. During early Pueblo III times this eastern part of the Virgin area apparently experienced the same population decrease that occurred in the western part. Hall suggested that there was probably a movement of people from the north to the south rim of the Grand Canyon at this time, but such a movement could not have accounted for all the Virgin people. Furthermore, archaeologists who have worked on the south rim subsequently have apparently all failed to identify the inhabitants of late sites there as migrants from the north rim (McGregor, 1951; Schwartz, 1956; Wheat, 1955).

The absence of evidence showing that the Fremont culture, and apparently the Sevier and Virgin cultures as well, moved to another area suggests that these cultures underwent a change to permit the people to survive under the changed conditions. Once they were faced with the need to move frequently in order to obtain food, their material culture inventory may have become much like that of the Plateau Shoshoneans found in the same area in historic times.

There are striking similarities (figs. 17–19) between the history of the Plateau Shoshoneans as reconstructed by Lamb (1958), Hale (1958), and Romney (1957), on the basis of linguistic data, and the development of the Virgin, Fremont, and Sevier cultures as postulated by Gunnerson (1960 a). On the basis of these similarities, Gunnerson (1962 a) suggested that these three archaeological complexes represent prehistoric speakers of Plateau Shoshonean. His argument proceeded as follows:

"The area occupied by Virgin Branch Anasazi suggests itself as the probable homeland of the proto-Plateau Shoshoneans for several reasons.

"1. It is centrally located along the southern edge of the area of Plateau Shoshonean distribution, that is, the edge nearest the rest of the Uto-Aztecans. It seems remarkable, however, that linguistic and archæological evidence suggested homelands for proto-Plateau Shoshonean as close together as Death Valley and the Virgin Area.

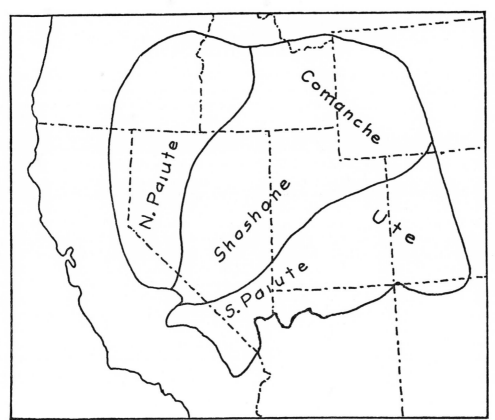

Fig. 17. Location of Plateau Shoshonean people *ca.* A.D. 1700. After Gunnerson (1962 a, fig. 1); based on Kroeber (1934), Steward (1941 b), and Stewart (1942).

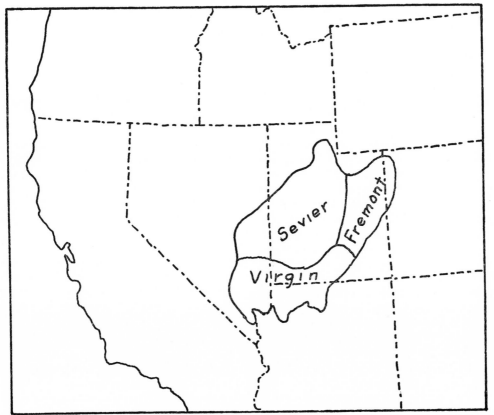

Fig. 18. Location of Virgin, Sevier, and Fremont cultures *ca.* A.D. 1050–1150. After Gunnerson (1962 a, fig. 2); based on Gunnerson (1960 a) and Rudy (1953).

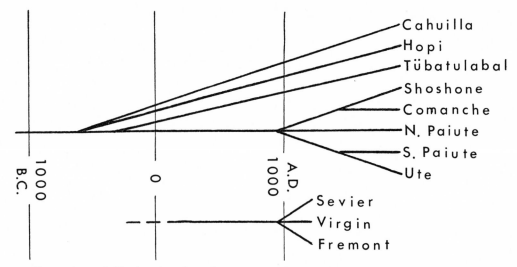

FIG. 19. Comparison of Shoshonean glottochronology with suggested archaeological reconstruction. After
Gunnerson (1962 a, fig. 3); based on Hale (1958) and Gunnerson (1960 a).

"2. The long in situ development and late spread attributed to the Virgin branch is compatible with the long period during which proto-Plateau Shoshoneans spoke a common language (Hale) or, alternatively, shared a small area (Lamb).

"3. The postulated outgrowth of the Fremont and Sevier cultures from the Virgin branch apparently began about A.D. 950, the time postulated by Hale for the first, three-way linguistic split among the Plateau Shoshoneans. Lamb, too, found this point in time significant, for he suggested it as a date of dispersal for the Numic peoples.

"The postulated cultural and temporal relationships of Virgin, Fremont, and Sevier could be equated, then, with either Hale's chronology or Lamb's reconstruction, which are difficult to compare in detail, but do not seriously contradict one another. Moreover, if the Virgin, Fremont, and Sevier peoples became Plateau Shoshoneans, they changed their way of life in the 1200's and expanded their territory beyond the area in which Pueblo-like sites are found. It seems reasonable that these changes would have led to the final linguistic differentiations that, according to both Lamb and Hale, took place in recent centuries." (Gunnerson, 1962 a, p. 43).

The fact that Plateau Shoshonean is generally regarded as having three major subdivisions suggested the possibility of equating these with Virgin, Sevier, and Fremont. Tentatively, the Fremont culture was equated with the Ute–Southern Paiute, the Sevier culture with the Shoshone-Comanche, and the Virgin

branch with the Northern Paiute, primarily on the basis of geographical distribution. These are the identifications that would necessitate a minimum movement of peoples except for expansion from their assumed homelands. Conceivably additional linguistic work will result in a modification of the genetic linguistic model that will permit a more satisfactory equating of historically known language groups and archaeological complexes. Considering the basic similarities of the Virgin, Fremont, and Sevier cultures and the very sudden changes which they would have had to undergo to become the historic Plateau Shoshoneans, it seems unlikely that archaeological evidence will be of much help in identifying the particular prehistoric complex from which a particular historic band came. To complicate matters even more, Steward (1940) has noted that the Plateau Shoshoneans have taken on a great deal of the color of their neighbors, so that the westernmost Shoshoneans have a culture closely resembling cultures in California while the easternmost Shoshoneans have a strong increment of Plains traits. This might be expected, especially in a group that had lost much of its own culture.

Although the tentative equating of major linguistic subdivisions and archaeological complexes is done primarily on the basis of geographical distribution, it is done with the complete realization that much shifting of groups could have taken place between A.D. 1200 and historic times, and that other identifications that now seem less likely may eventually be established.

The possibility that the Plateau Shoshoneans developed from the prehistoric Puebloan people has probably been considered by every anthropologist who has worked in the area, and more appear to have favored such a deculturation than to have rejected it. Among the first, if not the first, specifically to suggest such an origin for the Plateau Shoshoneans was Shimkin (1940, p. 20) who presented the idea in a paper read in the summer of 1939.

Writing at about the same time, Steward (1940, p. 478) considered and ruled out the possibility that the Shoshoneans received their Basketmaker-like culture from the "Northern Periphery" because: "1, it lacks a true Basket Maker culture; 2, it lacks any suggestion of an early Shoshonean culture . . . ; and 3, it is impossible to assume actual descent of Shoshoneans from the Puebloans because in addition to differences in physical type an enormous degree of deculturation would have to be postulated." The archaeological work done since 1940 has answered, at least in part, these three points. The Basketmaker traits retained by the cultures of this area could have provided the source of the Shoshonean traits just as well as a pure Basketmaker culture could. The fact that traits appropriate to a sedentary horticultural economy did not continue when the subsistence pattern changed back to one based predominantly, and in some cases exclusively, on hunting and gathering is to be expected.

As for Steward's second point, there would be no early sites (prior to the end of the Puebloan occupation) showing the Shoshonean culture if Shoshonean cultures developed from the Virgin, Sevier, and Fremont cultures as here postulated. And if the transition was as sudden as I believe, the likelihood of finding a site that appeared transitional would be very remote.

In western Utah, however, Rudy (1953) and in eastern Utah Gunnerson (1957 a) found numerous small camp sites that are probably assignable to the Sevier and Fremont cultures since many of them contain diagnostic pottery. In both cases these sites were considered to be related to hunting and gathering activities because of their small size and remoteness from large villages and tillable land. Since there is no obvious way to date these small sites, it is quite possible that some of them represent scattered occupation shortly after the termination of a horticultural way of life rather than temporary, perhaps seasonal, use during the height of the Sevier and Fremont cultures.

With regard to Steward's point concerning the differences in physical types between the Puebloid people and the Shoshoneans, the data are still very few, but the Puebloid people now appear to be very heterogeneous so it is unlikely that physical anthropology can help us much.

Furthermore, the degree of deculturation could hardly be called "enormous" as suggested by Steward, and the changes certainly would not be impossible, especially for a group that had retained and was actively using a wide variety of hunting and gathering techniques along with their agricultural practices. In historical records, one can find accounts of even the Hopi leaving their villages to live off the land when drought conditions precluded farming. On November 1, 1779, Governor de Anza of New Mexico wrote Teodoro de Croix, Commander General of the Interior Provinces:

"The scarcity of seasonal rains experienced in this kingdom for two years past and during the present one has brought such conditions of hunger to the province of Moqui, that according to conversations and frequent news of the month of August last, until today, its dwellers have seen themselves forced to abandon entirely or in greater part their idolatrous pueblos, dividing themselves into many groups among the woods and hills to seek in them wild sustenance. For this reason also they have submitted to various nations whom before they had enriched with what they now lack, their calamities reaching such an extreme that they have sold or are selling their children to procure sustenance" (Thomas, 1932, p. 145).

The Fremont, Sevier, or Virgin people would probably have been even more inclined to such a course of action since they appear to have been far less committed to a horticultural way of life than were the Hopi. If, after nearly a century too dry for crop growing, they did not resume a settled horticultural way of life it is not surprising.

Culture changes of a magnitude equal to or greater than what has been postulated for the Shoshoneans occurred in the Plains, where the Cheyenne, for example, gave up a settled farming way of life and adopted the horse-nomad, bison-hunting culture that characterized the High Plains in the middle 1800's. And finally, not only is the postulated deculturation possible, it seems to have been the only alternative available to at least the majority of the Fremont, Sevier, and probably Virgin people.

The postulated derivation of the Plateau Shoshoneans from the Virgin-Sevier-Fremont block involves a several-fold increase in territory occupied, and such an increase would have been necessary to permit the change unless one also postulates a drastic decrease in population. In spite of the small proportion of the Fremont area that could be successfully cultivated, agriculture along with hunting and gathering would have supported a far denser population than could hunting and gathering without crops. After about two centuries of growth, the Fremont population was probably approaching a balance with its environment and technology. Since drought conditions would adversely affect the amount of available wild food, it is obvious that a great increase in territory would be necessary to support the same population on wild foods alone. The dispersal of the population would continue until the population was again in balance with its environment and technology, or until further expansion was blocked.

The population dispersal was effectively blocked to the south and southeast by other Pueblo farmers who were probably beginning to feel or perhaps were already suffering from drought conditions. To the east, the territory could not expand very far because of the formidable Rocky Mountains. This left the west, northwest, and north as the only directions for a significant dispersal. It seems unlikely that the areas into which the Virgin-Fremont-Sevier people would have spread were entirely devoid of inhabitants at about A.D. 1200, although we know virtually nothing about them. We can assume that if there were people living in these surrounding areas they were hunt-

ers and gatherers, probably with a way of life very much like the Desert culture.

It is safe, therefore, to assume that our expanding Plateau Shoshonean block did encounter hunting and gathering peoples and acquired new traits from them at different points on the circumference. A badly deculturated people would be more ready to adopt traits that were apparently successfully used by their neighbors than would a well-integrated successful people. Such borrowing would account for the wide cultural differences associated with close linguistic relationship noted by Steward and others for the Plateau Shoshoneans. Whereas there were apparently no definable cultural boundaries anywhere within the Plateau Shoshonean region, there were great cultural variations on opposite sides of this huge area. Between the contrasting cultures there was a smooth gradient.

Steward (1940) sees the Plateau Shoshoneans as having a basically Basketmaker culture to which various traits have been added in different areas. The groups that differ most from a generalized Plateau Shoshonean culture are those on the east, such as the Shoshoni and Ute, who have taken on much of the late bison-horse complex of the Plains. Steward feels, however, that these eastern, most deviant groups previously had a culture much more like that found farther west, although the Northern Paiute, who occupy the westernmost part of the Plateau Shoshonean area, apparently acquired a number of traits from California tribes even farther west.

Among wandering hunters and gatherers one would not expect much effort to be expended on the construction of dwellings. Pottery, which is hard to transport because of its fragility, and heavy stone artifacts such as metates, rarely play a significant role in nomadic cultures that have only foot transport. But even these traits are not completely lacking among the Plateau Shoshoneans.

For this reason, comparisons of the Plateau Shoshoneans with Virgin-Fremont-Sevier are not altogether unrewarding. Romney (1957, p. 38) found in reconstructed proto-Uto-Aztecan terms for "planting stick, mano, metate, two terms for maize, and one for planted field." Thus, horticulture had apparently been known to the Plateau Shoshoneans for at least

4000 years, the time that has elapsed since the Uto-Aztecan dispersal. In 1776 Escalante found crops and fields with irrigation ditches near St. George, Utah (Auerbach, 1943, p. 85). Nearly a century later in 1868, Major Powell's expedition observed crops and irrigated fields thought to belong to Paiutes (Bradley, 1947, p. 69; Powell, 1875, p. 96).

Steward (1941 b, p. 338) and Stewart (1942, pp. 231–232) collected ethnographic information indicating that the Utes and Paiutes were and had been farmers, although there are suggestions that the Utes might have adopted agriculture recently. Even though some of the Plateau Shoshoneans, especially the Southern Paiute, practiced horticulture in early historic times, there could well have been a hiatus of a century or so during the height of the 13th century drought when farming was at a minimum, or dormant. Linguistic evidence cited earlier shows that farming was not entirely forgotten. It is not possible, however, to say how completely and how long farming was absent. By the late 1700's it was apparently well established again in southwestern Utah, but did not provide a base upon which a culture with permanent villages of substantial dwellings and a well-developed ceramic complex could be established. In the more ecologically precarious areas to the north that had once supported the Fremont and Sevier cultures, farming had regained even less of a foothold.

Substantial, although not elaborate, houses were constructed by some of the Plateau Shoshoneans. Steward (1933 c, pp. 263–266) reports several types of structures among the Owens Valley Paiute including some up to 25 feet in diameter built over excavations 2 feet deep and having earth-covered roofs supported by two posts set in the floor and connected by a ridgepole. A fireplace was located in the center of the floor, directly under a smoke hole through the roof. Entrance was by means of a sloping passageway to the east. Such a structure would not differ radically from the earlier Virgin, Fremont, and Sevier pithouses. Among the Owens Valley Paiute, the sweat houses, which were the most substantial, served as men's dormitory, "club house," and community center.

Steward (1933 c, pp. 334–335) also reports a number of archaeological sites in the Owens Valley area that he assumes, or at least implies, are of Paiute origin. Several of these sites have "low rings, 10 to 12 feet in diameter, of unshaped boulders, piled two or three high," which appeared to Steward to be bases of houses. Associated with most, but not all, of these sites was pottery. At another site he found pits that were "probably the remains of post-Caucasian semisubterranean, earth-covered lodges," and glass beads. From a rock shelter he reports a slab-lined cist, about 3 feet in diameter and 18 inches deep. All of these, and especially the rock rings, are very reminiscent of sites in the Fremont area. And since Paiute informants could not explain them, they are probably at least moderately old. It would be worthwhile to excavate some of these to determine whether they are actually old Paiute sites.

A few other specific traits found in various Plateau Shoshonean groups are of particular interest when examined in the light of the archaeological complexes being considered here. Similar traits cannot be taken as proof of relationship, but when added to the many broad basic similarities, they increase the plausibility of a relationship.

T-shaped stone pipes are very common in other parts of North America, especially east of the Rocky Mountains, but they are rare in the Southwest and the Great Basin. A unique specimen of this type was found in a pithouse at Paragonah (Meighan et al., 1956, p. 66). Steward (1941 b, fig. 4 c) shows a similar pipe that he calls a monitor or platform pipe from the Diamond Valley Shoshoni. The Paragonah specimen differs from the one obtained by Steward in that the long stem portion has a hole through its full length and a stone plug closing one end, whereas the Shoshoni specimen has a hole through only one arm of the stem or base portion. Stewart (1942, p. 344) was told by informants that the Pahvant Utes of the Sevier River area received monitor stone pipes from the Utes in the Uinta basin and that Utes near Cimarron, New Mexico, received similar pipes from the Plains just before the arrival of the whites. Among the northern and Gosiute Shoshoni Steward (1943, p. 278) found monitor (T-shaped), L-shaped, and tubular stone pipes. Tubular pipes, however, appear to have been by far the most common among the Plateau Shoshoneans as they were among the Fremont, Sevier, and Virgin people, and both stone and clay were used on both time levels. Steward (1933 c) describes one Mono pipe made of clay in which the bowl meets the stem at a 45° angle, a shape very suggestive of the elbow pipes of the Fremont and Sevier cultures.

Steward (1940, p. 486) points out that the Northern Paiute and some of the Southern Paiute used fiber sandals of a Southwestern type while elsewhere the Plateau Shoshoneans wore moccasins of hide when they could get the hide or sometimes substituted moccasins of fiber when they could not. It is interesting that sandals were found most commonly among the Northern Paiute, the group that Gunnerson (1962 a) suggested might be the descendants of the Virgin people, who also used fiber sandals.

Whether any of the various styles of Plateau Shoshonean moccasins (Steward, 1941 b, fig. 13; 1943, p. 255) could have been derived from the Fremont moccasin is uncertain, but this problem would repay a detailed examination. The moccasins worn by several of the eastern tribes, for example, the Ute, Comanche, and Shoshoni, are of Plains style and were probably not adopted until about 1700 after the introduction of the horse had brought about increased contact with the Plains. In any case, the acceptance of a new and better (?) style of skin moccasin would probably be easier for a group that was accustomed to wearing hide moccasins than for one that was not.

The problem of "Paiute" and "Shoshoni" pottery is complex as well as important. There is no doubt that pottery was made by many of the Plateau Shoshoneans. It has been reported ethnographically by Steward (1933 c, pp. 266-268; 1941 b, p. 242; 1943, p. 273; 1940), Stewart (1942, p. 273), and Lowie (1924, pp. 25–26). By the late 1800's, however, it had become quite uncommon and very few specimens have been collected by ethnographers.

Baldwin (1950) described "Southern Paiute Utility Ware" on the basis of pottery that he had collected archaeologically. It is the general belief that this ware was made by the

Southern Paiute, although the identification rests primarily upon its post-Pueblo age and its geographical distribution, which corresponds closely to the area occupied by the Southern Paiute. Moreover, Baldwin quotes Harrington (1926 b, p. 229) to the effect that "This pottery we have been able to identify as of Paiute origin, and we learned from the Indians that such vessels were manufactured by the Moapa band as late as 1890." Unfortunately, the full range of types collected archaeologically is not represented by the ethnographic specimens.

Other archaeological pottery that is probably of Plateau Shoshonean origin has been reported from western Colorado by Huscher and Huscher (1940) and Wormington and Lister (1956), from western Utah by Rudy (1954 b, pp. 94–98), and from Wyoming by Wedel (1954). Wedel calls attention to the similarity in shape between the clay and steatite vessels of northwestern Wyoming and suggests a Shoshoni authorship for both. These specimens are flat-bottomed with a flange surrounding the bottom and have nearly straight flaring walls. Rudy reports vessels similar in shape from northern Utah.

With regard to Ute pottery, Opler (1939, p. 162) reports that it was made by "the coiling method after a base had been molded by hand on a flat stone. After the coiling, it was smoothed down by hand and later the surface was further polished with a flat stick." The most common vessel shape described "was that of the typical twined basketry waterjug of the Ute." The larger vessels were similar in shape but had a wider neck. These two types were sometimes crudely ornamented along the upper edge with cross hatching or vertical lines. Both vessel shape and decoration are reminiscent of Fremont pottery. Other vessel shapes reported by Opler are "triangular, open-neck bowls" and flat shallow bowls.

Huscher and Huscher (1940), in describing a possible Ute pot, suggest that the polishing with a flat stick described by Opler's informant actually refers to the use of a paddle-and-anvil technique for thinning, a technique reported by Barber (1876, p. 452) for the Utes on the basis of information secured from John H. Moss, his guide, who had lived among the Utes. Thus, the Ute pottery made during the past century may represent a blending of ceramic traditions such as is apparently present in Paiute pottery. However, while pottery attributed to other Plateau Shoshonean groups resembles that of the Southern Paiute in some respects, it is not nearly as abundant. None of the "Shoshonean" pottery resembles pottery of Pueblo tradition, such as that of the Fremont or Virgin cultures, really closely. Essentially the only traits shared are coiling and the use of fingernail punctations to decorate some specimens of Fremont and Sevier pottery and some specimens of Paiute and Ute pottery. Admittedly, decadence would have gone a long way to change the good pottery of Pueblo tradition into the very much cruder pottery generally considered to be of Shoshonean manufacture. Yet this could have happened. If Steward (1933 c, p. 269) is correct when he suggests that the two quite different wares he found in the Owens Valley area were both of Paiute manufacture, then we may have two degrees of such a degeneration. Certainly the thinner, smoothed, round-bottomed pot that he illustrates in plate 5a has a vessel form closely resembling the most common jar forms of the Virgin-Fremont-Sevier block and differs radically from the more characteristic bowls, pointed-bottom jars, flat-bottom jars, and conical vessels generally attributed to the Paiute and Shoshoni.

With regard to possible transitions from Puebloan to Shoshonean pottery, one statement made by Malouf (1946, p. 119) is of special interest. In discussing the archaeology of the Deep Creek area, which lies near the western edge of the Sevier area at about the middle of the Utah-Nevada state line, Malouf observed that it is often very difficult to distinguish between sherds of Shoshoni pottery and sherds of Great Salt Lake Buff, a Puebloan type which Rudy (1953, p. 83) subsumes under Great Salt Lake Gray. It may be that such marginal areas will disclose even more suggestions of transition from a basic Puebloan complex into the Shoshonean complex.

Still another foreign element in Paiute pottery is use of the paddle-and-anvil technique, along with the characteristic Pueblo scraping technique, for the thinning of vessel walls. The paddle-and-anvil technique could have been acquired from Indians on the lower Colorado River, where such a technique is common.

If these various Shoshonean wares do not represent a decadent Pueblo pottery, then they must either have been derived from some as yet undiscovered ancestral ceramic tradition or they must represent a local development or developments. If these wares were strictly imitations of stone vessels in clay, then one would not expect to see the great variety of shapes or the use of coiling. If they came from the lower Colorado River area where the paddle-and-anvil technique was used, they represent degeneration from the standards of quality that existed in that area. Far to the east, across the Rocky Mountains, were other pottery traditions, but there is little to link the Plateau Shoshoneans with this area until historic times and there is no Plains ceramic tradition at the proper time that would appear to be a likely ancestor.

Perhaps the largest single problem in explaining the various "Shoshonean" wares is the lack of good dating information. At many sites, especially in southern Nevada and northwestern Arizona, both Pueblo and Paiute pottery has been found, but apparently in no single instance has it been possible to demonstrate conclusively that the Paiute pottery was left during the Pueblo occupation. At a number of caves, both types of pottery were found in the upper level in apparent association, but dry caves are notorious for permitting specimens of radically differing ages to become mixed. Since the locations for both Pueblo and Paiute farming sites were usually chosen for the same reasons, especially available water, it is not surprising that many Puebloan sites were reoccupied by the Paiute. One of the few indubitable associations was in a burial where a Paiute vessel and a Washington Black-on-gray vessel were both included. Since the painted vessel was probably made between A.D. 700 and 900, the most probable explanation is that the burial is Paiute and that with it was included a "collected" earlier vessel. The A.D. 700–900 date of the Puebloan pot is earlier than dates generally assigned to the questionable Paiute-Pueblo associations.

The differences between the pre-1200 pottery and the various wares attributed to Plateau Shoshoneans of later times could also reflect the same hiatus suggested for farming.

As would be expected, the Paiute pottery is most abundant in areas where farming was reintroduced. Perhaps after a century or so, during which little or no farming was done and little or no pottery was made, most of the old techniques of pottery making had been lost and new ceramic traits were devised or borrowed. The change in shape from round-bottomed vessels to pointed-bottomed or conical vessels probably reflects to some extent changes in cooking methods. For a pointed-bottom pot to be kept upright, it could best be set in a small pit in sand or loose dirt, a condition more probably found by an open campfire than by a fire in a fireplace on the floor of a house. The fact that Shutler (1961) classified many sherds as "Southern Paiute Corrugated" provides a tantalizing implication of continuity of some sort with the previous Pueblo pottery in the area. However, it is difficult to see how one could produce corrugated pottery while using a paddle-and-anvil thinning technique. The use of a paddle-and-anvil technique may prove to be an alien trait accepted by some Southern Paiute potters at a relatively late time and, if so, a very useful trait in dating Paiute sites.

A number of other interesting problems regarding Paiute and Shoshonean pottery in general present themselves, but unfortunately it is now only possible to ask a few questions. Has there been a gradual change in vessel shape from globular through globular with a pointed bottom to conical with a pointed bottom? The vessels thought to be the earliest Paiute ware in the Owens Valley area were round-bottomed, while the relatively recent Paiute vessels (from southern Utah) in the Peabody Museum referred to by Baldwin (1950, p. 54) are essentially conical. In his description Baldwin includes a variety of vessel shapes: "large deep bowls, and tall narrow jars, both with pointed or semi-pointed bases and more or less conical in form; also rather large jars with very wide mouths." Therefore, within this collection we may have variations with time represented.

Another trait possibly related to variations with time may be the presence of fingernail indentations over most of the surface. The one nearly complete vessel illustrated by Baldwin that has such decoration is essentially globular with an only slightly pointed bottom, while the conical bowl he illustrates and the Paiute vessels, also conical, in the Peabody Museum are without such over-all decoration. One vessel in the Peabody Museum has a single line of fingernail impressions around it.

In order better to determine the course of development of this ware it is highly desirable that an effort be made to collect a variety of Southern Paiute vessels that can be accurately dated. It would be equally desirable to secure well-dated examples of other Shoshonean vessels, but since pottery-making elsewhere among the Shoshoneans was relatively rare, the likelihood of finding such specimens is far more remote.

Baldwin (1950), along with various other people, has suggested a possible relationship between Paiute pottery and that made by other Shoshonean groups as well as by the Western Apache and Navaho. He further suggests that Paiute pottery is of a general Woodland type, rather than of a Pueblo or Hohokam type. Since the time Baldwin wrote, the derivation of these wares from the Plains has received very little concrete support. The Promontory Point pottery, which has a general resemblance to Paiute and Shoshonean pottery, was thought by Steward (1937 b) to be of possible Athabascan manufacture. On the basis of comparisons with Plains Apache pottery (Gunnerson, 1956 d; 1960 d) this idea is supported, but a date of *ca.* A.D. 1700 is suggested for Promontory Point material. So, unless the Plateau Shoshonean pottery proves more recent than this, the Promontory Point complex can be ruled out as a link between the Great Basin and the Plains and as a source for these pottery traits. Furthermore, the Promontory Point culture does not appear to have become established in the Great Basin. Rather, it appears to represent a temporary occupation by bison hunters who probably followed the herds across South Pass. Such an interpretation would help explain the hundreds of worn-out moccasins in the Promontory caves. Perhaps they were discarded after a long hike across the Rocky Mountains. Here again, in trying either to establish or to rule out possible Promontory-Shoshonean connections, we are greatly handicapped by the lack of a good chronological framework.

Thus with regard to the origin and development of Plateau Shoshonean pottery, our data are still too few and too poorly dated to permit any positive statements. My very tentative suggestion, and this is little more than a considered opinion, is that it is basically decadent Pueblo (Virgin, Fremont, Sevier) pottery that received influence from other pottery traditions and from an outside stone-vessel tradition and that underwent some further changes in response to changing cooking techniques. A change in pottery tradition under the disruptive conditions that would have followed reverting to a hunting and gathering economy is not difficult to understand. Under much less traumatic conditions, the Taos, for example, made nearly as great a shift about 1680 when they gave up their traditional pottery styles and started making their characteristic micaceous ware, probably taken over from the Jicarilla Apache with whose pottery it is virtually identical (Gunnerson, 1959 e, pp. 6–8). This shift among the Taos took place without their even leaving the pueblo that they had long occupied.

Once traits such as permanent dwellings, good pottery, and heavy metates are eliminated from the Pueblo and Pueblo-like complexes, there are relatively few traits left that do not appear in the Plateau Shoshonean complexes as well. Projectile points with small straight-to-tapered stems, which became common during the latest phases of the Sevier and Virgin cultures, but not in Fremont, are generally thought to be absent from the Plateau Shoshonean assemblages. However, most of the projectile points collected by Edward Palmer from the Paiute of southern Utah in 1875 are of this type. These points, which are in the Peabody Museum at Harvard (Catalogue No. 9452), could have been "collected" by the Paiutes from archaeological sites, but since they were obtained at an early date they may be more representative than data obtained later. Moreover, the triangular unnotched or side-notched points generally attributed to the Plateau Shoshoneans were standard for the Sevier and Virgin cultures prior to their latest phase, and were always characteristic of the Fremont Culture.

From the scant evidence at hand, there appears to have been a degeneration in clay figurines after *ca.* 1200. And, although it is impossible to date most pictographs with any degree of accuracy, there was probably a great decline in such art, especially with regard to the very elaborate anthropomorphic figures and the figures of colossal proportions. If these artistic efforts were associated with crop fertility ritual, as presumed, one would expect their loss along with the loss of horticulture. Furthermore, if the finest of the pictographs were the work of specialists, as they may well have been, the lack of enough surplus food to support such specialists would have curtailed such endeavors.

Steward (1940, p. 466), in discussing the origin of the Plateau Shoshoneans, concluded: "If the Shoshoneans were not in the Northern or Western Peripheries, they must have been in western Nevada, where, through contact with Basket Maker cultures, they acquired some but not all of its elements. The picture provided by Lovelock Cave fills the bill perfectly." On the same page he states that "The recent work of Robert Heizer, of the University of California, and Alex Krieger will probably supplement and correct some details of the Lovelock sequence. The general implications of Lovelock Cave will, however, doubtless stand." (This seems to have been a reversal of an earlier opinion since three years earlier Steward (1937 b, p. 86) comments in a footnote that "the latest occupants of Lovelock Cave seem not to have been Shoshonean.")

Heizer and Krieger (1956, pp. 87–90), however, in reporting the archaeology of Humboldt Cave, which closely resembles that of Lovelock Cave, seriously question the Northern Paiute affiliation of the major part of the "Lovelock culture." In Humboldt cave, which was excavated with far better control than was possible at Lovelock Cave, Paiute occupation was thought to be present in only the upper 20 inches of deposit, which included such objects as iron arrowheads. "The complex represented by the main body of Humboldt Cave remains, therefore, is composed of certain generic western culture forms, a strong element, shared with—but not necessarily derived from—the Southwest culture province, a somewhat lesser connection with trans-Sierran California, and a definite, though weaker, connection with southern Oregon" (Heizer and Krieger, 1956, p. 90).

Thus it seems more likely that specific similarities between Plateau Shoshonean traits and Lovelock traits which do not have a widespread distribution represent borrowings by the Plateau Shoshoneans rather than traits inherited by them from ancestors with either the Lovelock or a closely related culture.

For example, the most spectacular trait found in Lovelock Cave that also occurs in Northern Paiute culture is stuffed duck decoys. The significance of the duck decoys at Humboldt, Ocala, and Lovelock caves was discussed by Heizer and Krieger (1956, p. 76) who pointed out that, although they were used by the Northern Paiute, they were also used by the Washo (Hokan speakers) and have their closest parallels in central California.

The conclusions arrived at by Heizer and Krieger are compatible with a tradition of the Northern Paiutes (Loud and Harrington, 1929, p. 1) that Lovelock Cave had not been occupied by them but by another tribe for which they used the name Sai-i, the name by which they call the Pit River Indians. Tradition also has it that the Northern Paiute both fought this other tribe and took some of its members into their families.

In the light of the conclusions arrived at by Heizer and Krieger, which are supported by Northern Paiute traditions, it seems unlikely that the Lovelock culture is ancestral to the Plateau Shoshonean cultures.

In the wanderings of the Southern Paiute it is reasonable to assume that they might have encountered ruins not long abandoned either at Paragonah or in the Moapa Valley. If the Southern Paiute are descendants of the Fremont people, they would have had no previous connection with the ruins in these two areas, and there would be no reason for them to claim one.

The archaeological evidence from the Virgin area has been interpreted, by Schroeder (1955, 1961) and Shutler (1961) for example, as showing a friendly encroachment of Shoshoneans with their distinctive pottery that took place prior to the end of the Pueblo occupation. The occurrence together of Pueblo and Paiute pottery, both at open sites and in the upper layers of rock shelters, has been interpreted as evidence of contemporaneity,

possibly joint occupation. It has also been interpreted as evidence of reuse of sites. Primarily on the basis of these data the date for the entry of the Shoshoneans (Paiutes) into the Virgin area has been placed at various points after about A.D. 850 but probably before A.D. 1150, the approximate terminal date of the Pueblo culture. Schroeder (1961, p. 113) opposes the idea that the Fremont people became Paiutes, whom he sees as coming from some northern reservoir of Basketmaker-like people. In the Virgin area specifically, Gunnerson (1962 a) postulated that there might have been an exodus of Virgin people (to the northwest) and a movement of Fremont people into the area. While Gunnerson postulated the replacement of Virgin people by Fremont people because it was the simplest way to account for the present linguistic distribution, this explanation also satisfies the conditions of complete replacement seen by Schroeder, who suggests that the Virgin branch ended perhaps 50 years before the date advanced by Gunnerson for the end of the Fremont culture. There is, however, no way to reconcile the conflicting views on the probable beginning date for the Southern Paiute culture, or more specifically, for the beginning date of the Southern Paiute Brown ware. This question, fortunately, can probably be solved eventually through additional field work by verifying or refuting the occurrence of Paiute pottery in good association in Virgin sites or by tree-ring dates for early pure Paiute sites.

Over the years, there has been a great deal of discussion in archaeological reports of an invasion of the Pueblo area in the early 1200's by enemy nomads. The evidence for such an invasion consists primarily of defensive features at many sites and the abandonment of many sites. In some cases evidence of violence has been found. The main candidates for the "Enemy Nomads" have been the Southern Athabascans, since they were nomads and late arrivals in the Southwest. The Athabascans have been fairly well vindicated, however, because no direct evidence has been found showing them to have been in the Southwest prior to about A.D. 1500, and various other lines of evidence summarized by D. A. Gunnerson (1956) support this as their approximate date of arrival.

The other most popular explanation of the

Pueblo III defensive features is that worsening drought conditions caused a great deal of intervillage rivalry for the best agricultural land and possibly food-stealing raids. This appears to the present author as the most probable explanation. However, if there were any outside people harassing the Pueblos in the Four Corners area, they were probably Fremont and/or Virgin people who had been forced to give up farming in their own territories. It is probably not without significance that the Utes, here considered descendants of the Fremont people, still live in the Mesa Verde area and own and occupy a considerable part of Mesa Verde itself.

Moreover, in this connection it is very interesting to note that, according to a Hopi informant, "the traditional enemies of the Hopi are not the Navaho who surround them now, but the Paiute." In fact, even now when a Hopi child misbehaves he is called a "little Payuche."

THE LEXICO–ARCHAEOLOGICAL MATRIX OF THE FREMONT CULTURE

It is now time to consider how the tentative identification of the Fremont, Sevier, and Virgin cultures as Plateau Shoshonean fits in with the archaeological and linguistic picture of the western part of the United States in general.

Fortunately, the linguistic history of the western United States has recently been examined by Taylor (1961), who presented a carefully considered reconstruction of a possible sequence of language movements that would take into account linguistic and archaeological evidence. Although, as it stands, Taylor's reconstruction is incompatible with the suggestions that have been made in this paper, a slight modification of his views would bring the two together. In brief, Taylor sees an ancient movement into the area of Hokaltecan peoples who are represented archaeologically by the Desert culture. Much later two related groups, the Uto-Aztecans and Penutians, moved south along the western side of the Rocky Mountains at about the same time. One must decide, on the basis of circumstantial evidence, which came first. Taylor chose to have the Penutians come first and then be pushed to the west by the Uto-Aztecans who followed. In his scheme, the Plateau Shoshoneans would have been the last Uto-Aztecans to arrive from the north, and they would never have gone farther south than their territory of early historic times.

To modify Taylor's reconstruction to fit my suggestions, it is necessary only to choose the alternative he rejected and let the Uto-Aztecans precede the Penutians into the area west of the Rocky Mountains. The historical distribution of the Penutians, all of whom are to the west or northwest of the northernmost Uto-Aztecans (the Plateau Shoshoneans), can be explained better by their being the last to arrive. Their presence in this area could represent in part their original location, "on top of" and somewhat down the western side of the Uto-Aztecan block, and in part a compression into this area by the Plateau Shoshoneans during their later territorial expansion to the north. Furthermore, if the Uto-Aztecans had followed the Penutians from the north into the western part of the United States, pushing them out of their way as they came, one would expect to find remnants of the Penutians to the south, where they would have been pushed ahead of the entering Uto-Aztecans. Taylor (1961, fig. 1) shows many such isolated enclaves of Hokaltecans but none of Penutians.

Taylor considers the suggestion by Romney (1957) and Lamb (1958) that there was a center for Uto-Aztecan dispersal somewhere in the middle of the ultimate Uto-Aztecan area, perhaps in southern Arizona, but rejects it on the basis that such a history, with a major reverse movement to the north, would have been too complicated. He feels, moreover, that if the Yuman block was in the Colorado River valley before this reverse movement, a circuitous route would have to be postulated to get the Uto-Aztecans into southern California. One very feasible route for such a northward movement of the Shoshoneans from a point in southern Arizona would have been north along any route through the eastern half of Arizona to the Kayenta area, where the ancestors of the Hopi could have dropped off. The rest of the proto-Shoshoneans could then have moved west across the Colorado River, dropping off the ancestors of the Plateau Shoshoneans in the Virgin area. The ancestors of such groups as the Cahuilla and the Tubatulabal could then have moved on farther west to take up residence in southern California. It seems unlikely that the dispersal happened in precisely this way, but such movements could easily have occurred and they are compatible with archaeological and linguistic evidence. And to judge by Hale's glottochronology dates, this northern dispersal of the Shoshoneans would have taken place within a span of perhaps a thousand years, ending about the middle of the first millennium before Christ—perfect timing so far as the archaeological picture is concerned.

If Penutian speakers followed the Uto-Aztecans down the western side of the Rocky Mountains as the present suggested revision of the Taylor hypothesis would suggest, then one might expect to find Penutian archaeological sites in the Upper Colorado Plateau and eastern Great Basin that predate the Plateau Shoshonean reoccupation of this area. Although the identification of such possible Penutian sites is beyond the scope of this paper, a few archaeological complexes suggest themselves by their deviation from the patterns of both the Desert culture and the Virgin-Fremont-Sevier–Plateau Shoshonean tradition. Could the Uncompahgre complex represent a Penutian variant of the Desert culture (which, according to Taylor, was probably of Hokaltecan affiliation)? Could part of the material from Mantle's Cave, including the California-

like flicker headdress (Hewes, 1952) and the greater emphasis on variations of basketry techniques, represent a Penutian group that was contacted by the Fremont culture when it spread to its northeasternmost boundary?

Many unusual artifacts, including bone harpoon heads and various eccentric flints, have been found by a collector near Ferron, Utah (Gunnerson, 1962 b). Although the area of these finds is rich in Fremont sites, the artifacts are out of place in the Fremont inventory. Perhaps this unusual material, which has many counterparts in California, will eventually be shown to have Penutian affiliations.

One of the most baffling archaeological complexes found in Utah is that on Fremont Island in the Great Salt Lake (Rudy and Stoddard, 1954). This complex is characterized by numerous shallow stone bowls, by eccentric ground stone artifacts, and by various projectile points and blades. Artifacts of obsidian, which are presumed to be part of the same complex as the bowls and eccentric slate forms, have been dated by the obsidian weathering method (Friedman and Smith, 1960, p. 522) at 1600 to 13,000 years old. Most of the dates cluster between 2600 and 5500 years old, however, and this seems a more reasonable range. The artifacts from Fremont Island are vaguely reminiscent of some material in the Peabody Museum from islands off the coast of California near Los Angeles. Thus, this site, too, could have Penutian affiliations, but it is not obvious at present how such identifications can be established or refuted.

SUMMARY

The history of trans-Colorado Puebloan archaeology presented here has shown how interpretations of the archaeological data have changed through time. Those who visited sites and collected artifacts in the area in the late 1800's and early 1900's accepted the archaeological manifestations there as part of the widespread Southwestern Pueblo culture in general, but because this culture appeared somewhat attenuated north of the Colorado River, that area became known as the "Northern Periphery."

The Fremont culture, especially, was considered anomalous because, although it dated from Pueblo II times, it exhibited a number of traits that characterized the Basketmaker III period in the San Juan Anasazi area. Interpretations in the 1930's and 1940's were concerned chiefly with how and where a mixture of such disparate traits could have been formed, and it was generally assumed that the mixture had been carried into the area by migration.

Although no suitable point of origin could be found, the migration theory was held until further developments in archaeological thinking turned popular opinion in another direction. It had long been realized that Pueblo culture as such had developed slowly in the Southwest from a generalized hunting and gathering base. In the 1950's, the Fremont culture was recognized to be very similar to the Sevier culture, which reached into an area in western Utah and eastern Nevada where the existence of an ancient and more or less continuous Desert culture pattern could be demonstrated. Thereupon, the Fremont and Sevier cultures were thought to have developed *in situ*, from a Desert culture base, with the addition of Pueblo traits from the south.

But soon interpretations took another turn. The Fremont culture was dated by tree rings and trade pottery at *ca.* A.D. 950–1200. And intensive areal survey proved that the picture of the Fremont culture had been somewhat distorted because the sites from which it was best known were largely caves or atypical open sites on the margins of the Fremont area. Open villages were found that exhibited a variety of approaches to architecture, pottery-making, and other aspects of material culture. Moreover, additional information on the named but still poorly known Virgin branch of Anasazi, Fremont's neighbor to the southwest, showed that it possessed the right mixture of traits, at the right time, to have been the source of the Fremont culture complex.

Again a migration of Anasazi peoples into the Fremont (and Sevier) areas began to seem probable. When, at last, this reconstruction of Virgin-Fremont-Sevier culture history, with its tree-ring dates, was compared with reconstructions of Plateau Shoshonean prehistory based on glottochronology, remarkable similarities were apparent. As a result, it was postulated that the area occupied by the Virgin branch of Anasazi was the homeland of the proto-Plateau Shoshoneans, that some of them moved out of the Virgin area into the Fremont area at *ca.* A.D. 950, and that, at about the same time, others moved into the Sevier area. Here they lived by means of horticulture combined with hunting and gathering until *ca.* A.D. 1200, when drought forced them to abandon their crop lands and disperse as hunters and gatherers to the limits of the area occupied by Plateau Shoshoneans in early historic times. Such dispersion effected the final linguistic separations of the various subgroups.

At this point, the "what," "when," and "where" of the reconstruction were based on fairly sound archaeological data. The "who," while speculative, gained support from the convergence of two lines of evidence and the internal consistency of the hypothesis. But, for the time being, the implications of the data seemed exhausted.

However, one body of relevant data remained unreported. Since it represented four seasons' work in the Fremont area, largely in sections never resampled by archaeologists, the

195

unpublished data collected by the Claflin-Emerson Peabody Museum expeditions to north-eastern Utah (1927–1931) offered, *per se*, both a challenge to existing interpretations and a possible source of new information.

As it turned out, this material contributed, among other things, new data on Fremont material culture. It also shed some light on the relationships of Fremont and Mesa Verde, and thereby accounted for some of the differences between Fremont and Virgin. Most important, however, it provided a collection of maize specimens which, when studied, gave a probable answer to the "why" of the Fremont and Sevier cultures. The analysis of Fremont corn suggests that it was the introduction of germplasm from a race of maize having an ultimate origin in the highlands of South America that triggered the entire Pueblo II expansion of which the Fremont culture was a part.

Thus, the material obtained by the Claflin-Emerson expeditions has made this theoretical reconstruction of trans-Colorado culture history complete by providing what the archaeologist is so often forced to do without—a plausible reason for the events he reconstructs.

On the basis of the information that exists, and the reasonable inferences drawn therefrom, it may not be unwarranted to offer A Just So Story of How the Fremont People Got Their Culture and Then Proceeded to Lose Much of It.

About 5000 years ago the ancestors of the Uto-Aztecans migrated from the north and settled in the Southwest, perhaps somewhere in southern Arizona. There they acquired maize and a knowledge of horticulture. Then, about 2500 years ago, part of them moved to northeastern Arizona, where some stayed to become the Kayenta and later the Hopi people. The rest of this group moved on to the west. Some settled down in the Virgin River drainage to become the ancestors of the Plateau Shoshoneans, while the remainder moved on into southern California.

Those who settled in the Virgin River drainage gradually developed into the Virgin branch of the Anasazi. Before and after Pueblo I times, they were influenced by their relatives in the Kayenta area. During the Pueblo I period, however, there seems to have been little contact between these groups, perhaps because their cultures were so basically similar that trade offered few advantages. Whatever the reason, the Virgin branch culture complex of *ca.* A.D. 700–900 suggests virtual isolation from the Pueblo developments farther east.

At about A.D. 700, germplasm from a new race of maize that had developed in the highlands of South America entered the northern part of Mexico and the southern part of the Southwest. When it blended into the maize that had been evolving there for a few thousand years, the result was a new hybrid that not only gave a greater yield but was much easier to mill. Consequently, by Pueblo II times, the Pueblo population had increased. The new hybrid maize probably reached the Virgin area about A.D. 900, and the resulting increase in population there soon led some of the people to push out beyond the limits that the environment had imposed on the successful cultivation of their old maize. Their migrations were made possible by the fact that the new maize, having developed originally at high altitudes, could thrive at higher latitudes.

Migrants from the Virgin branch carried Puebloan culture northward on both sides of the Wasatch Mountains even beyond the northern border of Utah. West of the mountains these new frontiersmen, although they kept in touch with the parent Virgin branch, developed their own culture, the Sevier complex. East of the Wasatch Mountains they developed the Fremont culture, but did not maintain close ties with the Virgin branch. They did, however, borrow traits from the other groups with whom they came in contact.

In their new homeland, the Fremont people depended heavily upon the corn, beans, and squash that they raised, but they never became irrevocably committed to horticulture as a means of subsistence. Included in their cultural heritage from the Virgin branch were many techniques for hunting and gathering, as well as for processing wild food. For the Virgin people, throughout their long history, had retained old traits even when they adopted new artifacts and practices that served the same general purpose.

For about 250 years the Fremont people prospered and developed a vigorous and distinctive but unspecialized culture, whose exuberant nature manifested itself in elaborate and colorful pictographs, highly adorned clay figurines, and the variety of its techniques for pottery decoration.

By about A.D. 1200, after the Fremont population had increased to a point where it was more or less in balance with its environment and technology, the climate began to get drier and crop failures more common. Bickering over rights to the best-watered land, or over water rights, grew into quarrels, and those who raised a crop had to take added precautions to protect their stores of food from those who did not.

Eventually, drought forced all the Fremont people to give up farming, and since similar conditions prevailed in other areas where horticulture was still possible, Fremont refugees were unwelcome there. Any attempts to move into the large pueblos to the south and southeast were met by resistance and walled-up outside doors.

The hungry Fremont people, faced with starvation, scattered out in small groups to live off the land. Since the drought that had ended farming had also decreased the supply of wild food, they had to disperse over a large territory and move often to secure enough food.

It was no longer worthwhile to build substantial houses. Their heavy metates had to be abandoned. It was impractical to carry fragile pottery or, if they did so, they took little pains with its manufacture because of the greater chance of breakage.

Meanwhile, the Virgin and Sevier people had suffered the same fate. As these three Plateau Shoshonean groups spread thinly over the Basin-Plateau area, further linguistic differentiation took place. Moreover, at the margins of the inhospitable land they finally covered, they encountered other groups, and from them accepted many new traits. Thus, when white men came into the Great Basin and Upper Colorado Plateau, they found that any one Plateau Shoshonean tribe was likely to have a culture more like that of his non-Plateau Shoshonean neighbor than like that of his close linguistic relatives who lived at a distance.

The earliest white explorers also found some of the Plateau Shoshoneans farming and making pottery, so they had either readopted these practices or had somehow managed, here and there, now and then, and on a small scale, to keep these practices alive. They had not, however, returned to the same sedentary pattern that existed before the great drought.

Within two thousand years, then, Plateau Shoshonean culture first developed slowly until a new food resource made life easier and allowed the population to grow in numbers and develop new marginal lands. Then a slight but natural change in climate eliminated the new prosperity. But the frontier farmers, never having had things too easy, knew all the ways to make a living that the land allowed. Thus they survived.

Appendix I

FREMONT MAIZE

Walton C. Galinat and James H. Gunnerson

IN conjunction with a study of all the maize collected by the various Claflin-Emerson expeditions, including that conducted by Morss (1931), Galinat and Gunnerson (1963) re-examined the entire problem of the development and spread of maize in the Southwest with special emphasis on Fremont maize. Much of that paper will be repeated here with only a minimum of change. In addition, the basic information regarding the maize in the Claflin-Emerson collections is included (tables 2, 3).

It is now apparent that most if not all of the southwestern maize came from adjoining areas in Mexico, although a part of this maize may have come originally from South America, as will be discussed later. Both Mexico and the Southwest had the same ancient indigenous race, "Chapalote," which underwent a slow evolutionary change for several thousands of years until two separate and sudden evolutionary spurts were triggered by two new elements—first teosinte, a wild relative of maize, and later an unrelated eight-rowed race of maize which survives in a mixed form in a race called "Harinoso de Ocho" in northwestern Mexico (Mangelsdorf and Lister, 1956).

Apparently Chapalote reached the Bat Cave area in New Mexico from central or southern Mexico about 3600 B.C. (Mangelsdorf, 1954) and, after a gradual evolutionary change leading to increased size of ear and number of kernel rows, it formed the Basketmaker maize which became the subsistence base of the prehistoric Pueblo culture. The addition of teosinte germplasm to Chapalote occurred probably not later than 500 B.C., as shown at Bat Cave (Mangelsdorf and Smith, 1949), and apparently it had spread as far north as Durango, Colorado, by A.D. 46 to 330 (tree-ring

dates). A re-examination of the eight-rowed cobs from the Durango Basketmaker site, reported by Jones and Fonner (1954), has now revealed that their eight-rowed condition, cupule shape, and glume characters give strong evidence of teosinte introgression. This introgression can be estimated in archaeological cobs and such estimates have been correlated with various changes in the morphology of the cob (Galinat et al., 1956). These effects include a tremendous increase in variability as well as an apparent heterotic effect on plant growth (Galinat and Ruppé, 1961). In addition, the teosinte germplasm in maize seems to have allowed an extension of maize culture into new and more arid regions.

Apparently at about A.D. 700 (Mangelsdorf and Lister, 1956), a third element, the race of maize "Harinoso de Ocho," entered upon the evolutionary scene and conferred new benefits in the form of higher yield, easier milling, and adaptability to a far greater range of environments. Some of the differences between eight-rowed cobs involving teosinte introgression in their origin, such as those from Durango, and this new eight-rowed race are apparent in figure 45A (compare a-d with e-l). The Harinoso de Ocho element is manifest in its thick straight cobs, sometimes swollen at the base, wide cupules, and wide, crescent-shaped kernels. In describing this race, Wellhausen et al. (1952) postulated that it was introduced into Mexico from South America in pre-Columbian times. Its South American progenitor was subsequently found in Colombia and identified by Roberts et al. (1957) as "Cabuya," an eight-rowed race which is tripsacoid and also has nearly knobless chromosomes (averages 2.2 knobs). Grobman et al. (1961) have suggested that these two features might result from indirect

Table 2: Characteristics of all Maize Ears and Cobs from Sites Investigated by the Claflin-Emerson Expedition. Cobs to which Kernels are Still Attached are Checked in the "With Kernels" Column.

Site	Frequency	With Kernels	Row Number								Ear Shape			Tripsacoid			
			4	6	8	10	12	14	16	18	Straight	Intermediate	Tapered	Slight	Medium	High	Faciated
A 6-1	2	–	–	–	x	–	–	–	–	–	x	–	–	x	–	–	–
	2	x	–	–	–	–	x	–	–	–	–	x	–	–	x	–	–
	3	x	–	–	–	–	–	x	–	–	–	x	–	–	x	–	–
	1	x	–	–	–	–	x	–	–	–	–	–	x	–	–	x	–
	3	–	–	–	–	x	–	–	–	–	–	x	–	x	–	–	–
	4	–	–	–	–	–	x	–	–	–	–	x	–	x	–	–	–
	8	–	–	–	–	–	–	x	–	–	–	x	–	x	–	–	–
	5	–	–	–	–	x	–	–	–	–	–	x	–	–	x	–	–
	1	–	–	–	–	–	x	–	–	–	–	x	–	–	x	–	x
A 6-2	2	–	–	–	–	–	x	–	–	–	–	x	–	x	–	–	–
	1	–	–	–	–	x	–	–	–	–	–	x	–	–	x	–	–
A 6-5	1	–	–	–	–	x	–	–	–	–	–	x	–	x	–	–	–
A 6-6	1	–	–	–	–	–	x	–	–	–	–	x	–	x	–	–	–
	1	–	–	–	–	–	–	x	–	–	–	x	–	x	–	–	–
	1	–	–	–	–	–	x	–	–	–	–	x	–	–	x	–	–
	1	–	–	–	x	–	–	–	–	–	–	x	–	–	–	x	–
	1	–	–	–	–	x	–	–	–	–	–	x	–	–	–	x	–
	1	–	–	–	–	–	x	–	–	–	–	x	–	–	–	x	–
A 12-1	2	–	–	–	–	x	–	–	–	–	–	x	–	x	–	–	–
	2	–	–	–	–	–	x	–	–	–	–	x	–	x	–	–	–
	1	–	–	–	–	–	–	x	–	–	–	x	–	x	–	–	–
	1	–	–	–	–	–	–	–	–	x	–	x	–	x	–	–	–
	1	–	–	–	x	–	–	–	–	–	–	x	–	–	–	x	–
ET 6-3	1	–	–	–	x	–	–	–	–	–	–	x	–	–	x	–	–
	15	–	–	–	–	x	–	–	–	–	–	x	–	–	x	–	–
	1	–	–	–	–	x	–	–	–	–	–	x	–	x	–	–	–
	8	–	–	–	–	x	–	–	–	–	–	x	–	–	x	–	–
	1	–	–	–	–	–	x	–	–	–	–	x	–	–	x	–	–
	2	–	–	–	–	x	–	–	–	–	–	x	–	–	–	x	–
	1	–	–	–	–	–	x	–	–	–	–	x	–	–	–	x	–
	1	–	–	–	x	–	–	–	–	–	–	–	x	x	–	–	–
DT 6-7	3	–	–	–	–	–	x	–	–	–	–	x	–	x	–	–	–
	1	–	–	–	–	–	–	x	–	–	–	x	–	x	–	–	–
	4	–	–	–	–	x	–	–	–	–	–	x	–	–	x	–	–
	1	–	–	–	–	–	x	–	–	–	–	x	–	–	x	–	x
	1	–	–	–	–	x	–	–	–	–	–	x	–	–	–	x	–
	1	–	–	–	–	–	x	–	–	–	–	x	–	–	–	x	x
	1	–	–	–	–	x	–	–	–	–	–	–	x	–	–	–	–
	3	–	–	–	–	–	x	–	–	–	–	x	–	–	x	–	–
	2	–	–	–	–	x	–	–	–	–	–	x	–	–	x	–	–
	1	–	–	–	–	x	–	–	–	–	–	x	–	–	–	x	–

Site	Frequency	With Kernels	Row Number 4	6	8	10	12	14	16	18	Ear Shape Straight	Intermediate	Tapered	Tripsacoid Slight	Medium	High	Faciated
ET 6-10	1	–	–	–	–	–	x	–	–	–	–	–	x	–	–	–	–
ET 6-24	1	–	–	–	–	–	x	–	–	–	–	x	–	x	–	–	–
	2	–	–	–	–	–	–	x	–	–	–	x	–	x	–	–	–
FL 12-4	1	–	–	–	x	–	–	–	–	–	x	–	–	x	–	–	–
	1	–	–	–	–	x	–	–	–	–	x	–	–	–	–	–	–
	1	–	–	–	–	–	x	–	–	–	x	–	–	–	–	–	–
	1	–	–	–	–	–	x	–	–	–	–	x	–	x	–	–	–
H 7-2	1	–	–	–	–	x	–	–	–	–	x	–	–	–	–	–	–
PR 4-6	1	–	–	–	–	–	x	–	–	–	–	x	–	x	–	–	–
PR 4-25	1	–	–	–	–	x	–	–	–	–	–	x	–	–	–	x	–
	2	–	–	–	–	–	x	–	–	–	–	–	x	–	–	–	–
	3	–	–	–	–	–	x	–	–	–	–	x	–	–	x	–	x
PR 4-27	4	–	–	–	x	–	–	–	–	–	x	–	–	–	–	–	–
	1	–	–	–	–	x	–	–	–	–	x	–	–	–	–	–	–
	3	–	–	–	x	–	–	–	–	–	–	x	–	x	–	–	–
	3	–	–	–	–	x	–	–	–	–	–	x	–	x	–	–	–
	4	–	–	–	–	–	x	–	–	–	–	x	–	x	–	–	–
	5	–	–	–	–	–	x	–	–	–	–	–	x	–	–	–	–
	1	–	–	–	–	–	–	x	–	–	–	–	x	–	–	–	–
PR 4-28	1	–	–	–	–	x	–	–	–	–	x	–	–	–	–	–	–
	1	–	–	–	–	–	x	–	–	–	x	–	–	–	–	–	–
	3	–	–	–	–	x	–	–	–	–	–	x	–	–	x	–	–
PR 4-31	1	x	–	–	–	x	–	–	–	–	–	–	x	x	–	–	–
	2	–	–	–	x	–	–	–	–	–	–	x	–	–	–	x	–
	2	–	–	–	x	–	–	–	–	–	–	x	–	–	–	x	–
	1	–	–	–	–	–	x	–	–	–	–	x	–	x	–	–	x
	9	–	–	–	–	–	x	–	–	–	–	x	–	x	–	–	–
	2	–	–	–	–	x	–	–	–	–	–	x	–	–	x	–	–
	5	–	–	–	x	–	–	–	–	–	–	x	–	–	–	x	–
	4	x	–	–	–	x	–	–	–	–	–	–	x	x	–	–	–
	1	x	–	–	–	–	x	–	–	–	–	–	x	x	–	–	–
	1	x	–	–	–	–	–	x	–	–	–	–	x	x	–	–	–
	4	–	–	–	x	–	–	–	–	–	–	x	–	x	–	–	–
	9	–	–	–	–	x	–	–	–	–	–	x	–	x	–	–	–
	1	–	–	x	–	–	–	–	–	–	–	x	–	–	–	x	–
	1	–	–	–	–	–	–	x	–	–	–	–	x	–	–	–	–
	1	–	–	–	x	–	–	–	–	–	x	–	–	–	x	–	–
	1	–	–	–	–	–	–	x	–	–	–	x	–	x	–	–	–
	1	–	–	–	–	x	–	–	–	–	–	–	x	–	–	–	–
	1	–	–	–	x	–	–	–	–	–	–	x	–	–	–	–	–

Site	Frequency	With Kernels	Row Number 4	6	8	10	12	14	16	18	Ear Shape Straight	Intermediate	Tapered	Tripsacoid Slight	Medium	High	Faciated
PR 8-1	1	–	–	–	–	x	–	–	–	–	–	x	–	x	–	–	–
	4	–	–	–	–	–	x	–	–	–	–	x	–	x	–	–	–
	1	–	–	–	–	x	–	–	–	–	–	x	–	–	–	x	–
	1	–	–	–	–	–	–	x	–	–	–	x	–	x	–	–	–
	1	–	–	–	–	–	–	x	–	–	–	–	x	–	–	–	–
PR 8-4	1	–	–	–	–	x	–	–	–	–	x	–	–	–	–	–	–
	1	–	–	–	–	x	–	–	–	–	–	x	–	–	x	–	–
PR 12-6	3	–	–	–	–	–	x	–	–	–	–	x	–	x	–	–	x
	2	–	–	–	–	–	–	x	–	–	–	x	–	x	–	–	x
	1	–	–	–	–	x	–	–	–	–	–	x	–	–	–	x	x
	1	–	–	–	–	–	x	–	–	–	–	–	x	–	–	–	–
	1	–	–	–	–	–	–	x	–	–	–	–	x	–	–	–	–
PR 12-19	1	–	–	–	–	–	x	–	–	–	–	x	–	x	–	–	–
	2	–	–	–	–	x	–	–	–	–	–	x	–	–	x	–	–
PR 12-20	1	–	–	–	–	x	–	–	–	–	x	–	–	x	–	–	–
SR 16-6	1	–	–	–	–	x	–	–	–	–	–	–	x	–	–	–	–
	3	–	–	–	–	–	x	–	–	–	–	–	x	–	–	–	–
	1	–	–	–	–	–	–	x	–	–	–	–	x	–	–	–	–
SR 12-? (Barrier Canyon)	2	–	–	–	–	–	x	–	–	–	–	x	–	–	x	–	–
	1	–	x	–	–	–	–	–	–	–	–	x	–	–	–	x	–
	1	–	–	x	–	–	–	–	–	–	–	x	–	–	–	x	–
	1	–	–	–	–	x	–	–	–	–	–	x	–	–	–	x	–
Morss 13	2	–	–	–	–	–	x	–	–	–	–	x	–	x	–	–	–
	1	–	–	–	–	–	–	x	–	–	–	x	–	x	–	–	–
	1	–	–	–	–	x	–	–	–	–	–	x	–	–	x	–	–
	1	–	–	–	–	–	x	–	–	–	–	x	–	–	x	–	–
Morss 19	1	–	–	–	–	–	–	x	–	–	–	x	–	x	–	–	–
	1	–	–	–	–	–	–	–	x	–	–	x	–	x	–	–	–
	1	–	–	–	–	–	x	–	–	–	–	x	–	–	x	–	–
	1	–	–	–	–	x	–	–	–	–	–	–	x	–	–	–	–
Morss 21	1	–	–	–	x	–	–	–	–	–	x	–	–	–	–	–	–
	1	–	–	–	–	–	x	–	–	–	–	x	–	x	–	–	–
Morss 36	1	–	–	–	–	–	x	–	–	–	–	x	–	x	–	–	–
Morss 37	1	–	–	–	x	–	–	–	–	–	x	–	–	–	–	–	–

TABLE 3: CHARACTERISTICS OF SELECTED EARS OF MAIZE. MEASUREMENTS ARE IN MILLIMETERS.
A-ABSENT, S-SLIGHT, M-MEDIUM, H-HIGH

Site No. and Catalog No.	Denting	Tripsacoid	Cupule Depth	Cupule Width	Kernel Thickness	Kernel Width	Kernel Length	Cob Diameter	Ear Diameter	Ear Length	Ear Shape Tapered	Ear Shape Intermediate	Ear Shape Straight	Race Near Chapalote	Race Fremont Dent	Race Maiz de Ocho	Row Number
A 6-1 A7936	M	M	2	9.3	4.5	8.5	10	30	38	160	–	x	–	–	x	–	14
A 6-1 A7944	M	M	1	11	4.3	7	6	24	34	80+	–	x	–	–	x	–	12
A 6-1 A7944	M	H	2	9	4.7	5	5	26	33	110	x	–	–	–	x	–	12
A 6-1 A7944	M	M	1	8	3.5	6	6	28	34	130	–	x	–	–	x	–	14
PR 4-31 A7743	M	M	2	9.5	4.5	7	9	30	42	110+	–	x	–	–	x	–	12
SR 16-6 10-264	S	S	1	5	3.8	7	8	23	31	126	x	–	–	x	–	–	12
Morss 19 A6520	M	M	1.5	11	3.8	8	8	25	37	130+	–	x	–	–	x	–	12
Morss 19 A6478	M	S	1.5	9	3.6	8	7	30	35	115	–	x	–	–	x	–	16
Morss 21 A6466	A	S	0.5	7	3.2	8	6	18	33	120	–	x	–	–	–	x	12
Morss 37 A6819	A	S	1.5	10	4.4	9	8	20	30	160	–	–	x	–	–	x	8

introgression, by way of Sabanero (1.5 knobs), from a South American species of *Tripsacum*, *T. australe*, which, as shown by Graner and Addison (1944), is unlike its knobby Central and North American relatives in being almost knobless.

The blending of these three diverse germplasms, Chapalote, teosinte, and Harinoso de Ocho, produced in Mexico and the American Southwest new and more productive races of maize which increased adaptability sufficiently to permit maize cultivation to spread north to northern Utah in the Great Basin, north into the Dakotas in the Plains east of the Rocky Mountains and east across the northern United States into New England. The eight-rowed race which asserted itself across the northern part of the eastern United States eventually went on to aid in the formation of the world's most productive maize, the "Corn-Belt Dent."

There has been some confusion surround-ing the origin and identity of the new eight-rowed race. This confusion seems to stem from the fact that pure forms of the eight-rowed race are either rare or hidden by the great diversity of maize in the Southwest, while eight-rowed maize was abundant and often the only archaeological maize in the North or Northeast. Accordingly, most references to this race follow Carter's (1945) early term of "Eastern Complex," a term which was coined to indicate an Eastern origin. Others (Brown and Anderson, 1947) have referred to the same race as "Northern Flint," a term which seems to be better than that used by Carter because it does at least indicate the "Life Zone" where this eight-rowed race attained its greatest distribution. But in examining both the prehistoric and historic evidence concerning the distribution of this eight-rowed race, we find that its origin can be traced back to the Southwest, as first suggested by Mangelsdorf and Reeves (1939) and southward to the race "Harinoso de Ocho" in Mexico. The Spanish term "harinoso" refers to the floury character of its kernels, while "ocho" refers to the eight-rowed condition of its ears. In the east and northeast this race has acquired "flinty" kernels instead of the original floury ones. We proposed a more general name, "Maíz de Ocho," for this race in which we included both the "Northern Flints" and "Harinoso de Ocho." The Spanish name was chosen to give recognition to its Mexican point of dispersal.

An excellent historic record on the geographic distribution of the eight-rowed flint was made by C. S. Plumb in 1898, a record which is the more significant because at this early date, before the advent of extensive commercial maize hybridization, the races and their distribution more closely approximated the prehistoric condition. This survey data revealed that "Maíz de Ocho" was best adapted to the humid part (Alleghenian area) of the Transition Life Zone, presumably because of suitable conditions of temperature and moisture; that is, especially to the Allegheny region, Ontario, New England, New York, Pennsylvania, Michigan, Wisconsin, and Minnesota. This race also extended down through the arid part of the Transition Zone, where it received some natural irrigation from rivers or from other local conditions in parts of Nevada, Wyoming, Colorado, Utah, New Mexico, and northwestern Mexico. But although this eight-rowed race was not well adapted to the Southwest, it did grow there which is in sharp contrast to its almost complete absence in the Lower Austral Zone in the Southeast. These historic data suggest that Maíz de Ocho arrived in the Northeast by way of the Southwest.

Convincing evidence that Maíz de Ocho did indeed come from the Southwest became apparent when we extended the map of Brown and Anderson (1947), showing the prehistoric distribution of Maíz de Ocho so as to include all of the United States rather than just that part east of the Mississippi. With these archaeological data added to the data of Plumb, we found that Maíz de Ocho follows the Transition Life Zone from New England across the northern United States and down through the Southwest into Mexico.

Furthermore, the data on which this distribution is based showed that the closer one gets to Mexico, the earlier the dates for Maíz de Ocho.

If Maíz de Ocho did originate in the highlands of Colombia, then its poor adaptation to the lowlands in the southern part of the Southwest might be expected. But a flow of germplasm from local races such as Chapalote, Reventador, and Tabloncillo has apparently tended to acclimatize it to this area. Thus, Harinoso de Ocho, as it lingers on, is extremely variable and mixed. Each ear from two collections of Harinoso de Ocho recently received from the Rockefeller Foundation in Mexico is different in size and shape and has thin dented kernels rather than thick floury kernels, as described for this race by Wellhausen et al. (1952). Although the kernels of Harinoso de Ocho are thinner (4.4 mm.) than those of Cabuya (6.36 mm.), they still are thicker than those of all other Mexican races except one, Cacahuacintle, which is also thought to be from South America and related to Cabuya (data from Wellhausen et al., 1952, and Grobman et al., 1961). The mixed nature of Maíz de Ocho is also apparent in archaeological collections from northwestern Mexico (Mangelsdorf and Lister, 1956) and adjoining areas of the Southwest, as in a collection from several sites in southwestern New Mexico reported by Cosgrove (1947). This collection shows the distinct ingredients which were blended during the evolution of maize in the Southwest as follows: Chapalote, tripsacoid Chapalote, and Maíz de Ocho, as well as their hybrid product, probably the Pima-Papago race or Maíz Blando.

As Maíz de Ocho moved northward and eastward from the Southwest, it would have encountered colder soils and shorter growing seasons. As a result, natural selection, especially during germination, would have increased the frequency of the hard, flinty kernels and early maturing kernels. Also, natural selection for the reassertion of a residual preadaptation to growing conditions in the North and Northeast must have been carried over through the poorly adapted Harinoso de Ocho in Sonora from the introduced highland race Cabuya of Colombia. Apparently, during its northward migration from the Southwest, we had the well-known substitution of latitude for altitude adaptation, resulting in this reassertion of the original South American heritage.

This new eight-rowed race had certain advantages over the indigenous Chapalote race in that its larger and softer kernels were easier to grind for flour. When the problem of adaptability was overcome by hybridization with indigenous maize, the new superior type of grain must have spread rapidly. The hybrid called Maíz Blando de Sonora by Wellhausen et al. (1952) remained in Mexico. It has floury kernels approaching those of Harinoso de Ocho in size and a twelve-rowed ear approaching that of Chapalote. Just to the north, the counterpart of this hybrid is called "Pima-Papago" after the Indians who cultivated it (Anderson and Cutler, 1942). Teosinte introgression seems to have also played a role in the spread of this hybrid, especially in the Fremont area of Utah, where the kernels become strongly dented and the glumes indurated (fig. 45B). That denting is one of the effects which can result from teosinte introgression is indicated by its correlation with the number of chromosome knobs, which in turn is related to tripsacoid characteristics in the maize from western Guatemala (Mangelsdorf and Cameron, 1942), and in that from the United States (Brown, 1949).

Although most collections of Fremont Dent appear to be just a dented version of the Pima-Papago race, apparently some of its northern isolates have acquired slightly more pointed kernels and shorter ears than the Pima-Papago race and, therefore, have some superficial resemblance to the race called Zapalote Chico. In fact, it has been suggested that Zapalote Chico jumped about one thousand miles from central Mexico to the Castle Park area in northwestern Colorado (Anderson, 1959).

The most Zapalote Chico–like specimen which we were able to pick out of the Peabody Museum collection from Fremont sites is from Vernal, Utah, not far from Castle Park. This specimen matches very closely the "Zapalote Chico" ears from Castle Park illustrated by Anderson (1959), but its resemblance to Zapalote Chico is not convincing when it is compared with actual specimens

obtained through Dr. E. J. Wellhausen of the Rockefeller Foundation in Mexico (fig. 45C). Any similarities which exist between the Castle Park maize and Zapalote Chico may stem from the fact that Zapalote Chico and our candidate, the Pima-Papago race, have some similarities in their ancestry, as pointed out by Mangelsdorf (personal communication). That is, Nal Tel, which is one parent of Zapalote Chico, is apparently related to or the actual precursor of Chapalote, which is one parent of Maíz Blando (Pima-Papago). Furthermore, both hybrid races involve teosinte introgression, coming by way of the race Tepecintle in the case of Zapalote Chico and coming in more directly during the origin of Maíz Blando from Harinoso de Ocho and Chapalote (see Wellhausen et al., 1952).

ARCHAEOLOGICAL IMPLICATIONS

This re-examination of the origin and spread of Maíz de Ocho has far-reaching implications for the archaeology of the Southwest, especially the Pueblo II expansion; for the beginnings of sedentary cultures in the Plains east of the Rocky Mountains, and across the northern part of the United States as far as the Atlantic Ocean. Considering the very limited data with which we are dealing and the inherent imprecision of radiocarbon dating, which provides much of our chronological framework, it cannot be stressed too strongly that the reconstructions here outlined, especially those concerning the Eastern United States, are of a tentative nature.

It has already been pointed out that Chapalote, the maize introduced from Mexico into the American Southwest some 5000 years ago, developed quite slowly until teosinte was introduced, also from Mexico, by about 500 B.C. Pre-Chapalote has been recovered from the earliest, but undated, levels at Swallow Cave in Chihuahua (Mangelsdorf and Lister, 1956) and from the earliest, 5000-year-old level, at Bat Cave in southwestern New Mexico (Johnson, 1951; Mangelsdorf, 1954).

More evolved, teosinte-contaminated, early Chapalote was recovered from a 2300-year-old level at Tularosa Cave in southwestern New Mexico, not far from Bat Cave (Martin et al., 1952; Johnson, 1951). The highly variable hybrids that resulted from the blending of Chapalote and teosinte provided the base for the Basketmaker and Pueblo development. By the beginning of the Christian era, the Basketmaker horticultural way of life had spread north into southern Utah and southwestern Colorado. A number of sites in this area that have yielded Early and Evolved Chapalote showing varying amounts of teosinte contamination have been dated by dendrochronology. Among these are Cave du Pont (A.D. 217) in south-central Utah (Collins, *in*: Nusbaum, 1922; Schulman, 1949); White Dog Cave (A.D. 312), as well as other sites in the Marsh Pass area of northeastern Arizona (Kidder and Guernsey, 1919; Guernsey and Kidder, 1921; Gladwin, 1957, p. 37); and the Durango Basketmaker site (A.D. 46–330) near Durango in southwestern Colorado (Morris and Burgh, 1954).

At about A.D. 700 the new race of maize which we have named Maíz de Ocho made its appearance in northern Mexico (Mangelsdorf and Lister, 1956), where it survives in a race called Harinoso de Ocho. Our data are still too few to establish definitely the routes by which Harinoso de Ocho traveled. No evidence of its influence has been noted between its postulated homeland in South America and northern Mexico. From the location of the few sites in the latter area where it has been found, the most likely route would have been up the west coast of Mexico. It seems probable that it was also introduced into Central America and southern Mexico, but since this race is especially well suited to high latitudes or altitudes, it is not surprising that no evidence of it can be seen in the maize of this tropical area. Once it reached northern Mexico, however, it apparently spread very rapidly throughout the Southwest, where it occurs at Tularosa Cave at about the same time that it appears in Chihuahua. Since it was crossing an area which had long contained other maize, the new germplasm probably spread in the form of a hybrid in most cases.

Our re-examination of some of the charred cobs from the Durango, Colorado, Basketmaker site that were originally thought to show a significant amount of "Eastern" (Maíz de Ocho) influence, led to the conclusion that the traits in question were more probably the result of teosinte introgression. Thus, with the cancellation of this material as evidence of Maíz de Ocho in a Basketmaker context, we can apparently rule out its occurrence in the Southwest prior to *ca.* A.D. 700, when it entered the Mogollon area. So far as we can determine from the literature and other evidence available, very little Maíz de Ocho is present in maize from Anasazi sites prior to the end of the Pueblo I period, *ca.* A.D. 900, but the data are very few. It seems likely that sometime during this two-century-long period Maíz de Ocho made its first appearance in the Anasazi area, and it might have contributed to the increase in population that apparently took place during Pueblo I times.

The addition of this new race appears to have provided a second and even more potent impetus to the development of the already well-adapted maize in the Southwest. By sometime between about A.D. 950 and 1100, the area occupied by the Pueblo cultures reached its maximum extent with what is known as the Pueblo II expansion; and throughout the Southwest, after about A.D. 950, the archaeological maize shows a blending of Chapalote, teosinte, and Maíz de Ocho. The occurrence of Maíz de Ocho along with other maize that is strongly Chapalote-affiliated is dramatically shown at Painted Cave, northeastern Arizona (Haury, 1945 a, plate 36).

The reason for the Pueblo II expansion into areas not previously occupied by horticulturalists has not been satisfactorily explained. A period of more favorable rainfall has generally been accepted as one factor. It is suggested here that a more important factor was the introduction of the new race of maize, Maíz de Ocho, which, when blended with the previously cultivated maize, resulted in a hybrid that not only produced more abundant yields of a grain that was more easily milled, but was also better suited to a wider range of environments, particularly higher elevations and latitudes. Thus the introduction of Maíz de Ocho appears to have provided a food resource that resulted in a population increase, and a maize sufficiently adaptable to higher latitudes to permit this increased population to carry the Pueblo farming way of life an additional 250 miles farther north than had previously been possible. Although the

Pueblo area spread limited distances both east and west during this period (*ca.* 900–1100), the most dramatic expansion was to the north, with the movement of the Fremont and Sevier (probably Plateau Shoshonean) peoples into the northern 85 per cent of Utah (Gunnerson, 1960 a, 1962 a).

Certain changes that took place in the Pueblo II period, when considered along with the advent of Maíz de Ocho, raise questions such as the following. Did the greater ease with which the new maize could be milled cause changes in the design of manos and metates such as the use of mealing bins and the graded coarseness of the metates? Did the increased yields provided by the new maize result in changes of settlement pattern and village plan, as well as changes in architectural styles such as increased size of storage rooms? Did the increased yields make the Pueblo people overly dependent upon maize horticulture so that the occasional inevitable crop failures, especially when they occurred for several consecutive years, caused severe hardships and increased intervillage competition for the most desirable farm land, and even raids against villages which did harvest a successful crop by another village which did not? Was the moving of storage rooms into large multiroomed structures a device for protecting the surpluses that could now be amassed? These and many other questions can probably be answered by additional field work and a re-examination of data now available.

APPENDIX II

USE OF PLANT MATERIALS OTHER THAN MAIZE

BY

MARGARET A. TOWLE

An examination of the plant material other than maize collected by the Claflin-Emerson expedition to northeastern Utah provided information on the use of nine different plants. Some of these had been used for only a single purpose while others had been used in a wide variety of ways.

The most versatile appears to have been *Yucca*. Fiber of this plant was made into cord that was used either alone or as the core of the warp elements of both feather and fur cloth. One of the few traits that were consistent throughout the collection studied was the use of yucca fiber as the bundle in half-rod-and-bundle foundation coiled basketry. Yucca leaves were woven into sandals of common Anasazi types and also served to hold together the moccasin-like sandal made chiefly of bent sticks and grass that was found at Site SR 16-6. A rather crude bag was made of yucca leaves and a fragment of a mat made from yucca stems was recovered. One of the fiber-ring pot rests is of yucca leaves. The fact that all the knotted pieces of plant material are yucca leaves suggests that they were used for incidental tying. The several quids of well-masticated yucca leaves found at two sites attest to their use even for food.

Juniper bark was almost as useful as yucca. It, too, was made into cord that was used either alone or as the core for the elements of fur and feather cloth. The bundle foundation of one coiled basket is of juniper bark, as are two fiber-ring pot rests. Juniper bark had been made into a brush at one site and had served as the innersole for sandals or moccasins at two others.

Rhus (squawbush) and *Salix* (willow) were used primarily for basketry and appear to have been essentially interchangeable. In the most common type of basketry (coiled with a half-rod-and-bundle foundation) the half-rod is always of one or the other and the stitching material apparently always consists of strips of bark from the same plant as the rod. Strips of bark from both served as the stitching material in coiled baskets with a bundle foundation. The single split-twig animal figurine recovered is of *Salix*.

Phragmites communis was also used for a variety of purposes. Long sections of this reed served as arrowshafts, and short tubes, deliberately cut off, may have been beads. The leaves were woven into mats and were twisted together to form the bundle foundation for coiled baskets.

Apocynum was apparently used only for cordage. The one bundle of loose apocynum fiber found was probably raw material from which cord was to have been made. A single fragment of what is tentatively identified as *Asclepias* sp. was also in the form of cord.

Cucurbita are represented by many small fragments of shell, but only one specimen had definitely been fashioned into a container. Most of the specimens of cucurbita probably represent food refuse. Maize (Appendix I) and beans are obviously plants cultivated for food.

A list of the specimens made from plant material, the identifications of the plants, and the sites at which they occurred is presented in table 4.

TABLE 4: DISTRIBUTION OF SPECIMENS OF IDENTIFIED PLANT MATERIALS.

SPECIMENS AND MATERIAL	SITES
Arrowshaft	
Phragmites communis	SR 15-5

Specimens and Material	Sites	Specimens and Material	Sites
Basketry, coiled		Innersoles	
Half-rod-and-bundle foundation		*Juniperus* sp.	PR 4-31
Half-rod and stitching			SR 12-5
Rhus sp. (?)	A 6-1	Knotted plant material	
	PR 4-31	*Yucca* sp.	LS 13-11
Salix sp. (?)	FL 12-2 (?)		SR 12-5
	SR 16-6		SR 16-6
			SR 16-10
Half-rod foundation			
Foundation and stitching		Matting, plaited	
Rhus trilobata (?)	A 6-1	*Yucca* sp.	E 12-7 (?)
Bundle foundation		*Phragmites communis*	LS 14-8
Foundation		Matting, twined	
Juniperus sp.	A 6-1	Warp elements	
Phragmites communis (?)	A 6-1	*Scirpus* sp.	H 3-8 (?)
Stitching			LS 13-11
Salix sp.	A 6-1		PR 4-31
Rhus sp. (?)	A 6-1		SR 12-5
Bag fragment		Weft cord	
Yucca sp.	SR-16-6	*Apocynum* sp.	PR 4-31
Basketry material		*Juniperus* sp.	PR 4-31
Salix sp.	PR 4-31		SR 12-5
Brush		*Scirpus* sp.	H 3-8 (?)
Juniperus sp.	FL 12-2	*Scirpus* sp. (?)	LS 13-11
Cord		Quids, masticated	
Apocynum sp.	SR 16-6	*Yucca* sp.	SR 15-2
	SR 16-10		SR 16-10 (?)
Apocynum sp. (?)	ET 6-10		
Apocynum sp. and *Juniperus* sp.	PR 4-31	Ring pot rest	
Asclepias sp. (?)	ET 6-10	*Juniperus* sp.	LS 13-1
Juniperus sp.	A 6-2		SR 12-5
	LS 13-11	*Yucca* sp.	LS 13-11
	PR 4-6	Sandals	
	PR 4-27	*Yucca* sp.	LS 13-11
	PR 4-28		SR 12-5
	PR 4-31	*Yucca* sp., wood and grass	SR 16-6
	SR 16-6	Split-twig animal figure	
Yucca sp.	LS 13-11	*Salix* sp.	SR 16-6
	PR 4-6	Tubes	
	PR 4-31	*Phragmites communis*	PR 4-31
	PR 12-19		SR 16-10
	SR 16-6	*Phragmites communis* (?)	A 6-1
	SR 16-10	Unmodified plant material	
Feather cloth (core)		Squash shell fragments	
Juniperus sp. and *Yucca* sp.	SR 12-5	*Cucurbita* sp.	A 6-1
Yucca sp.	SR 16-6		A 6-6
Fiber, separated but unspun			LS 13-11
Apocynum sp.	SR 16-6		PR 4-25
Fur cloth (core)			PR 4-28
Juniperus sp.	SR 16-9		PR 4-31
Yucca sp.	SR 4-31	Beans and pod	
"Gourd" container		*Phaseolus vulgaris*	ET 6-7
Cucurbita sp.	SR 12-15		

THE RASMUSSEN CAVE SKELETON:
OBSERVATIONS AND MEASUREMENTS

JAMES H. GUNNERSON

THE skeleton found at Rasmussen Cave (PR 4-31) is nearly complete, but it is impossible to determine whether the missing mandible and the right femur, fibula, and patella were lost before or after excavation. A small amount of dry tissue still adheres to most of the bones, and enough is attached to the vertebrae to hold together most of those in the thoracic section.

The skeleton is that of an adult male, probably well over 50 years of age. He had been moderately rugged and well muscled, with the bones of the right arm noticeably larger and better muscled than those of the left. The margins of the bodies of the cervical and lumbar vertebrae show extensive osteo-arthritic lipping, although in no place does it appear to be great enough to have seriously impaired movement. One obvious anomaly was the failure of the vertebral arch to fuse to the body in the fifth lumbar vertebra. In most of the bones of the postcranial skeleton there is evidence of adsorption and demineralization, apparently all due to advancing age.

The skull (fig. 46) is dolichocephalic (cephalic index of 74) and shows no evidence of artificial deformation. The mastoid processes are large, but muscular attachments in general, as well as the brow ridges, are of only medium size.

The teeth of this individual show a great deal of wear and rampant caries. The right second premolar is almost entirely decayed away and the first and second right molars are nearly as bad. All that remains of the left first molar is one (lingual) root and its surface shows wear. The left second molar appears to have been entirely lost long before the time of death, since most of the buckle portion of the socket is smoothly absorbed.

There is also a perforation through the buckle portion of the socket of the first molar.

Immediately under the right infraorbital foramen is a honeycomb-like area 1 cm. in diameter that is obviously some sort of bone lesion. When the skull was examined with a very bright light placed inside it, the lesion was seen to have perforated the anterior wall of the right maxillary sinus which was thinner (more translucent) than that of the left maxillary sinus. Thus, more of the sinus than just the lesion appears to have been affected. Since the lesion is directly above three badly decayed teeth, it may have resulted from an abscess that started in the teeth and spread into the sinus.

The cranium measurements (Hooton, 1946, pp. 736–738) that it was possible to take are as follows.

Glabello-occipital length	18.9 cm.
Maximum width	14.0
Basion-bregma height	12.2
Thickness of left parietal	0.5
Minimum frontal diameter	9.0
Maximum diameter bi-zygomatic	14.0
Prosthion-nasion height	7.5
Basion-nasion	10.0
Basion-prosthion	10.0
Nasal height	5.3
Nasal breadth	2.3
Nasalia—upper breadth	1.0
Nasalia—lower breadth	1.5
Orbits—height, right	3.7
Orbits—height, left	3.7
Orbits—breadth, right	4.0
Orbits—breadth, left	4.0
Interorbital breadth	2.0
Bi-orbital breadth	9.9
Palate—external length	5.5
Palate—external breadth	6.7

The maximum lengths of the long bones are as follows:

Left femur	47.7 cm.
Left tibia	40.2
Left fibula	38.8
Right humerus	34.0
Left humerus	33.5
Right ulna	28.1
Left ulna	27.7
Right radius	25.8
Left radius	25.8

Calculations to determine stature of the individual by using various of the formulae given for males by Hooton (1946, p. 728) indicate that he had been about 172 cm. (5 ft. 8 in.) tall.

BIBLIOGRAPHY

ABEL, L. J.
1955 Pottery Types of the Southwest. *Museum of Northern Arizona Ceramic Series*, no. 3 B. Flagstaff.

ADAMS, W. Y.
1960 Ninety Years of Glen Canyon Archaeology, 1869–1959. *Museum of Northern Arizona, Bulletin* 33. Flagstaff.

ALTER, J. C.
1936 Section 21-Eastern Utah. *Climatic Survey of the United States*, Revised Edition. United States Department of Agriculture, Weather Bureau. Washington.
1941 Climate of Utah. In: Hambidge (1941), pp. 1147–1158. Washington.

AMBLER, J. R.
1959 A Preliminary Note on 1959 Excavations at the Coombs Site, Boulder, Utah. *Utah Archeology*, vol. 5, no. 3, pp. 4–11. Salt Lake City.

ANDERSON, E.
1948 Racial Identity of the Corn from Castle Park. Appendix I in: The Archaeology of Castle Park Dinosaur National Monument, by Burgh and Scoggin. *University of Colorado Studies, Series in Anthropology*, no. 2, pp. 91–92. Boulder.
1959 Zapalote Chico: An Important Chapter in the History of Maize and Man. *Actas del 33 Congreso Internacional de Americanistas*, pp. 230–237. San José, Costa Rica.

ANDERSON, E., AND CUTLER, H. C.
1942 Races of Zea Mays: I. Their Recognition and Classification. *Annals of the Missouri Botanical Garden*, vol. 29, pp. 69–86. St. Louis.

ANDERSON, K. M.
1963 Ceramic Clues to Pueblo-Puebloid Relationships. *American Antiquity*, vol. 28, no. 3, pp. 303–307. Salt Lake City.

AUERBACH, H. S.
1943 Father Escalante's Journal 1776–77, Newly Translated with Related Documents and Original Maps. *Utah Historical Quarterly*, vol. 11. Salt Lake City.

BALDWIN, G. C.
1947 An Archaeological Reconnaissance of the Yampa and Green Rivers. *The Kiva*, vol. 12, pp. 31–36. Tucson.
1949 Archaeological Survey in Southeastern Utah. *Southwestern Journal of Anthropology*, vol. 5, no. 4, pp. 393–404. Albuquerque.
1950 The Pottery of the Southern Paiute. *American Antiquity*, vol. 16, no. 1, pp. 50–56. Menasha.

BARBER, E. A.
1876 Ancient Pottery of Colorado, Utah, Arizona, and New Mexico. *American Naturalist*, vol. 10, no. 8, pp. 449–464. Salem, Mass.

BECKWITH, F.
1931 Some Interesting Pictographs in Nine Mile Canyon, Utah. *El Palacio*, vol. 31, no. 14, pp. 216–222. Santa Fe.
1932 Serpent Petroglyphs in Nine Mile Canyon. *El Palacio*, vol. 33, nos. 15–16, pp. 147–149. Santa Fe.
1935 Ancient Indian Petroglyphs of Utah. *El Palacio*, vol. 38, nos. 6-7-8, pp. 33–40. Santa Fe.

BLAIR, W. C.
1949 Additional Data on Crania From the Warren Mounds, Utah. *American Antiquity*, vol. 14, no. 3, pp. 224–225. Menasha.

BRADLEY, G. Y.
1947 George Y. Bradley's Journal, May 24–August 30, 1869. Edited by: W. C. Darrah. *Utah Historical Quarterly*, vol. 15, pp. 31–72. Salt Lake City.

BREW, J. O.
1946 Archaeology of Alkali Ridge, Southeastern Utah. *Peabody Museum, Harvard University, Papers*, vol. 21. Cambridge.

BROWN, W. L.
1949 Number and Distribution of Chromosome Knobs in United States Maize. *Genetics*, vol. 34, pp. 524–536. Princeton.

BROWN, W. L., AND ANDERSON, E.
1947 The Northern Flint Corns. *Annals of the Missouri Botanical Garden*, vol. 34, pp. 1–28. St. Louis.

BULLARD, W. R., JR.
1962 The Cerro Colorado Site and Pithouse Archi-

tecture in the Southwestern United States Prior to A.D. 900. *Peabody Museum, Harvard University, Papers*, vol. 44, no. 2. Cambridge.

BURGH, R. F.
1950   A Fremont Basket Maker House in Dinosaur National Monument. *Tree-Ring Bulletin*, vol. 16, no. 3, pp. 19–20. Tucson.

BURGH, R. F., AND SCOGGIN, C. R.
1948   The Archaeology of Castle Park, Dinosaur National Monument. *University of Colorado Studies, Series in Anthropology*, no. 2. Boulder.

CARTER, G.
1945   Plant Geography and Culture History in the American Southwest. *Viking Fund Publications in Anthropology*, vol. 5. New York.

CHRISTENSEN, R. T.
1949   On the Prehistory of Utah Valley. *Proceedings, Utah Academy of Science, Arts, and Letters*, vol. 25, pp. 101–111. Salt Lake City.

CLAFLIN, W. H.
n.d.   *An Archaeological Reconnaissance into Southern Utah.* Manuscript, Peabody Museum. Cambridge.

COLTON, H. S.
1939   Prehistoric Culture Units and their Relationships in Northern Arizona. *Museum of Northern Arizona, Bulletin* 17. Flagstaff.
1942   Archaeology and the Reconstruction of History. *American Antiquity*, vol. 8, no. 1, pp. 33–40. Menasha.
1952   Pottery Types of the Arizona Strip and Adjacent Areas in Utah and Nevada. *Museum of Northern Arizona Ceramic Series*, no. 1. Flagstaff.
1955   Pottery Types of the Southwest. *Museum of Northern Arizona Ceramic Series*, no. 3 A. Flagstaff.
1956   Pottery Types of the Southwest. *Museum of Northern Arizona Ceramic Series*, no. 3 C. Flagstaff.

COSGROVE, C. B.
1947   Caves of the Upper Gila and Hueco Areas in New Mexico and Texas. *Peabody Museum, Harvard University, Papers*, vol. 24, no. 2. Cambridge.

CUMMINGS, B.
1910   The Ancient Inhabitants of the San Juan Valley. *Bulletin of the University of Utah*, vol. 3, no. 3, pt. 2. Salt Lake City.

DAY, K. C.
1962   Preliminary Report of the Flaming Gorge

Survey. *Utah Archeology*, vol. 8, no. 4, pp. 3–7. Salt Lake City.

DOUGLAS, F. H., AND D'HARNONCOURT, R.
1941   *Indian Art of the United States.* Museum of Modern Art, New York.

DOYLE, C. B.
1941   Climate and Cotton. In: Climate and Man, *Yearbook of Agriculture, United States Department of Agriculture*, pp. 348–363. Washington.

ENGER, W. D.
1942   Archaeology of Blackrock 3 Cave, Utah. *Archaeology and Ethnology Papers, Museum of Anthropology, University of Utah*, no. 7. (Republished as *University of Utah Anthropological Papers*, no. 7). Salt Lake City.

ENGER, W. D., AND BLAIR, W. C.
1947   Crania from the Warren Mounds and their Possible Significance to Northern Periphery Archaeology. *American Antiquity*, vol. 13, no. 2, pp. 142–146. Menasha.

FARMER, M., AND DESAUSSURE, R.
1955   Split-Twig Animal Figurines. *Plateau*, vol. 27, no. 4, pp. 13–23. Flagstaff.

FERGUSON, C. W., JR.
1949   Additional Dates for Nine Mile Canyon, Northeastern Utah. *Tree-Ring Bulletin*, vol. 16, no. 2, pp. 10–11. Tucson.

FEWKES, J. W.
1917a   Prehistoric Remains in New Mexico, Colorado, and Utah. *Smithsonian Miscellaneous Collections*, vol. 66, no. 17, pp. 76–92. Washington.
1917b   Archaeological Investigations in New Mexico, Colorado, and Utah. *Smithsonian Miscellaneous Collections*, vol. 68, no. 1. Washington.
1919   Prehistoric Villages, Castles, and Towers of Southwestern Colorado. *Bureau of American Ethnology, Bulletin*, no. 70. Washington.

FRIEDMAN, I., AND SMITH, R. L.
1960   A New Dating Method Using Obsidian: Part I, The Development of the Method. *American Antiquity*, vol. 25, no. 4, pp. 476–522. Salt Lake City.

GALINAT, W. C., AND GUNNERSON, J. H.
1963   Spread of Eight-Rowed Maize From the Prehistoric Southwest. *Botanical Museum Leaflets, Harvard University*, vol. 20, no. 5. Cambridge.

GALINAT, W. C., MANGELSDORF, P. C., AND PIERSON, L.

1956 Estimates of Teosinte Introgression in Archaeological Maize. *Botanical Museum Leaflets, Harvard University*, vol. 17, pp. 101–124. Cambridge.

GALINAT, W. C., AND RUPPÉ, R. J.
1961 Further Archaeological Evidence on the Effects of Teosinte Introgression in the Evolution of Modern Maize. *Botanical Museum Leaflets, Harvard University*, vol. 19, no. 8, pp. 163–181. Cambridge.

GAUMER, A. E.
1937 Basketmaker Caves in Desolation Cañon, Green River, Utah. *The Masterkey*, vol. 11, no. 5, pp. 160–165. Los Angeles.
1939 A Fremont River Culture Cradle. *The Masterkey*, vol. 13, no. 4, pp. 139–140. Los Angeles.

GILLIN, J.
1938 Archaeological Investigations in Nine Mile Canyon, Utah. *University of Utah Bulletin* 28, no. 11. (Republished 1955, *University of Utah Anthropological Papers* no. 21.) Salt Lake City.
1941 Archaeological Investigations in Central Utah. *Peabody Museum, Harvard University, Papers*, vol. 17, no. 2. Cambridge.

GLADWIN, H. S.
1957 *A History of the Ancient Southwest*. The Bond Wheelwright Company, Portland, Maine.

GLADWIN, W., AND GLADWIN, H. S.
1934 A Method for Designation of Cultures and their Variations. *Medallion Papers*, no. 15. Globe.

GRANER, E. A., AND ADDISON, G. O.
1944 Meiose em *Tripsacum australe* Cutler e Anderson. Anais Escola Superior Agric. "Luis Queiroz" vol. 1, pp. 213–224.

GREEN, D. F.
1961 *Archaeological Investigations at the G. M. Hinckley Farm Site, Utah County, Utah 1956–1960*. Brigham Young University Press, Provo.

GROBMAN, A., SALHUANA, W., SEVILLA, R., IN COLLABORATION WITH MANGELSDORF, P. C.
1961 Races of Maize in Peru. *National Academy of Sciences, National Research Council, Publication 915*. Washington.

GROSSCUP, G. L.
1962 Excavations in the Hill Creek Area, Grand County, Utah. *Utah Archeology*, vol. 8, no. 3, pp. 3–7. Salt Lake City.

GUERNSEY, S. J.
1931 Explorations in Northeastern Arizona. *Peabody Museum, Harvard University, Papers*, vol. 12, no. 1. Cambridge.

GUERNSEY, S. J., AND KIDDER, A. V.
1921 Basket-Maker Caves of Northeastern Arizona. *Peabody Museum, Harvard University, Papers*, vol. 8, no. 2. Cambridge.

GUNNERSON, D. A.
1956 The Southern Athabascans: Their Arrival in the Southwest. *El Palacio*, vol. 63, nos. 11–12, pp. 346–365. Santa Fe.

GUNNERSON, J. H.
1955 Archeological Evidence of Hunting Magic. *Utah Archeology*, vol. 1, no. 3, pp. 5–8. Salt Lake City.
1956a A Fluted Point Site in Utah. *American Antiquity*, vol. 21, no. 4, pp. 412–414. Salt Lake City.
1956b 1956 Archeological Activities of the University of Utah. *Utah Archeology*, vol. 2, no. 3, pp. 4–14. Salt Lake City.
1956c Fremont Ceramics. "Papers of the Third Great Basin Archeological Conference," *University of Utah Anthropological Papers* no. 26, pp. 54–62. Salt Lake City.
1956d Plains-Promontory Relationships. *American Antiquity*, vol. 22, no. 1, pp. 69–72. Salt Lake City.
1956e Utah Statewide Survey Activities — 1955. *Utah Archeology*, vol. 2, no. 1, pp. 4–12. Salt Lake City.
1957a An Archeological Survey of the Fremont Area. *University of Utah Anthropological Papers*, no. 28. Salt Lake City.
1957b Uinta Basin Archeology. *Guidebook to the Geology of the Uinta Basin, Eighth Annual Field Conference, Intermountain Association of Petroleum Geologists* (Otto G. Seal, Editor), pp. 15–16. Salt Lake City.
1957c Preliminary Report of 1957 Work at Snake Rock. *Utah Archeology*, vol. 3, no. 4, pp. 7–12. Salt Lake City.
1957d Prehistoric Figurines from Castle Valley. *Archaeology*, vol. 10, no. 2, pp. 137–140. Brattleboro, Vermont.
1958 Archeological Survey of the Kaiparowits Plateau — A Preliminary Report. *Utah Archeology*, vol. 4, no. 3, pp. 9–20. Salt Lake City.
1959a An Enigmatic Unfired Clay Disk. *El Palacio*, vol. 66, no. 3, pp. 107–108. Santa Fe.
1959b Archeological Survey in the Dead Horse Point Area. *Utah Archeology*, vol. 5, no. 2, pp. 4–9. Salt Lake City.
1959c 1957 Excavations in the Glen Canyon Area.

University of Utah Anthropological Papers, no. 43. Salt Lake City.

1959d Archeological Survey of the Kaiparowits Plateau. *University of Utah Anthropological Papers*, no. 39, pp. 319–469. Salt Lake City.

1959e Archeological Survey in Northeastern New Mexico. *El Palacio*, vol. 66, no. 5, pp. 145–154. Santa Fe.

1960a The Fremont Culture: Internal Dimensions and External Relationships. *American Antiquity*, vol. 25, no. 3, pp. 373–380. Salt Lake City.

1960b Highway Salvage Archeology: St. George, Utah. *University of Utah Anthropological Papers*, no. 60, pp. 45–65. Salt Lake City.

1960c Archeological Survey in the Hammond Canyon Area, Southeastern Utah. *University of Utah Anthropological Papers*, no. 60, pp. 9–44. Salt Lake City.

1960d An Introduction to Plains Apache Archeology — The Dismal River Aspect. *Bureau of American Ethnology, Bulletin* 173 (*Anthropological Paper*, no. 58) pp. 129–260. Washington.

1962a Plateau Shoshonean Prehistory: A Suggested Reconstruction. *American Antiquity*, vol. 28, no. 1, pp. 41–45. Salt Lake City.

1962b Unusual Artifacts from Castle Valley, Central Utah. *University of Utah Anthropological Papers*, no. 60, pp. 67–91. Salt Lake City.

1962c Three Wooden Shovels from Nine Mile Canyon. *University of Utah Anthropological Papers*, no. 60, pp. 1–8. Salt Lake City.

n.d. *Archeological Excavations at Snake Rock, Central Utah*. Manuscript. Department of Anthropology, University of Utah, Salt Lake City.

GUNNERSON, J. H., LIPE, W., LISTER, R. H., AND SUHM, D. A.

1959 Findings. In: The Glen Canyon Archeological Survey. *University of Utah Anthropological Papers*, no. 39, pp. 14–26. Salt Lake City.

HALE, K.

1958 Internal Diversity in Uto-Aztecan: I. *International Journal of American Linguistics*, vol. 24, no. 2, pp. 101–107. Baltimore.

HALL, E. T., JR.

1942 Archaeological Survey of Walhalla Glades. *Museum of Northern Arizona, Bulletin* 20. Flagstaff.

HAMBIDGE, G. (EDITOR)

1941 Climate and Man. *U.S. Department of Agriculture, Yearbook of Agriculture for 1941*. Washington.

HARRINGTON, M. R.

1926a A Pre-Pueblo Site on the Colorado River. *Museum of the American Indian, Heye Foundation, Indian Notes*, vol. 3, pp. 274–284. New York.

1926b Western Extension of Early Pueblo Culture. *El Palacio*, vol. 20, no. 11, pp. 227–231. Santa Fe.

1927 A Primitive Pueblo City in Nevada. *American Anthropologist*, n.s. vol. 29, no. 3, pp. 262–277. Menasha.

1928 Tracing the Pueblo Boundary in Nevada. *Museum of the American Indian, Heye Foundation, Indian Notes*, vol. 5, pp. 235–240. New York.

1930 Archeological Explorations in Southern Nevada. *Southwestern Museum Papers*, no. 4, pp. 1–25. Los Angeles.

1937 Some Early Pit-Dwellings in Nevada. *The Masterkey*, vol. 11, no. 4, pp. 122–124. Los Angeles.

HAURY, E. W.

1936 Some Southwestern Pottery Types, Series IV. *Gila Pueblo, Medallion Papers*, no. 19. Globe.

1945a The Excavation of Los Muertos and Neighboring Ruins in the Salt River Valley, Southern Arizona. *Peabody Museum, Harvard University, Papers*, vol. 24, no. 1. Cambridge.

1945b Painted Cave, Northeastern Arizona. *The Amerind Foundation, Inc.*, no. 3. Dragoon, Arizona.

HAYDEN, I.

1930 Mesa House. *Southwestern Museum Papers*, no. 4, pt. 2, pp. 26–92. Los Angeles.

HEIZER, R. F.

1954 Notes on the Utah Utes by Edward Palmer, 1866–1877. *University of Utah Anthropological Paper*, no. 17. Salt Lake City.

HEIZER, R. F., AND KRIEGER, A. D.

1956 The Archaeology of Humboldt Cave, Churchill County, Nevada. *University of California Publications in American Archaeology and Ethnology*, vol. 47, no. 1, pp. 1–190. Berkeley.

HENDERSON, R.

1946a Glyph Hunters in the Indian Country. *Desert Magazine*, vol. 10, no. 1, pp. 11–16. Palm Desert, Calif.

1946b We Explored Dark Canyon. *Desert Magazine*, vol. 10, no. 2, pp. 5–9. Palm Desert, Calif.

1957 We Camped in the Land of the Standing Rocks. *Desert Magazine*, vol. 20, no. 10, pp. 5–11. Palm Desert, Calif.

HERNANDEZ X., E.
1949 Maize Granaries in Mexico. *Botanical Museum Leaflets, Harvard University*, vol. 13, no. 7. Cambridge.

HEWES, G. W.
1952 Californian Flicker-Quill Headbands in the Light of an Ancient Colorado Cave Specimen. *American Antiquity*, vol. 18, no. 2, pp. 147–154. Salt Lake City.

HIBBEN, F. C.
1938 The Gallina Phase. *American Antiquity*, vol. 4, no. 2, pp. 131–136. Menasha.

HOLMES, W. H.
1886 Pottery of the Ancient Pueblos. *Smithsonian Institution, Bureau of American Ethnology, Annual Report*, no. 4, pp. 257–360. Washington.

HOOTON, E. A.
1946 *Up From the Ape.* Macmillan Company, New York.

HUNT, A. P.
1953 Archeological Survey of the La Sal Mountain Area, Utah. *University of Utah Anthropological Papers*, no. 14. Salt Lake City.

HUNT, A. P., AND TANNER, D.
1960 Early Man Sites Near Moab, Utah. *American Antiquity*, vol. 26, no. 1, pp. 110–117. Salt Lake City.

HUSCHER, B. H., AND HUSCHER, H. A.
1940 Potsherds from a Piñon Tree! *The Masterkey*, vol. 14, no. 4, pp. 137–142. Los Angeles.
1943 The Hogan Builders of Colorado. *Southwestern Lore*, vol. 9, no. 2. Gunnison, Colorado.

JACKSON, W. H.
1878 Report on the Ancient Ruins Examined in 1875 and 1877. *United States Geological and Geographical Survey, Tenth Annual Report*, pp. 411–450. Washington.

JAMESON, S. J. S.
1958 Archeological Notes on Stansbury Island. *University of Utah Anthropological Papers*, no. 34. Salt Lake City.

JENNINGS, J. D.
1953 Danger Cave: A Progress Summary. *El Palacio*, vol. 60, no. 5, pp. 179–213. Santa Fe.
1957 Danger Cave. *University of Utah Anthropological Papers*, no. 27. Salt Lake City.
1960 Early Man in Utah. *Utah Historical Quarterly*, vol. 28, no. 1, pp. 3–27. Salt Lake City.

JENNINGS, J. D. (EDITOR)
1956 The American Southwest: A Problem in Cultural Isolation. In: Seminars in Archaeology: 1956. *Society for American Archaeology, Memoir*, no. 11, pp. 61–127. Salt Lake City.

JENNINGS, J. D., AND NORBECK, E.
1955 Great Basin Prehistory: A Review. *American Antiquity*, vol. 21, no. 1, pp. 1–11. Salt Lake City.

JOHNSON, F. (COMPILER)
1951 Radiocarbon Dating. *Society for American Archaeology, Memoir*, no. 8. Salt Lake City.

JONES, C. H.
1958 A Puebloid Site in Utah Valley. *Utah Archeology*, vol. 4, no. 2, pp. 7–13. Salt Lake City.
1961 *An Archaeological Survey of Utah County, Utah.* Privately printed, Provo.

JONES, V. H., AND FONNER, R. L.
1954 Plant Materials from Sites in the Durango and LaPlata Areas, Colorado. In: E. H. Morris and R. F. Burgh, Basketmaker II Sites near Durango, Colorado. *Carnegie Institution of Washington, Publication* 604, pp. 93–115. Washington.

JUDD, N. M.
1916 Archeological Reconnaissance in Western Utah. *Smithsonian Miscellaneous Collections*, vol. 66, no. 3, pp. 64–71. Washington.
1917 Archeological Reconnaissance in Western Utah. *Smithsonian Miscellaneous Collections*, vol. 66, no. 17, pp. 103–108. Washington.
1918 Archeological Work in Arizona and Utah. *Smithsonian Miscellaneous Collections*, vol. 68, no. 12, pp. 74–83. Washington.
1919 Archeological Investigations at Paragonah, Utah. *Smithsonian Miscellaneous Collections*, vol. 70, no. 3, pp. 1–22. Washington.
1920 Archeological Investigations in Utah and Arizona. *Smithsonian Miscellaneous Collections*, vol. 72, no. 1, pp. 66–69. Washington.
1926 Archeological Observations North of the Rio Colorado. *Bureau of American Ethnology, Bulletin* 82. Washington.
1940 Progress in the Southwest: In: "Essays in Historical Anthropology of North America." *Smithsonian Miscellaneous Collections*, vol. 100, pp. 417–444. Washington.

KIDDER, A. V.
1910 Explorations in Southeastern Utah in 1908. *American Journal of Archaeology*, vol. 14, no. 3, pp. 337–360. Norwood, Mass.
1924 An Introduction to the Study of Southwestern Archaeology. *Papers, Southwestern Expedition, Phillips Academy, No. 1.* Yale University Press, New Haven.

KIDDER, A. V., AND GUERNSEY, S. J.
1919 Archeological Explorations in Northeastern Arizona. *Smithsonian Institution, Bureau of American Ethnology, Bulletin 65.* Washington.

KLIMEK, S.
1935 The Structure of California Indian Culture, Culture Element Distributions I. *University of California Publications in American Archaeology and Ethnology*, vol. 37, no. 1, pp. 1–70. Berkeley.

KROEBER, A. L.
1934 Uto-Aztecan Languages of Mexico. *Ibero-Americana*: 8. Berkeley.

LAMB, S. M.
1958 Linguistic Prehistory in the Great Basin. *International Journal of American Linguistics*, vol. 24, no. 2, pp. 95–100. Baltimore.

LEH, L. L.
1936 Prehistoric Pueblo Ruins in Range Creek Canyon, Utah. *University of Colorado Studies*, vol. 23, no. 2, pp. 159–168. Boulder.

LIPE, W. D.
1960 1958 Excavations, Glen Canyon Area. *University of Utah Anthropological Papers*, no. 44. Salt Lake City.

LIPE, W. D., SHARROCK, F. W., DIBBLE, D. S., AND ANDERSON, K. M.
1960 1959 Excavations, Glen Canyon Area. *University of Utah Anthropological Papers*, no. 49. Salt Lake City.

LISTER, R. H.
1951 Excavations at Hells Midden, Dinosaur National Monument. *University of Colorado Studies, Series in Anthropology*, no. 3. Boulder.
1958a The Glen Canyon Survey in 1957. *University of Utah Anthropological Papers*, no. 30. Salt Lake City.
1958b A Preliminary Note on Excavations at The Coombs Site, Boulder, Utah. *Utah Archeology*, vol. 4, no. 3, pp. 4–8. Salt Lake City.
1959a The Glen Canyon Right Bank Survey. *University of Utah Anthropological Papers*, no. 39, pp. 27–161. Salt Lake City.
1959b The Coombs Site. *University of Utah Anthropological Papers*, no. 41. Salt Lake City.
1959c The Waterpocket Fold: A Distributional Problem. *University of Utah Anthropological Papers*, no. 39, pp. 285–316. Salt Lake City.

LISTER, R. H., AMBLER, J. R., AND LISTER, F. C.
1960 The Coombs Site, Part II. *University of Utah Anthropological Papers*, no. 41. Salt Lake City.

LISTER, R. H., AND LISTER, F. C.
1961 The Coombs Site, Part III, Summary and Conclusions. *University of Utah Anthropological Papers*, no. 41. Salt Lake City.

LOUD, L. L., AND HARRINGTON, M. R.
1929 Lovelock Cave. *University of California Publications in American Archaeology and Ethnology*, vol. 25, no. 1, pp. 1–183. Berkeley.

LOWIE, R. H.
1924 Notes on Shoshonean Ethnography. *American Museum of Natural History Anthropological Papers*, vol. 20, pp. 185–314. New York.

MALOUF, C.
1939 Prehistoric Exchange in Utah. *Archaeology and Ethnology Papers, Museum of Anthropology, University of Utah*, no. 1. (Republished as *University of Utah Anthropological Papers*, no. 1) Salt Lake City.
1940 Prehistoric Exchange in the Northern Periphery of the Southwest. *American Antiquity*, vol. 6, no. 2, pp. 115–122. Menasha.
1946 The Deep Creek Region, The Northwestern Frontier of the Pueblo Culture. *American Antiquity*, vol. 12, no. 2, pp. 117–121. Menasha.

MALOUF, C., DIBBLE, C. E., AND SMITH, E. R.
1940 Archaeology of the Deep Creek Region, Utah. *Archaeology and Ethnology Papers, Museum of Anthropology, University of Utah*, no. 5. (Republished as *University of Utah Anthropological Papers*, no. 5). Salt Lake City.

MANGELSDORF, P. C.
1954 New Evidence on the Origin and Ancestry of Maize. *American Antiquity*, vol. 19, pp. 409–410. Salt Lake City.

MANGELSDORF, P. C., AND CAMERON, J. W.
1942 Western Guatemala: A Secondary Center of Origin of Cultivated Maize Varieties. *Botanical Museum Leaflets, Harvard University*, vol. 10, pp. 217–252. Cambridge.

MANGELSDORF, P. C., AND LISTER, R. H.
1956 Archaeological Evidence on the Evolution of Maize in Northwestern Mexico. *Botanical Museum Leaflets, Harvard University*, vol. 17, pp. 151–177. Cambridge.

MANGELSDORF, P. C., AND REEVES, R. G.
1939 The Origin of Indian Corn and its Relatives. *Texas Agricultural Experiment Station, Bulletin 574.* College Station.

MANGELSDORF, P. C., AND SMITH, C. E., JR.
1949 New Archaeological Evidence on Evolution in Maize. *Botanical Museum Leaflets, Harvard University,* vol. 13, pp. 213–247. Cambridge.

MARTIN, P. S., RINALDO, J. B., BLUHM, E., CUTLER, H. C., AND GRANGE, R., JR.
1952 Mogollon Cultural Continuity and Change. *Chicago Natural History Museum, Fieldiana: Anthropology,* vol. 40. Chicago.

MASON, O. T.
1904 Aboriginal American Basketry: Studies in a Textile Art Without Machinery. *Annual Report of the Smithsonian Institution for 1902.* Washington.

McGREGOR, J. C.
1951 *The Cohonina Culture of Northwestern Arizona.* University of Illinois Press, Urbana.

MEIGHAN, C. W., COLES, N. E., DAVIS, F. D., GREENWOOD, G. M., HARRISON, W. M., AND MACBAIN, E. H.
1956 Archeological Excavations in Iron County, Utah. *University of Utah Anthropological Papers,* no. 25. Salt Lake City.

MONTGOMERY, H.
1894 Pre-historic Man in Utah. *The Archaeologist,* vol. II, pp. 227–234, 298–306, 335–342. Waterloo, Indiana.

MORRIS, E. H.
1939 Archaeological Studies in the La Plata District, Southwestern Colorado and Northwestern New Mexico. *Carnegie Institution of Washington, Publication* no. 519. Washington.

MORRIS, E. H., AND BURGH, R. F.
1941 Anasazi Basketry, Basketmaker II Through Pueblo III; a Study Based on Specimens from the San Juan River Country. *Carnegie Institution of Washington, Publication* no. 533. Washington.
1954 Basket Maker II Sites Near Durango, Colorado. *Carnegie Institution of Washington, Publication* 604. Washington.

MORSS, N.
1931 The Ancient Culture of the Fremont River in Utah. *Peabody Museum, Harvard University, Papers,* vol. 12, no. 3. Cambridge.
1954 Clay Figurines of the American Southwest. *Peabody Museum, Harvard University, Papers,* vol. 49, no. 1. Cambridge.
1957 Appendix I, Figurines. In: D. C. Taylor, "Two Fremont Sites and Their Position in Southwestern Prehistory." *University of Utah*

Anthropological Papers, no. 29, pp. 167–170. Salt Lake City.

MURDOCK, G. P. AND OTHERS
1950 Outline of Cultural Materials. 3rd Revised Edition. *Behavior Science Outlines,* vol. 1. New Haven.

NEWBERRY, J. S.
1876 Report of the Exploring Expedition from Sante Fe, New Mexico, to the Junction of the Grand and Green Rivers of the Great Colorado of the West, in 1859. *U.S. Engineering Department.* Washington.

NUSBAUM, J. L.
1922 A Basket-Maker Cave in Kane County, Utah: with Notes on the Artifacts by A. V. Kidder and S. J. Guernsey. *Museum of the American Indian, Heye Foundation, Indian Notes and Monographs, Miscellaneous,* no. 29. New York City.

O'BRYAN, D.
1949 Methods of Felling Trees and Tree-Ring Dating in the Southwest. *American Antiquity,* vol. 15, no. 2, pp. 155–156. Menasha.

OPLER, M. K.
1939 Southern Ute Pottery Types. *The Masterkey,* vol. 13, no. 5, pp. 161–163. Los Angeles.

OSBORNE, D.
1941 Archeological Reconnaissance in Western Utah and Nevada, 1939. *The Masterkey,* vol. 15, no. 5, pp. 189–195. Los Angeles.

PALMER, E.
1876 Exploration of a Mound in Utah. *American Naturalist,* vol. 10, no. 8, pp. 410–414.
1878 Cave Dwellings in Utah. *Reports of the Trustees of the Peabody Museum,* vol. II, no. 2, pp. 269–272. Cambridge.

PENDERGAST, D. M.
1960 The Frei Site, Santa Clara, Utah. *University of Utah Anthropological Papers,* no. 60, pp. 127–163. Salt Lake City.
1961 1960 Test Excavations in the Plainfield Reservoir Area. *University of Utah Anthropological Papers,* no. 52, Addendum, pp. 1–12. Salt Lake City.

PENDERGAST, D. M., AND MEIGHAN, C. W.
1959 Folk Traditions as Historical Facts: A Paiute Example. *Journal of American Folklore,* vol. 72, no. 284, pp. 128–133. Montpelier, Vt.

PEPPER, G. H.
1902 The Ancient Basket Makers of Southeastern Utah. *American Museum of Natural History*

Journal, vol. 2, no. 4. Supplement. New York City.

PIERSON, L. M.
1962 Archaeological Resources of the Needles–Salt Creek Area, Utah. *Utah Archeology*, vol. 8, no. 2, pp. 1–3. Salt Lake City.

PLUMB, C. S.
1898 The Geographic Distribution of Cereals in North America. *U.S. Department of Agriculture, Division of Biological Survey, Bulletin* 11, pp. 1–24. Washington.

POWELL, J. W.
1875 *Exploration of the Colorado River of the West and its Tributaries. Explored in 1869, 1870, 1871, and 1872, Under the Direction of the Secretary of the Smithsonian Institution.* Washington.

PRUDDEN, T. M.
1903 The Prehistoric Ruins of the San Juan Watershed in Utah, Arizona, Colorado, and New Mexico. *American Anthropologist*, n.s., vol. 5, no. 2, pp. 224–288. Lancaster, Pa.

PUTNAM, F. W.
1876 *Reports of the Peabody Museum, Harvard University*, Volume I (1868–1876). Cambridge.
1880 *Reports of the Peabody Museum, Harvard University*, Volume II (1876–1879). Cambridge.

REAGAN, A. B.
1931a Some Archaeological Notes on Nine Mile Canyon, Utah. *El Palacio*, vol. 31, no. 4, pp. 45–71. Santa Fe.
1931b Ruins and Pictographs in Nine-Mile Canyon, Utah. *Transactions of the Illinois Academy of Science*, vol. 24, no. 2, pp. 369–370. Springfield.
1931c Some Archaeological Notes on Hill Canyon in Northeastern Utah. *El Palacio*, vol. 31, no. 15, pp. 223–244. Sante Fe.
1931d Additional Archaeological Notes on Ashley and Dry Fork Canyons in Northeastern Utah. *El Palacio*, vol. 31, no. 8, pp. 122–131. Santa Fe.
1931e The Pictographs of Ashley and Dry Fork Valleys in Northeastern Utah. *Transactions of the Kansas Academy of Science*, vol. 34, pp. 168–216. Topeka.
1931f Archaeological Notes on the Brush Creek Region, Northeastern Utah. *The Wisconsin Archaeologist*, vol. 10, no. 4, pp. 132–138. Madison.
1931g Some Notes on the Ancient Earthlodge Peoples of the Willard Stage of Pueblo Culture in the Uintah Basin, Utah. *El Palacio*, vol. 30, nos. 19–20, pp. 236–241. Santa Fe.

1931h Collections of Ancient Artifacts from the Ashley–Dry Fork District of the Uintah Basin, with some Notes on the Dwellings and Mortuary Customs of the Ouray Indians of the Ouray (Utah) Region. *El Palacio*, vol. 31, no. 26, pp. 407–413. Santa Fe.
1933 Anciently Inhabited Caves of the Vernal District with some Additional Notes on Nine Mile Canyon, Northeastern Utah. *Transactions of the Kansas Academy of Science*, vol. 36, pp. 41–70. Topeka.
1934 Additional Archeological Notes on the Uintah Basin in Northeastern Utah. *Transactions of the Kansas Academy of Science*, vol. 37, pp. 39–54. Topeka.

ROBERTS, L. M., GRANT, U. J., RAMIREZ, E., HATHEWAY, W. H., AND SMITH, D. L. IN COLLABORATION WITH MANGELSDORF, P. C.
1957 Races of Maize in Colombia. *National Academy of Sciences, National Research Council, Publication* 510, pp. 1–153. Washington.

ROMNEY, A. K.
1957 The Genetic Model and Uto-Aztecan Time Perspective. *Davidson Journal of Anthropology*, vol. 3, no. 2, pp. 35–41. Seattle.

RUDY, J. R
1953 An Archeological Survey of Western Utah. *University of Utah Anthropological Papers*, no. 12. Salt Lake City.
1954a University of Utah Archaeological Field Work, 1952–1953. *Southwestern Lore*, vol. 19, no. 4, pp. 13–15. Boulder.
1954b Pine Park Shelter, Washington County, Utah. *University of Utah Anthropological Papers*, no. 18. Salt Lake City.
1955 Archeological Excavations in Beef Basin, Utah. *University of Utah Anthropological Papers*, no. 20. Salt Lake City.

RUDY, J. R, AND STIRLAND, R. D.
1950 An Archeological Reconnaissance in Washington County, Utah. *University of Utah Anthropological Papers*, no. 9. Salt Lake City.

RUDY, J. R, AND STODDARD, E.
1954 Site on Fremont Island in Great Salt Lake. *American Antiquity*, vol. 19, no. 3, pp. 285–290. Salt Lake City.

RUDY, S. S.
1957 Textiles. In: Danger Cave by J. D. Jennings. *University of Utah Anthropological Papers*, no. 27, pp. 235–264. Salt Lake City.

RUSSELL, F.
1908 The Pima Indians. *Bureau of American Ethnology, Annual Report* no. 26. Washington.

SCHELLBACH, L., III
1927 Ancient Bundles of Snares from Nevada. *Museum of the American Indian, Heye Foundation, Indian Notes*, vol. 4, pp. 232–240. New York.

SCHROEDER, A. H.
1953 Statement on the Early History and Archaeology of the Gunnison River Basin. *Southwestern Lore*, vol. 19, no. 3, pp. 3–11. Boulder.
1955 Archeology of Zion Park. *University of Utah, Anthropological Papers*, no. 22. Salt Lake City.
1961 The Archeological Excavations at Willow Beach, Arizona, 1950. *University of Utah Anthropological Papers*, no. 50. Salt Lake City.

SCHULMAN, E.
1948 Dendrochronology in Northeastern Utah. *Tree-Ring Bulletin*, vol. 15, no. 1/2, pp. 2–14. Tucson.
1949 An Extension of the Durango Chronology. *Tree-Ring Bulletin*, vol. 16, no. 2, pp. 12–16. Tucson.
1950 A Dated Beam from Dinosaur National Monument. *Tree-Ring Bulletin*, vol. 16, no. 3, pp. 18–19. Tucson.
1951 Miscellaneous Ring Records. III. *Tree-Ring Bulletin*, vol. 17, no. 4, pp. 28–29. Tucson.
1956 *Dendroclimatic Changes in Semiarid America*. University of Arizona Press, Tucson.

SCHWARTZ, D. W.
1956 Demographic Changes in the Early Periods of Cohonina Prehistory. In: Willey, G. R. (Editor), "Prehistoric Settlement Patterns in the New World." *Wenner-Gren Foundation Publications in Anthropology*, no. 23, pp. 26–31. New York.
1963 An Archaeological Survey of Nankoweap Canyon, Grand Canyon National Park. *American Antiquity*, vol. 28, no. 3, pp. 289–302. Salt Lake City.

SCHWARTZ, D. W., LANGE, A. L., AND DESAUSSURE, R.
1958 Split-Twig Figurines in the Grand Canyon. *American Antiquity*, vol. 23, no. 3, pp. 264–274. Salt Lake City.

SEVERANCE, M. S.
1874 Preliminary Ethnological Report. In: G. M. Wheeler, *Progress Report upon Geographical and Geological Explorations and Surveys West of the One Hundredth Meridian, in 1872*, Appendix F. Washington.

SHARROCK, F. W., ANDERSON, K. M., FOWLER, D. D., AND DIBBLE, D. S.

1961 1960 Excavations, Glen Canyon Area. *University of Utah Anthropological Papers*, no. 52. Salt Lake City.

SHARROCK, F. W., AND KEANE, E. G.
1962 Carnegie Museum Collection from Southeast Utah. *University of Utah Anthropological Papers*, no. 57. Salt Lake City.

SHIMKIN, D. B.
1940 Shoshone-Comanche Origins and Migrations. *Proceedings of the Sixth Pacific Science Congress of the Pacific Science Association*, vol. IV, pp. 17–25. Berkeley.

SHUTLER, R., JR.
1961 Lost City: Pueblo Grande de Nevada. *Nevada State Museum Anthropological Paper* no. 5. Carson City.

SMILEY, T. L.
1951 A Summary of Tree-Ring Dates from some Southwestern Archaeological Sites. *University of Arizona Laboratory Bulletin of Tree-Ring Research*, no. 5. Tucson.

SMILEY, T. L. (EDITOR)
1958 Climate and Man in the Southwest. *University of Arizona Program in Geochronology, Contribution* no. 6. Tucson.

SMITH, E. R.
1934 A Brief Description of an Indian Ruin Near Shonesburg, Utah. *Zion and Bryce Nature Notes*, vol. 6, no. 1. (Reprinted as: *Museum of Anthropology, University of Utah, Archaeology and Ethnology Paper* no. 4, 1940; and *University of Utah Anthropological Paper* no. 4, 1950, Salt Lake City)
1941 The Archaeology of Deadman Cave, Utah. *University of Utah Bulletin*, vol. 32, no. 4. Salt Lake City.
1952 The Archaeology of Deadman Cave, Utah: A Revision. *University of Utah Anthropological Papers*, no. 10. Salt Lake City.

SMITH, W.
1952 Kiva Mural Decorations at Awatovi and Kawaika-a. *Peabody Museum, Harvard University, Papers*, vol. 37. Cambridge.

SPENCER, J. E.
1934 Pueblo Sites of Southwestern Utah. *American Anthropologist*, vol. 36, no. 1, pp. 70–80. Menasha.

STALLINGS, W. S., JR.
1941 A Basketmaker II Date from Cave du Pont, Utah. *Tree-Ring Bulletin*, vol. 8, no. 1, pp. 3–6. Tucson.

STEEN, C. R.

1937 Archeological Investigations at Natural Bridges National Monument. *Monthly Report, Southwestern Monuments,* pp. 329–337. Santa Fe.

STEWARD, J. H.

1929 Petroglyphs of California and Adjoining States. *University of California Publications in American Archaeology and Ethnology,* vol. 24, no. 2. Berkeley.

1931 Archaeological Discoveries at Kanosh in Utah. *El Palacio,* vol. 30, no. 8, pp. 121–130. Santa Fe.

1933a Early Inhabitants of Western Utah, Part I— Mounds and House Types. *University of Utah Bulletin,* vol. 23, no. 7. Salt Lake City.

1933b Archaeological Problems of the Northern Periphery of the Southwest. *Museum of Northern Arizona, Bulletin* no. 5. Flagstaff.

1933c Ethnography of the Owens Valley Paiute. *University of California Publications in American Archaeology and Ethnology,* vol. 33, no. 3, pp. 233–350. Berkeley.

1936 Pueblo Material Culture in Western Utah. *University of New Mexico Bulletin,* no. 287. Albuquerque.

1937a Petroglyphs of the United States. *Smithsonian Institution, Annual Report for 1936,* pp. 405–425. Washington.

1937b Ancient Caves of the Great Salt Lake Region. *Bureau of American Ethnology, Bulletin* 116. Washington.

1938 Basin-Plateau Aboriginal Sociopolitical Groups. *Bureau of American Ethnology, Bulletin* 120. Washington.

1940 Native Cultures of the Intermontane (Great Basin) Area. In: "Essays in Historical Anthropology of North America." *Smithsonian Miscellaneous Collections,* vol. 100, pp. 445–502. Washington.

1941a Archeological Reconnaissance of Southern Utah. *Bureau of American Ethnology, Bulletin* 128, pp. 277–356 (Anthropological Paper, no. 18). Washington.

1941b Current Element Distributions: XIII, Nevada Shoshone. *University of California Anthropological Records,* vol. 4, no. 2, pp. 209–359. Berkeley.

1943 Culture Element Distributions: XXIII, Northern and Gosiute Shoshoni. *University of California, Anthropological Records,* vol. 8, no. 3, pp. 263–392. Berkeley.

1955 Review of Rudy "Archeological Survey of Western Utah." *American Antiquity,* vol. 21, no. 1, pp. 88–89. Salt Lake City.

STEWART, O. C.

1941 Culture Element Distributions: XIV, Northern Paiute. *University of California, Anthropological Records,* vol. 4, no. 3, pp. 361–446. Berkeley.

1942 Culture Element Distributions: XVIII, Ute-Southern Paiute. *University of California Anthropological Records,* vol. 6, no. 4, pp. 231–354. Berkeley.

SUHM, D. A.

1959 Extended Survey of the Right Bank of The Glen Canyon. *University of Utah Anthropological Papers,* no. 39, pp. 163–284. Salt Lake City.

TAYLOR, D. C.

1954 The Garrison Site. *University of Utah Anthropological Papers,* no. 16. Salt Lake City.

1955 Archeological Excavations Near Salina, Utah. *Utah Archeology,* vol. 1, no. 4, pp. 3–7. Salt Lake City.

1957 Two Fremont Sites and Their Position in Southwestern Prehistory. *University of Utah Anthropological Papers,* no. 29. Salt Lake City.

TAYLOR, W. W.

1958 A Brief Survey through the Grand Canyon of the Colorado River. *Museum of Northern Arizona, Bulletin* 30, pp. 18–30. Flagstaff.

1961 Archaeology and Language in Western North America. *American Antiquity,* vol. 27, no. 1, pp. 71–81. Salt Lake City.

THOMAS, A. B.

1932 *Forgotten Frontiers: A Study of the Spanish Indian Policy of Don Juan Bautista de Anza, Governor of New Mexico, 1777–1778.* Norman.

WEDEL, W. R.

1954 Earthenware and Steatite Vessels from Northwestern Wyoming. *American Antiquity,* vol. 19, no. 4, pp. 403–409. Salt Lake City.

WELLHAUSEN, E. J., ROBERTS, L. M., AND HERNANDEZ X., E. IN COLLABORATION WITH MANGELSDORF, P. C.

1952 Races of Maize in Mexico. *The Bussey Institution of Harvard University.* Cambridge.

WETHERILL, B. W.

1934 Summary of Investigations by the Zion National Park Archaeological Party. *Zion and Bryce Nature Notes,* vol. 6, no. 1, pp. 1–9. Zion National Park.

WHEAT, J. B.
  1955 Prehistoric People of the Northern South-west. *Grand Canyon Natural History Association, Bulletin* no. 12. Grand Canyon.

WHEELER, S. M.
  1936 A Pueblo II Site in the Great Basin Area of Nevada. *The Masterkey*, vol. 10, no. 6, pp. 207–211. Los Angeles.

  1938 A Fremont Moccasin from Nevada. *The Masterkey*, vol. 12, no. 1, pp. 34–35. Los Angeles.

  1939 Split-Twig Figurines. *The Masterkey*, vol. 13, no. 1, pp. 42–45.

  1942 *Archeology of Etna Cave, Lincoln County, Nevada.* Carson City.

  1949 More About Split-Twig Figurines. *The Masterkey*, vol. 23, no. 5, pp. 153–158. Los Angeles.

WOODBURY, A. M., DURRANT, S. D., AND FLOWERS, S.
  1959a Survey of Vegetation in the Glen Canyon Reservoir Basin. *University of Utah Anthropological Papers,* no. 36. Salt Lake City.

WOODBURY, A. M., and others
  1959b Ecological Studies of the Flora and Fauna in Glen Canyon, *University of Utah Anthropological Papers,* no. 40. Salt Lake City.

WOODBURY, R. B.
  1954 Prehistoric Stone Implements of Northeastern Arizona. *Peabody Museum, Harvard University, Papers,* vol. 34. Cambridge.

WORMINGTON, H. M.
  1955 A Reappraisal of the Fremont Culture. *Denver Museum of Natural History, Proceedings,* no. 1. Denver.

WORMINGTON, H. M., AND LISTER, R. H.
  1956 Archaeological Investigations on the Uncompahgre Plateau in West Central Colorado. *Denver Museum of Natural History, Proceedings,* no. 2. Denver.

FIGURES 20–51

Fig. 20*A*. Structure at Site LS 13-2 in Ruin Park.

Fig. 20*B*. Portion of structure at Site LS 13-4 in Ruin Park.

FIG. 21A. Structures at Site LS 14-11 in Salt Creek Canyon. Donald Scott in foreground.

FIG. 21B. Detail of construction at Site LS 13-12 in Bobby's Hole just north of Ruin Park.

FIG. 22A. Two-story storage structure at Site LS 13-11 in Spring Canyon, a tributary of Salt Creek Canyon.

FIG. 22B. Remains of structures at Site LS 14-10 in Salt Creek Canyon.

Fig. 23A. Distant view of Fort Bottom Ruin (LS 9-1).

Fig. 23B. Fort Bottom Ruin (LS 9-1), Colorado River.

Fig. 24*A*. Structures at Site SR 8-5 on Woodruff Bottoms, Green River.

Fig. 24*B*. Cists 2, 3, 7, and 8 at Cottonwood Cave (SR 16-6), Willow Tank Canyon.

FIG. 25A. Pictographs at Site H 3-4 in North Wash (Crescent Creek).

FIG. 25B. Pictographs at Site FL 4-1, Rochester Creek at junction with the Muddy River.

Fig. 26A. General view of Great Gallery in Barrier Canyon (SR 12-4).

Fig. 26B. Continuation to right of fig. 26A.

Fig. 27*A*. Details of figures in Great Gallery (SR 12-4).   Fig. 27*B*. Details of figures in Great Gallery (SR 12-4).

Fig. 27C.   Details of figures in Great Gallery (SR 12-4), Barrier Canyon.

FIG. 28*A*. Details of figures in Great Gallery (SR 12-4).

FIG. 28*B*. Details of figures in Great Gallery (SR 12-4), Barrier Canyon.

Fɪɢ. 29A. Details of figures in Great Gallery (SR 12-4).

Fɪɢ. 29B. Details of figures in Great Gallery (SR 12-4), Barrier Canyon.

FIG. 30*A*. Details of figures in Great Gallery (SR 12-4).

FIG. 30*B*. Details of figures in Great Gallery (SR 12-4), Barrier Canyon.

Fig. 31*A*. Small pictograph figures resembling Fremont figurines at unnumbered site in Barrier Canyon.

Fig. 31*B*. Pictographs at Horseshoe Shelter (SR 12-5), Barrier Canyon.

Fig. 32*A*. Excavation in progress at Horseshoe Shelter (SR 12-5), Barrier Canyon.

Fig. 32*B*. Ring of basalt boulders outlining a structure prior to its excavation at Site FL 11-2 near Torrey, Utah.

FIG. 33A. Nordell's Fort (PR 4-11), located on end of narrow ridge overlooking Nine Mile Canyon.

FIG. 33B. Storage structure at Site PR 4-13, in Nine Mile Canyon.

Fig. 34*A*. General view of Rasmussen's Cave (PR 4-31), facing northwest.

Fig. 34*B*. Burial *in situ* at Rasmussen's Cave (PR 4-31), Nine Mile Canyon.

FIG. 35A. Crude stone walls at Site ET 6-2 in Hill Creek Canyon. Donald Scott.

FIG. 35B. Small stone-and-adobe storage structure at Site ET 6-3, near mouth of Horsecorn Canyon.

FIG. 36A. General view of Long Mesa Ruin (ET 6-7) and fields in Hill Creek Canyon.

FIG. 36B. Details of masonry at Long Mesa Ruin (ET 6-7). J. O. Brew standing in rear room.

FIG. 37*A*. General view of Rock House Ruin (ET 6-26). L. to r., Alfred Kidder II, William Bowers, and Waldo Emerson Forbes.

FIG. 37*B*. Details of masonry at Rock House Ruin (ET 6-26), Hill Creek.

FIG. 38*A*. Ascent to Pinnacle Rock (ET 6-4), Hill Creek; wall remnants may be seen on the rock. On top, Dafton Thompson, one of the wranglers; on the way up, Donald Scott.

FIG. 38*B*. Excavation at Site A 9-2, northeast of Fort Duchesne, near the Uinta River.

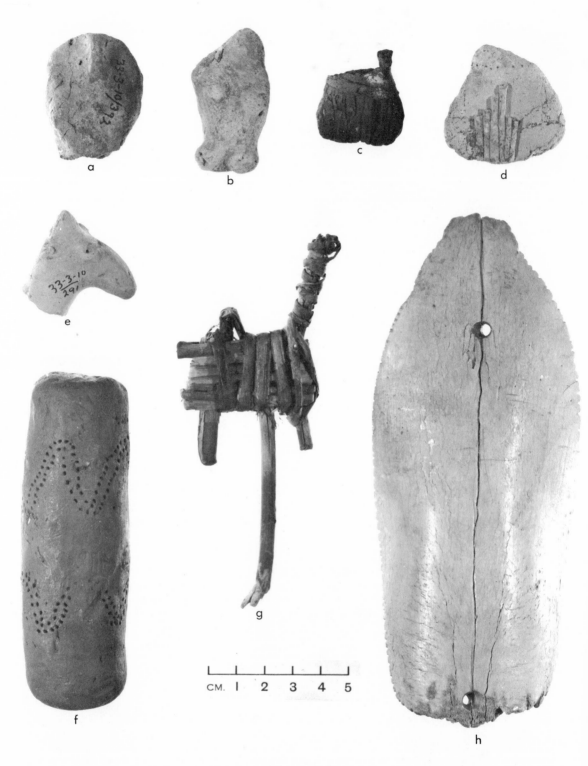

Fig. 39. Miscellaneous artifacts. *a-d*, figurine fragments from SR 12-5; *e*, clay animal head from SR 16-10; *f*, pigment from SR 16-6; *g*, split-twig animal figure from SR 16-6; *h*, worked bone object from SR 16-12. Peabody Museum Catalogue nos.: *a*, 33-3-10/392; *e*, 33-3-10/291; *g*, 33-3-10/260.

Fig. 40. Miscellaneous artifacts. *a*, digging stick from A 6-6; *b*, wooden sickle (?) from SR 16-6; *c*, horn sickle from SR 12-5; *d*, horn sickle (?) from FL 12-5; *e*, grass-filled leather pad from SR 16-6; *f*, sandal from LS 14-11; *g*, sandal from SR 12-5; *h*, sandal from SR 16-6.

Peabody Museum Catalogue nos.: *a*, A7987; *b*, 33-3-10/263; *c*, 33-3-10/438; *d*, A6892; *e*, 33-3-10/239; *f*, 33-3-10/313; *g*, 33-3-10/268; *h*, 33-3-10/401.

FIG. 41.   Artifacts found with burial at Site PR 4-31. *a-d,f*, chipped stone blades; *e*, chipped stone drill; *g*, flaker (?) of horn; *h*, grooved bear (?) canine; *i*, bone awl; *j*, bone flesher (?); *k,l*, wooden spear foreshafts without points; *m,n*, wooden spear foreshafts with chipped stone points; *o*, hide pouch containing hematite; *p*, single hide moccasin used as a pouch or medicine bundle; *q*, one of a pair of moccasins; *r*, atlatl; *s*, wooden spear shaft (portion); *t*, flaker (?) (portion), note bone and hide attached to end of wooden shaft.

Peabody Museum Catalogue nos.: *a-d*, A7797; *e*, A7799; *f*, A7798; *g*, A7815; *h*, A7793; *i*, A7790; *j*, A7818; *k*, A7795; *l*, A7816; *m,n*, A7794; *o*, A7814; *p*, A7813; *q*, A7811; *r*, A7822; *s*, A7825; *t*, A7824.

FIG. 42. Chipped stone artifacts from Myton Bench sites (U 16-1-7) representative of crude blades or choppers and (n) pebble tools.

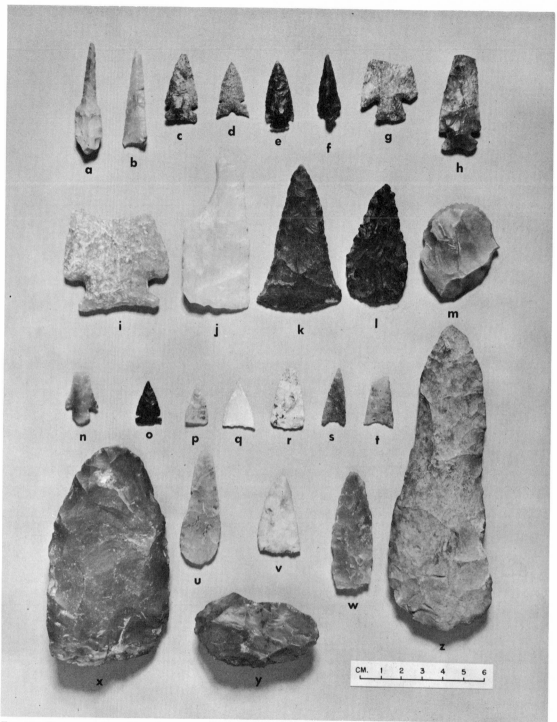

FIG. 43. Representative chipped stone tools from sites with Fremont culture components. *a*, drill; *b-f*, *n-t*, projectile points; *g-i*, notched blades, *j-l*, *u-w*, unnotched blades; *m*, "saw" or serrated scraper; *x-z*, crude blades or choppers.

Provenience: *a*, ET 6-7; *b*, FL 7-1; *c,e*, U 16-1-7; *d*, U 11-1; *f*, PR 4-31; *g*, SR 10-4; *h*, SR 16-5; *i*, FL 4-4; *j*, FL 7-1; *k*, FL 12-5; *l*, PR 4-31; *m*, FL 16-1; *n*, SR 16-5; *o-z*, SR 12-5.

Peabody Museum Catalogue nos.: *a*, A7648; *b*, A6849; *c*, A7902; *d*, A7911; *e*, A7902; *f*, A7836; *g*, A6869; *h,n*, 33-3-10/271; *i*, A6855; *j*, A6848; *k*, A6887; *l*, A7854; *m*, 33-2-10/202; *o,p,s*, 33-3-10/366; *q,t*, 33-3-10/360; *r*, 33-3-10/376; *u*, 33-3-10/362; *v*, 33-3-10/367; *w*, 33-3-10/370; *x*, 33-3-10/346; *y*, 33-3-10/359; *z*, 33-3-10/329.

Fig. 44. Miscellaneous containers. *a*, pottery vessel from PR 4-31; *b*, squash shell from SR 12-5; *c-e*, baskets from A 6-1.

Peabody Museum Catalogue nos.: *a*, A7744; *b*, 33-3-10/453; *d*, A7955; *e*, A7942.

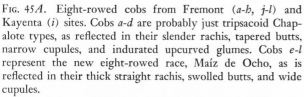

FIG. 45*A*. Eight-rowed cobs from Fremont (*a-h*, *j-l*) and Kayenta (*i*) sites. Cobs *a-d* are probably just tripsacoid Chapalote types, as reflected in their slender rachis, tapered butts, narrow cupules, and indurated upcurved glumes. Cobs *e-l* represent the new eight-rowed race, Maíz de Ocho, as is reflected in their thick straight rachis, swolled butts, and wide cupules.

Provenience: *a-d*, PR 4-31; *e*, ET 6-3; *f*, A 6-1; *g-h*, PR 4-27; *i*, Cave 8, northwest of Kayenta, Arizona (Guernsey and Kidder, 1921, p. 34); *j*, FL 12-4; *k*, Site 21 (Morss, 1931); *l*, Site 37 (Morss, 1931).

Peabody Museum Catalogue nos.: *a,d*, A7800; *c*, A7761; *e*, A7612; *f*, A7945; *g,h*, A7984; *i*, A3520; *j*, 33-2-10/196; *k*, A6466; *l*, A6819.

FIG. 45*B*. Dent maize from various prehistoric sites in the Fremont area. *d*, from Basketmaker Site SR 16-6, shows slight denting that sometimes occurs in Chapalote. The rest of the specimens, all of which show a blend of Maíz de Ocho, Chapalote, and teosinte, are from Fremont sites: *a*, Site 21 (Morss, 1931); *b*, PR 4-31; *c,i-l*, A 6-1; *e-g*, Site 19 (Morss, 1931); *h*, PR 4-28.

Peabody Museum Catalogue nos.: *a*, A6466; *b*, A7769; *c,j-l*, A7944; *d*, 33-3-10/264; *e,f*, A6478; *g*, A6520; *h*, A7736; *i*, A7936.

FIG. 45*C*. A comparison of the most Zapalote Chico–like specimen in the collection studied with a modern ear of Zapalote Chico. *b*, Peabody Museum Catalogue no. A7944.

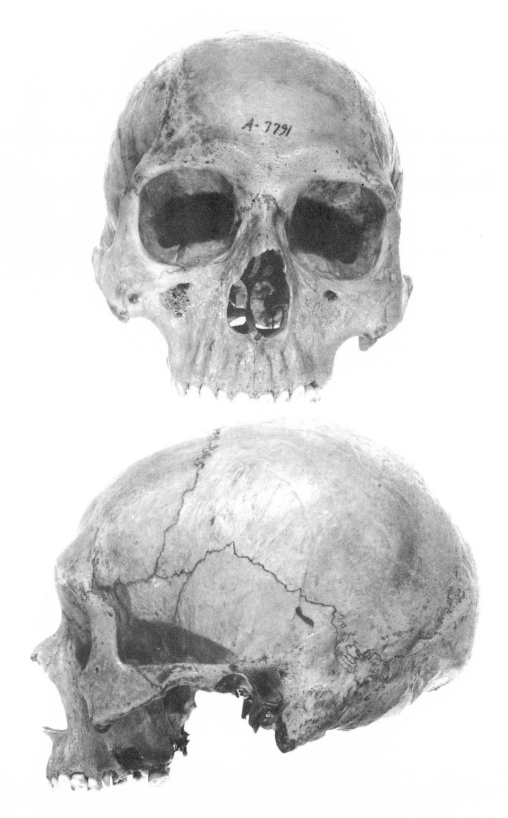

Fig. 46. Skull from burial at Site PR 4-31. Peabody Museum Catalogue no. A7791.

Fig. 47*A*. Part of pack train on top of Water Pocket Fold, 1929.

Fig. 47*B*. Starting down from the top of Water Pocket Fold, 1929.

Fig. 47*C*. Quicksand in Hoxie Creek, 1929. The horse was "salvaged."

Fig. 47*D*. Pack train coming out of Hoxie Creek, 1929.

FIG. 48A. The expedition boarding the current ferry on the Green River en route from Hill Creek to Nine Mile Canyon, 1931.

FIG. 48B. Donald Scott in The Devil's Pocket, "The Needles" in the background, 1930.

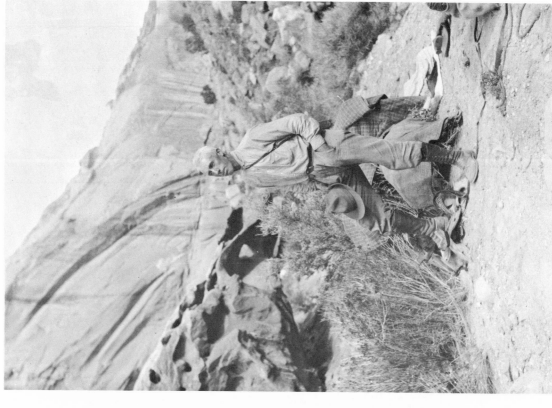

Fig. 49B. The late Dave Rust; packer, guide, and friend and advisor to the expedition throughout its various seasons. Shows characteristic topography in the Water Pocket Fold country.

Fig. 49A. William H. Claflin in The Muley Twist, Water Pocket Fold, 1929.

FIG. 50B. Climbing to a cliff ruin, 1930. At top, Donald Scott, Jr.; below, Henry B. Roberts.

FIG. 50A. A Colorado River trail, 1930. Donald Scott in the rear.

FIG. 51A. Part of the pack train on the trail up the Green River. Alfred Kidder II is the tail rider.

FIG. 51B. Camp in the Uinta foothills, 1931. L. to r., Alfred Kidder II, Donald Scott, Ivan Thorne, cook, with pot of coffee.